MW00652064

Real Estate Appraisal

4th Edition

Joseph F. Schram, Jr.

Rockwell
PUBLISHING

Rockwell Publishing Company

By Rockwell Publishing, Inc.
13218 N.E. 20th
Bellevue, WA 98005
(425)747-7272 / 1-800-221-9347

Fourth Edition

ISBN: 978-1-887051-52-1

PRINTED IN THE UNITED STATES OF AMERICA

Graphic art: Minh Nguyen, Dai Pham, James Love
Cover design: Alisa Oh

Table of Contents

1 Introduction to Appraisal

Overview

The appraisal of real estate fulfills a vital economic function in our society. Appraisals are used in hundreds of different ways in both government and the private sector. The importance of the appraiser's role is reflected in the standards of professionalism established by the industry itself, and the increasing government regulation of appraisal practices. In order to fill their vital role, real estate appraisers must have a solid understanding of what an appraisal is, as well as the nature of real estate and real property rights. After completing this chapter, you should be able to:

- define the terms "appraisal," "appraisal report," and "appraisal practice" as they apply to the appraisal profession;
- describe the kinds of services that real estate appraisers perform and list some common uses of real estate appraisals;
- define the terms "real estate" and "real property" as they are used in real estate appraisal practice;
- describe the various components of real estate and explain how real estate is distinguished from personal property;
- list the major types of real property interests and describe their characteristics; and
- describe the three powers of government that limit private property rights.

Appraisal

The term **appraisal** can be defined in a number of different ways. One of the most common definitions of appraisal is "an opinion of value." Appraisal can also be defined as "the act or process of developing an opinion of value."

The two key words in these definitions are "opinion" and "value." An appraisal is an **opinion** because it relies significantly on the appraiser's judgment and experience. There is no mechanical process or mathematical formula that can determine the exact value of a property, and two different appraisers may arrive at two somewhat different, but equally valid, opinions of value for the same property.

> **Example:** A common appraisal technique is to analyze the sales prices of properties that are comparable (similar) to the subject property (the property being appraised), in order to arrive at an indication of the subject property's value. In this technique, the choice of which "comparable" sale to use in the analysis has a large impact on the resulting value indicator. Appraisers follow well-established rules in selecting comparable sales, but may be presented with a large number of recent sales from which to choose.
>
> The appraiser must rely on his or her experience and knowledge of the market in order to select the particular comparable sales that are most likely to result in a reliable indication of value for the subject property. Thus, two appraisers may choose different comparable properties and arrive at somewhat different opinions of value.

The second key term in the definition of appraisal is "value." There are many different types of **value** (market value, insurable value, investment value, etc.), and each type may be defined in a number of different ways. Defining the type of value is a critical element of any appraisal assignment. An appraisal is always related to a particular defined value. (Concepts and definitions of value are discussed in detail in Chapter 2.)

Appraisal Practice

In common conversation, the term "appraisal" is often used to refer to all of the work or services performed by appraisers. A more precise term is **appraisal practice**, which encompasses not only appraisal (developing an opinion of value), but also appraisal consulting and appraisal review (which may or may not require the appraiser to develop an opinion of value).

Appraisal consulting is distinguished from a simple appraisal by the fact that in consulting, the opinion of value is only part of a larger problem. Appraisers often provide consulting services in connection with studies of marketability, development feasibility, and land use, and also in connection with investment analysis.

The third type of work performed by some appraisers is **appraisal review**. In a review, the appraiser analyzes an opinion of value that has been prepared by someone else, and forms opinions regarding the adequacy and relevance of the data, analysis, and opinions contained in the appraisal.

An **appraisal report** is the communication (either written or oral) of an appraisal, appraisal review, or appraisal consulting service that is provided at the completion of an assignment.

History of Appraisal

The roots of the modern real estate appraisal industry in the United States can be traced back to the Great Depression in the 1930s. Prior to that time, appraisal was not viewed as a specific occupation. Few people specialized in appraisal practice, and those who did often lacked a good understanding of value theories. Commonly accepted standards and guidelines for the appraisal process were virtually non-existent.

In 1929, the first nationally recognized standards for appraisal practice were published by the Appraisal Division of the National Association of Real Estate Boards (now known as the National Association of REALTORS®). The first professional appraisal associations in the U.S. were also founded at about the same time, including the American Institute of Real Estate Appraisers, the Society of Residential Appraisers, and the American Society of Farm Managers and Rural Appraisers. (The Society of Residential Appraisers later became known as the Society of Real Estate Appraisers. In 1990, this organization merged with the American Institute of Real Estate Appraisers to form the Appraisal Institute.)

Over the next 50 years, the demand for professional appraisal services grew, stimulated in part by the requirements of federal agencies such as the Federal Housing Administration (FHA), the Department of Veterans Affairs (VA) and the Federal National Mortgage Association (FNMA or Fannie Mae), which required independent verification of property values. However, the appraisal industry was still only minimally regulated, and no uniform standards existed for appraiser qualification or appraisal practice. Professional appraisal associations took on the responsibility of certifying the competency of individual real estate appraisers.

The savings and loan crisis of the 1980s resulted in sweeping changes for the appraisal industry. As a result of federal legislation that was passed in the aftermath of the S&L crisis, appraisers are now subject to significant government regulation, including state licensing and certification. This legislation also established a requirement for nationwide competency standards and uniform standards of practice for professional appraisers.

In response to the S&L crisis and subsequent legislation, the major appraisal organizations in the country jointly founded The Appraisal Foundation. This nonprofit corporation is responsible for the Uniform Standards of Professional Appraisal Practice (USPAP), as well as national qualification standards for appraiser certification. (The Uniform Standards of Professional Appraisal Practice are discussed throughout this book. For more information regarding professional appraisal associations, the Appraisal Foundation, and government regulation of appraisers, refer to Chapter 14.)

Purposes and Uses of Appraisals

In appraisal practice, a distinction is drawn between:

1. the purpose of an appraisal, and
2. the intended use (and intended users) of an appraisal.

The **purpose** of an appraisal refers to the information that the client wants the appraiser to provide. In most cases, the client wants the appraiser to provide an opinion about a defined type of value for a specific property interest in a specific parcel of real estate as of a specific date.

Example: The purpose of an appraisal may be to develop an opinion of the market value of the fee simple interest in a particular residential property, as of September 1 of this year. (The appraisal itself would include precise definitions of the terms "market value" and "fee simple interest," as well as a complete legal description of the particular parcel of real estate.)

In contrast to the purpose of an appraisal, the **use** of an appraisal refers to the reason that the client wants to know the information. The uses of appraisals are many and varied. Real estate buyers and sellers use appraisals to help them decide how much to offer or ask for a property. Financial institutions use appraisals in connection with their lending activities, to evaluate property that is offered as loan security. Governments use appraisals for purposes of taxation and condemnations. Appraisals are also frequently used to guide investment decisions and help with business planning.

Identifying the purpose, use, and users of an appraisal assists the appraiser in determining the scope of work required to produce a credible and meaningful result.

Career Opportunities

Most appraisers are employed in one of two basic categories. **Staff appraisers** are employed by a business, government agency, or other organization to perform appraisal services that relate to the employer's operations. For example, a staff appraiser may be an employee of an insurance company and perform appraisals related to the company's insurance business.

In contrast, **independent fee appraisers** are either self-employed or work for companies whose primary business is to provide appraisal services to others. They may perform appraisals for many different clients. Independent fee appraisers (or the appraisal companies that employ them) normally charge a separate fee for each appraisal assignment. Staff appraisers, on the other hand, are compensated in the form of hourly wages or salary.

Some of the most important employers of appraisers include:

- independent fee appraisal companies;
- federal, state, and local government agencies concerned with taxation, land use, land or property management, construction, or loan guarantees;
- real estate lenders, such as commercial banks, savings and loan associations, credit unions, and mortgage companies;
- insurance companies;
- real estate developers; and
- large corporations with significant real estate assets.

The Real Estate Financing Industry

Regardless of the type of work they do, appraisers need to have an understanding of the real estate financing industry. The industry is divided into two "markets" that supply the funds available for real estate loans—the primary market and the secondary market. In the primary market, lenders make mortgage loans to borrowers, enabling the borrowers to buy real estate. In the secondary market, lenders sell the mortgage loans that they've made to investors.

The lenders that make loans in the **primary market** include mortgage companies, commercial banks, savings institutions (also known as savings and loan associations or thrifts), and credit unions. With the exception of mortgage companies, these are **depository institutions**. A depository institution accepts deposits from account holders and then, in most cases, uses the deposited funds to make loans to borrowers. The institution pays interest to its account holders to attract deposits; to earn a profit, it collects a higher rate of interest from its borrowers.

Whether a depository institution is a commercial bank, a savings institution, or a credit union depends on its **charter**. A charter is essentially a license to operate a depository institution, granted by either the federal government or a state government. For example, a depository institution might be a federally chartered savings and loan association, or it might be a state-chartered credit union. The type of charter determines which state or federal agencies have regulatory authority over the institution and which rules apply to its operations.

In the **secondary market**, real estate loans are treated as investments, just like stocks or bonds. A primary market lender can sell its loans to secondary market investors and then use the proceeds from those sales to make new loans in the primary market. Since the secondary market operates on a national scale, it serves to smooth out imbalances in the supply of and demand for real estate financing on a local level, moderating the impact of local real estate cycles.

In practice, loans usually aren't sold directly from lenders to investors in the secondary market. A primary market lender sells the loans to a middleman, who then "packages" or "securitizes" the loans into investments called **mortgage-backed securities**. It is these

Fig. 1.1 **Mortgage funds flow from the secondary market, to lenders, to home buyers**

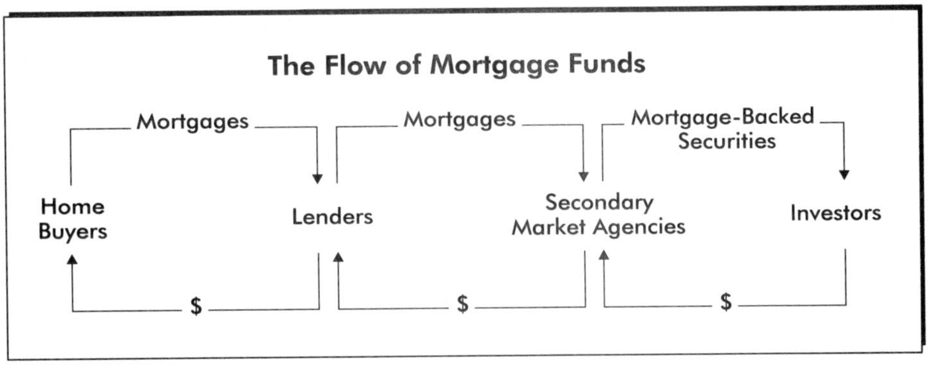

securities that are then sold to investors on the open market. The three largest "middlemen" (intermediary agencies) in the secondary market are **Fannie Mae** (the Federal National Mortgage Association, or FNMA), **Freddie Mac** (the Federal Home Loan Mortgage Corporation, or FHLMC), and **Ginnie Mae** (the Government National Mortgage Association, or GNMA).

Exercise 1

1. What is the definition of an appraisal?

   An opinion of value. The act or process of developing an opinion of value.

2. What three types of services are included in the definition of appraisal practice?

   Appraisal, Appraisal Consulting, Appraisal Review.

3. The nonprofit corporation that is responsible for the Uniform Standards of Professional Appraisal Practice, as well as national qualifications standards for appraiser certification, is called:

   The Appraisal Foundation

4. List three common uses of appraisals.

   a. Real Estate Buyers and Sellers - What to offer?

   b. Financial Institutions - in connection w/ lending

   c. Government - taxation and condemnation

Real Estate

Earlier in this chapter, we saw that the purpose of most appraisals is to develop an opinion of a defined type of value for a particular interest in a particular property as of a specified date. Obviously, the concept of property is of vital importance in the appraisal process. In general, property can be defined as anything that can be owned. Appraisers develop opinions of value for many different sorts of property, including land, buildings, businesses, artwork, and antiques, among other things. For the purposes of this book, however, we are concerned only with the appraisal of real estate.

Definitions of Real Estate

In appraisal practice, the term **real estate** has a very specific meaning. The Uniform Standards of Professional Appraisal Practice define real estate as "an identified parcel or tract of land, including improvements, if any." For appraisal purposes, a parcel or tract of land is identified by its formal **legal description**, which precisely locates the boundaries of the parcel. (Legal descriptions are discussed in detail in Chapter 4.)

In theory, a parcel of **land** consists of an **inverted pyramid**, with its peak at the center of the earth and its sides extending through the surface boundaries of the parcel and out into space. (See Figure 1.2.) So ownership of land includes ownership of the subsurface below and the air space above, as well as ownership of the surface of the land. Things that occur naturally on or in the land, such as minerals, vegetation, or bodies of water, are often considered part of the land as well.

The second component of real estate, in addition to land, is **improvements**. An improvement is something that is added to the land by human effort, such as utilities or buildings or landscaping. It is something that was not originally part of the real estate, but has become so by virtue of being attached to the land or closely associated with it in some way. Improvements are often referred to as **fixtures**, because they are usually affixed to the land (or to other fixtures on the land such as buildings) in a relatively permanent fashion.

Fig. 1.2 The Inverted Pyramid

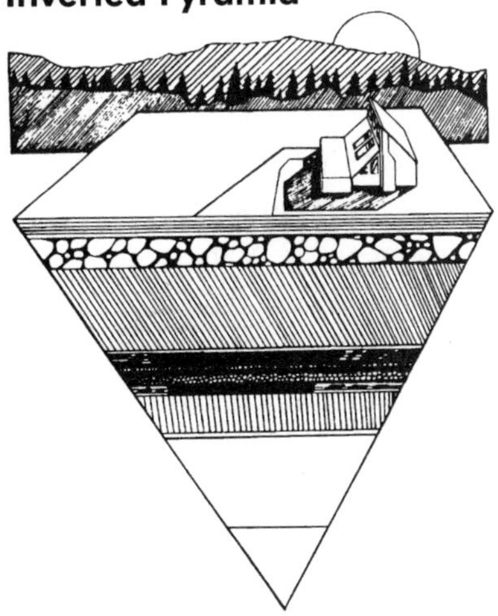

Example: A stack of lumber sitting in a garage is not an improvement. But if the lumber is used to build a fence on the property, it becomes attached to the land and constitutes an improvement or fixture that is part of the real estate.

Distinguishing Real Estate from Personal Property

Real estate or real property is distinguished from **personal property**, which is defined by the USPAP as "all tangible property that is not classified as real estate." Typically, the value of personal property is excluded from an appraisal of real property. So an appraiser must be able to distinguish between items that are part of the real estate, and items that are personal property. While most items fall squarely into one category or the other, the distinction between real estate and personal property is not always easy to make.

The legal tests for determining whether an item is real estate or personal property vary somewhat from state to state, but they all tend to address the same basic issues. A key consideration is the **method of attachment** of the item to the real estate. Movable items are usually personal property; immovable items are usually real estate. The harder it is to remove something from the land, the more likely it is to be considered real estate, and vice versa.

Example: A mobile home that is mounted on wheels and connected to temporary utility hookups is likely to be viewed as personal property. But the same mobile home, if attached to a permanent foundation in the same location, would probably be considered part of the real estate.

A second consideration in distinguishing real estate from personal property is the **adaptation** of the item to the real estate. Items are more likely to be deemed part of the real estate if they are specially adapted or designed to function as part of it.

Example: Even though they are not physically attached in any way, the keys to a house are normally considered part of the real estate, because their function is so closely tied to that particular property.

The third major factor that affects classification of items as real estate or personal property is the **intention of the interested parties**. In the sale of a house, for example, the buyer and seller may agree that a certain antique light fixture is not part of the real estate, and will be removed and taken away by the seller.

The intention of the parties can be determined from their expressed agreement (as in the case of the light fixture above), or by the surrounding circumstances. For example, tenants often install fixtures in rented properties, with the intention of removing them at the conclusion of the lease. In the absence of any agreement to the contrary, such tenant-installed items are usually considered the personal property of the tenant, even though they are attached to the real estate.

Fixtures that are installed by a tenant in connection with the operation of a business on the leased property are known as **trade fixtures**. It is commonly accepted that such fixtures remain the personal property of the tenant (unless specifically agreed otherwise), and may be removed by the tenant when the lease expires. The tenant is, however, responsible for repairing any damage caused to the real estate by removing the items.

Exercise 2

1. Property is anything that can be owned.

2. The USPAP defines "real estate" as:

   an identified parcel or tract of land including improvements, if any.

3. Equipment installed by a tenant in connection with the operation of a business on the leased property is known as:

   Trade fixtures.

4. Which of the following items would ordinarily be considered real estate?

X	a. fence		f. portable air conditioner
	b. furniture		g. swing set
X	c. shrubbery	X	h. water heater
X	d. detached garage	X	i. wall-to-wall carpeting
X	e. custom window blinds		j. picnic table

Real Property

The terms real estate and real property are often used interchangeably, and in fact they have the same legal definitions in many jurisdictions. Traditionally, however, appraisers have drawn a distinction between:

- real estate, which is the physical land and improvements, and
- real property, which refers to the interests, benefits, and rights inherent in the ownership of real estate.

The basic legal rights of property ownership, called the **bundle of rights**, include the right to use, lease, enjoy, encumber, will, sell, or do nothing with the property. The ownership rights to a particular parcel may also include **appurtenant rights**. An appurtenance is something that goes along with ownership of land. Examples include easements, mineral rights, and water rights.

Example: A property that lacks direct access to a public street will usually have an easement for right-of-way across some adjacent parcel. The right to use the easement for access is an appurtenant right that goes along with ownership of the property.

Because real estate appraisals are always concerned with a defined real property interest, appraisers need to understand the characteristics of the different types of interests, which we'll discuss next. One fundamental distinction is that some types of interests give the holder the right to possess the real estate and other types do not. Possessory interests in real property are called **estates**, while nonpossessory interests are known as **encumbrances**.

Estates

An **estate** is a real property interest that includes the right of possession—the exclusive right to occupy and use the real estate, either in the present or at some point in the future. For example, an owner who leases her property gives up the right of possession to the tenant for the term of the lease. However, the owner still has an estate, because she is entitled to regain possession in the future, when the lease expires.

There are two main categories of estates: freehold estates and leasehold estates. A **freehold estate** includes title; in other words, the holder of a freehold estate owns the property. A **leasehold estate** does not include title—the estate holder is only a tenant.

Freehold Estates. The most common freehold estate is the **fee simple**, often referred to simply as the **fee**. The fee simple is the most complete and comprehensive form of real property interest; it includes the entire bundle of rights. It is also the most commonly appraised interest in residential real estate appraisals.

A second (and far less common) type of freehold estate is the **life estate**. A life estate terminates automatically upon the death of a specified person—either the person holding the life estate (the **life tenant**), or some other person designated as the **measuring life**.

Example: Ramirez deeds a piece of property "to Gray for the life of Carter." Gray is the life tenant, and Carter is the measuring life. Gray owns the property during Carter's lifetime. When Carter dies, Gray's life estate ends.

When a life estate is created, a future interest is created at the same time. The future interest is an **estate in reversion** if the property will revert to the grantor when the life estate ends. It's an **estate in remainder** if the property will go to a third party instead.

Example: Ramirez deeds property "to Gray for the life of Carter, and then to Hollins." Hollins has an estate in remainder; he is referred to as the remainderman. When Carter dies and Gray's life estate ends, Hollins will own the property in fee simple. If Ramirez had not named a remainderman in the deed, the property would have reverted to her (or, if Ramirez had died in the meantime, to her heirs).

Leasehold Estates. A tenant or lessee under a lease has a real property interest called a leasehold estate. The rights that accompany a leasehold estate are determined by the terms of the lease agreement. The most important of these rights is the exclusive right to use and occupy the leased real estate for the specified lease term, but the lease agreement may give the lessee other rights with respect to the property as well. For example, the lease may specify that the lessee is entitled to transfer or sublease his interest to a third party.

Leases are classified according to how and when they are terminated. A lease that terminates on a specific date (such as a lease for six months or one year) creates a **tenancy for years**. A lease that automatically renews itself until one of the parties takes action to terminate it (such as a month-to-month lease) creates a **periodic tenancy**.

If a tenant remains in possession of the leased property after the termination of a tenancy for years or a periodic tenancy, the result is a tenancy at will or a tenancy at sufferance. In a **tenancy at will**, the landlord agrees to let the tenant remain in possession for an indefinite period of time, usually until agreement can be reached on the terms of a new lease. A **tenancy at sufferance** arises if the tenant remains in possession without the consent of the landlord.

The ownership rights retained by the landlord are called the **leased fee**. For example, an owner who leases her property transfers the right to occupy and use the property for a limited period of time, but retains the right to receive rental payments during the lease period. She will regain possessory rights at the end of the lease term.

Fig. 1.3 Types of Estates

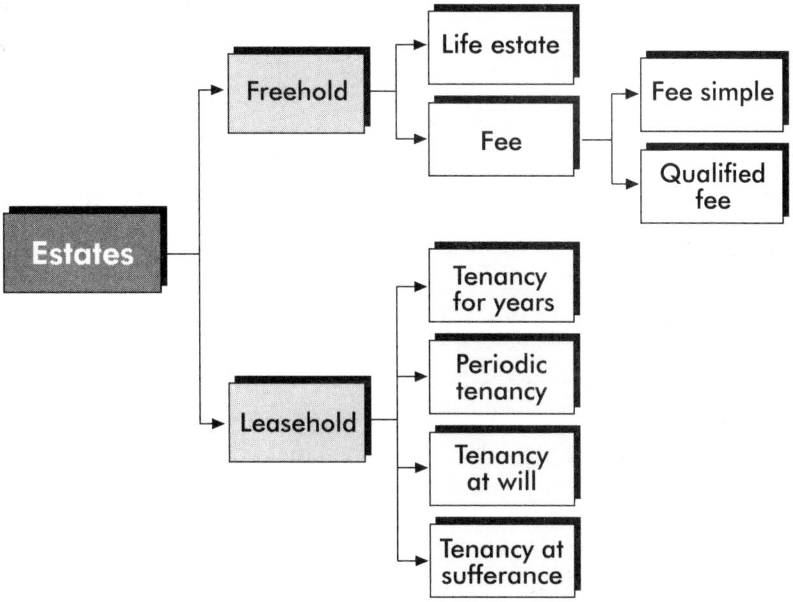

Appraisers may be called upon to develop an opinion of the value of leasehold estates. Appraisals of the ownership interest in the leased fee are also common. Appraisal of leasehold and leased fee estates is discussed in detail in Chapter 13.

Exercise 3

1. The most complete form of real estate ownership is the:

   Fee Simple Estate

2. An estate is a real property interest that includes the right to: (Right of Possession)

   Occupy and use the Real Estate, either in the present or some point in the future

3. The type of estate that does not include title to property is called a/an:

   A Leasehold Estate

4. The interest of a tenant under a month-to-month lease is a/an:

   Periodic tenancy

5. A nonpossessory interest in real estate is known as a/an:

   Encumbrance

Encumbrances

The second major category of real property interests is **encumbrances**. Encumbrances are interests that do not include the exclusive right to use and occupy real estate; in other words, they are nonpossessory interests. Encumbrances may be financial interests such as mortgages, or nonfinancial interests such as easements.

Financial Encumbrances. Financial encumbrances are commonly known as **liens** or **security interests**. A lien is a nonpossessory interest that is held by a creditor in property owned by a debtor. It gives the creditor the right to sell the debtor's real estate and use the proceeds of the sale to pay off the debt, in the event that the debtor does not pay the debt according to its terms. The forced sale of security property to satisfy a debt is referred to as **foreclosure**.

Fig. 1.4 Types of Encumbrances

Financial Encumbrances	Nonfinancial Encumbrances
Mortgages Deeds of trust Construction liens Judgment liens Attachment liens Property tax liens Other tax liens	Easements Profits Private restrictions

Liens can be classified as either voluntary or involuntary, and also as either general or specific. A **voluntary lien** is a security interest that is created voluntarily by the debtor. Mortgages and deeds of trust that are used to secure loans are common examples of voluntary liens. **Involuntary liens** arise through the operation of law. They include such liens as tax liens, judgment liens, and construction liens.

A **general lien** is a lien that affects all of the property owned by the debtor, including real estate. Judgment liens are usually general liens, since they apply to any property that the judgment debtor may happen to own. **Specific liens**, on the other hand, apply only to a particular property or group of properties. Voluntary liens (such as mortgages) are usually specific liens, since they usually specify the particular property or properties that will serve as security for the mortgage debt. Some types of involuntary liens (such as property tax liens or construction liens) are also specific to a particular property.

Nonfinancial Encumbrances. Unlike financial encumbrances, nonfinancial encumbrances affect the use of real estate. The three most common forms of nonpossessory use rights are:

1. easements,
2. profits, and
3. private restrictions.

Easements. An **easement** is a nonexclusive right to use someone else's property for a particular purpose. A property that is subject to (burdened by) an easement is referred to as the **servient tenement**. The property that benefits from the easement is referred to as the **dominant tenement**.

Example: If your neighbor has a right-of-way easement across your property for purposes of access, your property (Lot A) is the servient tenement. Your neighbor's property (Lot B) is the dominant tenement.

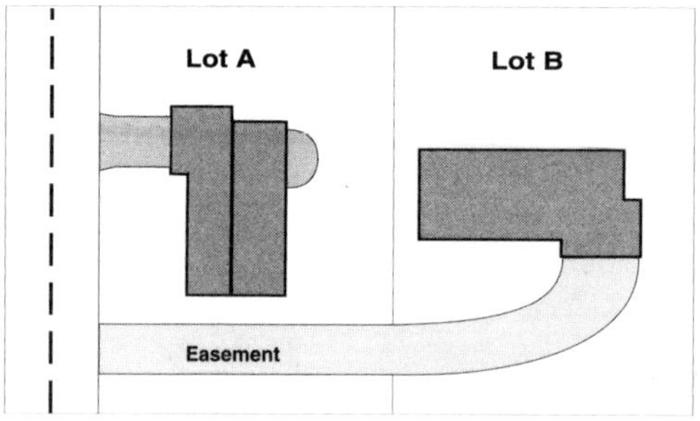

In the example above, the right-of-way is an **appurtenant easement**, because it burdens one parcel of land for the benefit of another. The easement right is appurtenant to ownership of the benefited parcel. If the benefited property were sold, the easement right would pass to the new owner along with the rest of the ownership rights in the property. Similarly, the easement is considered an encumbrance on the servient tenement. If the servient property were sold, the encumbrance would pass to the new owner as a restriction on the use of the property.

In contrast to appurtenant easements, **easements in gross** don't benefit a particular parcel; they benefit a person or an organization. An easement granted to a utility company for installation and maintenance of utility lines is a common example of an easement in gross.

Profits. Another type of nonfinancial encumbrance is a profit. A **profit** is the right to take something (usually a renewable resource such as timber or gravel) from someone else's property.

Private Restrictions. Some of the most common nonfinancial encumbrances for residential real estate are private restrictions, which may take the form of **deed restrictions** limiting the use of an individual property, or **covenants, conditions, and restrictions (CC&Rs)** affecting properties in a condominium or subdivision.

Deed restrictions are typically created by a prior owner to limit the future use of the property. These restrictions can be used for a variety of purposes, such as limiting structures to one story, or prohibiting tree heights from interfering with neighboring views. Like easements, private restrictions can "run with the land," binding all subsequent owners of the property.

CC&Rs are usually established when a subdivision is created. The subdivision developer records a declaration of CC&Rs, and includes a reference to it in the deeds that transfer ownership of each of the condominium units or subdivision lots to their individual owners.

Private restrictions are a form of land use regulation similar to zoning. They can cover a wide range of subjects, including building sizes and styles, fence heights, landscaping, parking, and even what sort of pets may be kept on the property. The big difference between private restrictions and zoning is that private restrictions are not enforced by the government. Instead, they are enforceable by private owners or homeowners associations.

Exercise 4

1. Which of the following real property interests are possessory?

   X a. life estate
   ___ b. easement
   X c. leasehold
   ___ d. lien
   ___ e. profit
   X f. fee simple

2. Financial encumbrances are also known as:

   liens

   or Security interests

3. Indicate whether each of the following types of liens is specific or general (S/G) and voluntary or involuntary (V/I).

S/G	V/I	
G	I	judgment lien
S	V	mortgage
S	I	property tax lien
S	V	deed of trust
S	I	construction lien

4. Name the type of easement that does not benefit a particular parcel of real estate.

   Easement in gross

5. The instrument used to create private restrictions is a/an:

   Deed Restrictions, CC+R's

Government Restrictions on Property Rights

Earlier in this chapter, we saw that the fee simple interest in real estate is the most complete and comprehensive form of real property interest. But even though the fee simple owner has the full bundle of ownership rights, his or her control of the real estate is not absolute. All private ownership rights are subject to the legitimate powers of government, including the powers of eminent domain and taxation and the police power.

Eminent Domain. The government may use its power of **eminent domain** to take private property for public use, as long as it pays just compensation to the private property owner for the taking. If a government agency cannot acquire needed property through a voluntary sale by the owner, it may use the power of eminent domain to file a condemnation lawsuit, forcing the owner to give up the property in return for just compensation. Condemnation lawsuits commonly require the services of appraisers to give expert testimony regarding the market value of the condemned property.

Taxation. Ownership of real estate is subject to taxation in the form of general property taxes and special assessments. **General property taxes** are usually assessed on an annual basis, and they apply to all properties that are not exempted by law. Because they are based on the value of the real estate, they are often referred to as **ad valorem** taxes, which is Latin for "according to value." General property taxes are levied by the individual states, each of which has its own separate laws governing tax rates, assessments, exemptions, and other details.

Special assessments are taxes that are levied against particular properties in order to cover the cost of public improvements that benefit those properties. The properties that are subject to the assessments comprise a special assessment district (also called a local improvement district). Properties outside the district are not subject to the special assessment tax. Unlike general property taxes, special assessments are a one-time tax. They expire once sufficient tax revenue has been collected to pay for the improvements.

Police Power. The government's power to make and enforce regulations for the protection of the public health, safety and welfare is referred to as the **police power.** This broad power is exercised in many forms and often affects real estate values significantly. It is the basis for land use regulations such as community planning ordinances and zoning laws, and also for building codes, subdivision development regulations, and environmental protection legislation.

Escheat. If a person dies without leaving a will or heirs, any real property owned by that person will **escheat**. This means that title to the property passes to the state or county government. To obtain title, the government must follow certain legal procedures. The government may also use escheat to obtain title to abandoned property.

Exercise 5

1. The government's power to take private property for public use is called eminent Domain. This power is exercised through the process of Condemnation, and requires the government to pay Compensation to the private property owner.

2. A temporary tax levied only on certain properties in order to cover the cost of public improvements that benefit those properties is called a/an:

   Special assessment

3. General property taxes are sometimes referred to as "ad valorem" taxes, because:

   they are based on the value of the RE

4. List three common exercises of the police power as it affects real estate:

   a. Basis for land use regulations.

   b. Building Codes

   c. Environmental protection legislation

5. When a person dies without a will or heirs, his or her property passes to the state through the process of:

   Escheat

Key Terms

Ad valorem—A Latin phrase meaning "according to value." Used to describe general property taxes that are levied on the basis of a property's assessed value.

Appraisal—The act or process of developing an opinion of value; an opinion of value (USPAP definition). A form of appraisal practice.

Appraisal assignment—The task of appraising a particular property under specified terms and conditions.

Appraisal consulting—The act or process of developing an analysis, recommendation, or opinion to solve a problem, where an opinion of value is a component of the analysis leading to the assignment results (USPAP definition). A form of appraisal practice.

Appraisal practice—Valuation services performed by an individual acting as an appraiser, including but not limited to appraisal, appraisal review, or appraisal consulting (USPAP definition).

Appraisal review—The act or process of developing and communicating an opinion about the quality of another appraiser's work that was performed as part of an appraisal, appraisal review, or appraisal consulting assignment (USPAP definition). A form of appraisal practice.

Appurtenance—Something that goes along with ownership of real estate, such as mineral rights or an easement.

Assessment—1. The valuation of property for property tax purposes. 2. The amount of a property tax. 3. The process of levying a property tax.

Bundle of rights—A description of property ownership in terms of the various rights that ownership conveys.

Charter—A license to operate a depository financial institution, granted by either the federal government or a state government.

Depository institution—A financial institution that accepts deposits from its account holders. Includes savings institutions (also known as savings and loan associations or thrifts), commercial banks, and credit unions.

Easement—A nonexclusive right to use someone else's property for a particular purpose. A type of nonfinancial encumbrance. Appurtenant easements benefit a particular piece of real estate. Easements in gross benefit individuals or organizations.

Eminent domain—The power of government to take private property for public use upon payment of just compensation. This power is exercised through the process of condemnation.

Encumbrance—A real property interest that does not include the present or future right of possession. Financial encumbrances (such as mortgages) affect title to the real estate. Nonfinancial encumbrances (such as easements) affect the use of the real estate.

Escheat—Reversion of property to the state when the owner dies without leaving a will or heirs.

Estate—A real property interest that includes the right of possession, i.e., the exclusive right to occupy and use the real estate. Estates may be freehold estates (ownership) or leasehold estates (tenancy).

Fee appraiser—An appraiser who is self-employed, or who works for a company whose primary business is to provide appraisal services to others

Fee simple—A freehold estate that is the most complete and comprehensive form of real property interest, including the entire bundle of rights.

Freehold—An estate that includes the rights of ownership or title, either presently or in the future. Freehold estates include the fee simple, the life estate, the estate in remainder, and the estate in reversion.

General property tax—A property tax levied against all non-exempt property, usually on the basis of a property's value (ad valorem).

Improvement—An item of personal property that is added to the land by human effort, in such a way as to become part of the real estate. Also called a fixture.

Land—The surface of the earth, together with all that it contains.

Leased fee—The real property interest of the landlord (owner) under a lease, which includes ownership but not the immediate right of possession.

Leasehold—A non-freehold estate, which includes the right of possession during the term of the lease, but not ownership or title. The real property interest held by a tenant under a lease. Also known as a tenancy. Leasehold estates include the tenancy for years (created by a term lease), the periodic tenancy (created by a period-to-period lease), and the tenancy at will (created when a tenant remains in possession with the landlord's consent after expiration of a valid lease).

Legal description—A description of a parcel of real estate in a form that is legally approved in the state where the property is located. Common systems of legal description include the metes and bounds, government (rectangular) survey, and lot and block systems.

Lien—A financial encumbrance. The holder of a lien has the right to force the sale (foreclosure) of the liened property and use the proceeds of the sale to satisfy a debt, in the event that the debt is not paid according to its terms. Specific liens (such as mortgages) apply only to a particular piece of real estate, while general liens (such as judgment liens) apply to all real estate owned by the debtor.

Life estate—A freehold estate that terminates automatically upon the death of the person designated as the measuring life.

Personal property—All tangible property that is not classified as real estate (USPAP definition).

Police power—The power of government to make and enforce regulations for the protection of the public health, safety, and welfare. It is the basis for zoning laws, land use regulations, building codes, etc.

Primary market—The market in which financial institutions (or other real estate lenders) make real estate loans to home buyers.

Purpose of appraisal—The information that a client wants the appraiser to provide in an appraisal assignment. The purpose of most appraisals is to estimate a defined value for a specific real property interest in a specific parcel of real estate as of a specific date.

Private restriction—A type of nonfinancial encumbrance that limits the types of uses that an owner may make of real estate. They are most commonly created by developers at the time of subdivision, and are enforced by other property owners, often through a homeowners association. Also called a deed restriction.

Real estate—An identified parcel or tract of land, including improvements, if any (USPAP definition).

Real property—The interests, benefits, and rights inherent in the ownership of real estate (USPAP definition).

Report—Any communication, written or oral, of an appraisal, appraisal review, or appraisal consulting service that is transmitted to the client upon completion of an assignment (USPAP definition). The means by which an appraiser's value conclusions are communicated to the client.

Secondary market—The market in which real estate loans are packaged and resold to investors. The major secondary market organizations are FNMA, FHLMC and GNMA.

Servient tenement—A parcel of land that is subject to an easement.

Special assessment—A form of property tax levied against properties in a special assessment district or local improvement district, in order to cover the cost of certain public improvements that benefit those properties. It is a one-time tax that expires when sufficient tax revenue has been collected to pay for the improvements.

Staff appraiser—An appraiser employed by a business, government agency, or other organization to perform appraisal services that relate to the employer's operations.

Trade fixture—A fixture installed by a tenant in connection with the operation of a business on leased property. Usually considered to be the personal property of the tenant, and not part of the real estate.

Use of appraisal—The reason why a client wants to know the information that an appraiser will provide in an appraisal assignment.

Value—The monetary relationship between properties and those who buy, sell, or use those properties (USPAP definition). The theoretical worth of something, expressed in terms of something else, usually money.

Summary

I. An appraisal is an opinion of value.

A. The appraiser's judgment and experience are vital factors in developing an opinion of value.

B. An appraisal is always related to a particular defined value.

C. Appraisal practice includes appraisal, appraisal consulting, and appraisal review.

D. The appraisal profession has come under increasing government regulation in recent years, including requirements for licensing and certification, and Uniform Standards of Professional Appraisal Practice (USPAP).

E. The purpose of an appraisal is to develop an opinion of a defined value for a specific real property interest in a specific parcel of real estate, as of a specific date.

F. The use of an appraisal refers to the reason that the client (user) wants to know the appraisal information. Appraisals have a wide variety of uses by many different kinds of clients.

G. Staff appraisers provide appraisal services to meet the needs of their employers. Independent fee appraisers provide appraisal services to others on a contract basis.

II. Property is anything that can be owned. Appraisers develop opinions of the value of all types of properties, including real estate and personal property.

A. Real estate consists of land and improvements.

1. Land can be viewed as an inverted pyramid, including the surface, subsurface and airspace. Things that occur naturally on or in the land are part of the real estate as well.
2. Improvements are man-made objects that are attached to the land or closely associated with it, so as to become part of the real estate. They are sometimes called attachments or fixtures.

B. Personal property includes all property that is not classified as real estate. Personal property is usually movable, while real estate is usually immovable.

1. Whether an item is real estate or personal property depends on its method of attachment, its adaptation to the real estate, the intent of the interested parties, and any agreement between the parties.
2. Trade fixtures are usually considered to be the personal property of the tenant.

III. Real property consists of a bundle of rights. These rights may be divided in various ways, creating different types of real property interests.

A. Possessory interests (estates) include the exclusive right to use and occupy the real estate, either now or at some time in the future.

1. Freehold estates include the fee simple, which is the most complete form of real property interest, and the life estate.

2. Leasehold estates include the right of possession, but not title. They are created by lease agreements. The most common leasehold estates are the tenancy for years (term lease) and the periodic tenancy (periodic lease).

B. Nonpossessory interests are referred to as encumbrances. They may be financial or nonfinancial in nature.

1. A financial encumbrance (lien or security interest) gives the holder the right to sell the property to satisfy a debt. The sale is accomplished through foreclosure. Liens may be general or specific, and voluntary or involuntary.

2. An easement gives the holder a nonexclusive right to use someone else's property for a particular purpose. Easements that benefit one parcel of land while encumbering another are called appurtenant easements. Easements that do not benefit a parcel of land are called easements in gross.

3. A profit gives the holder the right to take something from the land of another.

4. Private restrictions are common in subdivision developments and condominiums.

C. Private property interests are limited by the powers of government.

1. Eminent domain is the power to take private land for public use, with payment of just compensation. If necessary, this power is exercised through the legal process of condemnation.

2. States have the power to imposes taxes on real estate. General real estate taxes apply to all non-exempt property, and are assessed regularly on the basis of property values. Special assessments apply only to properties that benefit from some public improvement, and are levied only to the extent necessary to cover the cost of the improvement.

3. Police power is the power of government to make laws for the public health, safety and welfare. Planning and zoning, building codes, subdivision development regulations, and environmental protection laws are examples of police power regulations.

Chapter Quiz

1. According to the USPAP, appraisal practice includes:
   a. appraisal only
   b. appraisal and review
   c. appraisal and consulting
   d. appraisal, consulting, and review

2. An appraisal assignment that called for analysis of real estate data and recommendations other than an opinion of value, would be considered:
   a. appraisal
   b. appraisal practice
   c. consulting
   d. Both b) and c)

3. The organization that is responsible for national qualification standards for appraiser certification and for the Uniform Standards of Professional Appraisal Practice is the:
   a. Appraisal Institute
   b. Appraisal Foundation
   c. Federal Appraisal Council
   d. Federal National Mortgage Association

4. An appraiser who performs appraisal services for others on a contract basis is known as a/an:
   a. staff appraiser
   b. temporary appraiser
   c. independent fee appraiser
   d. commission appraiser

5. According to the USPAP, real estate includes land and:
   a. nothing else
   b. improvements
   c. improvements and encumbrances
   d. improvements and trade fixtures

6. The interest of a landlord in leased property is known as:
   a. a fee simple
   b. a leasehold
   c. a leased fee
   d. None of the above

7. The power of government to regulate for the public health, safety, and welfare is known as:
   a. the police power
   b. the power of eminent domain
   c. states' rights
   d. sovereignty

8. An item that is not part of the real estate is considered to be:
   a. a fixture
   b. an appurtenance
   c. an improvement
   d. personal property

9. A possessory estate that includes title to the real estate is a/an:
   a. freehold estate
   b. easement estate
   c. leasehold estate
   d. tenancy estate

10. A mortgage lien is an example of a lien that is:
    a. general and voluntary
    b. general and involuntary
    c. specific and voluntary
    d. specific and involuntary

11. The term "ad valorem" refers to:
    a. the calculation of just compensation for eminent domain purposes
    b. the effect on property value that results from location in a special improvement district
    c. the manner in which general property taxes are assessed
    d. the general nature of judgment liens

12. Smith and Jones are neighbors. There is an easement across Jones' property to provide access to Smith's parcel. If Jones sells his property to Brown:
    a. Smith must negotiate a new easement agreement with Brown
    b. Smith may continue to use the easement without interruption, regardless of the sale
    c. Smith may continue to use the easement unless Brown objects
    d. Smith must notify Brown of the existence of the easement

13. An easement granted to a utility company for the purpose of installing and maintaining utility lines for a residence is an example of a/an:
    a. appurtenant easement
    b. dominant easement
    c. servient easement
    d. easement in gross

14. Which of the following would be most likely to be considered personal property?
    a. Keys to a house
    b. Standard kitchen refrigerator
    c. Built-in oven
    d. Storm windows

15. The opinion of a defined value for a specific real property interest in a specific parcel of real estate, as of a specific date, is the:
    a. purpose of an appraisal
    b. definition of an appraisal
    c. use of an appraisal
    d. practice of appraisal

Quiz Answers

1. d) Appraisal practice, according to the USPAP, includes appraisal, consulting, and appraisal review.

2. d) If an appraisal assignment includes making recommendations in addition to providing an estimate of the property's value, it would be considered consulting. According to the USPAP, consulting is a form of appraisal practice.

3. b) The Appraisal Foundation is the organization responsible for establishing professional standards for appraisers and updating the Uniform Standards of Professional Appraisal Practice.

4. c) An appraiser who is independently employed and performs appraisal services for a variety of clients is an independent fee appraiser.

5. b) The USPAP definition of real estate includes land and improvements. This is an important distinction from the definition of real property, which is defined as all interests, benefits, and rights inherent in the ownership of real estate (which would include appurtenances).

6. c) A landlord who leases property holds an interest known as a leased fee.

7. a) The government's power to regulate property for public health, safety, and welfare is known as the police power.

8. d) Any item that is not classified as part of the real estate is considered to be personal property.

9. a) The highest form of ownership is a freehold estate, which includes title to the property and the right to possess the property.

10. c) Because a mortgage pertains to one particular property and is a lien that a home buyer chooses to accept, it is considered a specific and voluntary lien.

11. c) "Ad valorem" is a Latin phrase meaning "according to value," which is appropriate since property taxes are levied according to the assessed value of the property.

12. b) An easement appurtenant runs with the land, and the benefits and burdens will continue to apply even if the servient tenement is sold.

13. d) An easement held by a utility company for maintenance purposes is an easement in gross, which applies only to the utility company and does not run with the land.

14. b) A refrigerator, while large, is usually not permanently attached to the real estate. A built-in oven and storm windows, by contrast, are permanently attached. House keys are considered part of the real property because they are specifically adapted to that particular property, even though they are not physically attached.

15. b) An appraisal is defined as the opinion of a defined value of a specific property as of a specific date.

Exercise Answers

#1
1. An estimate of value; the act or process of estimating value
2. Appraisal; appraisal consulting; appraisal review
3. The Appraisal Foundation
4. Valuation of property for sale or tax purposes; evaluating property offered as loan security; guiding investment decisions

#2
1. Property
2. An identified parcel or tract of land, including improvements, if any
3. Trade fixtures
4. a, c, d, e, h, i

#3
1. Fee simple
2. Possession
3. Leasehold
4. Periodic tenancy
5. Encumbrance

#4
1. a, c, f
2. Liens; security interests
3. G,I; S,V; S,I; S,V; S,I
4. Easement in gross
5. Deed

#5 1. Eminent domain; condemnation; just compensation

2. Special assessment

3. They are levied according to the value of the taxed property

4. Planning ordinances; zoning laws; building codes; subdivision development regulations; environmental protection legislation

5. Escheat

2 Understanding Value

Overview

The appraiser's job is to estimate value. Therefore, it is essential for appraisers to have a good understanding of the meaning of value, how it is created, and the forces that affect it. After completing this chapter, you should:

- be able to define value and identify the factors that interact to create it;
- be able to distinguish between value, price, and cost;
- understand the concepts of markets, supply and demand, substitution, competition, change, and anticipation, and how they affect real estate values;
- understand the concepts of agents of production, balance, surplus productivity, contribution, increasing and decreasing returns, highest and best use, consistent use, and conformity, and their application to real estate appraisal;
- be able to define market value and list its essential characteristics;
- be able to define use value, investment value, liquidation value, assessed value, and insurable value; and
- understand the ways in which social, economic, governmental, and environmental forces influence real estate values.

What is Value?

In its simplest form, the term "value" refers to the relative worth of a thing, expressed in terms of some other thing. In our society, value is expressed in terms of the accepted medium of exchange: dollars and cents. Thus, a common definition of value is "the monetary relationship between properties and those who buy, sell, or use those properties" (USPAP definition).

Although the concept of value seems simple on its face, it has been (and continues to be) the subject of a great deal of study. The modern concept of value has evolved over centuries, and the principles of value that appraisers use today took a long time to become widely accepted. As you learn about those principles, keep in mind that they are all dependent on one another. The theory of value should be viewed as a unified whole.

In this chapter, we will first consider the four factors of value and discuss the distinction between value, price, and cost. We will then explore the economic principles that help describe how value is created in the marketplace, and look at some of the rules used by appraisers as they apply those economic principles. Finally, we will examine how social, economic, governmental, and physical or environmental forces can influence the value of real estate.

Four Factors of Value

According to economic theory, value is not intrinsic. In other words, the value of something is not inherent in the thing itself, but is created by certain conditions or circumstances known as the **four factors of value**. These are:

- utility,
- scarcity,
- desire, and
- effective purchasing power.

The four factors of value interact to affect the relationship between supply and demand. (We'll discuss the principle of supply and demand in detail later in the chapter.) A thing—a property, a product, or a commodity—will not have value unless all four factors are present.

Utility. For something to have value, it must first have **utility**. This means it must satisfy some want or need that potential buyers have. Real estate generally has considerable utility; it can satisfy many different needs. For example, it may be a site for permanent structures that serve a wide variety of purposes (homes for shelter, factories for industrial production, and so on); it may be put to recreational use; it may produce agricultural or

Fig. 2.1 The Four Factors of Value

1. Utility
2. Scarcity
3. Desire
4. Effective purchasing power

mineral products; or it may generate income for the property owner. However, in certain circumstances a particular piece of real estate might have little utility.

> **Example:** An undersized vacant lot is subject to zoning rules and private restrictions that prevent it from being used in the same way that surrounding properties are used. As a result, the property lacks utility.

Scarcity. The second factor of value is **scarcity**. Even if a thing has utility, it will not have value if it is overabundant. For example, while air is certainly very useful, it is so abundant as to have no monetary value. This is an extreme illustration of the principle of supply and demand. When the supply of a commodity or a product far outstrips the demand for it, value becomes negligible.

> **Example:** Waterfront property is more valuable than non-waterfront property because of its scarcity. If every home in a community had water frontage, then waterfront property would not be scarce, and it would not command a premium price.

Desire. While utility and scarcity are concerned with attributes of the property, product, or commodity, the other two factors of value concern characteristics of potential purchasers. The third factor is **desire**. For something to have value, there must be potential purchasers who have a desire to own it.

Effective Purchasing Power. Desire alone is not enough; it must be coupled with the fourth factor of value, **effective purchasing power**. In other words, a thing cannot have value unless there are potential purchasers who have the ability to pay for it. Purchasing power is measured in terms of current economic conditions such as inflation, unemployment, and wage scales, and it has a tremendous impact on real estate values.

Exercise 1

Choose the factor(s) of value that is or are lacking from each property described. (The same factor may be used more than once.)

1. ___ remote desert land		a. utility
2. ___ a condominium in an overbuilt neighborhood		b. scarcity
3. ___ a lot that is not buildable because of zoning restrictions		c. desire
4. ___ a house in a community where the primary employer has announced the closing of the local factory		d. purchasing power

Value Distinguished from Price and Cost

The terms value, price, and cost are often used interchangeably in everyday conversation, but they have distinct meanings for appraisal purposes. **Value** refers to what a piece of property is theoretically worth under certain circumstances. **Price**, on the other hand, refers to the actual amount paid for an item by a particular buyer to a particular seller in an actual transaction. Value is a concept; price is a fact.

> **Example:** A purchaser buys a house for $400,000. Similar homes in the neighborhood were selling for $415,000, but the seller lowered his price because he needed to sell quickly. Although the price is $400,000, the value of the house is probably more than $400,000. In any event, an appraiser could not determine its value solely on the basis of the price.

The term **cost** is used most often to refer to the production of an item, as opposed to price and value, which refer to an exchange. In the context of real estate, cost is the sum of money required to develop and/or build improvements on the land.

> **Example:** A homeowner pays $20,000 to install a swimming pool. The home is located where the weather is suitable for swimming only eight weeks out of the year. The cost of the improvement is $20,000. Its value is likely to be much less, since the improvement has such limited utility.

Exercise 2

A developer buys a vacant lot and builds a house on it. He spends a total of $175,000 on the purchase price and construction costs. The developer then lists the improved property for sale and a buyer agrees to pay $195,000 for it.

1. What is the cost of the property? $175,000
2. What is its price? $195,000
3. What is the property's market value? Cannot be determined w/o other factors.

Types of Costs Encountered in Appraisal. There are many different types of costs. Costs are sometimes categorized as either direct costs or indirect costs. **Direct costs** refer to the costs of labor and materials used to build an improvement. **Indirect costs** refer to other costs incurred in the construction process. Examples of indirect costs include contractor's overhead, architectural fees, financing costs, and permit fees.

Appraisers also distinguish between development costs and construction costs. **Development cost** refers to the cost to create a project, such as a housing development. **Construction cost** is the cost to build an improvement, such as a house. Development cost may include the construction cost for each individual improvement that is a part of the development, such as the construction cost of each house in a subdivision.

Example: The following costs are associated with the creation of a single family residential property:

$30,000	raw land
12,000	site utilities, clearing, grading, etc.
7,000	architectural fees
80,000	construction cost for house
+ 4,000	construction loan interest
$133,000	total development cost

The construction cost for the residence is $80,000. The development cost for the project is the total of all the costs, or $133,000.

For appraisal purposes, an important distinction is drawn between the terms replacement cost and reproduction cost. The **replacement cost** of a building is the cost to create a substitute building of equivalent function and utility, using current methods, materials, and techniques. **Reproduction cost** is the cost to create an exact replica of the building, using the same design, materials, and construction methods as were used in the original. The distinction between replacement cost and reproduction cost is explained in detail in Chapter 8.

Types of Value

There are several different types of value. For appraisal purposes, it is vital to distinguish between the different types of value, and to identify the particular type of value the appraiser is estimating. This is so critical, in fact, that appraisal reports always contain a specific definition of the value being estimated. The various types of value that may be estimated in real estate appraisals include market value, investment value, value in use, assessment value, insurable value, liquidation value, and going concern value.

Market Value

The type of value that is most often estimated in real estate appraisals is market value. Market value is sometimes referred to as **exchange value** or **value in exchange**. It is the value of property as determined by the open market. Market value is defined by federal agencies such as Fannie Mae and Freddie Mac as:

"The most probable price which a property should bring in a competitive and open market under all conditions requisite to a fair sale, the buyer and seller each acting prudently and knowledgeably, and assuming the price is not affected by undue stimulus. Implicit in this definition is the consummation of a sale as of a specified date and the passing of title from seller to buyer under conditions whereby: (1) the buyer and seller are typically motivated; (2) both parties are well informed or well advised, and acting in what they consider their best interests; (3) a reasonable time is allowed for exposure in the open market; (4) payment is made in terms of cash in United States dollars or in terms of financial arrangements comparable thereto; and (5) the price represents the normal consideration for the property sold unaffected by special or creative financing or sales concessions granted by anyone associated with the sale."

In other words, market value refers to the amount of cash (or cash equivalent) that is most likely to be paid for a property on a given date in a transaction that takes place under normal conditions. A sale can generally be considered to have taken place under normal conditions if:

- it was an arm's length transaction (a sale between unrelated parties, as opposed to family members, friends, or business associates);
- neither the buyer nor the seller was subject to unusual pressure to act (undue stimulus);
- both the buyer and the seller acted prudently and knowledgeably, and in his or her own best interests; and
- the property was exposed on the open market for a reasonable length of time.

Market Value in Non–Cash Equivalent Transactions. As a practical matter, very few real estate transactions are all cash. When the financing for a transaction is comparable to the financing typically available in the market, it is considered the equivalent of cash. However, if the financing includes concessions that are not typical in the market (such as a below-market interest rate in a seller-financed transaction), the terms that are not cash equivalent must be identified by the appraiser in the appraisal report, and their effect on value must be taken into account.

Other Definitions of Market Value. The term market value has been in use for many years, and has been subject to varying interpretations by economists, judges, and legislatures. As a result, market value does not necessarily mean the same thing in all situations. For example, state laws pertaining to condemnation—the taking of private property for a public purpose—and tax assessment frequently include definitions of market value. When performing an appraisal for purposes governed by state or federal law, the appraiser should use that law's definition of market value.

Value in Use

Value in use (also called **use value**) refers to the value of a property when used only for a particular purpose. This is in contrast to market value, which assumes that the market will set the value of the property in light of all of its possible uses. In addition, use value

Fig. 2.2 Types of Value

1. Market value
2. Value in use
3. Investment value
4. Liquidation value
5. Assessed value
6. Insurable value
7. Going concern value

is commonly viewed in terms of a property's value to an individual or a particular ongoing business operation. Thus, use value is affected by the subjective viewpoint of the potential user or by the business climate in which the business is operating.

Example: A manufacturer places a high use value on its factory located in Commerce City, partly because the location is near the manufacturer's primary supplier of raw materials. If the supplier were to close down or relocate to another area, the use value of the factory to the manufacturer would be diminished, since the manufacturer would now have to pay higher shipping charges to obtain its raw materials.

Value in use appraisals are usually ordered for commercial properties and are most often encountered in three types of situations:

1. industrial property may be appraised for its value in use to the industrial operation, for example, when valuing the assets of a business;
2. governments sometimes grant property tax relief to property used for certain purposes (such as agriculture) by assessing the property at its value in use for those purposes, regardless of the property's highest and best use; and,
3. value in use may be the most appropriate valuation when no competitive market exists for a property, as is often the case for properties with limited markets, such as large factories, schools, and public buildings.

A property may have both a market value and a use value. The appraiser must bear this distinction in mind when asked to estimate the market value of a property for which there is a limited market. Even if no market exists for the property, the appraiser may not substitute a use value estimate for the requested market value. The appropriate procedure in these circumstances is to either report that market value cannot be determined, or to attempt to estimate market value on the basis of data other than current market data (for example, by determining replacement cost).

Investment Value

Investment value is the value of a property to a particular investor with specific investment criteria. Thus, when estimating investment value, it is important that the appraiser clearly understand the investment requirements of the particular investor. Because the goals of the individual investor have a significant effect on the value estimate, investment value is inherently subjective in nature. By comparison, market value is said to represent a more objective standard.

Example: An investor has purchased five of the six parcels it needs in order to develop a planned condominium complex. In addition, the investor has already spent thousands of dollars on development studies and preliminary planning for the complex. Because of its unique circumstances, this investor may be willing to pay a premium to acquire the sixth parcel that it needs for the development. If the current owner of the sixth parcel is aware of the developer's situation, he or she may hold out for an offer of greater than market value for the property.

Liquidation Value

Liquidation value is a form of market value. The primary distinction is that liquidation value assumes that the property must be sold in a limited period of time, which rarely constitutes reasonable exposure to the market. Liquidation value is typically sought when a financial institution is considering foreclosure.

Assessed Value

Assessed value is set by state taxing authorities for the purpose of assessing ad valorem property taxes—annual property taxes that are based on the value of the property. The tax proceeds are used to support general government services. To determine assessed value, the appraiser must first estimate market value (as defined by the tax law), then apply a certain percentage rate (called the assessment ratio) as specified under the assessment statute.

$$\textit{Assessed Value} = \textit{Market Value} \times \textit{Assessment Ratio}$$

For example, one state may specify that property is to be assessed at 100% of market value, while another assesses property at 10% of market value. A $100,000 property would be assessed at $100,000 in the first state (100% × $100,000), and at $10,000 in the second state (10% × $100,000).

Insurable Value

Insurable value is defined by the terms of a particular insurance policy. It refers to the value of property for purposes of reimbursement under the policy.

Going Concern Value

Going concern value is the total value of a proven, ongoing business operation, which includes real property as an integral part of the operation. Going concern value is normally inapplicable to residential real estate.

Exercise 3

Place a check mark next to each transaction in which the sales price is indicative of the market value of the property being transferred (in other words, each sale under normal conditions for the equivalent of cash).

1. A property is sold in a foreclosure sale. ______
2. A property is sold for 5% less than the listing price after being on the market for eight weeks. __✓__
3. A property is sold to the listing agent, for 10% less than the listing price, after the property has been on the market for six months, and after the agent has fully disclosed all the details of the purchase and how much profit he expects to make from the sale to the seller. __✓__
4. A property is sold for $10,000 over the listing price to a family who is new to the area and very eager to settle in before the school year begins. ______
5. A mother sells her house to her daughter in a private sale. ______
6. A seller accepts the first offer he receives for his house, because he needs to raise some cash in a hurry. ______

Principles of Value

We have seen that value requires utility, scarcity, desire, and effective purchasing power. We have also discovered that value is a concept, as opposed to price and cost, which are established facts. Next we will turn our attention to the **principles of value** that are fundamental to the development of a credible real estate appraisal. The principles of value are a series of rules that describe how value is created in the real estate market. These principles have their roots in basic economic theory and are widely accepted by the real estate industry.

Underlying each principle of value is the concept of markets. Broadly speaking, the term **market** refers to buyers and sellers interacting to exchange property. A market is typically defined in terms of a particular type of product or service that is bought and sold for money (or exchanged for other assets) within a particular geographical area. In real estate, we speak of the market for a particular type of property (single-family homes, residential building lots, high-rise apartments, vacation condominiums, etc.) in a particular location, district, or region.

Example: The definition of a market can be very specific, such as the market for "single-story ranch-style homes between $250,000 and $280,000, located within five miles of the city center." Or a market can be broadly categorized, as in the market for "income-producing properties in the western United States," or simply "the United States real estate market."

No matter how a market is defined, it always refers to the actions of buyers and sellers in the exchange of ownership.

Principle of Supply and Demand

One of the most basic principles of value is that of supply and demand. **Supply** refers to the amount of a certain type of property being offered for sale in a given market at a given price. **Demand** is the amount of that same type of property that buyers want to purchase at that same price. The principle of supply and demand states that the value of the property

Fig. 2.3 Principles of Value

1. Supply and demand	7. Surplus productivity
2. Substitution	8. Contribution
3. Competition	9. Increasing and decreasing returns
4. Change	10. Highest and best use
5. Anticipation	11. Consistent use
6. Balance	

in a competitive market is strongly affected by the relative levels of supply and demand. Property does not have an inherent or intrinsic value; rather, it is worth more when demand exceeds supply, and worth less when supply exceeds demand.

The principle of supply and demand is constantly at work in the residential real estate market. When demand for housing in a community is on the rise, two things can happen. If vacant land is available for new construction, home builders become more active, increasing the supply of housing to meet the increasing demand. On the other hand, if supply cannot be increased because the area is already built up, prices will rise as more and more buyers compete for the limited supply of housing. When demand for housing is declining, the normal result is a drop in both prices and new construction activity.

Example: Many people have recently discovered that Montana is a wonderful place to build a vacation home. This has created an increased demand for what was previously considered mere range land. As predicted by the law of supply and demand, the price of such land has skyrocketed as a result of the surge in demand.

The supply side also affects real estate values. Overbuilding by too many competing housing contractors can saturate a market, depressing prices. Conversely, a new zoning law that prevents new housing from being developed on vacant land (thus limiting the supply) can cause the values of existing properties to rise.

Example: During an economic boom, builders rushed to erect dozens of new office towers and complexes, anticipating an increase in demand for office space. But the economy cooled, and the expected demand did not materialize. Because of the resulting oversupply, many of the new buildings remained vacant, and office rents (and values) plummeted in the frantic competition to attract tenants.

Appraisers must be well-informed regarding the supply of and demand for properties in their area of expertise. Equally important, they must be aware of the actions of the many forces that cause supply and demand to change over time in the marketplace.

Exercise 4

1. A county has just passed a new zoning ordinance that will require all new development to be located in designated urban areas.

   a. Is the value of the undeveloped land within the designated urban area likely to increase or decrease?

      increase
      ____

b. Is the value of the undeveloped land outside the designated urban areas likely to increase or decrease?

decrease

2. The city government has just condemned an area of undeveloped land for use as a park and public golf course. Is the value of the five acres of undeveloped land immediately adjacent to this area likely to increase or decrease?

increase

3. Inventions, Inc., a major company located in Spring City, has just obtained a patent on an important new invention that will make the company a fortune. To prepare for the production and sales of the new product, Inventions, Inc. has hired hundreds of new employees. Will overall housing prices in Spring City increase or decrease because of the new jobs?

increase

Market Principles

The rule of supply and demand is the fundamental principle of value. When we examine the workings of the market, we can see that the rule of supply and demand operates because of certain fundamental characteristics of markets. The principles of substitution, competition, change, and anticipation describe some of these fundamental characteristics.

Principle of Substitution. According to the principle of **substitution**, the value of a property cannot exceed the value of equivalent substitute properties that are available in the market. In other words, reasonable buyers will compare similar properties in the market, and choose the least expensive one that meets their requirements.

Example: Units in a condominium complex are selling for about $145,000. An owner who needs to make a quick sale might list her condo for $140,000. The lower price would make her condo more likely to sell than the comparable but higher priced units.

The principle of substitution is applied by appraisers in each of the three approaches to estimating value (which will be described in detail in subsequent chapters). The appraiser compares the prices of substitute existing properties in the sales comparison approach, compares the cost to build a new substitute property in the cost approach, and compares the cost to acquire a substitute income investment in the income approach.

In applying the principle of substitution, the appraiser must be keenly aware of what constitutes an "equivalent" substitute property in the particular market.

Example: Two houses may be physically identical, but may not be equivalent because they are in different neighborhoods. And homes in the same neighborhood with the same number of rooms and square footage may not be equivalent because they vary significantly in the quality of their construction.

By studying the actions of the market, the appraiser can discern those characteristics—and thus properties—that are deemed "equivalent" by the market, and those that are not.

Principle of Competition. The rule of supply and demand operates because of competition in the market. **Competition** occurs when supply and demand are out of balance. When supply is greater than demand, sellers must compete for buyers. Conversely, buyers are in competition when demand exceeds supply. Competition tends to bring supply and demand back into balance. When buyers compete, prices rise, which stimulates supply and reduces demand. When sellers compete, prices fall, which stimulates demand and dampens supply.

Example: If an oversupply of housing exists, sellers may be forced to reduce prices to attract buyers. Price reductions improve marketability because, theoretically, they will either stimulate more demand by increasing the purchasing power of buyers, or reduce supply as sellers take their properties off the market to wait for better times. It is the competition between sellers that drives the price reductions and restores the balance of supply and demand.

Competition can also correct an excess of demand as well as supply. When buyers must compete, prices are driven up, which has the effect of reducing demand. An increase in prices decreases the purchasing power of buyers and also increases the supply as more sellers enter the market to take advantage of the higher selling prices.

Appraisers must be aware of the competitive status of the real estate market, and also be alert for signs of excess competition, which can have a negative effect on value. **Excess competition** is essentially an overreaction or overcorrection by the market, brought on by the lure of excess profit. Seeking to take advantage of this profit, sellers and builders bring so much new property to the market that supply outstrips demand, and values decline.

Principle of Change. The principle of **change** recognizes that the forces of supply and demand are in constant flux. It states that supply and demand fluctuate in response to changes in social, economic, and other conditions that influence value. This is the fundamental reason for the requirement that appraisers estimate value as of a specific date.

The principle of change is especially important in regard to the sales comparison approach to value. Yesterday's selling price does not necessarily indicate today's value. When an appraiser examines an equivalent property (called a **comparable property**, or

comparable) to estimate the value of the property being appraised, the appraiser must take into account market conditions in effect when the comparable property was sold, and make adjustments for any changes in the market between the sale date of the comparable and the appraisal date. Thus, the more recently the comparable property sold, the more reliable it is as an indicator of current value.

> **Example:** An appraiser identifies three properties that are comparable to the subject property. The first comparable sold three months ago for $185,000. Subsequently, the county announced plans to build a medium security prison near the neighborhood. The second and third comparables sold after this announcement, for $158,000 and $161,000 respectively. The appraiser must adjust the value of the first comparable to reflect the change in the market resulting from the anticipated prison construction.

One kind of change in real estate is described as the neighborhood real estate cycle. The first stage of the cycle is the **development** stage (sometimes called **integration**), when values increase as raw land is improved. This is followed by a stage of relative stability in value, called **maturity** (or **equilibrium**), and then a stage of progressive **decline** (sometimes called **disintegration**). The cycle may then be repeated, substituting a **revitalization** stage for the initial development stage.

> **Example:** In a new subdivision, property values tend to increase as raw land is developed into home sites and homes (development stage). Once the subdivision development is completed, values will normally remain fairly stable for some period of time (maturity stage). Eventually, though, the homes will begin to deteriorate with age, and their value may also suffer from competition with newer, more modern developments in the surrounding area (decline stage). If homes in the neighborhood are then renovated or replaced with newer structures (revitalization stage), values will once again rise, starting a new cycle.

The phenomenon of **gentrification** is an example of revitalization. Gentrification occurs when properties in a lower class neighborhood are purchased and renovated or rehabilitated by more affluent (middle and upper class) buyers.

Principle of Anticipation. The principle of **anticipation** is related to the principle of change. It states that value is affected by the expectations of buyers regarding the future benefits to be gained from property ownership. Specifically, value is affected by buyers' anticipation of the utility of owning property, and of the gain (or loss) to be realized on reselling the property. For example, investment buyers rely on the anticipation of future rental income when making purchase decisions.

> **Example:** If buyers expect an economic slump in the near future, property values will tend to decline. On the other hand, if buyers are anticipating the arrival of a large employer into town, property values will tend to increase.

Exercise 5

Choose the market principle listed on the right that best matches the situation described on the left. Each principle may be used more than once.

1. b A new development contains ten houses, each with the same size lot, same square footage, same style and quality of construction, etc. All of the homes are listed for sale at the same price.

2. d A local economic slump has resulted in a decline in real estate values in the local community.

3. c The government has announced plans to build a new highway that will greatly improve access between a city and its suburbs. Even though the highway is not yet built, land values begin to increase in the suburban communities.

a. Substitution
b. Competition
c. Anticipation
d. Change

Production as a Measure of Value

We have seen that value is greatly affected by the forces of supply and demand in markets that operate according to the principles of substitution, competition, change, and anticipation. Now we will examine another concept that is also very important to an understanding of value: production.

Production—the ability to create wealth—can be used to measure the value of land and its improvements. As we shall see, the concept of production has many applications in the appraisal process.

Economists speak of four agents (or factors) that are capable of creating wealth. These are called the **four agents of production**. They are:

1. capital (financial resources, money),
2. land (natural resources),
3. labor, and
4. coordination (management or entrepreneurship).

These agents can work individually or in concert with each other to generate a return in the form of income or profit. It is the rate of this return (or profit) in relation to the amount of resources invested that is the measure of production, and consequently, a measure of value.

Example: In a real estate development, investors provide capital, the developer provides management (coordination), and construction crews provide labor. These three agents of production are combined with the fourth agent, land, to create something of value, such as a housing development.

Principle of Balance. According to the principle of **balance**, production (and value) is maximized when opposing or interacting factors are in equilibrium. Traditionally, this principle has been applied to the four agents of production as well as to supply and demand.

The value of an individual property that is overimproved or underimproved suffers because the agents of production are not in balance. Too much or too little capital, labor, or coordination has been invested in relation to the land.

Example: A certain building lot costs $20,000. If improved with a 1,000 square foot home costing $50 per square foot to build, it would sell for $77,000. This is a profit of $7,000, a 10% return on the investment of $70,000 ($20,000 for the land plus $50,000 for the home). If the lot were improved with a 2,000 square foot home, again at $50 per square foot cost, it would sell for $130,000, a profit of $10,000 and a return of about 8.3%. In this case, the larger home would represent an overimprovement, an imbalance among the agents of production. Even though the profit on the larger home is greater in terms of dollar amount, it is less in terms of a percentage rate of return: 8.3% as opposed to 10%.

The principle of balance can also be applied to neighborhoods or districts. Overdevelopment of office space in a city, for example, decreases the value of all office space in the city. Prices and rents will be depressed until the market is able to absorb the oversupply. In this case, too much labor, capital, and coordination has been invested in office space, relative to the demand for it. With the agents of production out of balance, values suffer.

The point at which the agents of production are no longer in balance is referred to as the **point of diminishing returns**. When this point is reached, additional expenditures for capital, labor, or management fail to increase productivity enough to offset the cost. The point of diminishing returns is explained in more detail below in the discussion of increasing and decreasing returns.

Principle of Surplus Productivity. Surplus productivity is a way of measuring the value of land that has been improved. It is assumed that the productivity (or net income) that is attributable to the agents of capital, labor, and coordination is equivalent to their costs. In other words, when the cost of capital, labor, and coordination is deducted from the total net income for a property, the remaining income (called the surplus productivity) can be attributed to the land. Thus, the surplus productivity indicates the value of the land. This concept forms the basis of residual techniques for estimating land value, which are discussed in Chapter 6.

> **Example:** A property has net income of $10,000 per year. If the costs of labor, capital, and management for the property total $8,000 per year, the remaining net income of $2,000 can be attributed to the value of the land.

Principle of Contribution. The value of an individual component of a property is measured according to the principle of **contribution**. The principle of contribution states that the value of a component, regardless of its cost, is equal to the amount of value it adds to the property as a whole (or the amount by which its absence decreases the value of the property as a whole).

> **Example:** By installing new siding on a house, the owner increased the value of the house by $5,000. $5,000 represents the value of the siding. This is true regardless of the cost of the siding, which may have been more or less than $5,000. If the siding cost less than $5,000, it added more value than it cost. If the siding cost more than $5,000, it added less value than it cost (and perhaps should not have been added at all).

This principle is particularly useful to the sales comparison approach to value. It is used to help answer questions such as: what is the difference in value between a lot that is 100 feet deep and one that is 120 feet deep? How does the absence of a garage affect the value of a house? How much is value increased by adding an extra bathroom or bedroom? Instead of relying on simple cost estimates, the principle of contribution directs the appraiser to analyze the market values of these various components to answer these and similar types of questions.

> **Example:** In a neighborhood of similar residential properties, homes with two bathrooms sell for $240,000, while homes with three baths sell for $245,000. The actual cost of adding a third bathroom is estimated to be $12,000.
>
> In this case, the contribution to value made by a third bathroom is $5,000. When adjusting the value of a comparable property to account for a difference in number of baths, the appraiser would base the adjustment on the $5,000 difference in value as determined by the market. This indication of market value would be given more weight in the appraisal than the actual cost of adding a third bath.

Principle of Increasing and Decreasing Returns. The principle of **increasing and decreasing returns** is related to the principle of contribution. Assume that the amount of one or more of the agents of production (land, for example) remains fixed. As the amount invested in the other agent(s) is incrementally increased, the rate of return on the investment will first increase at a progressively higher rate, then continue to increase but at a progressively lower rate, and finally begin to decrease (at the point of diminishing returns).

Example: A builder intends to develop a lot with a single-family residence, at a construction cost of $60 per square foot. By analyzing the local housing market, the builder estimates the likely sales price of the residence, based on various potential square footages. The following chart shows the effect of increased size of the house on the builder's overall rate of return (profit).

The amount of value added by each additional 100 square feet varies depending on the size of the residence, whereas the construction cost of each additional 100 square feet remains constant. At sizes up to 1,800 square feet, increasing the size of the house will increase the builder's profit and the size of the profit grows with each additional 100 square feet. At 1,900 square feet, the builder continues to profit but the amount of his profit per additional 100-square-foot increment begins to decrease. Above 2,100 square feet, the builder's costs exceed the increase in price realized on each 100-square-foot increment—the point of diminishing returns has been reached.

Size in sq. ft.	Est. sales price	Increase in sales price with additional 100 sq. ft.	Cost of adding 100 sq. ft.	Profits	Rate of return
1,500	$94,500	Base	Base	Base	5%
1,600	$101,800	$7,300	$6,000	$1,300	6%
1,700	$110,200	$8,400	$6,000	$2,400	8%
1,800	$119,900	$9,700	$6,000	$3,700	11%
1,900	$128,800	$8,900	$6,000	$2,900	13%
2,000	$136,800	$8,000	$6,000	$2,000	14%
2,100	$143,600	$6,800	$6,000	$800	14%
2,200	$149,200	$5,600	$6,000	<$400>	13%
2,300	$153,200	$4,000	$6,000	<$2,000>	11%

Exercise 6

Circle the principle(s) of value illustrated in each of the following situations.

1. An appraiser estimates the land value of an improved parcel by subtracting the costs of the improvements from the value of the property as a whole.

   Balance Contribution Increasing and Decreasing Returns

2. A homeowner spends $10,000 for new landscaping, but the value of the home is increased by only $5,000 as a result.

   Balance Contribution Increasing and Decreasing Returns

3. A developer determines that she will get a better return on her investment by building 2,500 square foot homes, even though she could sell 3,000 square foot homes for a higher price.

   Balance Contribution Increasing and Decreasing Returns

Effect of Use on Real Estate Value

Our discussion of the economic theory of value has covered the rule of supply and demand, market principles, and the use of production as a measure of value. We will conclude this discussion with a look at the interaction between the way real estate is used and its value.

Principle of Highest and Best Use. The principle of **highest and best use** is crucial to valuing real estate. This principle states that the market value of property should be determined according to the most profitable (and reasonably probable) use of the property. Thus, to determine market value for a property, the appraiser must first analyze its highest and best use.

A property's highest and best use must meet the following criteria:

1. physically possible,
2. legally permissible,
3. financially feasible, and
4. maximally productive.

A highest and best use must also be a legal use. This means that the use must be allowed under the applicable zoning restrictions or that a variance could easily be obtained for the use. When analyzing highest and best use, the appraiser must be aware of what uses are and are not permitted by local zoning laws.

When analyzing improved real estate for its highest and best use, the appraiser draws a distinction between the actual highest and best use, and the highest and best use that would apply if the site were vacant (i.e., unimproved). A property might have a different highest and best use if it were unimproved, but the property's current use may still be its highest and best use.

Example: A property is improved with a single family residence. The appraiser estimates that the value of the land for its current use is $50,000 and the value of the residence is

$70,000. In evaluating highest and best use, the appraiser determines that if vacant, the highest and best use of the land would be as a site for multi-family residential development, for which purpose the land is estimated to be worth $80,000. In this situation, the highest and best use of the land is its current use, since the current total value of the land and improvements ($50,000 + 70,000 = $120,000) exceeds the value of the land alone for a different use.

Example: Suppose we have the same circumstances as in the previous example, but the residence is run-down and estimated to be worth only $20,000. The total value of land and improvements for its current use would be $70,000. In this case, the appraiser could determine that the highest and best use of the land was for multi-family residential use, assuming the cost of removing the existing improvements was less than $10,000 ($80,000 value if vacant for new use less $70,000 value as improved for current use).

Principle of Consistent Use. The principle of **consistent use** relates to the appraisal of improved property. It requires both the land and the improvements to be valued for the same use, even if they are being valued separately. It is improper to value the land for one use and the improvements for a different use.

Example: The appraiser could not, in the two preceding examples, value the improvements for their current single-family residential use and value the land for multi-family residential use in the same appraisal. The land and the improvements must be valued consistently, either both for single-family use or both for multi-family use.

Principle of Conformity. According to the principle of **conformity**, property values are enhanced when the uses of surrounding properties conform to the use of the subject property. This is the rationale behind zoning regulations, which seek to group compatible uses together and to separate incompatible uses.

In practice, the principle of conformity is influenced by local perceptions of the kind of conformity that is desirable. Variation in architectural styles, for example, may be viewed favorably in one context, and unfavorably in another. A mix of commercial and residential uses in an urban setting could have a positive effect on values, where the same mix of uses in a suburban setting could have a negative effect. In applying the principle of conformity, the appraiser needs a sound appreciation for local customs and standards.

Note that the racial or ethnic composition of an area is not a consideration when applying the principle of conformity. The appraiser should never consider the presence or lack of ethnic diversity in an area to be an indicator of value. Not only has time proven that ethnic composition does not affect value, but to assume that it does would run afoul of antidiscrimination laws.

Principle of Progression/Regression. Progression and regression are terms used to describe the effect on value when a property does not conform to the level of improvement of surrounding properties. A property that is much more luxurious than surrounding properties suffers a decline in value that is called **regression**. By the same token, a modest home in an area of more expensive houses would see a relative increase in value called **progression**.

Exercise 7

Circle the principle(s) of value illustrated in each of the following situations.

1. Farmland surrounding a growing city is converted to housing developments as the city expands.

   Highest and best use   Consistent use   Conformity

2. An appraiser values a house and its lot, both for residential use, even though the lot would be worth more if used for commercial purposes.

   Highest and best use   Consistent use   Conformity

3. An old warehouse is restored and converted into a shopping mall.

   Highest and best use   Consistent use   Conformity

4. A homeowners association is created to enforce building restrictions in a subdivision.

   Highest and best use   Consistent use   Conformity

Forces Affecting Value

Value increases and decreases in response to changes in the balance between supply and demand. In turn, supply and demand are influenced by a broad range of external forces. These forces that affect value are frequently broken down into four general categories:

1. social,
2. economic,
3. governmental, and
4. environmental.

In actual practice, the various influences are interwoven, but the distinctions between them remain useful for purposes of discussion and analysis.

Social Forces

The numbers, characteristics, lifestyles, standards, and preferences of the people in a particular market constitute the social forces that influence value in that market. Real estate values are affected by changes in population, which may be due to changes in birth or death rates, or to migration into or out of an area. Demand for different types of properties is related to the age distribution of the population, the numbers of households of various sizes and compositions, and attitudes toward architectural style and utility. Social preferences with respect to recreational activities, religion, education, and cultural amenities also drive the forces of supply and demand for real estate.

Example: The trend toward smaller family size has increased the demand for smaller houses and decreased the demand for large ones. The aging of the population has greatly increased property values in desirable retirement areas by increasing demand. An overall increase in the population has contributed to a corresponding increase in average property values across the country.

The social characteristics of a market can be stable or volatile, but are always subject to the principle of change. The appraiser can stay informed about social forces in the market by studying census data and other statistical information collected by national, state, and local governments, as well as demographic studies published by business organizations, scholars, and other sources.

Economic Forces

The economic forces that most strongly affect real estate values relate to the availability and cost of money for real estate lending, construction, and investment, and the purchasing power of buyers in the real estate market. Money markets are influenced by relatively broad forces, such as the international investment climate, currency exchange rates, savings rates, inflation rates, national fiscal policy, and government borrowing.

Purchasing power tends to react to more localized influences, such as local wage and unemployment rates, the strength and diversity of the local economic base, local construction costs, and the local cost of living. But these local influences are often themselves affected by larger scale economic forces. Unemployment, for example, is often more closely tied to a particular industry than to a particular locality; it becomes a local force in areas that are dependent on the particular industry, but its causes are likely to be national or international.

Example: Communities dependent on oil and gas exploration for employment have undergone cycles of boom and bust for several decades. When oil prices are high, employment in the oil industry is also high, and property values rise in these communities. Conversely, when oil prices decline (with the resulting business failures and high unemployment rates), property values decline.

It is increasingly common for governmental forces to try to mitigate adverse economic conditions, to the point where it is often difficult to distinguish between economic and governmental forces. Examples include unemployment insurance, monetary and trade policies, government spending, taxes and tax exemptions, and government regulation of the financial market. In fact, few economic forces are without some governmental influence. When analyzing the effect of economic forces on real estate values, the appraiser must bear in mind the effects of governmental actions in the economic arena.

Governmental Forces

Aside from its direct intervention and influence on the economy, the government affects real estate values in a wide variety of ways. Zoning and other land use regulations limit the uses of property and shape the development of communities, with results that may either enhance or detract from values. Governments also provide community services such as police and fire protection, education, and health services; the level of these services can make property more or less desirable.

Example: Zoning to isolate residential areas from industrial pollution and other nuisances enhances the value of the residential property. Families with young children generally prefer to live in communities with good local school systems.

Environmental legislation is a growing area of government influence with a major impact on real estate values.

Example: Environmental restrictions may increase the cost of housing development by requiring developers to mitigate the adverse environmental effects of construction or to set aside land for open space. Government policies regarding the harvesting of timber from national and state lands affect the cost of lumber for construction.

The list of governmental forces influencing value also includes laws governing landlord-tenant relations (including rent control laws), laws that define the nature of ownership of property (such as condominiums, cooperatives, and timeshares), and laws specifying the methods and materials for building construction (occupational safety laws, building codes, etc.).

Environmental Forces

Environmental forces are those aspects of the physical environment, whether natural or man-made, that influence value. They include the character of the land itself: its topography, soil characteristics (stability and fertility), mineral wealth, vegetation, bodies of water, and so on. They also include climate (temperature, wind, rain, and snowfall), which not only influences the productivity of the land for various purposes, but affects local construction methods and costs, necessary services, and the extent to which the area is a desirable place to live.

Example: The trend of population movement from colder northern states to the warmer south is at least partly due to the attractions of a milder climate. Physical factors such as water frontage and spectacular views have traditionally enhanced property values. Land subject to natural disasters such as flooding or landslides may have little value except for agricultural purposes.

An important man-made environmental influence on real estate value is infrastructure. Transportation facilities such as airports, railroads, shipping facilities, highways, and bridges are examples of infrastructure that can influence value.

Example: A new freeway is built that allows commuters from a small town to reach jobs in the city in half the time it used to take. Suddenly it is practical for those with jobs in the city to live in the town, and property values increase.

Finally, environmental forces include the crucial element of "location." One of the most powerful influences on the value of real estate is its location relative to surrounding amenities, nuisances, and hazards. Location also determines views, neighborhood characteristics, access to employment, medical services, recreation, schools, churches, and public transportation, and proximity to incompatible uses or health or safety hazards.

Exercise 8

You work in a mid-size community called Viewmont. Viewmont is located about 30 minutes away from a large urban community. The population of Viewmont has increased an average of 8% in each of the previous seven years, and continues to grow. Property taxes have increased to pay for the extra schools and fire and police protection needed by the additional residents. Several small businesses have relocated to Viewmont because of tax incentives offered by the Viewmont government, thus opening up new jobs for residents. However, street construction and traffic control has been largely neglected, and increasing traffic problems have led to many complaints, especially from downtown merchants and those in prime residential neighborhoods.

Viewmont demographics show that a large portion of the community is made up of young families and retired people. Most of the city has a view of nearby rolling hills; however, the winter winds can cause significant damage. Because of its location, some experts have predicted a water shortage for residents within the next 25 years.

List the various forces that affect value that are currently operating in Viewmont.

1. Social forces:

 ____

2. Economic forces:

 ____

3. Governmental forces:

 ____

4. Environmental forces:

 ____

Key Terms

Agents of production—Capital, land, labor and coordination. In economic theory, these four agents work individually or in concert to create wealth.

Anticipation—A principle of value which holds that value is affected by the expectations of buyers regarding the future benefits to be gained from property ownership, including the utility to be derived from ownership and the potential gain or loss on resale of the property.

Arm's length transaction—A sale between unrelated parties.

Assessed value—The value used to calculate the amount of general property taxes. Each state has its own definition of assessed value for property tax purposes.

Balance—A principle of value which holds that value is maximized when the four agents of production are in balance. An overimproved or underimproved property suffers in value because of an imbalance in the agents of production.

Change—A principle of value which holds that the forces of supply and demand are in constant flux in response to the forces that influence value. Because of this, value can only be estimated as of a specific date.

Comparable—A property that has been sold in the same market that currently includes the subject property, and that appeals to the same sorts of buyers. Comparables are used in many different appraisal techniques.

Competition—The interactions between sellers or between buyers in a market. The principle of competition holds that competition helps to bring supply and demand into balance, either by raising prices when supply is low compared to demand, or by driving prices down when demand is relatively weak.

Consistent use—A rule of appraisal that requires both land and improvements to be valued for the same use.

Construction cost—The cost to build an improvement.

Contribution—The increase in overall property value that results from the presence of one component of the property. The principle of contribution holds that the value of a component of a property is equivalent to the amount by which it increases the value of the property as a whole.

Cost—The actual amount of expenditure necessary to acquire or produce something.

Demand—The amount of something that buyers in a market want to acquire at a given price.

Desire—When there are potential purchasers who want to own a property or a product. One of the four factors of value.

Development cost—The cost to create a project, such as a subdivision or housing development, including the construction cost of any improvements.

Direct costs—The costs for labor and materials used to build an improvement. Also called hard costs.

Economic forces—Forces that influence the availability and cost of capital and the purchasing power of buyers. Economic forces are often influenced by governmental forces.

Effective purchasing power—When potential purchasers have the ability to pay for a property or a product. One of the four factors of value.

Environmental forces—Those aspects of the physical environment, whether natural or man-made, that influence value, including the character of the land, climate, infrastructure, and location.

Excess competition—An overcorrection of an imbalance between supply and demand, usually as a result of the availability of excessive profits.

Going concern value—The total value of a proven, ongoing business operation, which includes real property that is an integral part of the operation.

Governmental forces—Laws, regulations, and public services that affect the value of property in the market.

Highest and best use—The use that is reasonably probable and results in the highest value for a property. It must be a use that is legally permitted, physically possible, and economically feasible.

Increasing and decreasing returns—If one or more of the agents of production remain fixed, an increase in the other agent(s) will first result in increasing rates of return for the property, but will eventually result in decreasing rates of return once the point of diminishing returns is reached.

Indirect costs—Costs other than direct costs (labor and materials) that are incurred in the process of building an improvement, such as overhead, architectural fees, construction financing interest, permit fees, etc. Also called soft costs.

Insurable value—The value of property for purposes of reimbursement under the terms of an insurance policy. Insurable value is defined by the insurance policy.

Investment value—The value of a property to a particular investor with specific investment goals. Investment value is inherently subjective.

Liquidation value—A form of market value that assumes the property must be sold in a limited period of time, which probably does not constitute "reasonable" exposure to the market.

Market—The interactions among a group of buyers and sellers who trade in a particular thing, such as real estate, within a particular area. The actions of the buyers and sellers in a market determine market value.

Market value—In general, the amount of cash (or cash equivalent) that is most likely to be paid for a property on a given date in a fair and reasonable open market transaction. Specific (but varied) definitions of market value can be found in USPAP and in many state laws. Also called exchange value or value in exchange.

Point of diminishing returns—The point at which the four agents of production are in balance. At this point, the cost of making additional improvements to the land becomes higher than the resulting increase in value.

Price—The actual amount paid by a particular buyer to a particular seller in an actual transaction.

Progression—The increase in the value of a property that is attributable to its location among more desirable properties.

Regression—The decline in value suffered by a property that is located in an area of less desirable properties.

Replacement cost—The cost to create a substitute improvement of equivalent function and utility, using current methods, materials, and techniques.

Reproduction cost—The cost to create an exact duplicate of an improvement, using the same design, materials, and construction methods as the original.

Scarcity—Limited availability or limited abundance. One of the four factors of value, and a key element in the principle of supply and demand.

Social forces—The numbers, lifestyles, standards, and preferences of the people in a particular market, which affect property values in that market.

Subject property—The property being appraised.

Substitution—A principle of value which holds that the value of a property cannot exceed the value of equivalent substitute properties that are available in the market.

Supply—The amount of something that is available for sale in a market at a given price.

Supply and demand—A principle of value which holds that the value of a property in a competitive market is determined by the relative levels of supply and demand. Property is worth more when demand is high compared to supply, and worth less when supply exceeds demand.

Surplus productivity—The amount of a property's income that remains after deducting the income attributable to capital, labor, and coordination. The remaining income is attributable to the land, and is used to indicate the value of the land.

Use value—The value of a property assuming it is used for a specific purpose. Also called value in use.

Utility—The ability to satisfy some want or need of potential buyers. One of the four factors of value.

Value—The monetary relationship between properties and those who buy, sell, or use those properties (USPAP definition). The theoretical worth of something, expressed in terms of something else, usually money.

Zoning—Government regulations which specify the allowable uses for a property. Zoning laws are an exercise of the police power, and are designed to enhance property values by preventing incompatible uses.

Summary

I. The Concept of Value

A. Value is "the monetary worth of property, goods, services, etc."

B. Value is not intrinsic; it is created by the four factors of value: utility, scarcity, desire, and effective purchasing power.

C. Value is not the same as price. Price refers to an actual fact in a transaction, whereas value is a concept.

D. Value is not the same as cost. Cost refers to the expenditures necessary to build or create a property, whereas value (and price) refer to the exchange of property.

    1. Replacement cost is the cost to create a substitute of equal utility; reproduction cost is the cost to create an exact replica.

II. Types of Value

A. Appraisal reports must define the type of value being estimated.

B. Market value is determined by the market in a sale under normal conditions.

    1. Buyer and seller must be typically motivated.
    2. Buyer and seller must be reasonably informed as to the conditions of the market and the property.
    3. Buyer and seller must be acting reasonably, for self-interest, and without duress.
    4. The property must be exposed to the market for a reasonable period of time.

C. Value in use is the value of property for a specific purpose only, and tends to be subjective in nature.

D. Investment value is the value to a particular investor, as opposed to value to the market.

E. Liquidation value is what a property would bring with limited exposure to the market, as in a foreclosure sale.

F. Assessed value is market value multiplied by the applicable assessment ratio.

G. Insurable value is value for purposes of reimbursement under an insurance policy.

H. Going concern value is the value of an ongoing business that includes real property as an integral part of its operations.

III. Appraisal Principles

A. The term "market" refers to the interactions between buyers and sellers with regard to the exchange of property.

B. Appraisal principles are rooted in economic theory. They include:

1. Principle of supply and demand: Values go up when demand exceeds supply, and go down when supply exceeds demand.
2. Principle of substitution: The value of a property cannot exceed the price of a substitute property of comparable utility.
3. Principle of competition: When supply and demand are out of balance, competition increases. Competition tends to bring supply and demand back into balance.
4. Principle of change: The forces of supply and demand are constantly subject to change.
    a. Change is manifested in the neighborhood life cycle, with value fluctuating as the cycle proceeds from development, to maturity, to decline and then revitalization.
5. Principle of anticipation: Value is dependent on the expectation of future benefits to be realized from property ownership.
6. Principle of balance: Value of a particular property or of all properties in a particular market is optimized when the four agents of production (capital, land, labor, and coordination) are in balance. The point where the agents of production are in balance is the point of diminishing returns.
7. Principle of surplus productivity: Surplus productivity is attributed to the land. It is what is left of the property's net income after deducting the costs of capital, labor and coordination.
8. Principle of contribution: The value of a component of a property is the amount by which its presence increases the value of the property as a whole, rather than its cost.
9. Principle of increasing and decreasing returns: Incremental increases in the investment of an agent of production in a property will first cause the rate of return to increase, but will eventually reach a point (the point of diminishing returns) where the return begins to decrease.
10. Principle of highest and best use: Property should be valued for its highest and best use, which is the reasonable and probable use that will yield the most profit.

11. Principle of consistent use: Both land and improvements must be appraised for the same (consistent) use.

12. Principle of conformity: A property's value is enhanced when the property's characteristics conform to the neighborhood.

IV. Forces Affecting Value

A. Value is affected by social, economic, governmental, and environmental forces.

B. Social forces include demographics, social standards, and lifestyles.

C. Economic forces affect real estate values by affecting the cost of capital and the purchasing power of buyers and investors.

D. Governmental forces include the many laws and regulations that affect value, such as zoning, taxes, environmental laws, financial regulations, and building codes.

E. Environmental forces include land characteristics, climate, infrastructure, and location.

Chapter Quiz

1. Market value is the same as:
   a. value in use
   b. value in exchange
   c. investment value
   d. None of the above

2. The concept of market value assumes that:
   a. the buyer is represented by a real estate agent
   b. property is normally sold within 90 days
   c. neither buyer nor seller is acting under duress
   d. All of the above

3. Which of the following is not one of the four factors of value?
   a. Utility
   b. Scarcity
   c. Desire
   d. Cost

   * Effective Purchasing Power

4. Which of the following is not a criterion for highest and best use?
   a. Legally permissible
   b. Financially feasible
   c. Physically possible
   d. Marginally productive

5. A property's value to a particular owner or for a particular purpose is called:
   a. value in use
   b. assessed value
   c. going concern value
   d. value in hand

6. According to the principle of substitution:
   a. appraisers should substitute the sales prices of comparable properties for the value of the subject property
   b. all other factors being equal, a buyer will choose the less expensive of two comparable properties
   c. lots of the same size in the same neighborhood are equivalent in value
   d. All of the above

7. Surplus productivity is attributed to:
   a. capital
   b. land
   c. labor
   d. coordination

8. The point where increased investment in the agents of production no longer results in increased profit is known as the point of:
   a. no return
   b. marginal productivity
   c. surplus productivity
   d. diminishing returns

9. Assessed value can be calculated as:
   a. market value times millage rate
   b. market value times effective tax rate
   c. market value times assessment ratio
   d. None of the above

10. An example of a social force that could affect real estate values is:
    a. wage levels
    b. population shifts
    c. climate
    d. unemployment

11. The principle of substitution is applied in which approach to value?

    a. Sales comparison approach
    b. Cost approach
    c. Income approach
    d. All of the above

12. When estimating market value, the appraiser should consider:

    a. the terms of financing for the sale
    b. the date of the appraisal
    c. the fact that the buyer and seller are related
    d. Both a) and b)

13. The principle of highest and best use holds that:

    a. improved property should always be appraised for its current use
    b. the land should always be appraised for its highest and best use, even if the improvements are appraised for some other use
    c. the market views the value of property in light of all possible legal uses
    d. commercial use is inherently more valuable than residential use

14. The cost to create an exact replica of an improvement is referred to as:

    a. replacement cost
    b. substitution cost
    c. insurable value
    d. reproduction cost

15. According to the principle of supply and demand, prices will tend to increase when:

    a. supply exceeds demand
    b. demand exceeds supply
    c. supply and demand are in balance
    d. competition increases

Quiz Answers

1. b) Market value is synonymous with value in exchange.
2. c) One of the assumptions underlying market value is that neither buyer nor seller is acting under duress.
3. d) The four factors of value are scarcity, utility, desire, and effective purchasing power.
4. d) A property's highest and best use must be maximally productive, as well as legally permissible, physically possible, and financially feasible.
5. a) A property's value to a particular user or its value for a particular use is called its value in use or use value.
6. b) The principle of substitution is based on the idea that, given a choice between two comparable properties, an informed buyer will purchase the less expensive option.
7. b) After subtracting for the costs of labor, capital, and coordination, any surplus productivity is attributed to the land.
8. d) The point after which additional investment in agents of production does not increase the profit margin is the point of diminishing returns.
9. c) Assessed value is determined by multiplying market value by the applicable assessment ratio.
10. b) Shifts in population are a social force that can influence property values.
11. d) The principle of substitution plays a role in all three approaches to value.
12. d) The terms of the financing are important in determining market value, since a buyer might pay a higher price to receive better financing terms. Likewise, the date of the sale is important, since market conditions may have changed since the sale was completed.
13. c) The highest and best use for a property is the most profitable use that is legally permissible and physically possible.
14. d) The cost to create a replica of an improvement, using the same materials and construction methods, is reproduction cost.
15. b) If demand exceeds supply, prices will increase as buyers compete with each other to buy available properties.

Exercise Answers

#1

1. a, c
2. b
3. a, c
4. d

#2

1. $175,000
2. $195,000
3. Market value cannot be determined without additional information regarding the forces acting in the market.

#3

1. No
2. Yes
3. Yes
4. No
5. No
6. No

#4

1. a. Increase
   b. Decrease
2. Increase
3. Increase

#5

1. a
2. d
3. c

#6

1. Contribution
2. All three
3. All three

#7

1. Highest and best use
2. Consistent use

3. Highest and best use
4. Conformity

#8 1. Population growth, age distribution
2. Nearby urban community, property tax levels, small business incentives
3. Property tax levels, small business incentives
4. Inadequate transportation system (roads), views, climate (winds), possible water shortage

3 The Appraisal Process

Overview

Development of an appraisal is guided by Standard 1 of the USPAP: "In developing a real property appraisal, an appraiser must identify the problem to be solved, determine the scope of work necessary to solve the problem, and correctly complete research and analyses necessary to produce a credible appraisal." Over the years, the process of developing an appraisal has been refined into a series of steps that serve as the appraiser's guide to reaching a competent and reliable estimate of value.

This chapter will present an overview of the steps in the appraisal process. The first three steps—defining the appraisal problem, determining the scope of work necessary to solve it, and collecting data—will be discussed in some detail. The remaining steps in the appraisal process will be described briefly, and then examined in more detail in later chapters.

After completing this chapter, you should be able to:

- identify each of the steps in the appraisal process;
- distinguish between the purpose and the use of an appraisal;
- understand the difference between the effective date of an appraisal (the valuation date) and the date of the appraisal report;
- identify the pieces of information that are essential to defining an appraisal problem, and understand why each one is necessary;
- understand the significance of assumptions and limiting conditions in an appraisal report;
- understand how an appraiser determines the scope of work that will be required in order to properly complete an appraisal assignment;
- understand the differences between general and specific data, and how each is used in an appraisal;
- understand the distinction between primary data and secondary data;
- define the meaning of the term "site" as it applies to real estate appraisal;

- identify the reasons for the separate valuation of the site and site improvements;
- identify the three approaches to value;
- understand the significance of the reconciliation process; and
- identify the various types of appraisal reports, and explain the major differences between them.

The Eight Steps of the Appraisal Process

Standards Rule 1-1(a) states: "In developing a real property appraisal, an appraiser must be aware of, understand, and correctly employ those recognized methods and techniques that are necessary to produce a credible appraisal." These "recognized methods and techniques" begin with the widely accepted eight steps of the appraisal process. It is therefore essential to understand and follow these steps of the appraisal process in order to arrive at a legitimate value estimate:

1. Define the appraisal problem.
2. Determine the scope of work.
3. Collect and verify the data.
4. Analyze the data.
5. Develop an opinion of the value of the site.
6. Apply the three approaches to value.
7. Reconcile the various value indicators to reach a final opinion of value.
8. Prepare and deliver an appropriate appraisal report.

Although we will discuss the steps in the appraisal process in the same order in which they are listed, this does not mean that the appraiser must always complete each step before

Fig 3.1 Steps in the Appraisal Process

1. Define the problem
2. Determine scope of work
3. Collect and verify data
4. Analyze data
5. Determine site value
6. Apply three approaches to value
7. Reconcile value indicators
8. Issue appraisal report

going on to the next one. As a practical matter, the various steps in the appraisal process often overlap. Data collection, for example, may begin even before the appraisal problem is fully defined, and data analysis may occur throughout the entire appraisal process. The steps in the appraisal process should not be seen as isolated tasks, but rather as components that make up the unified process of valuation.

Exercise 1

List the eight steps in the appraisal process.

1. Define the appraisal problem
2. Determine the Scope of work.
3. Collect and verify the data.
4. Analyze the data.
5. Develop an opinion of the value of the site.
6. Apply the three approaches to value.
7. Reconcile value indicators
8. Prepare and deliver an appraisal report.

Step 1: Defining the Appraisal Problem

The appraisal process begins with defining the appraisal problem. This step involves two important considerations. First, the appraiser must know why the client is hiring the appraiser (what the client wants to know). Second, and equally important, the appraiser must understand the terms and conditions of the appraisal assignment (how it will be carried out).

Defining the appraisal problem means answering some basic questions about the particular appraisal assignment, including:

1. What is to be appraised?
2. When is it to be appraised?

3. Why is it to be appraised?
4. How is it to be appraised?

To answer these questions, the appraiser must identify these essential elements of the appraisal problem:

- the identity of the real estate;
- the real property interest in question;
- the purpose of the appraisal (the type and the definition of value);
- the effective date of the appraisal;
- the date of the appraisal report;
- the identity of the client and other intended users of the appraisal;
- the intended use of the appraisal; and
- the assumptions and other conditions that apply to the assignment.

The first three items on this list answer the question, "What is to be appraised?" The next two address "When is it to be appraised?" The two after that correspond to "Why is it to be appraised?" And the last item addresses "How is it to be appraised?"

Exercise 2

1. List the essential elements that define an appraisal problem.

   a. the identity of the real estate

   b. the real property interest in question

   c. the purpose of the appraisal

   d. the effective date of the appraisal

   e. the date of the appraisal report

   f. the identity of the client + other users of the appraisal

   g. the intended use of the appraisal.

   h. the assumptions + other conditions that apply to the assignment.

2. To define an appraisal problem, the appraiser must understand the terms and conditions of the assignment and the client's reasons for hiring the

appraiser. Thus, to define an appraisal problem, what basic questions need to be answered?

What is to be appraised? When is it to be appraised? Why is it to be appraised? How is it to be appraised?

What is to be Appraised?

To determine what is to be appraised, the appraiser must identify three things:

1. the **real estate** that is the subject of the appraisal,
2. the **real property interest** that is the subject of the appraisal, and
3. the **type of value** that is to be estimated.

Identification of the Real Estate. Real estate is commonly identified by means of a street address or a building name. But in official documents, such as deeds or mortgages, real estate is identified by means of its **legal description**. Legal descriptions are the most accurate way to identify real estate; they leave the least room for ambiguity or confusion.

Fig. 3.2 Defining the Appraisal Problem

WHAT
- identity of real estate
- real property interest
- type of value

WHEN
- effective date of appraisal
- date of appraisal report

WHY
- identity of client and intended users
- intended use

HOW
- assumptions and conditions

A person reading a legal description can determine exactly what real estate is being described.

Since an appraisal report is an important document relating to real estate, appraisals also identify real estate by means of legal descriptions. The appraisal may, and often does, include the name or common address of the property, but should always include the legal description as well.

> **Example:** All of the following descriptions refer to the same piece of real estate. An appraisal might include all three descriptions, but should always include the legal description.
>
> | | |
> |---|---|
> | Building Name: | The Smith Tower, an office building |
> | Common Address: | 1024 Western Avenue
Seattle, Washington |
> | Legal Description: | Lot 17, Division 3, Pierce Addition, City of Seattle
County of King, as recorded in King County, Washington |

The legal description of the real estate is often provided by the appraiser's client. The appraiser can obtain (or verify) the legal description by consulting a copy of the property owner's deed. A copy of the deed can usually be obtained from the client, the property owner or manager, the real estate broker, or from the local county records office. (Copies of deeds, excise tax affidavits, and other county records are often available on the Internet through a county's website.) Unless otherwise agreed to between the appraiser and the client, the appraiser should not accept responsibility for the accuracy of the legal description, since this is beyond the training and expertise of most appraisers.

The three major categories of legal descriptions—metes and bounds, rectangular or government survey, and lot and block—are discussed in detail in Chapter 4.

Exercise 3

1. Why should an appraisal use a legal description to identify real estate?

   It is most accurate, least ambiguous + Confusing

2. List three possible sources where an appraiser might obtain a copy of a deed in order to verify a property description.

   a. the Client, Property owner or manager

   b. the real estate broker

   c. local County records office.

Personal property. It is normally assumed that the appraiser is estimating the value of real property only, and in many cases the client (such as a lender) will explicitly require this to be the case. However, in other cases, items of personal property need to be included in the appraisal as well. For example, an appraisal performed for a buyer might have terms of sale that include some equipment or furnishings. Because personal property is not normally included in an appraisal, it is important for the appraiser to identify any such items, and specify in the appraisal report that they are included in the value estimate.

Repairs and improvements. Identifying the real estate also involves identifying any repairs, improvements, or items of new construction that are to be completed. An appraiser valuing property in connection with a VA loan, for example, may assume that the repairs required to meet VA standards will be performed on the property. As in the case of personal property included in an appraisal, any repairs the appraiser assumes will take place must be identified and clearly specified in the appraisal report as influencing the estimate of value. In the case of new construction, adequate plans and specifications must exist to allow the appraiser to form a reasonable opinion of the value of the new improvements.

Exercise 4

1. Why is it important for an appraiser to identify any personal property items that are to be included in an appraisal?

   Because it Isn't normally included

2. Why is it important for an appraiser to identify any new real estate improvements that are to be included in an appraisal?

   ____

Identification of the Real Property Interest. Real estate is more than just the physical land and buildings; it includes the rights that go with the land. In addition to the identity of the subject real estate, the appraiser also must know what real property rights the client wants to have appraised. (For more information regarding real property rights, refer back to Chapter 1.)

Most appraisals estimate the value of the complete ownership rights, known as the **fee simple**. But appraisers may also estimate the value of partial freehold interests (such as a one-half partnership interest), or leasehold interests.

Fig. 3.3 Real Property Rights That May Be Appraised

1. Fee simple ownership
2. Life estate
3. Leasehold interest
4. Leased fee
5. Mineral or other subsurface right
6. Water rights, air rights
7. Rights of a co-owner (partner, spouse, or co-tenant)
8. Easement right

Example: An owner (landlord) of an office building may request an appraisal of the value of the various leasehold interests in the building in order to determine how much rent to charge. Leasehold interests are also frequently valued when business assets are appraised.

Obviously, the fee simple value of a property will not be the same as the value of a partial or limited interest. So it is vital to identify the real property interest that is the subject of the appraisal. (For a more detailed discussion of appraising partial or limited interests, refer to Chapter 13.)

In addition to knowing what property rights the client wants to have appraised, the appraiser must also identify any rights and restrictions that apply to the subject property. The property may include irrigation rights, for example, or the right to use an easement across adjoining property. On the other hand, property rights may be restricted by such things as zoning ordinances, public and private easements, rights-of-way, and private deed restrictions. The rights and restrictions that apply to the property may enhance or detract from its value.

Example: Property A and Property B are similar in all respects, except that Property A is crossed by a public right-of-way. Because the right-of-way limits the use of Property A, that parcel may have a lower value than Property B.

Property taxes are also a form of restriction on property rights. The appraiser must identify the taxes that apply to the subject property and analyze their effect on value. Property that is subject to a higher rate of taxation than other comparable properties, for example, may be less valuable.

The appraiser can identify many of the rights and restrictions that apply to a property by consulting the deed. Additional information can be found in a title abstract or title insurance policy. Information regarding zoning restrictions is available as a matter of public record from local zoning or planning offices. Similarly, property tax information may be obtained from local tax authorities. (In many localities, this information is available online.)

Exercise 5

1. List three examples of restrictions on property rights that can affect value.

   a. Zoning Ordinances

   b. Public and private easements, rights of way

   c. private deed restrictions

2. List three sources of information regarding restrictions on property rights.

   a. Deeds

   b. Title abstract or Title insurance Policy

   c. Local zoning or planning offices

Identification of the Type of Value to be Estimated. Next, the appraiser must define the **purpose** of the appraisal, or the **type of value** the appraiser is to estimate: market value, assessment value, insurable value, etc. In other words, what does the client want to know about the property? Regardless of the type of value the client is seeking, it should always be clearly defined in the appraisal report. (For more information on types and definitions of value, refer back to Chapter 2.)

Note that the purpose of the appraisal is not the same as the use of the appraisal. The purpose of the appraisal is the kind of value that the client wants estimated. The use of the appraisal is the reason the client wants to know the particular value.

> **Example:** A lender hires an appraiser to determine the market value of a property, because the lender wants to know whether it should approve a loan for the purchase of the property. In this case, the purpose of the appraisal is to determine the market value of the subject property. The use of the appraisal is to help the lender make a decision regarding the borrower's loan application.

Exercise 6

1. What three pieces of information must an appraiser have in order to define what the client wants to have appraised?

   a. Identity of the Real Estate

   b. Identity of the Real Property Interest

   c. Purpose of the appraisal

2. Why is it important to know the identity of the real property interest that the client wants to have appraised?

   Different interests have different Values

3. What is the difference between the purpose and the use of an appraisal?

   a. Purpose: the kind of value the Client wants estimated

   b. Use: the reason the Client wants to know the particular value.

When is it to be Appraised?

Once the appraiser knows what is to be appraised, she must identify the **effective date** (or **valuation date**) of the appraisal, and also the time frame in which the client requires the appraisal report.

Effective Date of Appraisal (Valuation Date). Value estimates are always made as of a specific date, which is called the **effective date** of the appraisal. This is because value typically changes over time. Market conditions, as well as the physical condition of the property, are subject to constant change, and both of these factors affect value.

Example: A residential property is appraised at $320,000 as of June 1. On June 2, the house is completely destroyed by a tornado, substantially reducing the value of the property. But the value estimate contained in the appraisal is still valid, because it was made as of a specific date, prior to the catastrophe. (The appraisal may also have included an assumption clause, stating that the value estimate was based on the assumption that the described improvements were in good repair.)

In most cases, the client will want to know the value as of the current date, but the appraiser may occasionally be asked to estimate value as of a past or future date. Appraisals of past value are possible if adequate data (comparable sales, etc.) exist for the period of time in question. Such data are often available, provided the valuation date is not too far in the past, so the process of estimating past value is normally not much different than the appraisal of current value. Appraisals of past value are most often required in connection with legal proceedings, such as divorce settlements, probate, or tax audits.

Example: The 2009 property taxes for a particular property are based on the assessed value of the property as of January 1, 2008. The property owner is informed of the assessed value in August 2008. In order to challenge the assessment, the owner may need to obtain an appraisal of the property as of January 1, 2008, the date of the assessment. An appraiser may make such a past value estimate, provided that adequate data are available for the time in question.

Unlike appraisals of past value, appraisals of future value are always speculative (theoretical), because it is impossible to predict future market conditions. Data simply do not exist, and must therefore be assumed. This type of appraisal requires the appraiser to clearly state the assumptions of future market conditions upon which the value estimate is based. An appraisal of future value is normally used in a business context to help someone decide whether to make a particular investment or whether to proceed with a particular project or development.

Example: An investor is considering the purchase of a vacant parcel of land, and wants to obtain an estimate of what the land will be worth five years from now. Such a value estimate will obviously be based on assumptions about future market conditions, economic trends, demographic changes, etc. In this case, it is vital that the appraiser spell out these assumptions clearly and in detail in the appraisal report.

Date of Appraisal Report. The appraisal report date, as opposed to the valuation date, does not directly affect the value estimate. It is simply the date on which the appraisal report is issued (the date on which the appraiser signed the report). In defining an appraisal problem, the report date is important for two reasons. First, the client needs to know that the appraisal will be issued in time to be of some use in the client's decision making process, and the appraiser needs to feel confident that the appraisal can be competently prepared within that time frame. Second, the report date shows whether the property is being valued as of the past (valuation date prior to report date), present (valuation date same as report date), or future (valuation date after report date).

Note that even in the case of an appraisal for current value, the valuation date and the report date are usually not identical. The report date may be the same as the valuation date, or it may be a somewhat later date. The difference is due to the time that is required to analyze the data and prepare the report. The valuation date is the date as of which value is estimated, commonly the date that the appraiser reviews the subject property. The appraisal report date is the date the appraiser completes and signs the report.

Exercise 7

1. Why are appraisals always made as of a specific valuation date?

Vallue typically changes over time

2. What two pieces of information does the appraisal report date indicate?

a. The Client needs to know the appraisal will be in time for use.

b. It shows whether the property is being valued as of the past present or future.

Why is it to be Appraised?

To proceed with the appraisal assignment, the appraiser must know why the appraisal has been requested; that is, what the appraisal will be used for. Appraisals are generally used to help make a particular decision. For example, lenders use appraisals to help decide whether to make a loan for a given amount; buyers and sellers use appraisals to help decide whether to buy or sell a property for a given price.

If a client or someone else makes a decision based on an appraisal, and that decision turns out to be a costly mistake, the injured party may try to hold the appraiser liable for the loss caused by the decision. To limit potential liability, the appraiser should clearly specify that the value estimate is valid only for its intended use by the intended user(s), and is not valid for any other use or any other user.

> **Example:** In an appraisal for property tax assessment purposes, the appraiser estimated a value that was $10,000 less than the true value of the property. If local property taxes are 1.5% of assessed value, then the consequences of the appraiser's error are a loss of tax revenue equal to 1.5% of $10,000, or $150. But if a home buyer were to rely on the same appraisal, the buyer's potential loss would be the full $10,000. By limiting the validity of an appraisal to the use for which it was intended, the appraiser helps control the extent of his or her liability.

The intended use of the appraisal can also have some effect on the appraisal process. If an appraisal is part of a borrower's loan application, for example, the lender is probably most concerned with the potential resale value of the property. Therefore, the appraiser may place greater emphasis on the sales comparison approach to value. On the other hand, the appraiser may tend to give more weight to the income approach to value if the client will be using the appraisal as part of an investment decision. By knowing how the appraisal will be used, the appraiser can make these kinds of judgment calls more competently.

In most cases, the intended user of an appraisal is the client, the person who engaged the appraiser's services. That's not always the case, however, so the appraiser should ask the client whether there are any other intended users.

Exercise 8

List two reasons why it is important for an appraiser to know how the client intends to use the appraisal.

1. ______________________________

2. ______________________________

How is it Being Valued?

Before proceeding with the appraisal, the appraiser and the client should discuss the assumptions and conditions that will apply to the appraisal assignment. Appraisers distinguish between general assumptions, extraordinary assumptions, hypothetical conditions, and limiting conditions.

Assumptions are assertions that the appraiser has assumed to be true but did not independently verify. Customarily, the appraisal report will state the assumptions on which the value estimate is based, and then specifically identify any exceptions to those assumptions.

Example: An appraisal report states that it is based on the assumption that title to the property is free and clear of any liens and encumbrances unless otherwise indicated. The report specifically notes that the property is subject to a utility easement, a fact that the appraiser took into consideration in arriving at the value estimate.

General assumptions are statements that are routinely included in appraisal reports to protect the appraiser from liability based on issues that wouldn't necessarily be discovered through reasonable inquiry or investigation. The assumption in the example, that the title is free of encumbrances except for those specifically listed in the report, would be considered a general assumption.

Extraordinary assumptions are assumptions that are directly related to the specific assignment; they concern uncertain information about the subject property or about other conditions that are critical to the valuation. The appraiser has no particular reason to doubt that the information is true, but it has not been verified, and the value estimate would be affected if it turned out to be false.

Example: A property is not known to have environmental contamination, but there hasn't been the kind of investigation that would be necessary to rule that out. If the appraisal is based on the assumption that the property is free of contamination, and if that assumption could have a significant effect on the appraiser's opinion of value, then it would be considered an extraordinary assumption.

In contrast, **hypothetical conditions** are conditions that are known to be contrary to fact, but that the appraiser treats as true for the purpose of the appraisal.

Example: An appraiser is asked to appraise property that is known to have environmental contamination as if it were uncontaminated. The appraiser agrees to provide an opinion of value based on the hypothetical condition that the property is free of contamination.

Any extraordinary assumptions or hypothetical conditions applied in the development of an appraisal must be clearly stated in the appraisal report, and the report should also state that they may have affected the opinion of value.

A **limiting condition** is a condition that limits the application of the conclusions contained in an appraisal report. Some of the main limiting conditions of an appraisal have been discussed above: the identity of the real estate, the real property interest in question, the purpose and the intended use of the appraisal, and the effective date of the appraisal. These are all limiting conditions because they set limits on the conclusions that may be drawn from the appraisal.

Step 2: Determining the Scope of Work

After the appraiser has defined the appraisal problem, the next step is figuring out what will be involved in solving the problem. This is called determining the scope of work. The USPAP defines the **scope of work** for an appraisal as "the type and extent of research and analyses in an assignment." Together, defining the appraisal problem and determining the scope of work are sometimes called the appraiser's **preliminary analysis**.

The scope of work must include whatever research and analysis is necessary in order to produce a credible opinion of value. An appraiser's opinion is considered credible if it's supported by the relevant evidence and by logic, evaluated in the context of the intended use of the appraisal. At a minimum, the appraiser's research and analysis must meet the expectations of regularly intended users of similar assignments, and it must include the actions that the appraiser's peers would perform in fulfilling similar assignments.

By evaluating the scope of work in advance, the appraiser can make sure the client is willing to authorize (and pay for) the work needed for a competent, credible appraisal. (If not, the appraiser shouldn't accept the assignment.) However, the scope of work may have to be reevaluated during the course of the assignment; determining the scope of work is an ongoing process.

An appraiser's initial evaluation of the scope of work for an assignment involves deciding what methods of appraisal should be used, what data will be needed, and how to go about obtaining that data.

Example: To appraise a house using the sales comparison approach, an appraiser needs data about houses similar to the subject property that have recently been sold. When determining the scope of work for the assignment, the appraiser might decide that he can produce credible results using information about comparable properties that's already on file at his office. Or he might decide that he can't arrive at a credible opinion of value for this particular assignment unless he locates additional comparables, inspects them himself, and investigates the conditions under which they were sold.

When determining the scope of work, the appraiser will also plan or schedule the tasks involved in completing the assignment. If the assignment is routine and all of the work will be done personally by the appraiser, the work plan may be nothing more than a mental review of the steps that must be taken. For more complex assignments, especially assignments that require the work of experts or assistants other than the appraiser, a written schedule may be useful to plan the work flow and insure timely completion of the appraisal.

Step 3: Collecting and Verifying the Data

The third step in the appraisal process is collecting and verifying the necessary data. The amount and types of data that must be collected will vary depending on the particular appraisal assignment. In every assignment, it is the appraiser's judgment that determines what data are necessary.

Sources of Data

Appraisers use data from many different sources. For some assignments, a large part of the necessary data may already be in the appraiser's files. For example, appraisers often maintain files containing regional, city, and neighborhood data for the area in which they customarily practice; data regarding local construction costs; and data on potential comparable properties. As we discussed, identifying the pertinent data that are already in the appraiser's possession, and those that are not, is one part of determining the scope of work for an assignment.

For data that aren't already on hand, the appraiser may need to personally investigate conditions and circumstances that could affect the subject property's value. The appraiser may also use sources of information such as:

- interviews with owners, brokers, lenders, and public officials;
- multiple listing services and other real estate data services; and
- reviews of statistical data published by government agencies, trade groups, and other research organizations.

Much of the information an appraiser needs is now available online. (Sources of information for appraisal data are discussed in more detail in Chapter 5.)

Types of Data

Next, we'll take a closer look at the types of data appraisers use. Data may be classified either as **general** data (pertaining to real estate values in general) or as **specific** data (pertaining to a particular property). Data are also categorized as **primary** or **secondary**, depending on whether they are generated directly by the appraiser or obtained from published sources.

Another way to categorize data is according to how they are used in the appraisal process. Appraisal data are gathered for four basic reasons:

- to identify relevant market trends that may affect real estate values,
- to identify the probable future supply and demand of competitive properties in the local market,
- to identify the relevant characteristics of the subject property, and
- to identify the characteristics of comparable properties that may affect their values.

Let's consider each of these types of data, beginning with market trend data.

Market Trend Data. The terms "market trend data" and "general data" essentially refer to the same thing: information about the ways that social, economic, governmental, and environmental (physical) forces interact to affect value.

> **Example:** In some markets, trends toward smaller households and two-income families may affect the desirability of certain types of homes. Smaller homes or low-maintenance homes are likely to gain in value, while larger homes may lose value because of lessening demand.

To identify the relevant general data, the appraiser must have a good understanding of the market, market trends, and the forces that are driving those trends. This is true for every appraisal, so appraisers are usually already aware of data pertaining to the conditions and influences operating in their markets. If this is not the case, an appraiser should consider consulting with another appraiser who has the appropriate expertise, or even declining the appraisal assignment.

Competitive Supply and Demand Data. Competitive supply and demand data are a form of market trend data, one that is more closely tied to a particular (local) market. These data concern trends in the supply of and demand for properties that are competitive with the subject property. A property is competitive if it is (or may become) available for the same potential uses as the subject property in the same market area.

> **Example:** In collecting data about the competitive supply of single-family residences in a market, an appraiser would consider the existing supply of houses, the supply of vacant land available for residential development, and also the supply of properties that might reasonably be converted to residential use in the future. All of these might prove competitive with the subject property in its future market.

Fig. 3.4 Ways to Categorize Appraisal Data

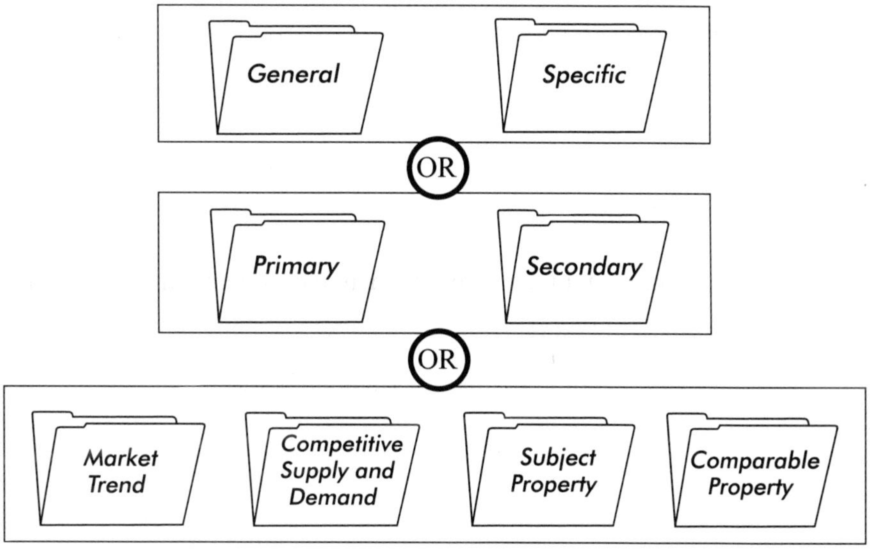

The appraiser must collect data about competitive demand as well as competitive supply. Demand data include factors such as wage and employment levels and population shifts, which drive demand in the local market.

Subject Property Data. Subject property data are any data that pertain specifically to the subject property. Which subject property data will be relevant depends on the purpose and the intended use of the appraisal. However, **relevant characteristics** typically include not only physical characteristics such as the size and the number of rooms, but also legal and financial characteristics, such as any private or public restrictions on the property's use, the terms of sale, or special financing arrangements.

Knowledge of the market will guide the appraiser in identifying the relevant data concerning the subject property. Certain property data, such as location, size, and condition of improvements, are always relevant to an estimate of value. But the relevance of other property data may depend on the market. For example, a corner lot location may be considered desirable in one market, undesirable in another, and of no relevance at all in a third.

Comparable Property Data. Much of the information required for an appraisal is about comparable properties. A **comparable property** is one that's similar to the subject property in regard to certain key characteristics. For a property to be truly comparable, it must:

- have physical characteristics similar to those of the subject property;
- be competitive with the subject property (that is, appeal to the same kinds of buyers in the market);

- be located in the same market area as the subject property; and
- have sold within a limited time from the valuation date (normally within the previous six months).

Example: If the subject property is a 3-bedroom, 2-bath ranch-style house located in a neighborhood of similar houses, the best comparables will be other 3-bedroom, 2-bath ranch-style houses in the same neighborhood that have sold within the last six months. A similar (or even identical) house in a different neighborhood may not be a true comparable, since its neighborhood characteristics may appeal to a different group of buyers.

The appraiser will use comparable property data in each of the three approaches to value. In the sales comparison approach, the appraiser analyzes the sales of improved properties that are comparable to the subject property. In the cost approach, the appraiser analyzes sales of vacant lots that are comparable to the subject property's lot. Sales prices and rents for comparable properties are the basis of the income approach.

An appraiser can begin to identify potential comparables as soon as a general description of the subject property is known. Often the appraiser will be familiar with the subject property's market, and will have some idea of the relative scarcity or abundance of suitable comparables. This knowledge is useful for assessing the amount of time and effort that will be necessary to complete the appraisal assignment.

The appraiser will usually review the subject property early in the appraisal process. The information obtained from this review, together with additional information gathered by the appraiser regarding the rights and restrictions that apply to the subject property, will allow the appraiser to refine the list of potential comparables, discarding those that are not truly comparable, and perhaps adding new ones that more clearly match the subject property's characteristics.

Exercise 9

1. What are the four main types of data used in an appraisal?

   a. Market Trend Data

   b. Competitive Supply and Demand Data

   c. Subject Property Data

   d. Comparable Property Data

2. List the four characteristics of comparable properties.

a. Physical characteristics similar to subject Property
b. Competitive w/ the Subject Property
c. located in the same market area as Sub. Prop.
d. have sold w/in limited time from valuation date. usually 6 mo's.

Verifying Data

All of the data that the appraiser collects must be verified in one way or another. Verification may take the form of a personal review, as when the appraiser verifies the dimensions of the subject property by physical measurement. Or it may mean cross-checking information—for example, interviewing the owner of a comparable property to verify the terms of the sale, or reviewing county records to validate the date and sale price.

The method of verifying information depends on the nature of the data and the scope of work involved in the appraisal. In general terms, the appraiser should verify all data to the extent reasonably possible and to the extent necessary for a credible opinion of value.

Example: The appraiser normally verifies building dimensions of the subject property by personally measuring the improvements. This is considered reasonable because the size of the subject property may have a significant impact on its value, and the measurement process does not involve any great expense.

In the case of comparable properties, however, verification of building size is usually accomplished by visual review only, without actual measurements being taken. In this case, the visual review should pick up any major discrepancies in building size data; smaller size differences are not as great a concern for comparable properties, since more than one comparable is relied on in the appraisal.

Steps 4 Through 8

The following discussion of Steps 4 through 8 is only a summary. Each of these last five steps will be explored in depth in later chapters.

Step 4: Analyzing the Data

Data analysis occurs throughout the appraisal process. As data are selected and collected, the appraiser not only verifies them (checks their accuracy), but also analyzes their relevance—their reliability as indicators of the subject property's value. The data then serve as the basis for the valuation of the property in the three approaches to value. And in the reconciliation step, the appraiser will again thoroughly review all of the data relied upon to reach the value estimate.

Two key aspects of the data analysis usually performed in the course of an appraisal are market analysis and highest and best use analysis. Market analysis is the evaluation of market trend data (including competitive supply and demand data) to determine their significance in regard to the subject property's value. Market analysis is covered in Chapter 5.

As discussed in Chapter 2, property is normally appraised at its highest and best use, the use that results in the greatest return on the investment. For an improved property, highest and best use is analyzed both for the property as improved and for the property as if vacant. The highest and best use analysis also indicates whether any existing improvements are contributing to the value of the land, or whether they should be removed to permit some more profitable use. Highest and best use is discussed more fully in Chapter 6.

Exercise 10

1. What does the term "relevance" refer to in connection with the data analysis for an appraisal?

   reliability as indicators of the subject property's value.

2. List two types of data analysis that are usually performed in the course of an appraisal.

   a. Market Analysis

   b. highest and best use analysis

Step 5: Valuing the Site

A site valuation is an estimate of the value of a property, excluding the value of any existing or proposed improvements. In the case of unimproved property, site valuation is the same as appraising the property as is. For improved property, site valuation means appraising the property as if vacant.

The term "site" refers to a parcel of land that has been improved by clearing, grading, and providing access and utilities. A site is land that has been prepared for some use, typically for the construction of some type of building. The term "site improvements" can be confusing, because not all site improvements are considered part of the land for appraisal purposes. Site improvements that are valued as part of the land, such as clearing and grading, are sometimes referred to as improvements "of" the site. In contrast, site improvements such as buildings and landscaping are called improvements "on" the site, and are valued separately from the land.

Reasons for Separate Site Valuation. There are three reasons why a separate site valuation may be necessary. First, site valuation is an integral part of analyzing highest and best use. By definition, analysis of the highest and best use of a property as if vacant implies a separate site valuation.

The second reason for a separate site valuation is to obtain data for certain valuation techniques. In particular, the cost approach to value and the building residual technique of income capitalization both require a separate estimate of site value. If either of these techniques is used in an appraisal, a separate site valuation is necessary. (The cost approach to value is covered in detail in Chapter 8. The building residual technique is discussed in Chapter 10.)

A separate valuation of site and improvements may also be required by law, particularly in appraisals for property tax assessment and condemnation purposes. In these cases, a separate site evaluation is required because of the intended use of the appraisal.

Step 6: Applying the Three Approaches to Value

Having collected data, analyzed highest and best use, and evaluated the site, the appraiser is ready to apply the three approaches to value: the cost approach, the sales comparison approach, and the income approach. Each of these approaches results in an indication of value, or **value indicator**. The appraiser will then reconcile these value indicators in Step 7, reconciliation.

Cost Approach. The first approach to value, the cost approach, assumes that the value of improved property is indicated by the value of the site, plus the cost (new) to construct the improvements, less any depreciation that the improvements have suffered. **Depreciation** is the difference in value between the cost (new) of the improvements and their current value, regardless of the reasons for the difference. The cost approach can be expressed by the formula:

Property Value = Site Value + Replacement Cost of Improvements – Depreciation

As noted earlier in this chapter, the cost approach requires a separate valuation of the site. The appraiser then estimates what it would cost to replace any existing structures, and adds this amount to the site value. The cost of replacing the structures is estimated as of the date of valuation.

Finally, the appraiser estimates any loss in value due to physical, functional, or external depreciation, such as physical deterioration of the improvements, or a loss in value due to an outdated design. The appraiser deducts this amount to arrive at the final value indicator.

Sales Comparison Approach. The sales comparison approach to value is also known as the **market approach** or **market data approach**. Under this approach, the value of the subject property is indicated by the values (sale prices) of similar properties in the market. These similar properties are referred to as **comparables**. The two keys to effective use of the sales comparison approach are:

1. identifying similar properties that are truly "comparable" to the subject property, and
2. making the proper adjustments to the sales prices of the comparable properties to account for any differences between the subject property and the comparables.

The considerations in identifying legitimate comparables were discussed earlier in this chapter. It is relatively rare, however, to find two properties that are so comparable that there is no difference in their values. For this reason, the adjustment process is central to the sales comparison approach. In the adjustment process, the sales price of the comparable property is adjusted (up or down) to reflect aspects of the comparable property that are viewed as less valuable or more valuable in comparison to the subject property.

Example: An appraiser identifies a comparable property that is similar to the subject property in all respects, except the subject property has only one bath, while the comparable has two. The comparable property sold recently for $145,000. Current market data indicate that an extra bath adds $5,000 to the values of homes similar to these. So the appraiser would subtract the value of the more desirable feature (the extra bath) from the price of the comparable, to arrive at an indicated value of $140,000 for the subject property.

The sales comparison approach may be summarized by the formula:

Subject Value = Comparable Sales Price +/– Adjustments

Income Approach. The third approach to value is the income approach, or **income capitalization approach**. This approach assumes that the value of property is indicated

Fig. 3.5 Reasons for Site Valuation

1. Necessary for highest and best use analysis
2. Provides data for certain valuation methods
3. May be required because of intended use of appraisal

by the amount of income that the property can generate: the greater the income, the greater the value. The income approach can be summarized by the following formula:

$$Value = Income \times Factor$$

It is obvious from this formula that the key to effective use of the income approach is identifying the amount of income, and choosing an appropriate factor to apply to the income. This factor may be an income multiplier or a capitalization rate, depending on the income approach technique being used. If the subject property is currently being used as income property, analyzing its income may be fairly simple. If the subject property is not currently used as income property, the appraiser will have to identify similar properties that are income-producing, and compare them to the subject property to estimate its potential rental income.

The factor or multiplier used in the income approach is obtained from analyzing market data. The appraiser compares the sales prices and incomes of similar properties in the market to arrive at the appropriate multiplier. For example, an appraiser may determine that properties similar to the subject property typically sell for 10.5 times their annual income. If the subject property's annual income were $30,000, its indicated value under the income approach would be $315,000 ($30,000 × 10.5).

Exercise 11

Identify the approach to value that is most closely associated with each of the following concepts.

1. b depreciation
2. c income multipliers
3. a sales of similar properties
4. b separate valuation of land and improvements
5. a adjustments to comparable sales

a. Sales comparison
b. Cost
c. Income

Step 7: Reconciling the Value Indicators

Each of the three approaches to value results in an separate indication of value for the subject property. In general, the greater the similarity among the three value indicators, the more reliable they are. However, it is very rare for all three value indicators to be identical.

When the value indicators are not identical, the appraiser must somehow resolve the value indicators into one estimate of value. This process is called **reconciliation**.

Reconciliation is the easiest when the value indicators are very similar. In that case, it is usually safe to assume that the value of the property lies somewhere between the lowest and highest value indicators.

Example: An appraiser arrives at the following value indicators:

Cost Approach:	$355,000
Market Approach:	$345,200
Income Approach:	$340,500

Since the value indicators are reasonably similar to each other, the value of the property is probably somewhere between $340,500 (the lowest indicator) and $355,000 (the highest indicator).

However, the process of reconciliation is not a simple averaging of the three value indicators. In fact, there is no set formula at all for reconciling the values. The process relies entirely on the judgment and ability of the appraiser to arrive at the most reliable estimate of value.

A primary consideration in the reconciliation process is the relative reliability of the three value indicators, especially when there is a wide disparity between the three indicators. For this reason, the reconciliation process requires a thorough review of the complete appraisal process. The appraiser must review the reliability of the data, the logic and analysis applied to the data, and the resulting value indicators. The more reliable indicators will receive more weight in the appraiser's analysis.

In addition to reviewing and considering the reliability of the various value indicators, the appraiser will also consider the use of the appraisal. For example, all things being equal, more weight may be placed on the value indicated by the income approach in the case of an appraisal that will be used by an investor who is looking for income property. On the other hand, if the appraisal is being used to help the owner-occupant purchaser qualify for a home loan, the sales comparison data approach may be considered the most reliable.

Step 8: Reporting the Value Estimate

The final step in the appraisal process is the preparation of the appraisal report. Standards Rule 2-2 of the USPAP provides for three options as to the content of written appraisal reports:

1. the self-contained report,
2. the summary report, and
3. the restricted use report.

The three types of reports differ in the level of detail required. Self-contained reports are the most comprehensive; summary reports are less detailed. Restricted use reports contain the least amount of information.

Regardless of the type of report used, USPAP Standard 2 requires that when reporting his or her results, the appraiser must communicate the information in a manner that is not misleading.

Note that even the simplest appraisal report should contain the elements described in USPAP Standards Rule 2-2, including:

- the identity of the client;
- the intended use of the appraisal;
- identification of the subject real estate;
- the real property interest to be appraised;
- the type and definition of value, with the source of the definition;
- the effective date of the appraisal and the date of the report;
- a description of the scope of work used to develop the appraisal;
- the appraisal methods and techniques used, and the value opinions and conclusions reached, along with an explanation of why certain methods were not used;
- the use of the property as of the date of valuation, the use reflected in the appraisal, and the appraiser's opinion of the highest and best use (if one was developed);
- extraordinary assumptions and hypothetical conditions that affect the appraisal; and
- a certification signed by the appraiser, as required by the USPAP.

Appraisal reports are prepared in one of three basic formats:

1. narrative report,
2. form report, and
3. oral report.

The **narrative report** is the most detailed form of appraisal report. It describes the data analyzed by the appraiser, the conclusions drawn, and the reasoning behind the stated conclusions. A self-contained appraisal report is most likely to be written in the narrative format.

The **form report** is probably the most commonly used format for residential appraisals. Form reports are used by many lenders and government agencies. The form report typically presents the data used by the appraiser and the appraiser's conclusions. The form has a limited amount of space for discussing the appraiser's reasoning. If necessary, the appraiser should use an addendum to provide additional information. Summary appraisal reports are typically form reports.

An **oral report**, as the term implies, is delivered to the client orally rather than in writing. The amount of detail contained in an oral report will depend on the circumstances and the needs of the client.

It is important to note that regardless of the type and format of the appraisal report, the appraiser should always maintain a **work file** with good detailed records of the data, analysis, and conclusions that form the basis of the appraisal.

Appraisal reports are discussed in greater detail in Chapter 12.

Exercise 12

Which type or types of appraisal reports would normally contain the following items?

1. abc identification of the real estate
2. ab description of data used in the appraisal
3. abc identification of the appraisal's effective date
4. a description of appraiser's analysis and reasoning
5. abc identification of the assumptions and limiting conditions

a. Narrative
b. Form
c. Oral

Key Terms

Assumptions—Assertions that are assumed to be true for the purposes of an appraisal, but that the appraiser does not independently verify. Assumptions concerning uncertain information that is critical to the valuation are referred to as extraordinary assumptions.

Comparable—A property that has been sold in the same market that currently includes the subject property, and that appeals to the same sorts of buyers. Comparables are used in many different appraisal techniques.

Cost approach—One of the three approaches to value in the appraisal process. In the cost approach, the value of the subject property is indicated by the cost to build the subject improvements, plus the value of the site, and minus any depreciation that affects the subject improvements.

Effective date of appraisal—The date as of which value is estimated, distinguished from the date the appraisal report is prepared. Value estimates are always made as of a specific date, because value can change over time.

Fee simple—A freehold estate that is the most complete and comprehensive form of real property interest, including the entire bundle of rights.

Form report—A written appraisal report prepared on a standardized form, usually with addenda.

General data—Data that relate to the real estate market in which a property is located, including regional, district, and neighborhood data.

Improvement—An item of personal property that is added to the land by human effort, in such a way that it becomes part of the real estate. Also called a fixture.

Income approach—One of the three approaches to value in the appraisal process. In the income approach, the value of the subject property is indicated by the amount of net income that the property can generate. Also called the income capitalization approach.

Legal description—A description of a parcel of real estate in a form that is legally approved in the state where the property is located. Common systems of legal description include the metes and bounds, government (rectangular) survey, and lot and block systems.

Limiting conditions—A statement or explanation in an appraisal report that limits the application of the conclusions contained in the report.

Oral report—An appraisal report that is delivered orally rather than in writing, as in a deposition or courtroom testimony.

Narrative report—A written appraisal report in narrative format; the most complete form of appraisal report, setting forth all the data relied on by the appraiser, and fully describing the appraiser's analysis and conclusions.

Personal property—All property that is not classified as real estate.

Primary data—Data that are generated by the appraiser, such as by a physical review of property or personal interviews.

Purpose of appraisal—The information that a client wants the appraiser to provide in an appraisal assignment. The purpose of most appraisals is to estimate a defined value for a specific real property interest in a specific parcel of real estate as of a specific date.

Real estate—An identified parcel or tract of land, including improvements, if any (USPAP definition).

Real property—The interests, benefits, and rights inherent in the ownership of real estate (USPAP definition).

Reconciliation—The process by which an appraiser reduces two or more value indicators to a single indicator or estimate of value.

Restricted use appraisal report—A written appraisal report that is prepared in accordance with USPAP Standards Rule 2-2(c).

Sales comparison approach—One of the three approaches to value in the appraisal process. In the sales comparison approach, the value of the subject property is indicated by the adjusted sales prices of similar properties (comparables) in the market.

Scope of work—The type and extent of research and analyses in an assignment (USPAP definition).

Secondary data—Data generated by someone other than the appraiser, and obtained by the appraiser via a review of published materials.

Self-contained appraisal report—A written appraisal report that is prepared in accordance with USPAP Standards Rule 2-2(a).

Specific data—Data that relate to a specific property, such as the subject property or a comparable.

Summary appraisal report—A written appraisal report that is prepared in accordance with USPAP Standards Rule 2-2(b).

Value—The monetary relationship between properties and those who buy, sell, or use those properties (USPAP definition). The theoretical worth of something, expressed in terms of something else, usually money.

Value indicator—A piece of data or a derived conclusion (such as the adjusted sales price of a comparable) that is relevant to the value of the subject property in an appraisal.

Summary

I. The appraisal process consists of eight steps that guide the appraiser to a competent estimate of value.

A. USPAP requires appraisers to "be aware of, understand, and correctly employ those recognized methods and techniques that are necessary to produce a credible appraisal."

II. Step 1—Defining the Appraisal Problem

A. Appraiser must know what the client wants, and the terms and conditions of the appraisal assignment.

B. What is to be appraised?

1. Identity of the real estate is established by the legal description.

   a. Appraiser must identify and consider any personal property that is included in the appraisal, as well as any repairs and improvements that will be made to the property.

2. The real property rights to be appraised will affect the value estimate. Most appraisals are concerned with the fee simple interest, but appraisals may be made for limited or partial interests as well.

3. The appraiser must consider all the rights that benefit the property, as well as all restrictions that may affect value.

4. The purpose of the appraisal is the type of value to be estimated. The value should always be defined.

C. When is it to be appraised?

1. Appraisals estimate value as of a specified date: the valuation date or effective date of the appraisal.

2. The valuation date may or may not be the same as the appraisal report date. Appraisals are sometimes made for past or future values, as well as current values.

D. Why is it to be appraised?

1. Knowing the intended use and intended users of the appraisal will affect the appraiser's selection of data, and also the appraiser's judgments in the reconciliation phase of the appraisal.

2. Knowing the intended use of the appraisal also allows the appraiser to limit liability arising from the appraisal.

E. How is it to be appraised?

1. Assumptions and conditions are stated in an appraisal report to help the reader understand the significance of the data and conclusions presented.

2. General assumptions are statements routinely included in appraisal reports to limit the appraiser's liability.

3. Extraordinary assumptions concern uncertain information about the subject property or other matters critical to the valuation. The opinion of value would be affected if the assumption turned out to be false.

4. Hypothetical conditions are conditions known to be contrary to fact, but treated as if they were true for the purposes of an appraisal assignment.

5. Limiting conditions limit the conclusions that can be drawn from an appraisal report.

III. Step 2—Determining the Scope of Work

A. Scope of work: the type and the extent of research and analysis needed to produce a credible opinion of value.

B. An opinion is credible if it:

1. is supported by the relevant evidence and by logic;

2. meets expectations of regularly intended users of similar assignments; and

3. is based on the actions that the appraiser's peers would perform in fulfilling similar assignments.

C. Appraiser evaluates what data will be needed, ascertains which of those are already in his or her files, and plans the work flow for the assignment.

IV. Step 3—Collecting the Data

A. Appraiser obtains some data through personal review and other data from published sources.

B. Types of data

1. General data concern real estate values in general; specific data concern a particular property.

2. Primary data are generated directly by the appraiser; secondary data are from published sources.

3. Market trend data (general data): information about social, economic, governmental, and environmental forces affecting real estate values.

4. Competitive supply and demand data: data about supply of and demand for properties competing with the subject property in the local market.

5. Subject property data: relevant characteristics may be physical, legal (such as zoning or other restrictions), or financial (such as the terms of sale).
6. Comparable property data: a property is comparable if it is physically similar to the subject property, appeals to the same kinds of buyers, is located in the same market area, and is sold within a limited period of time from the effective date of the appraisal.

C. The accuracy of data used in an appraisal must be verified, either by personal review or by cross-checking between sources.

V. Step 4—Analyzing the Data

A. Data analysis includes market analysis and highest and best use analysis.

B. For improved property, the appraiser must analyze the highest and best use of the property as improved, and also as if vacant.

VI. Step 5—Valuing the Site

A. A site is land that has been prepared for use or construction, by clearing, grading, and provision of access and utilities.

B. Site valuation may be necessary for highest and best use analysis, for application of certain appraisal techniques, and/or because of appraisal's intended use.

VII. Step 6—Applying the Three Approaches to Value

A. Cost approach indicates value by estimating the value of the land separately, then adding the estimated cost (new) of the improvements, and then subtracting depreciation that the improvements have suffered.

1. The older the improvements, the more difficult it is to estimate depreciation, and the less reliable the value indication given by the cost approach is.

B. Sales comparison approach (market data approach) indicates value by analyzing the sales of similar (comparable) properties.

1. The more similar the comparables are to the subject property, the more reliable they are as indicators of value.
2. Sales prices of comparables are adjusted for any differences from the subject property, including physical differences, changes in market conditions, and differences in the terms of sale.

C. Income approach (income capitalization approach) estimates value by multiplying a property's income (or potential income) by a multiplying factor.

1. Choice of the appropriate multiplying factor has a significant effect on the value indicated by the income approach. The factor is determined by analyzing sales prices and income from comparable properties.

VIII. Step 7—Reconciling the Value Indicators

A. Appraiser must reconcile any differences between the values indicated by the three approaches to value.

B. Reconciliation involves analysis of the reliability of the value indicators, and application of the appraiser's judgment as to the most reliable estimate of value.

IX. Step 8—Reporting the Value Estimate

A. The USPAP provides for three options for written appraisal reports: self-contained reports, summary reports, and restricted use reports. Self-contained reports contain the most detail, summary reports contain less detail, and restricted use reports contain the least detail.

B. Regardless of the form of an appraisal report, it must contain the elements required by the USPAP.

C. Appraisal reports are prepared in one of three formats: narrative reports, form reports, or oral reports.

1. The narrative report is the most detailed type of appraisal report. It sets out the data relied on by the appraiser, and explains the analysis of the data and the reasoning that led to the appraiser's final estimate of value.
2. Form reports include much of the data that support the appraiser's conclusion, but do not include an explanation of the appraiser's reasoning. Form reports are used by many lenders, insurers and government agencies.
3. Appraisal reports are sometimes given orally.

Chapter Quiz

1. The effective date of an appraisal is:
   a. the date of the appraisal report
   b. the date on which the appraiser accepts the appraisal assignment
   c. the date as of which value is estimated
   d. the date on which the appraiser reviews the subject property

2. The purpose of an appraisal refers to:
   a. the kind of value that the client wants to know
   b. the appraiser's desire to earn a fee
   c. the circumstances under which the client has ordered the appraisal
   d. the type of appraisal client

3. The site and improvements are valued separately under the:
   a. sales comparison approach
   b. cost approach
   c. income approach
   d. market data approach

4. In defining an appraisal problem, it is important to identify:
   a. the use of the appraisal
   b. the purpose of the appraisal
   c. the scope of work
   d. All of the above

5. An appraiser may analyze sales of comparable properties in the:
   a. sales comparison approach
   b. cost approach
   c. income approach
   d. All of the above

6. Which of the following is NOT a part of defining an appraisal problem?
   a. Identifying the real estate
   b. Identifying the real property interest
   c. Identifying the sources of data
   d. Agreeing on the limiting conditions

7. In an appraisal report, real estate is identified by means of its legal description because:
   a. it is the most commonly accepted way to do it
   b. it is required by law in all cases
   c. it is the most accurate way to describe the real estate
   d. it helps prevent unauthorized persons from understanding the appraisal report

8. Which of the following pairs of terms mean the same thing?
   a. Scope of work and use of the appraisal
   b. Purpose of the appraisal and use of the appraisal
   c. Valuation date and appraisal date
   d. Valuation date and effective date

9. In reconciling the value indicators from the three approaches to value, the appraiser:
   a. averages the value indicators
   b. applies a formula for the weighted average of the indicators
   c. reviews and analyzes the reliability of each of the value indicators
   d. None of the above

10. The assumptions and limiting conditions stated in an appraisal report are for the benefit of:

    a. the appraiser
    b. the client
    c. third parties
    d. All of the above

11. Which of the following would NOT be considered specific data?

    a. The location of a property
    b. Evidence of population shifts in a neighborhood
    c. The size of a lot
    d. The terms and conditions of a sale

12. The value of a site includes all of the following except:

    a. the value of the land
    b. the value of any landscaping
    c. the value of clearing and grading the land
    d. the value of providing access to the land

13. A site may be valued separately from its improvements:

    a. to provide data for certain valuation techniques
    b. because of the intended use of the appraisal
    c. as part of the highest and best use analysis
    d. All of the above

14. Which of the following types of appraisal reports would usually include a presentation of the data relied upon by the appraiser in reaching the value estimate?

    a. Narrative report
    b. Form report
    c. Letter of opinion
    d. Both a) and b)

15. In reconciling the value indicators from the three approaches to value, the appraiser should consider:

    a. the use of the appraisal
    b. the reliability of the indicated values
    c. Both of the above
    d. Neither of the above

Quiz Answers

1. c) The effective date of an appraisal is the date for which the valuation applies.
2. a) An appraisal's purpose refers to the type of value the appraiser is to estimate.
3. b) In the cost approach, the improvements and site are valued separately.
4. d) An appraiser must know the use and purpose of the appraisal and the scope of work in order to proceed.
5. d) While use of comparable properties is most commonly associated with the sales comparison approach, comparables are also used in the cost approach to determine the site value, and in the income approach to determine an appropriate multiplier or factor.
6. c) Identifying the sources of data is not a part of defining the appraisal problem; this is a separate step in the process.
7. c) A legal description is necessary since it provides an accurate description of the property's exact boundaries.
8. d) The valuation date and effective date of an appraisal are the same.
9. c) The reconciliation process does not involve averaging values or using a set formula. Instead, the appraiser will use her own judgment to analyze the reliability of each value indicator, and will weight them accordingly.
10. d) Assumptions and limiting conditions are stated in an appraisal report for the benefit of any reader, including third parties.
11. b) Population shifts within a neighborhood would not be considered specific data, since that information does not refer to a particular property.
12. b) Landscaping is considered an improvement, and is not included as part of the value of a site.
13. d) A site and improvements may be valued separately as part of a highest and best use analysis, to provide data for certain appraisal techniques (such as a residual technique), or because of the intended use of the appraisal (an appraisal for assessment purposes, for example).
14. d) A narrative report and a form report both present the data relied upon by the appraiser.
15. c) An appraiser should consider both the use of the appraisal and the reliability of the indicated values in reconciling the value indicators.

Exercise Answers

#1
1. Define the appraisal problem.
2. Determine the scope of work.
3. Collect and verify the data.
4. Analyze the data.
5. Estimate the value of the site.
6. Apply the three approaches to value.
7. Reconcile the various value indicators to reach a final value estimate.
8. Prepare and deliver an appropriate appraisal report.

#2
1. a. Identity of the real estate
   b. Real property interest in question
   c. Purpose of the appraisal (type and definition of value)
   d. Effective date (valuation date)
   e. Date of appraisal report
   f. Identity of client and other intended users
   g. Intended use of the appraisal
   h. Assumptions and other limiting conditions
2. The appraiser must determine what is to be appraised, when it is to be appraised, why it is to be appraised, and how it is to be appraised.

#3
1. Legal description is the most accurate way to describe real estate.
2. Legal descriptions are usually obtained from deeds or mortgages. These documents may be available from the property owner, real estate broker, lender, property manager or local records office.

#4
1. Personal property is not normally included in a real estate appraisal. If it is included, it must be identified because it can affect the value estimate.
2. Like personal property, new improvements can affect the value of real estate.

#5
1. Some of the more common restrictions on real property rights include: zoning laws, public and private easements, rights-of-way, and deed restrictions.

2. Restrictions on property rights can be identified by: examination of deeds, title insurance policies, and title abstracts, and by inquiring at the offices of local zoning, planning, and taxing authorities.

#6 1. a. Identity of the real estate

b. Identity of the real property interest

c. Purpose of the appraisal (type and definition of value)

2. The value in an appraisal depends on the interest that is being appraised. Different interests may (and usually do) have different values.

3. a. The purpose of an appraisal is the type of value the client wants to know.

b. The use of an appraisal is the reason the client wants to know the value.

#7 1. The forces that affect value are subject to change over time.

2. The appraisal report date gives an indication of the client's time requirements with respect to the appraisal, and (when contrasted with the valuation date) indicates whether the value to be appraised is past, current, or future.

#8 1. The use of the appraisal may affect the selection of data and also the appraiser's analysis of the data.

2. The appraiser can limit liability by specifying that the appraisal is valid only for its intended use.

#9 1. a. Market trend data

b. Competitive supply and demand data

c. Subject property data

d. Comparable property data

2. a. Similar physical characteristics

b. Appeal to same kinds of buyers

c. Located in same market area

d. Sold within 6 months of valuation date

#10 1. The reliability of the data as an indicator of the subject property's value.

2. a. Market analysis

b. Highest and best use analysis

#11 1. b

2. c

3. a

4. b

5. a

#12 1. a, b, c

2. a, b

3. a, b, c

4. a

5. a, b, c

4 Property Description and Appraisal Math

Overview

An appraiser should be able to read and understand a "legal" description of real estate, since most appraisals require a legal description in order to identify the subject property adequately. Appraisers must also be comfortable applying a variety of different mathematical techniques and formulas that are used in the valuation process. After completing this chapter, you should be able to:

- name the three major systems of land description used in the United States, and explain how land is described under each system;
- calculate the area and volume of complex figures;
- solve problems involving percentages, interest, capitalization rates, and income multipliers; and
- use a financial calculator or table to solve problems that involve discounting and annuities.

Property Description

In everyday life, real estate is normally identified by its street address, such as "111 Main Street" or "1517 Park Avenue." Some properties may also be known by a common name, such as "Empire State Building," or "South Fork Ranch." Although these methods of property description are suitable for many purposes, they are of little use when it comes to determining the exact boundaries of a parcel of real estate.

Standards Rule 1-2 of the USPAP requires the appraiser to "identify the characteristics of the property that are relevant" to the appraisal. One of these relevant characteristics is the property's location. To identify the subject property's location, the appraiser must use what is called a **legal description**: one that is adequate to identify the property's exact boundaries.

In most cases, a property's legal description is given to the appraiser by the appraisal client or obtained by the appraiser from legal records describing the property. It is not the appraiser's responsibility to verify the accuracy of the description or to survey the property. However, an appraiser should be able to recognize whether the description meets the local standards, and he or she should also be able to identify the real estate that is described in the legal description.

Three commonly used methods of legal description in the United States are:

1. the metes and bounds system,
2. the rectangular (government) survey system, and
3. the lot and block system.

Different areas of the country use different systems or combinations of systems, depending on local law and custom. An appraiser should have a basic understanding of each of the three methods.

Metes and Bounds

The metes and bounds system is the oldest of the three methods of legal description; it also tends to be the most complicated. This system describes real estate by describing its boundaries, similar to the way a surveyor would describe them. It gives directions and distances that could be followed by a surveyor to trace the boundaries of the property.

A metes and bounds description has three basic elements:

1. reference points,
2. courses, and
3. distances.

Reference Points. A **reference point** (sometimes called a **monument**) is an identifiable, fixed position from which measurements may be taken. A common example of a reference point is a fixed survey marker that has been permanently set in the ground. Natural or artificial landmarks such as trees, rocks, rivers, or roads are also used as reference points in metes and bounds descriptions.

All metes and bounds descriptions begin at a reference point that serves to locate the property with respect to adjoining surveys in the area. This initial reference point is known as the **point of beginning (POB)**. The term "point of beginning" can sometimes be confusing, since it can be used to refer to two different points: the initial reference point for the description, and the point at which the description of the actual property boundaries begins. Sometimes these two points coincide, but often they do not.

To distinguish between the initial reference point of the description and the first point on the actual property boundary, the latter is sometimes referred to as the **true point of beginning**. Figure 4.1 shows the relationship between the point of beginning, which is the initial reference point for the description, and the true point of beginning, which is the point at which the description of the actual boundaries of the property begins.

Fig. 4.1 True Point of Beginning

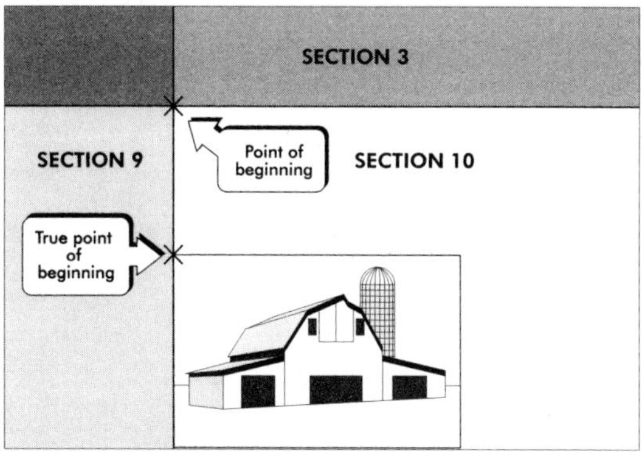

A metes and bounds description of this property would start by identifying the true point of beginning, in reference to the monument located at the northwest corner of Section 10: "Beginning at the Northwest corner of Section 10; thence south along the section line 900 feet to a true point of beginning..."

Courses and Distances. Once the true point of beginning is established, the metes and bounds description proceeds to describe each boundary of the property. The boundaries are described in sequential order, ending up back at the true point of beginning. Essentially, the description is a set of instructions that would enable someone to walk around the boundaries of the property. Each instruction corresponds to one boundary of the property; it tells which direction to go to follow the boundary (the course), and how far to go before changing to another direction (the distance).

Example: A typical instruction or "call" in a metes and bounds description might read: "North 36 degrees 30 minutes West, 267 feet." This tells the reader to proceed on a course that is 36° 30' to the west of due north, for a distance of 267 feet.

A course in a metes and bounds description may be stated in one of two ways. If the course is precisely along one of the four cardinal directions, it is usually stated as simply north, south, east, or west. All other courses are stated in terms of their quadrant (northeast, northwest, southeast, or southwest) and their angle in relation to a line running north and south.

Northwesterly and northeasterly courses are stated in terms of the angle from north; southwesterly and southeasterly courses are stated in terms of the angle from south. The angle is given in terms of degrees, minutes, and seconds. (In angular measurements, a degree (°) is equal to $^1/_{360}$ of a full circle; a minute (') is equal to $^1/_{60}$ of a degree; and a second (") is equal to $^1/_{60}$ of a minute or $^1/_{3600}$ of a degree.) The size of the angle is written in between the two cardinal directions that form the boundaries of the quadrant.

Fig. 4.2 Metes and Bounds Description

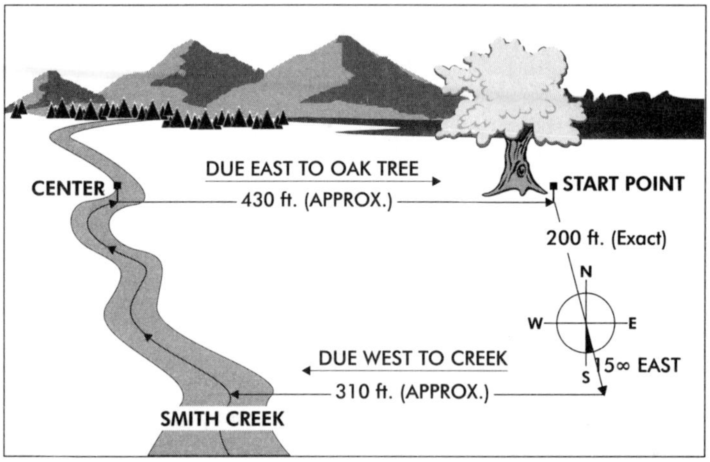

A tract of land located in Weller County, described as follows: Beginning at the oak tree, thence south 15° east, 200 feet, thence north 90° west, 310 feet more or less to the centerline of Smith Creek, thence northwesterly along the centerline of the creek to a point directly west of the oak tree, thence north 90° east, 430 feet more or less to the point of beginning.

Example: A northeasterly course that forms an angle of 40 degrees from due north would be stated as North 40 degrees East, or N 40° E. The angle is written between the two cardinal directions that identify the quadrant.

Metes and Bounds Descriptions in Appraisals. Metes and bounds descriptions can be very long and complex, which creates opportunities for errors whenever the description must be copied. For this reason, the description is often photocopied from a deed or other document, and the photocopy is attached as an addendum to the appraisal. This does not guarantee the accuracy of the description, but it at least prevents errors in its transcription.

Rectangular (Government) Survey

The second major system of property description is the rectangular survey system, also known as the government survey system. In this system, property is described in relation to a rectangular grid that has been established by federal government survey.

The rectangular survey system was established by law in 1785. It covers most areas of the country that were not already settled as of the date the system was established. As shown in Figure 4.3, separate rectangular grid systems have been surveyed for most areas of the country, the main exception being the eastern states.

Fig. 4.3 The Principal Meridians and Baselines in the United States

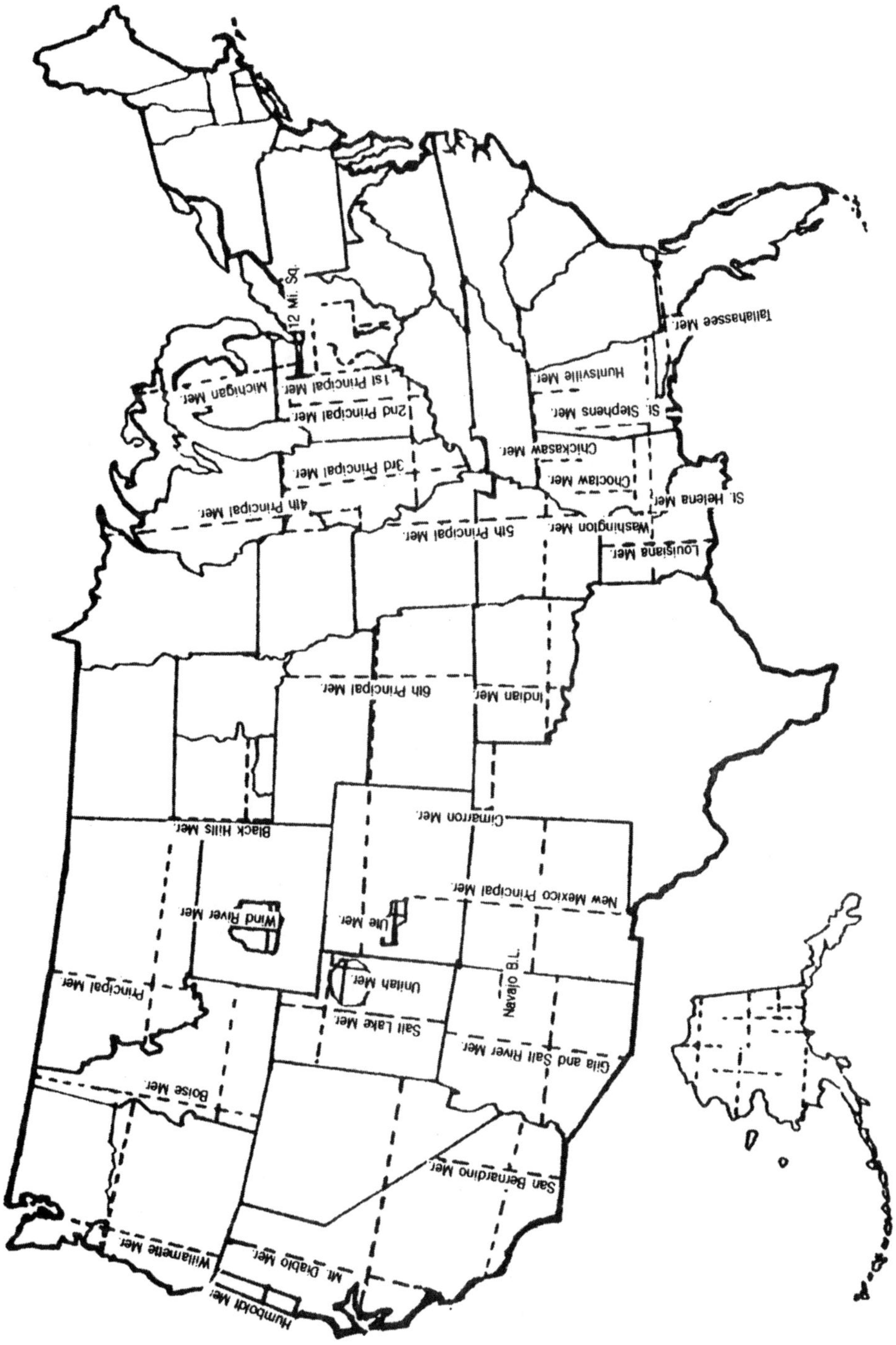

Base and Meridian. Each main grid in the rectangular survey system has an initial reference point, which serves as the basis for locating all properties in the grid. The initial reference point is the intersection between the **principal meridian**, running north and south, and the **base line**, which runs east and west.

Each grid system has its own unique name, corresponding to the name of its principal meridian. Property descriptions that use the rectangular survey system must refer to the name of the particular grid that is the reference for the description.

Example: The rectangular survey in southern California is based on the San Bernardino Principal Meridian and Base Line. A rectangular survey description in this area would refer to the "San Bernardino Base and Meridian," or "S.B.B.&M."

Townships. Each rectangular survey grid consists of a series of lines that run parallel to the principal meridian and the base line, at intervals of six miles apart. The east-west lines (running parallel to the base line) are called **township lines**; the north-south lines (parallel to the principal meridian) are referred to as **range lines**.

Township lines divide the land into a series of east-west strips, called **township tiers**. Range lines divide the land into north-south strips called **ranges**. Where a township tier intersects with a range, the result is a six-mile-square block of land known as a **township**. Townships are the main divisions of land in the rectangular survey system. Each township is identified according to its position relative to a principal meridian and base line.

Example: The township that is located at the intersection of the first township tier north of the base line, and the third range east of the principal meridian, is called "Township 1 North, Range 3 East," or "T1N, R3E."

Sections. Each six-mile-square township is divided into an even smaller rectangular grid, with grid lines (called **section lines**) spaced one mile apart. The section lines run both north-south and east-west within the township. The result is that each township contains 36 **sections**, each section measuring one mile on a side and containing 640 acres. The sections are numbered from 1 to 36, starting with Section 1 in the northeast corner of the township and continuing across and down in snake-like fashion to Section 36 in the southeast corner. This means that Section 1 is always located in the upper right-hand corner of the township and Section 36 is always located in the lower right-hand corner. (See Figure 4.4.)

Partial Sections. Sections may be broken down into even smaller rectangular blocks. This is done by first dividing the section into quarters, and then progressively dividing the quarter sections into quarters or halves, as shown in Figure 4.5. Partial sections are described by simply listing the sequence of the divisions, starting with the smallest one and ending with the largest.

Fig. 4.4 The Basic Components of the Government Survey System

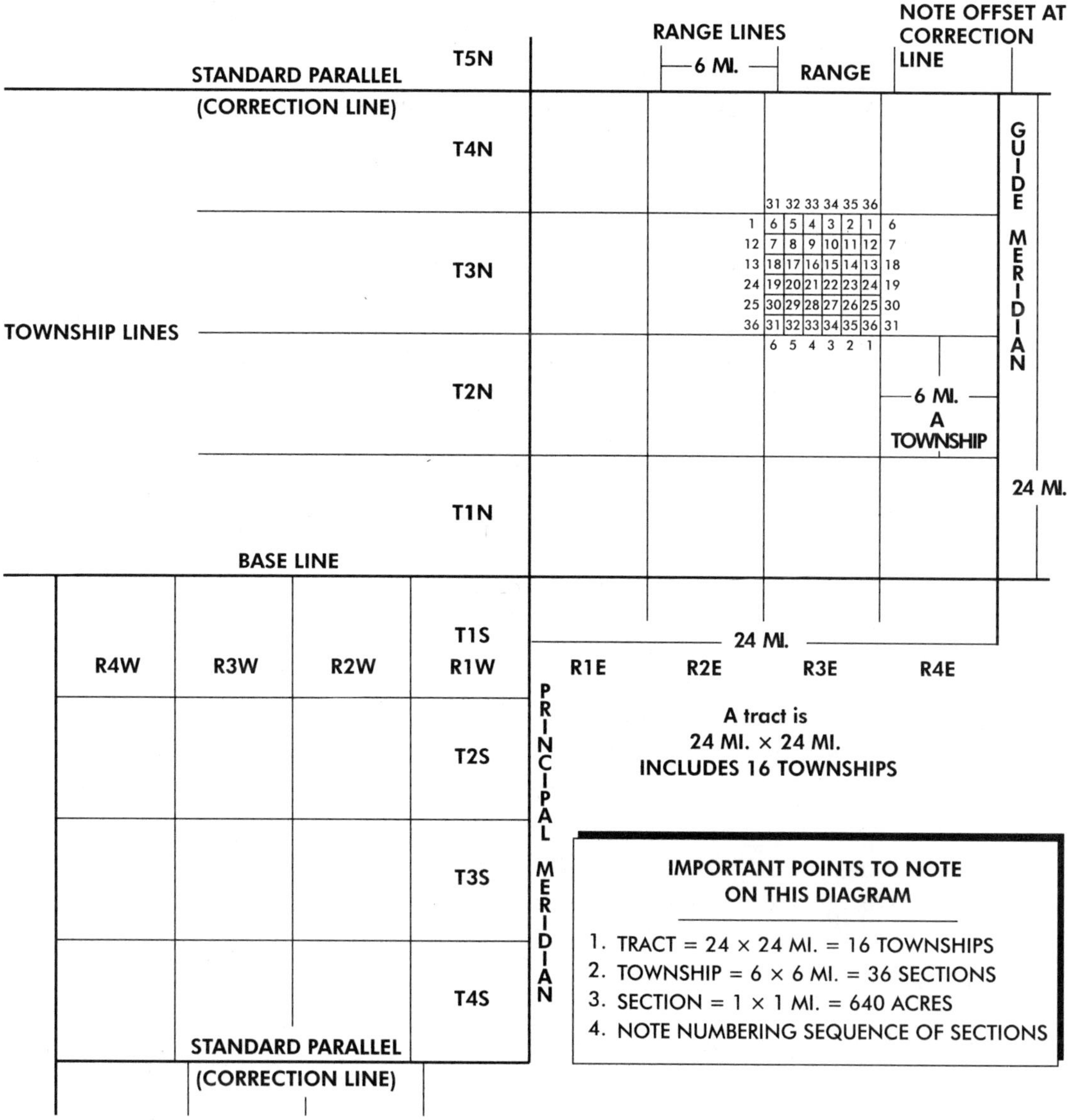

IMPORTANT POINTS TO NOTE ON THIS DIAGRAM

1. TRACT = 24 × 24 MI. = 16 TOWNSHIPS
2. TOWNSHIP = 6 × 6 MI. = 36 SECTIONS
3. SECTION = 1 × 1 MI. = 640 ACRES
4. NOTE NUMBERING SEQUENCE OF SECTIONS

Fig. 4.5 A Section Divided into Smaller Parcels

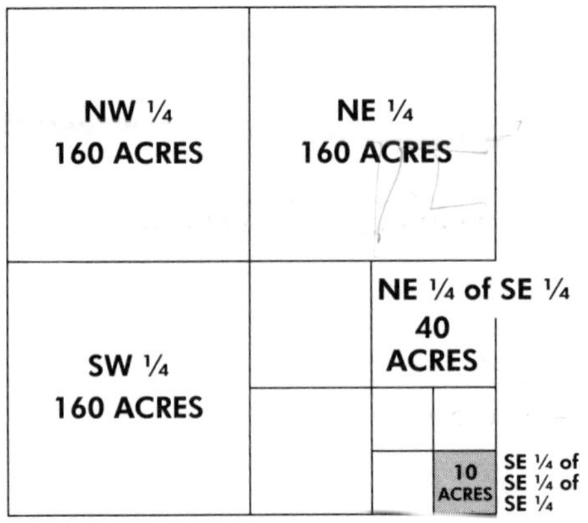

A section can be divided up into smaller parcels.

Example: The shaded partial section in Figure 4.5 would be described as "the Southeast quarter of the Southeast quarter of the Southeast quarter," or "the SE ¼ of the SE ¼ of the SE ¼."

Adjustments and Government Lots. The range lines in the rectangular survey are supposed to run true north and south. They are also supposed to be parallel, spaced six miles apart. Due to the fact that the earth is not flat, however, lines running north and south are not parallel to each other; they tend to converge (get closer together) as they approach the poles. To account for this convergence, the range lines in the rectangular survey must be adjusted.

Fig. 4.6 Government Lots

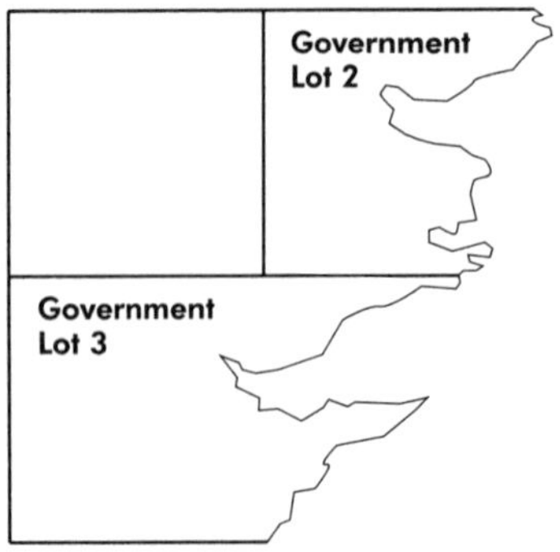

Government lots may be the result of a body of water intruding into a section.

Fig. 4.7 Dimensions Used to Measure Land

Distance:

1 mile = 8 furlongs = 80 chains = 320 rods = 1,760 yards = 5,280 feet
1 furlong = 1/8 mile = 10 chains = 40 rods = 220 yards = 660 feet
1 chain = 1/80 mile = 1/10 furlong = 4 rods = 22 yards = 66 feet
1 rod = 1/320 mile = 1/32 furlong = 1/4 chain = 5.5 yards = 16.5 feet

Area:

1 section = 640 acres = 1 square mile
1 quarter section = 160 acres
1 quarter quarter section = 40 acres
1 quarter quarter quarter section = 10 acres = 1 square furlong
1 acre = 43,560 square feet = 160 square rods

To maintain an approximate distance of six miles between range lines, they are adjusted at intervals of every 24 miles (every fourth township line) north and south of the base line. The township lines where the adjustments are made are referred to as **correction lines** or **standard parallels**. (See Figure 4.4.) Similarly, every fourth range line east and west of the principal meridian is referred to as a **guide meridian**.

Irregularities due to convergence or other factors are usually accounted for along the north and west boundaries of a township. For this reason, the quarter sections that lie along these boundaries are often somewhat irregular in size and shape. Irregular parcels in a township can also result when land abuts a body of water such as a river, lake, or ocean. An irregular parcel that does not constitute a full section or quarter section is known as a **government lot**, and is identified by a special government lot number. (See Figure 4.6.)

Rectangular Survey Descriptions. Land descriptions using the rectangular survey system are relatively simple. The standard procedure is to begin with the smallest division that identifies the parcel, and then list each larger division in sequence. At the end, the description must refer to the base and meridian that serve as the reference points for the grid.

Example: A typical rectangular survey description might read "The Northwest quarter of the Southwest quarter of Section 33, Township 6 South, Range 13 West, San Bernardino Base and Meridian," or "the NW ¼ of the SW ¼ of Sec. 33, T6S, R13W, S.B.B.&M."

Exercise 1

1. For each of the following described parcels, calculate the number of acres and the dimensions (in feet) of the parcel.

   a. The SE ¼ of the SW ¼ of Section 6.

   40 acres / 1320ft X 1320ft

   b. The N ½ of the NE ¼ of the NE ¼ of the SE ¼ of Section 4.

   5 acres / 330 ft x 660 ft.

   c. The E ½ of the NW ¼ and the NE ¼ of the SW ¼ of Section 35.

   120 acres / 1320 ft x 3960 ft

2. How far apart (in miles) are each of the following lines in the rectangular survey?

   a. correction lines 24 miles

   b. township lines 6 miles

   c. section lines 1 mile

   d. range lines 6 miles

   e. guide meridians 24 miles

3. For each of the following sections, identify the number of the section that lies directly to the north of it.

   a. Section 36 25

   b. Section 13 12

   c. Section 17 8

   d. Section 4 33

4. What is the minimum distance (in miles) from township T3N, R4W to the corresponding base line?

   12 miles

Fig. 4.8 A Plat Map

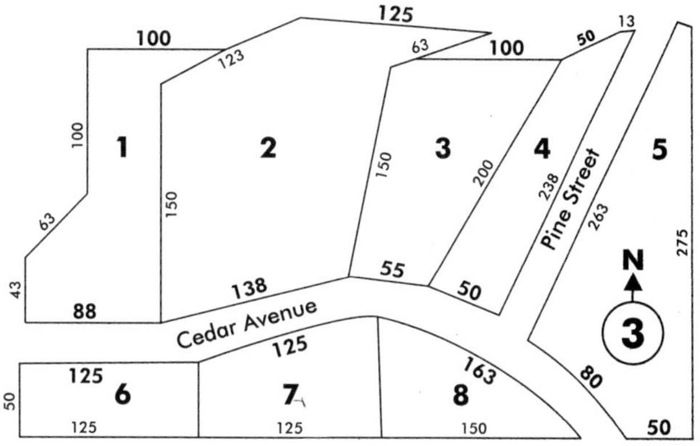

Lot and Block System

The rectangular survey method (described in the previous section of this chapter) is a simple and convenient way to describe large parcels of land. The lot and block system, on the other hand, is better suited for describing smaller parcels, such as building lots. This system allows a piece of land to be described by reference to an official map showing the boundaries of the plat or subdivision in which the property is located.

When a section or partial section is subdivided, the land is surveyed and a map is drawn to show the exact boundaries of each lot in the subdivision. The map is similar to a metes and bounds description: it shows a fixed reference point (such as a section corner) that locates the survey in relation to surrounding properties, and identifies the boundaries of each lot by course and distance.

Each lot on the subdivision map is identified by a number or letter. In some subdivisions, the lot may be further identified by reference to the block on which it is located. Once the map has been filed in the local county records office, a lot can be described by simply referring to its block and lot number, and identifying the map that contains its description.

Example: The description of a lot in a subdivision known as Maple Heights might read "Lot 7, Maple Heights Division #3, as recorded in Map 17-111 in Polk County, Oregon."

Appraisal Math

Appraisers use math in a wide variety of situations, from calculating the living area of a house to capitalizing the value of an income property. In the next part of this chapter, we will examine some of the more common applications of math in appraisal practice, including area and volume calculations, percentage and interest calculations, income capitalization, and financial calculations involving compound interest. The more advanced mathematical techniques that are used by appraisers, such as statistical analysis and regression techniques, are beyond the scope of this textbook.

Area and Volume

Appraisers are often called upon to determine the size of something, such as a lot or a building. The size may be a distance, an area, or a volume, depending on whether the thing to be measured has one, two, or three dimensions.

Distance is a measurement of one dimension only, such as the width of a lot or the height of a building. Distance is normally determined by direct measurement, as when an appraiser measures the perimeter walls of a house.

Area is the size of something in two dimensions. It doesn't matter what the dimensions are called: length and width, width and height, width and depth, length and height, and so on—what matters is that there are only two dimensions. Unlike distance, area cannot be measured directly; each of the two dimensions can be measured, but the area must be calculated mathematically.

Like area, **volume** is the size of something in more than one dimension. In the case of volume, the thing to be measured has three dimensions. Here again, it doesn't matter what the dimensions are called, it only matters that there are three of them. And as is the case with area, each of the dimensions may be measured directly, but the volume itself must be calculated. The following sections explain the procedures for calculating area and volume.

Area. The area of an object can be calculated from its dimensions. The formula used to calculate area depends on the shape of the object; different formulas are used to calculate the areas of rectangles, triangles, circles, and other shapes.

Area of a rectangle. A rectangle is any four-sided figure whose sides all meet at right angles (90 degrees). The area of a rectangle can be found by simply multiplying the dimensions of any two adjacent sides (the length and the width, for example).

$$Area\ of\ Rectangle = Length \times Width$$

Example: A rectangular garage measures 24 feet by 30 feet. The area of the garage can be calculated by multiplying the length by the width. 24 × 30 = 720, so the garage has an area of 720 square feet.

Fig. 4.9 Distance, Area, and Volume

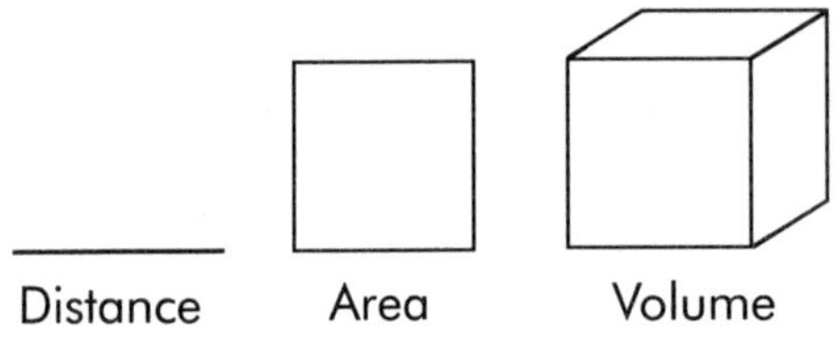

Units of area. As seen in the previous example, the result of an area calculation is expressed as **square** units. The units can be square inches, square feet, square yards, etc., depending on the units of distance (length) that are used to express the dimensions (length and width) of the object.

> **Example:** In the example of the garage above, the dimensions were expressed in feet, so the result of the calculation was an area in square feet. If the dimensions had been expressed in inches, the result would have been square inches; if the dimensions had been yards, the result would have been square yards.

The most common units of area are square inches, square feet, square yards, square miles, and acres. A **square inch** is equivalent to the area of a square that measures one inch on each side. Similarly, a **square foot** is equal to the area of a one-foot square, a **square yard** is equal to the area of a one-yard square, and a **square mile** is equal to the area of a square measuring one mile by one mile. An **acre** is an area that is equivalent to 43,560 square feet.

Converting units. When calculating areas, it is essential that the same units of distance be used to express each of the two dimensions. If one dimension is expressed in feet and the other is expressed in yards, for example, one of the dimensions will have to be converted to match the unit of the other before area can be calculated.

> **Example:** A rectangular building is 45 feet long and 7 yards wide. To calculate the floor area of the building, one of the dimensions must first be converted. One yard is equal to 3 feet, so 7 yards can be converted to feet by multiplying by 3.

7 yards × 3 (feet per yard) = 21 feet

Fig. 4.10 Units of Distance, Area, and Volume

Units of Distance

1 mile = 1,760 yards = 5,280 feet
1 yard = 3 feet = 36 inches
1 foot = 12 inches

Units of Area

1 square mile = 640 acres
1 acre = 4,840 square yards = 43,560 square feet
1 square yard = 9 (3 × 3) square feet
1 square foot = 144 (12 × 12) square inches

Units of Volume

1 cubic yard = 27 (3 × 3 × 3) cubic feet
1 cubic foot = 1,728 (12 × 12 × 12) cubic inches

Now both dimensions are expressed in feet, so the area can be calculated.

21 feet × 45 feet = 945 square feet

Instead of converting the width to feet, we could have converted length to yards. In this case the length of 45 feet is divided by 3 to get the equivalent number of yards.

45 feet ÷ 3 (feet per yard) = 15 yards

The area can then be calculated as follows.

15 yards × 7 yards = 105 square yards

In the preceding example, we got two different answers for the area of the building, depending on the units we used for the dimensions. When the dimensions were expressed as feet, the answer was an area in square feet; when the dimensions were expressed as yards, the answer was square yards. Units of area can be converted, just like units of distance. In this case, one square yard is equal to 9 square feet, so the calculated area of 105 square yards is equivalent to the calculated area of 945 square feet.

105 square yards × 9 (square feet per square yard) = 945 square feet

Sometimes, dimensions are expressed in a combination of units, such as 12 feet 4 inches (12'4"). Dimensions that use a combination of units cannot be used to calculate area; they must be converted to a single unit. Only one part of the dimension is converted, and then added to the other part to get the dimension in a single unit.

Example: To convert 12'4" to feet, only the 4" is converted.

4 inches ÷ 12 (inches per foot) = 0.33 feet

The result of the conversion is then added to the other part of the dimension (the 12 feet).

0.33 feet + 12 feet = 12.33 feet

If we wanted to convert 12'4" to inches, we would convert the 12 feet to inches and then add the result to 4 inches.

12 feet × 12 (inches per foot) = 144 inches

144 inches + 4 inches = 148 inches

Area of a triangle. A triangle is any three-sided figure whose sides are straight lines. To calculate the area of a triangle, two dimensions must be known: the base and the height. The base is simply the length of one of the sides of the triangle. The height is the perpendicular distance (the distance measured at a right angle—90 degrees—to the base) from the base to the opposite point (angle) of the triangle.

To calculate the area of a triangle, multiply the base by the height, then multiply the result by ½ (or divide by 2).

Fig. 4.11 Base and Height of a Triangle

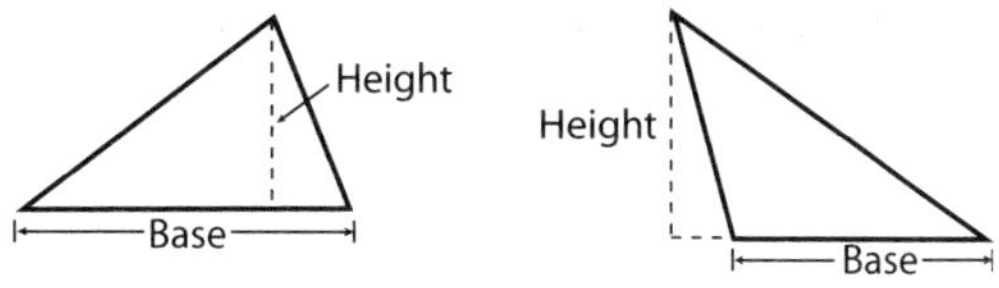

Area of a Triangle = ½ × Base × Height

Example: A triangular area has a base of 14 feet and a height of 10 feet. To find the area, multiply ½ times the base by the height.

½ × 14 feet × 10 feet = 70 square feet

As is the case with any area calculation, it is essential that both dimensions (the height and the base) be expressed in the same unit of measurement. If necessary, the dimensions may have to be converted to a common unit before calculating the area.

Example: A triangle has a base of 40 feet and a height of 10 yards. To calculate the area, first convert the dimensions to a common unit, then use the formula for the area of a triangle.

10 yards × 3 (feet per yard) = 30 feet

½ × 40 feet × 30 feet = 600 square feet

When calculating the area of a triangle, it does not matter which side of the triangle is used as the base. What is important is that the height measurement must correspond to the base measurement. In other words, the height must be the perpendicular distance from the base to the opposite point of the triangle.

Fig. 4.12 Using Any Side as the Base of the Triangle

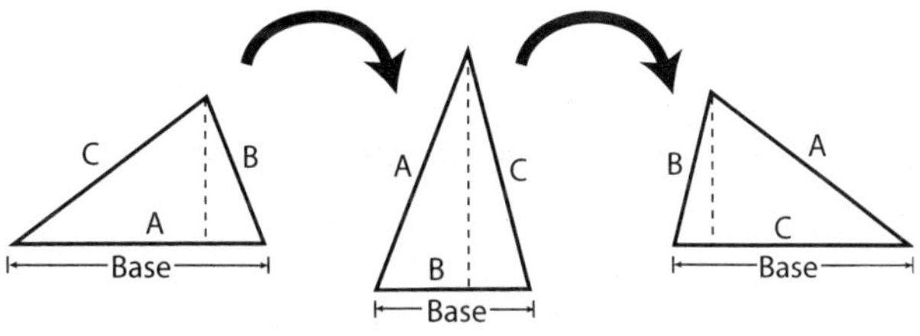

Right triangles. A right triangle is a triangle where two of the sides meet at a right angle (90 degrees). When calculating the area of a right triangle, the dimensions of the two sides that meet at a right angle can be used as the base and the height. The formula for calculating the area is the same as for any other triangle: Area = ½ × Base × Height.

Example: Because the triangle illustrated below contains a right angle, the dimensions of the two sides that meet at the right angle can be used as the base and the height to calculate the area of the triangle.

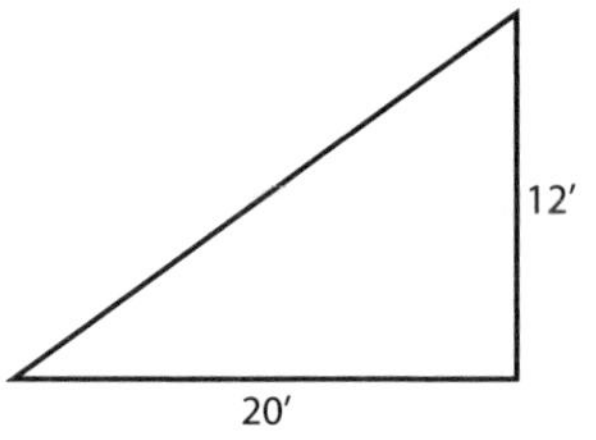

½ × 20 feet × 12 feet = 120 square feet

Areas of Complex Figures. To calculate the area of a complex figure (such as the building outlined in Figure 4.13), the figure is first divided up into simple shapes. Virtually any figure with straight sides can be divided into a series of rectangles and/or triangles. The area of each component rectangle and triangle is calculated individually, and then the areas of all the components are added together to get the total area of the figure.

Fig. 4.13 Calculating the Area of a Complex Figure

Step 1: Divide the figure into rectangles and triangles.

Step 2: Calculate the area of each component rectangle and triangle.

Step 3: Add the areas of the rectangles and triangles to find the figure's total area.

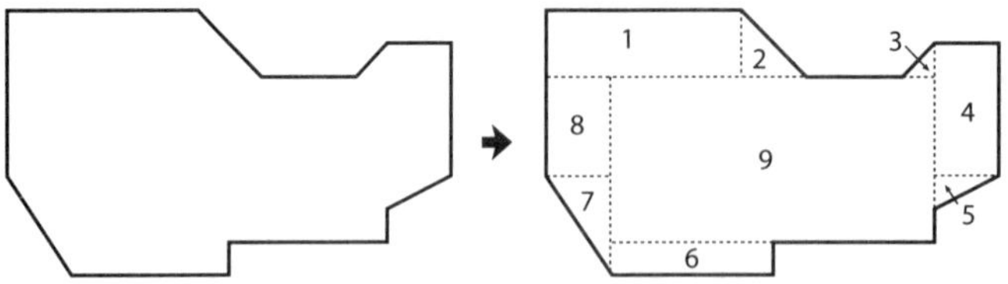

Example: The figure below shows the outline of a building. To find the area of the building, we must first divide it into rectangles and triangles. (See the figure below for one way to do this.) Next, we calculate the area of each component rectangle and triangle.

Rectangle "A" is 40' by 20', so its area is 40 feet × 20 feet = 800 square feet.

To find the area of rectangle "B," we must first find its height, which is not shown directly on the diagram. The height of rectangle "B" is equal to the length of wall "3" minus the length of wall "1": 30 feet – 20 feet = 10 feet. Now that we know the dimensions of rectangle "B," we can calculate its area: 10 feet × 22 feet = 220 square feet.

The final component of the figure is triangle "C." This is a right triangle, so we can use the dimensions of the two perpendicular sides for the base and the height. The horizontal side is equal to 40 feet (the length of wall "2") minus the width of rectangle "B" (the length of wall "4"), 22 feet, which equals 18 feet. The vertical side of the triangle is the same as the height of rectangle "B," which we know is 10 feet. So the area of "C" is ½ × 10 feet × 18 feet = 90 square feet.

Now we can add the areas of the three components to find the total area of the building.

800 square feet + 220 square feet + 90 square feet = 1110 square feet

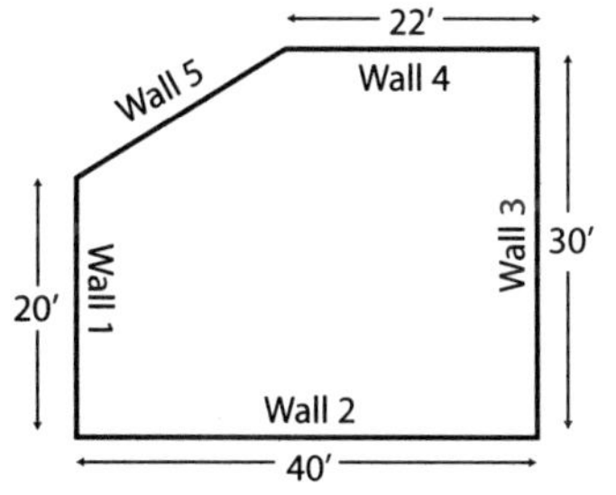

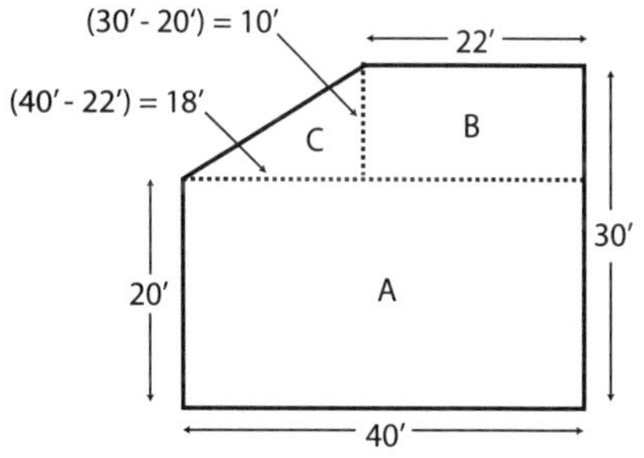

Exercise 2

1. Calculate the total area (in square feet) of the parcel of land shown below.

____

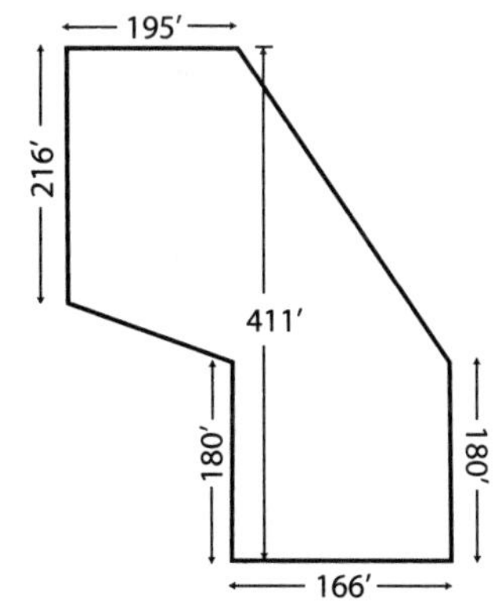

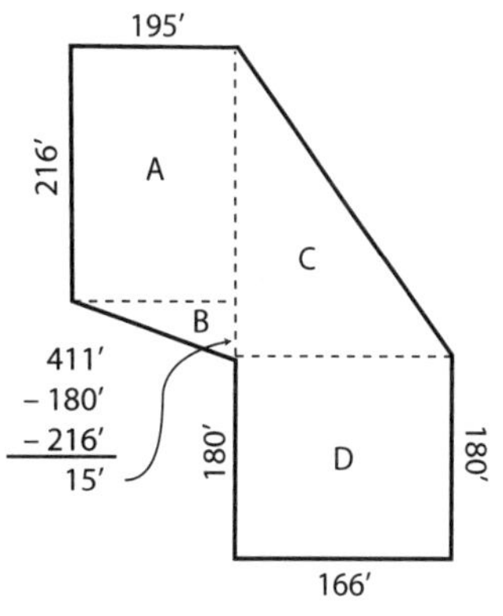

2. What is the area of the parcel in acres?

____

Volume. Volume is the size of an object in three dimensions. It is the amount of three-dimensional space that is enclosed or occupied by the object. Just as area can be calculated by multiplying two dimensions to find square units, volume is calculated by multiplying three dimensions to find cubic units. Cubic units are similar to square units, except that they have three dimensions instead of two: a cubic inch is equal to the volume of a cube measuring one inch on each side, a cubic foot is the volume of a cube with sides measuring 1 foot, etc.

The rule that all dimensions must be expressed in the same unit of measurement applies to volume calculations just as it does to area calculations. If all three of the dimensions are not expressed in identical units (all in feet, all in inches, etc.), then they must be converted to a consistent unit before the volume is calculated.

Prisms. In most cases where an appraiser needs to calculate volume, the object that must be measured is a prism. A **prism** is a three-dimensional figure with certain characteristics:

1. all of its edges are straight lines,
2. at least two of the faces (sides) of the figure are parallel to each other and have identical shapes and sizes, and
3. the edges of the non-parallel faces are formed by lines connecting the corresponding points (corners) of the two parallel faces.

Example: The living area of a house (from the floor to the ceiling) forms a prism. The floor and ceiling are parallel to each other and have identical shapes and sizes. Each corner of the structure forms a line that connects corresponding points of the floor and ceiling.

Fig. 4.14 Prisms

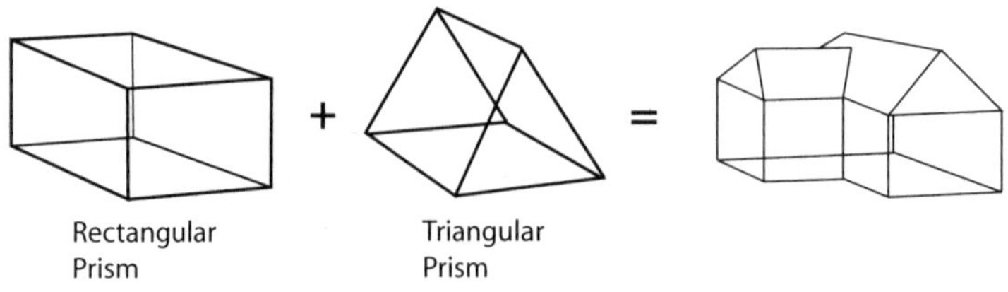

Assuming that the connecting edges of the prism are perpendicular (at right angles) to the matching parallel sides, the volume of the prism can be calculated by multiplying the area of one of the parallel sides by the length of one of the connecting edges.

Volume = Area of Parallel Side × Length of Connecting Edge

Example: A one-story house has a floor area of 1,500 square feet. If the walls are 8 feet high, the volume of the living area can be calculated by multiplying the floor area by the wall height.

1,500 square feet × 8 feet = 12,000 cubic feet (volume)

Exercise 3

1. Calculate the total volume (in cubic feet) of the house shown below, including the living space and attic area.

___

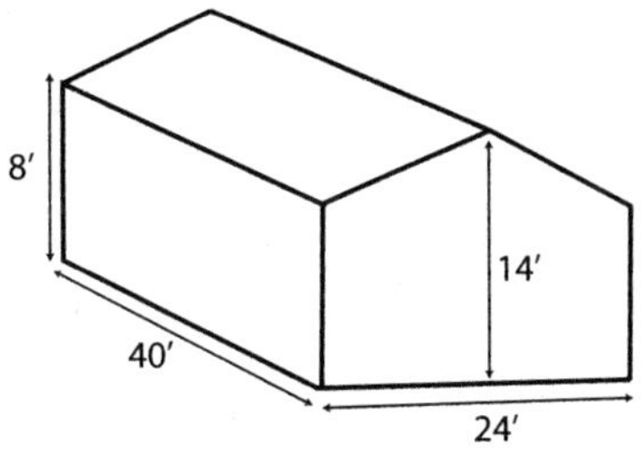

2. What is the volume of the house in cubic yards?

___

Reciprocals

The reciprocal of a number is equal to 1 divided by the number. For example, the reciprocal of 2 is equal to 1 divided by 2, which is ½ or 0.5. Reciprocals always come in pairs. If "A" is the reciprocal of "B," then "B" is also the reciprocal of "A."

Example: 0.5 is the reciprocal of 2. So 2 is the reciprocal of 0.5.

$1 \div 2 = 0.5$
$1 \div 0.5 = 2$

Reciprocals can be useful in performing multiplication and division calculations. Multiplication by a number is the same as division by its reciprocal, and division by a number is the same as multiplication by its reciprocal.

Example: Multiplication by 0.5 is the same as division by 2 (the reciprocal of 0.5). Division by 0.5 is the same as multiplication by 2.

$10 \times 0.5 = 5 \text{ or } 10 \div 2 = 5$

$10 \div 0.5 = 20 \text{ or } 10 \times 2 = 20$

Percentages

The use of percentages is common in appraisals. Allocation, direct capitalization, sales comparison, and many other appraisal techniques use percentages. In ordinary language, we often say that one number is a certain percentage of another number. In mathematics, "percent of" means "percent times," so the general formula for percent calculations is:

$$Part = Percentage \times (of)\ Whole$$

Example:

$10.00 is 10% of $100.00.

$Part = Percentage \times Whole$

$\$10.00 = 10\% \times \$100.00$

The symbol "%" is used to designate a percentage. "Percent" (or "%") means "divided by 100," so a percentage is simply a number divided by 100. For example, 10% means 10 divided by 100, or 0.10. In mathematical calculations using percentages, the percentage is always converted to a decimal number (by dividing by 100) before performing the calculation.

Because a percentage is nothing more than a number divided by 100, it is easy to convert percentages to decimals, and decimals to percentages. To convert a percentage to a decimal, move the decimal point two places to the left (adding zeros if necessary) and drop the percent sign. Reverse the process to convert a decimal to a percentage: move the decimal point two places to the right (again adding zeros if necessary), and add a percent sign.

Example: To convert 5% to a decimal, move the decimal point two places to the left and drop the percent sign.

$5\% = .05$

To convert 0.6 to a percentage, move the decimal point two places to the right and add the percent sign.

$0.6 = 60\%$

Any mathematical formula that can be written in the form A = B × C, such as the basic percentage formula (Part (A) = Percentage (B) × Whole (C)), can be solved in three different ways, depending on whether A, B, or C is the unknown quantity.

Example: A 1,500 square foot house is located on a 7,500 square foot lot. What percentage of the lot is occupied by the house?

We are looking for the percentage of the lot, so the lot represents the whole, and the house is the part.

Part (A) = Percentage (B) × Whole (C), so
Percentage (B) = Part (A) ÷ Whole (C)
Percentage = 1,500 square feet ÷ 7,500 square feet = 0.2

If we convert the decimal to a percentage, we can see that the house covers 20% of the lot area.

Direct Capitalization

Direct capitalization problems are very similar to percentage problems; they both use simple formulas that can be written in a form similar to A = B × C. In direct capitalization, two formulas are used, depending on whether the calculation involves a capitalization rate or an income multiplier.

Income (I) = Rate (R) × Value (V), or

Value (V)= Income (I) × Multiplier (M)

As is the case with percentage problems, these formulas can each be solved in three different ways, depending on the unknown variable.

Income = Rate × Value	*Value = Income × Multiplier*
Rate = Income ÷ Value	*Income = Value ÷ Multiplier*
Value = Income ÷ Rate	*Multiplier = Value ÷ Income*

It is interesting to note that for a given value and income, the corresponding capitalization rate and income multiplier are reciprocals of each other.

Example: Using a capitalization rate of 25%, a property with annual income of $40,000 would be assigned a value of $160,000.

Value = Income ÷ Rate
Value = $40,000 ÷ 25% (0.25) = $160,000

The corresponding income multiplier is 4, which is the reciprocal of 0.25 (1 ÷ 0.25 = 4).

Multiplier = Value ÷ Income
Multiplier = $160,000 ÷ $40,000 = 4

Interest

Interest problems are also similar to percentage and capitalization problems, but they involve an additional factor: time. The formula for calculating interest is:

$$Interest = Principal \times Rate \times Time$$

Instead of our usual A = B × C, we now have A = B × C × D. Fortunately, we can still use the same approach to solving for each of the four variables. The basic interest formula can be stated in four ways:

$$Interest\ (A) = Principal\ (B) \times Rate\ (C) \times Time\ (D)$$

$$Principal\ (B) = Interest\ (A) \div (Rate\ (C) \times Time\ (D))$$

$$Rate\ (C) = Interest\ (A) \div (Principal\ (B) \times Time\ (D))$$

$$Time\ (D) = Interest\ (A) \div (Principal\ (B) \times Rate\ (C))$$

An important point to keep in mind when solving interest problems is that an interest rate is always a rate per time period, such as 10% per year, or 2% per month. It is essential that the time variable in the interest equation be expressed in the same units as the time period of the interest rate. If necessary, either the rate or the time should be converted before performing the calculation.

Example: An investment earns 12% interest per year. How much interest will be earned in six months on an investment of $1,000? Here, the interest rate is an annual rate, but the time is given in months. Either the interest rate must be converted to a monthly rate, or the time must be converted to years.

Interest = Principal × Rate × Time

12% per year = 1% per month
Interest = $1,000 × 0.01 (1% per month) × 6 (months) = $60, or

6 months = 0.5 years
Interest = $1,000 × 0.12 (12% per year) × 0.5 (years) = $60

Exercise 4

1. Based on a capitalized annual income of $32,400, an appraiser derived a property value of $216,000. What capitalization rate did the appraiser use?

____

2. What annual income multiplier corresponds to the capitalization rate in question #1 above?

____

3. An investment pays interest at the rate of 8% per year. After six months, an investor has earned $10,000 on the investment. How much did the investor invest?

____

Financial Calculations

According to folk wisdom, "time is money." The value of $1 depends on when it is received. One dollar that is received today is worth more now than $1 that will be paid a year from now. The so-called "time value" of money is a critical factor in analyzing property values with the income approach.

In the past, financial calculations were performed using complex formulas and huge tables of factors. Nowadays, these manual techniques have been largely replaced by computer programs and inexpensive financial calculators. Financial calculations can now be performed accurately and quickly with the push of a few buttons.

Computer programs and financial calculators may simplify much of the work of financial calculations, but the appraiser still needs to understand the fundamental concepts that these computers are designed to apply. The following section will discuss the basic concepts that underlie all financial calculations.

Present and Future Value. If you put $100 into a savings account that pays 10% interest per year, after one year your account will hold $110: the original $100 plus one year's interest of 10%, or $10. In this case, the present value of $100 is equal to a future value of $110. **Present value** is the value of money today; **future value** is the value of money at some date in the future. The process of calculating the present value of a future payment amount is known as **discounting**.

The relationship between present value and future value depends on the amount of interest that can be earned between the present date and the future date. Earlier in this chapter, we saw that interest can be calculated with the formula: Interest = Principal × Rate × Time. This formula is used to calculate **simple interest**, which is interest that is earned by the principal only. However, most financial calculations involve compound interest.

Interest compounding. Compound interest is interest that is earned on both principal and accrued (paid) interest. In our savings account example, the initial $100 account balance grew to $110 after one year. If the account pays compound interest, the interest for the second year will be calculated on the new balance of $110 ($100 principal and $10 accrued interest). So in the second year, the account will earn interest of $11 (10% × $110), rather than just $10 as in the first year.

A critical factor in calculating compound interest is the **compounding period**. This is the interval at which interest is actually paid on the investment. If interest is compounded annually, for example, the interest payments are made once per year. With monthly compounding, interest is paid each month, so the balance of principal plus accrued interest grows each month.

Example: If the 10% interest on our savings account were compounded quarterly, an interest payment would be added to the account after each three months. 10% annual interest corresponds to 2.5% quarterly interest (10% ÷ 4 = 2.5%, or 0.025), so the interest on the account for one year would be calculated as follows.

$100.00 × 0.025 = $2.50 interest for 1st quarter
$100.00 + $2.50 = $102.50 account balance after 1st quarter
$102.50 × 0.025 = $2.56 interest for 2nd quarter
$102.50 + $2.56 = $105.06 account balance after 2nd quarter
$105.06 × 0.025 = $2.63 interest for 3rd quarter
$105.06 + $2.63 = $107.69 account balance after 3rd quarter
$107.69 × 0.025 = $2.69 interest for 4th quarter
$107.69 + $2.69 = $110.38 account balance after 4th quarter (1 year)

With quarterly compounding at a 10% annual rate of interest, the present value of $100 equals a future value (after one year) of $110.38.

Calculating Present and Future Value. We have seen that the relationship between present value and future value depends on the amount of interest that is earned between the present date and the future date. The amount of interest earned by an investment depends on two factors:

1. the interest rate per compounding period, and
2. the number of compounding periods during the life of the investment.

In the example above, we calculated the future value of $100, based on an interest rate of 2.5% per compounding period (10% annual interest with quarterly compounding), and a total of four compounding periods (1 year = 4 quarters). The basic process is fairly simple: for each compounding period during the life of the investment, the interest for the period is calculated and added to the investment balance. To calculate the present value of a future amount, the process is simply reversed.

Although the formulas for calculating present value and future value are fairly simple, the calculations can be quite lengthy. Imagine, for example, that we wanted to know the future value of our $100 savings account after 25 years, with monthly interest compounding. We would have to calculate the interest for 300 (12 × 25) compounding periods!

With a financial calculator or computer program, the appraiser need only enter the interest rate per compounding period and the total number of compounding periods. The computer will then automatically calculate the present or future value of any given dollar amount.

Present and future values can also be calculated using financial tables of **compound interest factors** and **reversion factors**. The tables list the factors that correspond to various interest rates, compounding periods, and investment terms. To find the future value of a present amount, the present amount is simply multiplied by the appropriate compound interest factor from the table. Likewise, present value can be calculated by multiplying a future amount by the appropriate reversion factor. (For a given interest rate, compounding period, and investment term, the corresponding compound interest factor and reversion factor are reciprocals of each other.)

Example: The compound interest factor for 10% interest with monthly compounding for 15 years is 4.45392. To find the future value of $1,000 invested at 10% for 15 years, with monthly compounding, just multiply the present amount by the factor.

$1,000 × 4.45392 = $4,453.92

Example: How much must be invested at 10% interest with monthly compounding in order to yield $10,000 after five years? The reversion factor for 10% interest with monthly compounding for five years is 0.607789, so the present value can be calculated as follows.

$10,000 × 0.607789 = $6,077.89

Annuities. An **annuity** is a series of payments that are made at regular intervals. Common examples of annuities include real estate loans with monthly payments of principal and interest, and leases that call for monthly or annual payments of rent.

Present or future value of an annuity. The present or future value of an annuity can be calculated in much the same way as the present or future value of a single investment amount (as described above). In fact, one way to calculate the present or future value of an annuity is simply to calculate the present or future value of each individual annuity payment and then add them together to find the value of the whole annuity.

When the payments under an annuity are all the same amount, the annuity is referred to as a **level annuity**. Calculation of the present or future value for level annuities does not require calculation of present or future value for each individual annuity payment. With a computer or financial calculator, the appraiser need only specify the annuity payment amount, the interest rate per compounding period, and the total number of annuity payments. (Annuity calculations assume that the compounding period for the annuity is equal to its payment interval: monthly compounding for monthly payments, annual compounding for annual payments, etc.)

Factors from financial tables can also be used to calculate annuity values. As with compound interest and reversion factors (described above), the factors used to determine annuity values are based on the interest rate, compounding period (payment interval), and investment term. **Level annuity factors** are used to calculate the present value of an annuity. **Sinking fund accumulation factors** give the future value of an annuity. In either case, the factor is simply multiplied by the annuity payment amount to find the present or future value.

Example: The level annuity factor for monthly annuities at 10% for eight years is 65.901488. At a yield rate of 10%, an investment that paid $1,000 per month for eight years would have a present value of:

$1,000 × 65.901488 = $65,901.49

Example: If you put $10,000 per year into a savings account that paid 10% interest, compounded annually, how much would you have in the account after ten years? The sinking fund accumulation factor for 10% interest, compounded annually for ten years, is 15.937425, so after ten years your account would contain:

$10,000 × 15.937425 = $159,374.25

Annuity payment amounts. Investors (and appraisers) sometimes want to know the annuity payment amount that corresponds to a particular value. A common example is a lender who needs to know the monthly payment amount that is required to amortize a loan. This is essentially the same calculation as finding the present or future value of an annuity, except in this case the present or future value is given, and the annuity payment is the unknown.

Fig. 4.15 Financial Formulas

Single Amount Values

Future Value = Present Amount × Compound Interest Factor
Present Value = Future Amount × Reversion Factor

Level Annuity Values

Future Value = Payment Amount × Sinking Fund Accumulation Factor
Present Value = Payment Amount × Level Annuity Factor

Annuity Payment Amounts

Payment Amount = Present Value × Direct Reduction Factor
Payment Amount = Future Value × Sinking Fund Factor

Financial calculators or computer programs can calculate level annuity payment amounts. The appraiser need only enter the interest rate per compounding period (per payment interval), the number of periods (payments), and the known present or future value. To perform the calculation with a financial table, **sinking fund factors** are used to calculate the payment amount for a given future value, and **direct reduction factors** are used to find the payment amount for a given present value. (For a given interest rate, compounding period and investment term, the sinking fund factor is the reciprocal of the sinking fund accumulation factor, and the direct reduction factor is the reciprocal of the level annuity factor.)

Key Terms

Acre—A unit of area equal to 43,560 square feet.

Annuity—A series of regular periodic payments, such as regular monthly rental payments under the terms of a lease.

Area—The size of a two-dimensional object. Area is expressed in square units (square feet, square yards, etc.) or in acres.

Compound interest—Interest that is calculated on both principal and accrued interest.

Correction line—East-west lines at intervals of 24 miles north and south of the base line in the rectangular survey system, where adjustments are made to account for convergence.

Direct capitalization—The process of estimating value on the basis of income from a single period, usually one year. The formula for direct capitalization is Value = Income ÷ Capitalization Rate, or Value = Income × Multiplier.

Future value—The value of something as of some future date.

Government lot—A division of the rectangular survey system. Irregular parcels that do not constitute a full section or quarter section are identified as government lots.

Guide meridian—North-south lines at intervals of 24 miles east and west of the principal meridian in the government survey system, where adjustments are made to account for convergence.

Interest—1. The amount earned by an investment; return on capital. 2. The amount earned by a debt investment (loan), as compared to the amount earned by an equity investment.

Legal description—A description of a parcel of real estate in a form that is legally approved in the state where the property is located. Common systems of legal description include the metes and bounds, government (rectangular) survey, and lot and block systems.

Lot and block system—A system of legal description of real estate, describing land by reference to an official map showing the boundaries of the parcel.

Metes and bounds system—A system of legal description of real estate, describing the boundaries of a parcel using reference points, courses (directions), and distances.

Monument—A natural or artificial object used as a reference point for land descriptions.

Rectangular survey system—A system of legal description of real estate, describing property in relation to a rectangular grid that has been established by federal government survey. The land is described by referring to the appropriate principal meridian, township, range, section and partial section. Also called the government survey system.

Point of beginning—The reference point from which a metes and bounds land description begins.

Present value—The value of something as of the present time. Expected future payments or benefits may be converted to their present value by discounting.

Principal meridian—The principal north-south line in a unit of the rectangular survey. The name of the principal meridian identifies the unit of the survey. Ranges are numbered in consecutive columns east and west of the principal meridian.

Range—A north-south strip of land bounded by two consecutive range lines in the rectangular survey system.

Range line—North-south lines running parallel to the principal meridian at intervals of six miles in the rectangular survey system.

Reversion factor—A factor used in financial calculations to calculate the present value of a future amount.

Section—A division of a township in the rectangular survey system. A section measures one mile on each side and contains 640 acres.

Simple interest—Interest that is calculated on the principal amount only, and not on accrued interest.

Township—A unit of the rectangular survey system, formed by the intersection of a range and a township tier, and identified by its position relative to the principal meridian and base line. A township measures six miles on a side, and contains 36 sections.

Township line—East-west lines running parallel to the base line at intervals of six miles in the government survey system.

Township tier—An east-west strip of land bounded by two consecutive township lines in the government survey system.

Volume—The size of something in three dimensions. Volume is expressed in cubic units (cubic feet, cubic yards, etc).

Summary

I. In appraisals, real estate is identified by its legal description.

A. A metes and bounds description describes the boundaries of a parcel of land by listing the course and distance for each boundary.

1. Reference points or monuments are natural or man-made landmarks that are used to locate property boundaries.
2. The point where the actual description of the property boundaries begins and ends is the true point of beginning.
3. Courses in a metes and bounds description are described according to their deviation from true north or south.

B. The rectangular (government) survey system subdivides land into rectangular grids for purposes of identification.

1. Each grid system is identified by the name of its principal meridian (north-south line) and base line (east-west line).
2. Township lines (east-west) and range lines (north-south) divide the land into townships measuring six miles on each side. The townships are numbered according to their distance from the principal meridian and base line, e.g., Township 3 North, Range 2 West.
3. Townships are divided into 36 numbered sections, each measuring 1 mile on a side and containing 640 acres.
4. Sections may be further divided into quarter sections, quarter-quarter sections, etc.
5. Adjustments to account for convergence are made at intervals of 24 miles north and south of the base line, at correction lines (standard parallels). The range lines at intervals of 24 miles east and west of the principal meridian are called guide meridians.
6. Partial sections (resulting from convergence, bodies of water, or other causes) may be identified as government lots, with a special identifying number.

C. The lot and block system identifies land by referring to a numbered parcel on a plat map that is kept in the local county records office.

II. Area is the size of something in two dimensions, measured in square units (square feet, square yards, etc.).

A. Area of a rectangle = length × width.

B. Area of a triangle = ½ × base × height.

1. The base can be any side of the triangle. The corresponding height is the perpendicular distance from the base to the opposite point of the triangle.

C. Irregular figures can be divided into component rectangles and triangles, and the areas of the components added together to find the area of the whole.

D. In area calculations, both dimensions must be expressed in the same unit of measurement.

III. Volume is the size of something in three dimensions, measured in cubic units (cubic feet, cubic yards, etc.).

A. Volume of a prism = area of matching parallel side × length of connecting edge.

B. In volume calculations, all three dimensions must be expressed in the same unit of measurement.

IV. The reciprocal of a number is equal to 1 divided by the number. Reciprocals always come in pairs, with each one of the pair being the reciprocal of the other.

V. Formulas in the form of A = B × C can also be expressed as B = A ÷ C or C = A ÷ B, depending on which variable is unknown.

A. The formula for percentage problems is Part = Percentage × Whole.

1. Percent (%) means "divided by 100."

B. The formula for capitalization is Income = Rate × Value, or Value = Income × Multiplier. The corresponding rate and multiplier are reciprocals of each other.

C. The formula for simple interest is Interest = Principal × Rate × Time. Rate and time must be expressed in corresponding units, e.g., 10% per year for five years.

VI. Financial problems involving compound interest are usually too complex to solve by hand. Most appraisers use computers, calculators, or tables of financial factors to solve these problems.

A. Most financial calculations involve the following variables: present value, future value, interest rate per compounding period, total number of compounding periods, and annuity payment amount. Given any four of these five variables, a financial computer program or calculator can calculate the missing fifth variable.

B. Factors from financial tables can also be used to solve financial calculations. Financial tables contain listings of factors that correspond to different combinations of interest rate, compounding period and investment term.

1. To find the future value of a single amount, multiply the present amount by the appropriate compound interest factor.

2. To find the present value of a single amount, multiply the future amount by the appropriate reversion factor.
3. To find the future value of a level annuity, multiply the annuity payment by the appropriate sinking fund accumulation factor.
4. To find the present value of a level annuity, multiply the annuity payment by the appropriate level annuity factor.
5. To find the annuity payment amount corresponding to a given present value, multiply the present value by the corresponding direct reduction factor.
6. To find the annuity payment amount corresponding to a given future value, multiply the future value by the corresponding sinking fund factor.

Chapter Quiz

1. The Southeast quarter of the Southwest quarter of Section 25 contains:
   a. 40 acres
   b. 80 acres
   c. 160 acres
   d. 640 acres

2. Courses in metes and bounds descriptions are given according to:
   a. the angle of deviation from north or south
   b. the angle of deviation from east or west
   c. Either of the above
   d. Neither of the above

3. The primary north-south line in a rectangular survey grid is called the:
   a. base line
   b. guide meridian
   c. principal meridian
   d. correction line

4. The system used to describe land by referring to a recorded map showing its boundaries is known as the:
   a. record title system
   b. registration system
   c. subdivision system
   d. lot and block system

5. A natural or man-made landmark that is used in a metes and bounds description is called a:
   a. marker
   b. monument
   c. base line
   d. point of beginning

6. If simple interest of 12% per year is paid on an account, how much interest will be earned after two years by an investment of $100?
   a. $12.00
   b. $24.00
   c. $25.44
   d. $124.00

7. A 4-inch-thick concrete slab is 20 feet wide and 30 feet long. How many cubic yards of concrete are contained in the slab?
   a. 7.4
   b. 22.2
   c. 200
   d. 240

8. How many acres are contained in a square parcel of land that measures 330' on each side?
   a. 2.5
   b. 5.0
   c. 7.5
   d. 10.0

9. A property was valued at $124,000, based on an annual direct capitalization rate of 13%. What is the property's annual income?
   a. $13,000
   b. $16,120
   c. $21,400
   d. None of the above

10. A house has a gross living area of 1,400 square feet. If the walls are 8 feet high, what is the volume of the living area?
    a. 1,400 cubic feet
    b. 1,400 cubic yards
    c. 11,200 cubic feet
    d. 11,200 cubic yards

11. In the sales comparison approach, an appraiser adjusted the sales price of a comparable by $10,000. If the comparable sales price was $200,000, what percentage of the sales price did the adjustment represent?

   a. 2%
   b. 5%
   c. 10%
   d. 20%

12. The factor used to calculate the future value of a level annuity is the:

   a. sinking fund factor
   b. level annuity factor
   c. sinking fund accumulation factor
   d. compound interest factor

13. A reversion factor would be used to calculate:

   a. the present value of a future amount
   b. the future value of a present amount
   c. the present value of an annuity
   d. the future value of an annuity

14. When performing financial calculations involving compound interest, the interest rate used for the calculations is the:

   a. annual interest rate
   b. annual percentage rate
   c. monthly interest rate
   d. interest rate per compounding period

15. An annual income multiplier of 6.67 is equivalent to a capitalization rate of:

   a. 7%
   b. 13%
   c. 15%
   d. 66%

Quiz Answers

1. a) A section contains 640 acres, so one-quarter of a quarter-section would be 40 acres.
2. a) In a metes and bounds description, the course is described in relation to either north or south.
3. c) The principal meridian is the primary north-south line in a rectangular survey grid.
4. d) The lot and block system makes reference to lots on a recorded map.
5. b) A landmark used in a metes and bounds description is a monument.
6. b) Simple interest means that the interest will not compound. As a result, in each year, the investment will earn $12 in interest ($100 × .12 = $12), for a total of $24.
7. a) Convert all of the measurements to yards (4 inches ÷ 36 inches per yard = .111 yards) (20 feet ÷ 3 feet per yard = 6.666 yards) (30 feet ÷ 3 feet per yard = 10 yards). The slab is 7.4 cubic yards (.111 × 6.666 × 10 = 7.399).
8. a) First, calculate the square footage of the property (330 feet × 330 feet = 108,900 square feet). The property is 2.5 acres (108,900 square feet ÷ 43,560 square feet per acre = 2.5 acres).
9. b) The property's income is $16,120 ($124,000 value × .13 rate = $16,120 income).
10. c) Multiply the area of the house by the height of the walls to find its volume is 11,200 cubic feet (1,400 square feet × 8 feet = 11,200 cubic feet).
11. b) The adjustment is 5% ($10,000 ÷ $200,000 = .05).
12. c) A sinking fund accumulation factor is used to calculate the future value of a level annuity.
13. a) A reversion factor is used to calculate the present value of a single future amount.
14. d) When calculating compound interest, the interest rate used is the rate per compounding period.
15. c) An income multiplier is the reciprocal of a capitalization rate, so a multiplier of 6.67 would equal a rate of 15% (1 ÷ 6.67 = .15).

Exercise Answers

#1
1. a. 40 acres; 1,320 feet × 1,320 feet
   b. 5 acres; 330 feet × 660 feet
   c. 120 acres; 1,320 feet × 3,960 feet
2. a. 24 miles
   b. 6 miles
   c. 1 mile
   d. 6 miles
   e. 24 miles
3. a. 25
   b. 12
   c. 8
   d. 33
4. 12 miles

#2
1. Rectangle A's dimensions are 195 feet by 216 feet, giving it an area of 195' × 216' = 42,120 sq. ft.

   Triangle B has a width of 195 feet, its shared side with A. To find the height, take the measurement of the lot's total height, 411 feet, and subtract the other known values of 216 feet and 180 feet. 411 – 216 – 180 = 15 feet. The triangle's area is ½ × 195' × 15' = 1,462.5 sq. ft.

   Triangle C is treated similarly, except this time we only need to subtract 180 feet from the total height of the lot, to give us the height of C. (You can also add the 15 feet just calculated back onto the 216 feet height of A.) Triangle C's dimensions are 166 feet wide and 231 feet high, giving an area of ½ × 166 × 231 = 19,173 sq. ft.

   Finally, Rectangle D's height is 180 feet and its base is 166 feet, for an area of 29,880 sq. ft.

   The total area is: 42,120 + 1,462.5 + 19,173 + 29,880 = 92,635.5 sq. ft.
2. There are 43,560 square feet in an acre. 92,635.5 ÷ 43,560 = 2.13 acres.

#3
1. Living space: 24' × 40' = 960 square feet floor area

   960 square feet × 8' = 7,680 cubic feet

   Attic space: ½ × 24' × 6' = 72 square feet area of gable end

72 square feet × 40' = 2,880 cubic feet

Total volume: 7,680 square feet + 2,880 square feet = 10,560 cubic feet

2. 10,560 cubic feet ÷ 27 (cubic feet per cubic yard) = 391.11 cubic yards

#4

1. Rate = Income ÷ Value = $32,400 ÷ $216,000 = 0.15, or 15%

2. 1 ÷ 0.15 = 6.67

3. Principal = Interest ÷ (Rate × Time)

   6 months = 0.5 years

   Principal = $10,000 ÷ (0.08 × 0.5) = $10,000 ÷ 0.04 = $250,000

5 Data Collection and Analysis

Overview

After completing the preliminary analysis for an assignment—defining the appraisal problem and determining the scope of work—the appraiser focuses on collecting and analyzing the data that will provide the basis for the opinion of value. Keep in mind, however, that data collection, selection, and analysis are an integral and ongoing part of virtually the entire appraisal process. As an appraiser estimates the value of property, he or she is constantly evaluating data, discarding data that are not reliable, selecting data that are most relevant to the appraisal problem, and gathering additional necessary data.

After completing this chapter, you should be able to:

- identify the types of forces that influence value at the regional, community, and neighborhood levels;
- identify common sources of general appraisal data;
- describe how appraisers define immediate market areas;
- describe the way appraisers define neighborhoods and neighborhood boundaries;
- list neighborhood characteristics that are important to appraisers;
- describe the data necessary for a site description;
- describe the data necessary for a building description;
- describe the data that are collected for comparable properties;
- know how to complete Page 1 (the property description) of the Uniform Residential Appraisal Report; and
- describe how an appraiser analyzes comparable sales data, cost data, and income and expense data.

Introduction

As discussed in Chapter 3, appraisal data may be classified in several different ways. Data may be classified as either **general** (pertaining to real estate values in general) or

specific (pertaining to a particular property). General data may be further categorized as broad market trend data or more localized competitive supply and demand data. Data are also categorized as **primary** or **secondary**, depending on whether they are generated directly by the appraiser or obtained from published sources.

In this chapter, we will consider data categorized according to a third method of classification used in the appraisal process. For our purposes here, types of appraisal data may be broken down into the following categories:

- regional and community data,
- market and neighborhood data,
- site data, and
- building data.

Regional and Community Data

Regional and community data reflect the effects of local social, economic, governmental, and physical forces on value. The interaction of these forces influences real estate values, either for better or for worse.

Example: Property values in an exclusive neighborhood of expensive homes may be enhanced by the scarcity of similar neighborhoods in a community. On the other hand, if the regional economy is in a slump, the demand for high-priced homes may lessen, causing neighborhood values to decline. In either case, the value of homes in the neighborhood cannot be analyzed without taking into consideration outside influences and trends at the regional and community level.

Use of Regional and Community Data in Appraisals

The collection and analysis of regional and community data is essential to the appraisal process for several reasons. First, it helps the appraiser identify the particular characteristics of properties that increase or decrease value.

Example: A region's climate has a significant effect on the desirability of various architectural styles and methods of construction. Buyers in areas with extreme winter or summer temperatures may place a high value on extra insulation and other energy-efficient construction details, while buyers in areas with more moderate climates may consider such features to be excessive and not worth their extra cost.

When included in an appraisal report, this type of data also helps the appraisal client or other reader to understand why buyers in that market value those specific property characteristics.

The study of regional and community data also helps an appraiser to identify large-scale patterns of value fluctuations and to anticipate shifts in the economy, either from a period

Fig. 5.1 Reasons for Regional and Community Data

1. Identify property characteristics that affect value
2. Identify economic and social trends that affect value
3. Provide context for analysis of local value influences

of growth to one of stagnation or decline, or vice versa. Social and political trends are also significant. For example, the general aging of the population is tied to population growth in certain areas, as more retirees seek out warmer places to live. And changing political winds, especially on state and local levels, may significantly affect value indicators such as property tax rates and economic climates.

Regional and community data also help provide a context for the analysis of local influences on value. Neighborhoods do not exist in isolation, but are part of larger communities and regions. To understand the desirability of a particular neighborhood, it must be viewed in the context of the surrounding area.

Example: A boom of new housing construction in a city may adversely affect property values in a neighborhood of older homes located in the same city. In addition to increasing the overall supply of housing, the new homes may have more modern designs and features that make the older homes seem less desirable by comparison.

Regional and Community Value Indicators

All data used in an appraisal are collected for one purpose: to help form a value estimate for a particular subject property. But this does not mean that the appraiser must collect new regional and community data for each appraisal assignment.

Regional and community data are often collected in advance, without reference to any particular subject property. Appraisers maintain files of such data pertaining to the geographic areas in which they practice. These files are updated on an ongoing basis, to reflect changes and developments in the market. When the appraiser receives a particular appraisal assignment, he or she simply determines which regional and community data are relevant to the appraisal problem.

Appraisers maintain data files on a wide range of subjects. Some of the more common regional and community value indicators—environmental, economic, social, and political factors—are discussed in this section.

Natural Environment. Natural environmental factors that can influence value include climate, topography (the shape of the land and the location of physical features such as lakes and streams), potential hazards (such as earthquakes, floods, or tornadoes), and the presence of natural resources.

Economic Characteristics. A major factor here is the area's **economic base**—the economic activities that support the people living in the area. Many areas depend on particular industries or a few large corporations to provide jobs and stimulate the local economy. The economic cycles in these industries can cause the region's economy to shift between growth and decline.

In addition to the economic base, other economic factors that affect values in a region or community include employment and unemployment levels, price levels, interest rates, construction activity, and government regulation and taxation of business and development.

Infrastructure. Infrastructure refers to public improvements that support basic needs, such as public transportation facilities, highways, power and water supplies, and sanitation facilities (sewage and waste disposal). Infrastructure contributes to the quality of life in an area, and can also have a major effect on business activity and regional growth.

The appraiser should be aware of the availability of these services in the area, their quality, their costs and benefits, and their capacity to support new growth.

Housing supply and demand. A fundamental rule of appraisal is that supply and demand affect value. Data about the supply of housing in an area include the existing supply of housing of various types and ages, the supply of vacant land for residential development, the current level of housing construction activity, the number of building permits being issued or processed, construction costs, and vacancy rates.

Social Attitudes. Population data such as age, income level, or household size and composition are important indicators of social attitudes in the community. For instance, percentage of homeownership, upkeep of properties, and level of community involvement all affect housing values.

Political Factors. Political factors that impact value include regional and local laws and regulations. For instance, high property taxes may reflect an anti-growth attitude in the community, while tax incentives to businesses or other groups may indicate a strong desire for growth in the region. Other governmental influences include zoning and building codes, the quality of public education, availability of social programs, the quality of police and fire protection, and the level of environmental legislation.

Exercise 1

Match the data items on the left with the appropriate category or categories of regional and community data on the right.

1. ___	climate	a.	natural environment
2. ___	economic base	b.	economic characteristics
3. ___	topography	c.	infrastructure
4. ___	wage levels	d.	housing supply and demand
5. ___	construction costs	e.	social attitudes
6. ___	average household size	f.	political factors
7. ___	population trends		
8. ___	transportation systems		
9. ___	development restrictions		
10. ___	property tax rates		
11. ___	utilities		
12. ___	supply of vacant land		

Sources of Regional and Community Data

Some regional and city data, such as climate and topography, can be gathered through direct observation by the appraiser. But for the most part, regional and community data come from published sources. Some of the more common sources of published regional and community data are listed below.

- City, county, and state public agencies—particularly agencies dealing with public records, planning, zoning, taxation, employment, housing and transportation—for information on environmental, zoning and building regulations, tax laws, tax assessments, ownership transfers, public improvements, building permits, current and proposed infrastructure, local industries and employment, and population and household statistics.
- Federal government agencies—in particular, the Department of Commerce, the Department of Housing and Urban Development, and the Department of Labor, the Council of Economic Advisors, and the Federal Reserve Board—for national, regional, and local statistics on business activity, income, employment, housing and housing construction, financial markets, population demographics, and price levels.

- Trade associations—such as Chambers of Commerce, Boards of Realtors, multiple listing services and home builders associations—for information on housing sales, housing costs and construction, financing, business activity, and demographics.

Note that many agencies and associations now make their information accessible over the Internet via their individual websites.

Market Area and Neighborhood Data

The value of a property depends on its position in the real estate market, so an appraiser must determine the market area in which the subject property competes. The **immediate market area** defines the area from which the appraiser can choose reliable comparable properties. This may be a particular geographic area, such as a neighborhood or a district, or a combination of neighborhoods and districts.

For appraisal purposes, a **neighborhood** can be defined as a geographical area in which land uses are complementary and in which all properties are influenced in a similar way by the forces affecting value. A neighborhood may have more than one type of use. For example, a neighborhood may include residences, schools, and retail shops, all of which complement each other. When a neighborhood includes only one type of land use, it is sometimes referred to as a **district**.

A property's relevant market area is often the neighborhood or district in which it is located. However, if the property competes with properties in other neighborhoods or districts, then the market area must include those areas as well. If the market area includes these additional areas, it may be necessary to make adjustments to the values of comparable properties during an appraisal, to account for the difference.

Defining Neighborhood Boundaries

Neighborhoods have some degree or type of uniformity that sets them apart from surrounding areas. The uniformity may relate to the age or architectural style of buildings in the neighborhood, to its zoning classification, to the economic status of its residents, or to some other factor or combination of factors.

Neighborhood boundaries are often (but not always) some type of physical feature. Common examples include highways or arterials, railroads, waterways, and other geographic boundaries. The boundaries can also be established by zoning differences, with one neighborhood ending and another beginning at the point where different land uses are permitted.

When defining a neighborhood boundary, an appraiser must keep in mind that just because a group of properties appears to be similar does not mean that they are all subject to the same value influences. Similarly, a physical barrier does not necessarily indicate the boundary of a neighborhood.

Example: A residential subdivision may contain homes of similar size, construction style, and lot size. At first glance, the subdivision may appear to be a distinct neighborhood. But if one side of the subdivision borders on a park or waterfront, while the other side borders on a busy freeway, the appraiser may decide that the subdivision is actually comprised of two or more distinct neighborhoods (or sub-neighborhoods), despite the superficial similarities between the homes.

It is important for the appraiser to establish and justify neighborhood boundaries for each subject property that is appraised. The boundaries established for the subject property's neighborhood will define the area for which neighborhood data will be gathered, and from which the most reliable comparable properties can be chosen.

Exercise 2

1. What is the definition of a neighborhood?

   ____

2. Indicate whether each of the following items would always (A), never (N), or sometimes (S) indicate a neighborhood boundary.

A	N	S	
_____	_____	_____	stream
_____	_____	_____	zoning district boundary
_____	_____	_____	city limit line
_____	_____	_____	change in architectural style
_____	_____	_____	railroad

Neighborhood Value Indicators

Neighborhood data help define the potential market for the subject property. Neighborhood data also help indicate the desirability of the subject property in relation to homes in competing neighborhoods. And if it becomes necessary to use comparable properties from other neighborhoods, neighborhood data help the appraiser identify similar neighborhoods, and adjust the values of the comparables for differences in neighborhood characteristics.

Example: An appraiser determines that the subject property neighborhood consists of an area of single-family, 2- and 3-bedroom homes, located two miles from the city center. Due to a shortage of recent comparable sales in the subject neighborhood, the appraiser must use comparables from another, similar neighborhood. The second neighborhood has homes of similar size, age, and appeal as the subject neighborhood, but is located five miles from the city center. In this case, the appraiser must investigate whether the added distance from the area business core has an effect on neighborhood values, and possibly adjust the sales prices of the comparables from the second neighborhood to account for any observed value difference.

The Uniform Residential Appraisal Report form contains a section for reporting neighborhood data (Figure 5.2). Data are frequently collected and entered directly on this form. Alternatively, the appraiser can use a separate neighborhood data form for the initial data collection, and then transfer the relevant data to the actual appraisal report. The neighborhood data form helps insure that no important neighborhood considerations are overlooked or omitted. A typical neighborhood data form is shown in Figure 5.3.

Important neighborhood data include the following items:

- neighborhood boundaries and adjoining uses;
- physical characteristics of the neighborhood (topography, views, climate, etc.);
- type of neighborhood (rural, suburban, or urban);
- percent of development of available sites;
- rate of growth (new construction);
- percent of owner occupancy;
- trend in property values (upward, downward, stable);
- relative supply and demand of housing in the neighborhood (excess supply, excess demand, balance);
- rate of change in ownership (turnover);
- average time between listing and sale (marketing time);
- typical terms of recent sales (financing concessions, etc.);
- percent of land devoted to various uses (single-family, two- to four-unit, multi-family, commercial, other);
- characteristics of properties in each existing use (price range, age range, size range, percent of vacancy);
- probable changes in land use, if any;
- degree of maintenance of improvements and landscaping;

Fig. 5.2 Neighborhood Section of the URAR

Note: Race and the racial composition of the neighborhood are not appraisal factors.

	Neighborhood Characteristics	One-Unit Housing Trends	One-Unit Housing		Present Land Use %	
NEIGHBORHOOD	Location ☐ Urban ☐ Suburban ☐ Rural	Property Values ☐ Increasing ☐ Stable ☐ Declining	PRICE	AGE	One-Unit	%
	Built-Up ☐ Over 75% ☐ 25–75% ☐ Under 25%	Demand/Supply ☐ Shortage ☐ In Balance ☐ Over Supply	$ (000)	(yrs)	2-4 Unit	%
	Growth ☐ Rapid ☐ Stable ☐ Slow	Marketing Time ☐ Under 3 mths ☐ 3–6 mths ☐ Over 6 mths	Low		Multi-Family	%
	Neighborhood Boundaries		High		Commercial	%
			Pred.		Other	%
	Neighborhood Description					
	Market Conditions (including support for the above conclusions)					

- occupant characteristics (family size, income levels, employment stability);
- distance (or time) to key services (employment, shopping, schools, places of worship, medical care, recreation, public transportation);
- access to major transportation routes;
- quality of public services (schools, police, fire, etc.);
- availability and cost of utilities (electricity, gas, water, sewer, storm sewer, phone, cable TV, garbage collection);
- property tax rates and special assessments; and
- negative value influences (heavy traffic, crime, pollution, exposure to hazardous substances, incompatible uses, flood zones, etc.).

Sources of Neighborhood Data

Many of the sources of neighborhood data are the same as the sources of regional and community data. In particular, local government agencies and trade associations can often provide useful data concerning neighborhood growth rates, zoning regulations, population characteristics, taxes and public services. Interviews with local real estate professionals (brokers, appraisers, lenders, and property managers) and property owners are another valuable source of neighborhood data. But to a far greater extent than is the case with regional and community data, the major source of neighborhood data is personal review by the appraiser.

Neighborhood Review. The appraiser's first task in reviewing a neighborhood is to determine its boundaries. The appraiser may already have some idea of the boundaries of the subject property's neighborhood, either from past experience or from secondary data sources. But it is important to review the area surrounding the subject property to note any unusual influences that may apply. Properties located near the edge of a neighborhood, for example, may be subject to greater value influences from adjoining uses than are properties located in the center of the neighborhood.

Fig. 5.3 Neighborhood Data Form

NEIGHBORHOOD DATA

Property adjacent to:

NORTH Plum Boulevard, garden apartments

SOUTH Cherry Street, single-family homes

EAST 14th Avenue, single-family homes

WEST 12th Avenue, single-family homes

Population: (increasing) decreasing stable

Life cycle stage: integration (equilibrium) disintegration rebirth

Tax rate: higher lower (same as competing areas)

Services: (police) (fire) (garbage) other:

Average family size: 3.5

Occupational status: White collar; skilled trades

Distance from:

Commercial areas 3 miles

Elementary school 6 blocks

Secondary school 1 mile

Recreational areas 2 miles

Cultural centers 3 miles

Places of worship Methodist, Catholic, Baptist

Transportation Bus stop 1 block; frequent service to downtown

Freeway/highway 10 blocks

Typical Properties	Age	Price Range	Owner-occupancy
Vacant lots: 0%			
Single-family homes: 80%	20 yrs	$175,000-$200,000	93%
Apartments, 2- to 4-unit: 15%	10 yrs		
Apartments, over 4 units: 5%	5 yrs		
Non-residential: 0%			

Nuisances (odors, noise, etc.) None

Environmental hazards (chemical storage, etc.) None

It may be helpful to outline the neighborhood boundaries on an area map. (A neighborhood map, showing the locations of the subject property and any comparables used in the appraisal, is usually attached as an exhibit to the appraisal.) In mapping the neighborhood boundaries, the appraiser should note the characteristics (physical barriers, land use changes, changes in school district, etc.) that define each boundary.

In addition to determining the boundaries of the neighborhood, the appraiser will observe and note its essential characteristics. Important data to be gathered or verified by review include:

- the type of neighborhood;
- physical characteristics and layout;
- percent of development;
- evidence of change (new construction, remodeling, degree of maintenance);
- quantity, age, and condition of various types of properties;
- traffic patterns;
- amenities such as parks, public beaches, etc.;
- convenience to shopping, employment centers, etc.;
- presence of negative value influences; and
- overall neighborhood quality and appeal.

Important features may be noted on the neighborhood map, either for later reference by the appraiser, or for inclusion in the appraisal report.

Fig. 5.4 Neighborhood Map

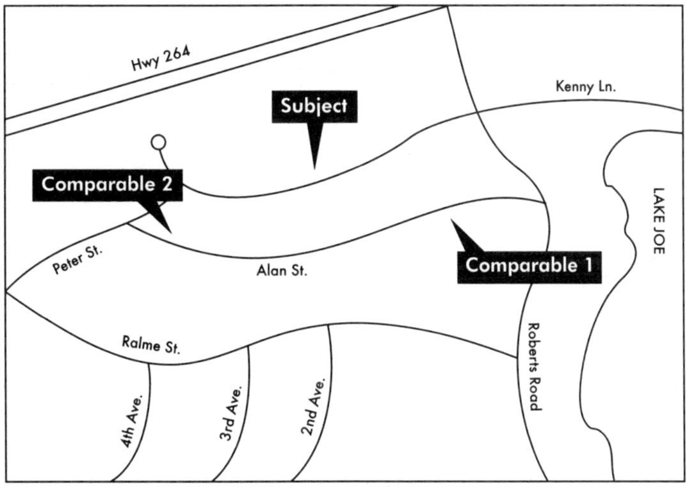

Exercise 3

List five neighborhood characteristics that may have an effect on property values.

1. ____________________

2. ____________________

3. ____________________

4. ____________________

5. ____________________

Site Data

Site data are specific data regarding the subject property site. As noted in Chapter 3, a **site** is defined as land that has been prepared for use by clearing, grading, and development of access and utilities. In an appraisal, the site is distinguished from its improvements (buildings, etc.) for several reasons:

1. for highest and best use analysis,
2. to provide data for certain valuation techniques (such as the cost approach to value), and
3. sometimes as a requirement of the appraisal assignment (as in appraisals for tax assessment purposes).

Important site data include the legal description of the property, property tax and zoning information, and data relating to the physical description of the property.

Legal and Tax Data

The legal description identifies the particular property that is the subject of the appraisal. Data for the legal description are often collected in the very early stages of the appraisal process, since identification of the real estate is an essential part of defining the appraisal problem (as discussed in Chapter 3). Using the legal description, the appraiser can prepare a plat map showing the subject site's boundaries. It is often possible to obtain such a plat by making copies of records from the county property records office.

In addition to the legal description, the appraiser gathers and verifies tax information for the subject property. This information includes the assessor's tax reference (or tax parcel) number for the property, the assessed value, the annual property taxes, and the annual amount of any special assessments that apply to the property. Since assessed value and tax rates may vary from year to year, the appraiser must also note the tax year for which the data is applicable. This should be the most recent tax year for which data is available.

The appraiser must also identify the specific zoning regulations that apply to the subject property. If the current use of the property does not conform to the zoning regulations, the appraiser must then determine whether the nonconforming use is legal (permitted under an exception to the zoning law) or illegal.

Physical Data

The majority of the data needed for the site description are generated by a personal review of the subject site. Physical site data include information about the land itself, its location, and any site improvements.

When preparing a site description, the appraiser should note whether the property boundaries appear to match the legal description of the property, and whether there are any apparent encroachments either by the subject upon adjoining properties, or vice versa. The appraiser should also note the location of any easements that benefit or burden the property. For example, the property may benefit from an access easement across adjoining land, or may be burdened by an easement for the installation and maintenance of underground utilities. The location of easements and encroachments is noted on the site map.

Fig. 5.5 Plat Map

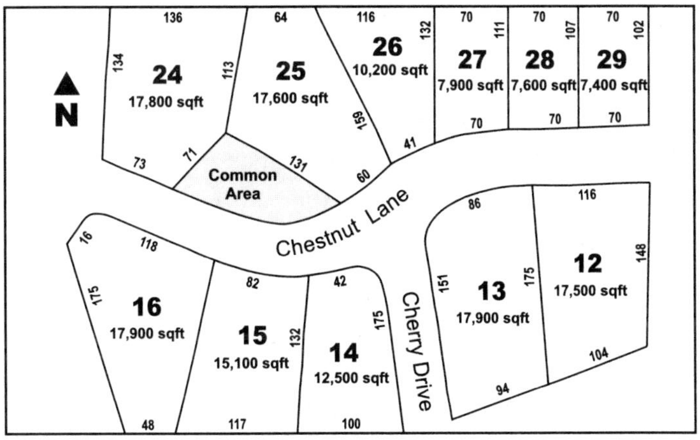

Fig. 5.6 Site Physical Data

Land Characteristics	Location
• width, depth, frontage, size	• orientation
• contour	• property access
• fertility	• distance to amenities
• soil support	• hazards and nuisances
• drainage	**Improvements**
• climate	• street improvements
• views	• utilities
	• site improvements

Site Dimensions. The appraiser will note the width and depth of the lot and also identify the location and dimension of any frontage. **Width** is the dimension of the site measured parallel to the street on which the site address is located. **Depth** is the opposite dimension, perpendicular to the street. For irregularly shaped lots, width or depth are sometimes stated as averages.

Frontage (or **front footage**) is the length of a property's boundary where it adjoins a street or body of water. It is sometimes used as a measure of value, but only when market data clearly indicate a relationship between frontage and value. Street frontage is normally more important for commercial properties than for residential properties.

> **Example:** In a residential neighborhood where street frontages vary from 80 feet to 100 feet, the difference in frontage will probably not affect value to any significant extent. On the other hand, residential properties bordering on a lake or stream may show significant value differences based on the amount of water frontage for each lot.

From the site map, the appraiser can calculate the size of the site. Size is normally described in square feet, or in acreage for larger sites. (One acre = 43,560 square feet.)

For irregularly shaped lots, the appraiser calculates the areas of different subsections of the lot, then adds these together to get the total area. (Refer to the section in Chapter 4 on calculating the area of irregularly shaped lots.)

Other land characteristics that are relevant to site description include the contour (slope) of the land, soil characteristics, and climate. The appraiser should note any characteristics that might pose problems such as steep slopes, poor drainage, or exposure to high winds, as well as favorable characteristics such as a sunny exposure, gently rolling topography, or pleasant views.

Fig. 5.7 Site Map

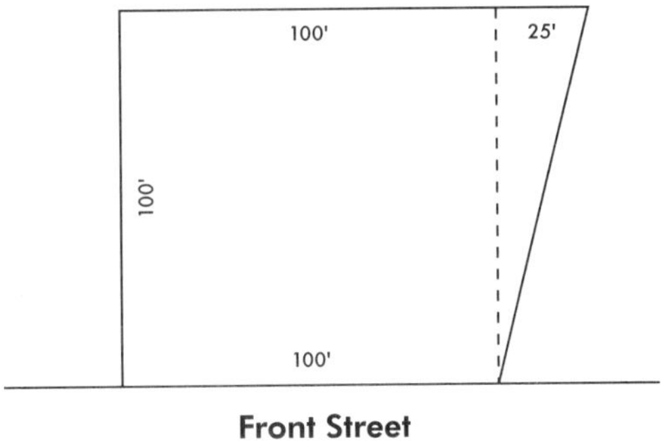

Location. Location data are collected for the subject site as well as for the neighborhood in general. The appraiser will note the type of lot (corner lot, inside lot, cul-de-sac lot, etc.), the access to the lot (public or private street, alley, or right-of-way easement), distance to arterial streets and to neighborhood amenities (schools, shops, etc.), and the presence of any hazards or nuisances such as heavy traffic, noise, or flood zones.

Improvements. The final category of site data relates to improvements that may benefit the site. These improvements may or may not be located on the subject property. Off-site improvements include streets and alleys (width, type, condition of surface, number of lanes, curbs and gutters, sidewalks, street lights, public or private ownership), and neighborhood utilities that are available to the subject property (water, sewer, storm drainage, electricity, gas, telephone, cable TV, garbage collection). Important on-site improvements include utilities that are actually connected to the subject site, as well as improvements such as driveways, parking, landscaping, and fences.

Site Data on the Uniform Residential Appraisal Report

The Site Data section of the Uniform Residential Appraisal Report is shown in Figure 5.8. As in the case of neighborhood data, site data may be entered directly onto the URAR form (or other appraisal form), or it may be collected on a separate site data form and later transferred to the actual appraisal form. Site data forms are useful as backup data for the appraiser's files, and they also remind the appraiser to investigate conditions that may not be specifically mentioned on the form report. A sample site data form is shown in Figure 5.9.

Fig. 5.8 Site Data Section of the URAR

SITE	Dimensions			Area		Shape		View	
	Specific Zoning Classification			Zoning Description					
	Zoning Compliance ☐ Legal ☐ Legal Nonconforming (Grandfathered Use) ☐ No Zoning ☐ Illegal (describe)								
	Is the highest and best use of the subject property as improved (or as proposed per plans and specifications) the present use? ☐ Yes ☐ No If No, describe								
	Utilities	Public	Other (describe)		Public	Other (describe)	Off-site Improvements—Type	Public	Private
	Electricity	☐	☐	Water	☐	☐	Street	☐	☐
	Gas	☐	☐	Sanitary Sewer	☐	☐	Alley	☐	☐
	FEMA Special Flood Hazard Area ☐ Yes ☐ No FEMA Flood Zone				FEMA Map #		FEMA Map Date		
	Are the utilities and off-site improvements typical for the market area? ☐ Yes ☐ No If No, describe								
	Are there any adverse site conditions or external factors (easements, encroachments, environmental conditions, land uses, etc.)? ☐ Yes ☐ No If Yes, describe								

Exercise 4

List five physical characteristics of a site that would be of interest to an appraiser.

1. ______________________________

2. ______________________________

3. ______________________________

4. ______________________________

5. ______________________________

Building Data

Building data for the subject property are collected for two main reasons. First, they are used to help identify and analyze comparable properties. A good comparable should not only be similar to the subject property in neighborhood and site characteristics, but in building characteristics as well. Knowledge of the detailed building data will also help the appraiser make any necessary adjustments for differences between the subject improvements and those of the comparables.

Fig. 5.9 Site Data Form

SITE DATA

Address 10157 - 13th Avenue

Legal description Lot 6, Block 4, Caldwell's Addition, vol. 72, pg. 25

Dimensions 50' x 200' Shape Rectangular

Square feet 10,000 Street paving Asphalt

Landscaping Adequate Topsoil Good

Drainage Good Frontage (Street)

Easements Utility S 15' Corner lot__ Inside lot x View__

Encroachments Fence on west property line?

Improvements: x Driveway x Sidewalks x Curbs __Alley

Utilities: x Electricity __Gas x Water x Sewers x Storm drains
x Telephone x Cable TV x High-speed Internet

Example: If the subject property is a 3-bedroom, 1-bath, ranch style house, the appraiser will look for other 3-bedroom, 1-bath ranch style houses to serve as comparables for the sales comparison approach to value. The appraiser will then adjust the values of the comparables to account for differences in building characteristics, such as differences in total square footage, building age, or quality of construction.

Specific building data are also used in the cost approach to value. These data are useful in estimating the reproduction or replacement cost of the improvements, and also in the analysis of depreciation due to deterioration or other causes.

Virtually all building data for the subject property are collected or verified by personal review, normally when the appraiser reviews the neighborhood and site. A solid knowledge of construction fundamentals is essential for this step in the appraisal process, since the appraiser must not only describe the improvements in terms of their size, style and materials, but must rate their quality and condition as well. (Aspects of residential construction are discussed in detail in Chapter 7.) If any blueprints are available for the building, these can be used to supplement personal observations.

Building data may be categorized in a number of ways, and no one way is considered superior. For our purposes here, we will categorize building data according to the following seven areas:

1. general data,
2. substructure data,
3. exterior data,
4. interior data,
5. equipment data,
6. energy efficiency data, and
7. miscellaneous data.

General Building Data

The first item of general data is a general description of the building: its overall size, number of living units, number of stories, architectural style, and placement on the site. General data also include a general description of each room in the structure, including its function (bedroom, living room, kitchen, etc.) and location (basement, first floor, second floor, etc.). In addition to counting rooms, the appraiser will also photograph the building. The front and rear view photos are taken at an angle to show the sides of the house and a view of the street. The appraiser may indicate the building's location on the site map, and make a sketch of the floor plan.

Building Dimensions. The overall size of a building is measured according to its outside dimensions. The appraiser measures each exterior wall of the structure, then calculates the **gross living area**. For purposes of this calculation, only above-grade living space is included; garage space, finished or unfinished basement space, or attic space is not considered part of the gross living area. Note that apartment and condominium units are typically measured according to interior dimensions.

Substructure Data

Substructure data (also known as **foundation** data) are information about the parts of the building that are below (or mostly below) grade level: the foundation and, if applicable, the basement or crawl space. The foundation must be described in terms of its type and condition. Common foundation types include slab-on-grade, full basement, and crawl space foundations (see Figure 7.7 in Chapter 7).

When reviewing the substructure, the appraiser should pay careful attention to evidence of settling (cracked, broken, or uneven foundation components), moisture penetration (damp foundation slabs or walls, accumulated water in crawl spaces or basements, presence of mold or fungus, moisture damage to wooden foundation members or floor framing), or infestation by termites, rodents, or other pests.

Fig. 5.10 Building Data

General Data
- building size
- number of living units
- number of stories
- architectural style
- placement on lot
- number and type of rooms

Exterior Data
- roofing material
- gutters and downspouts
- exterior wall covering and trim
- windows, screens, storm windows, skylights
- exterior doors

Equipment/Appliance Data
- electrical service
- plumbing and fixtures
- heating system
- cooling system
- kitchen appliances
- washer/dryer

Substructure Data
- type of foundation
- foundation settling
- moisture penetration
- pest infestation
- basement data (if applicable)
- size
- description of finished area
- water removal facilities
- outside access

Interior Data
- floor finishes
- wall and ceiling finishes
- bathroom and kitchen finishes
- cabinetry
- interior doors and trim

Energy Efficiency Data
- building insulation
- equipment insulation
- insulated doors and windows
- heating/cooling equipment efficiency
- solar design

Miscellaneous Data
- attic access
- attic improvements
- car storage
- porches, patios, decks
- fireplaces, stoves

In the case of basements, the appraiser will note the size of the basement area, and describe the ceiling, wall, and floor finishes of any finished areas of the basement. The appraiser should also describe any features (such as sump pumps or drains) designed to remove water from the basement. If the basement includes an outside access door, this fact is also noted.

Exterior Data

Important exterior building data include the type and condition of roofing materials, gutters and downspouts, exterior siding and trim, windows and window accessories, and exterior doors. Some types of roofing materials may last the lifetime of the building, but most tend to require replacement at some point, at a substantial cost. Thus the type and condition of the roofing material can significantly affect value. The appraiser should also note any damaged or missing shingles, as well as any evidence of rot or moss accumulation.

Gutters and downspouts are designed to carry runoff water from the roof. They should be in sound condition, with no leaks or broken connections, and water should drain through the downspouts in the opposite direction from the building, in a way that does not cause soil erosion.

Exterior wall materials come in a wide variety, including masonry (brick, block, stucco, concrete), wood (plywood, board siding, shingles), metal (steel, aluminum), and vinyl plastic. In addition to identifying the type (or types) of exterior wall covering, the appraiser looks for signs of damage or poor workmanship, such as cracks in masonry walls, moisture damage, warped, broken, rotten or missing boards, etc. The condition of any painted surfaces is also noted.

With regard to windows, the appraiser should identify the type of windows (casement, sliding, double-hung, etc.), the type of sash (wood, metal, vinyl-clad), and the type of glazing (single-pane, double-pane, etc.). If known, the window manufacturer's name may be noted. All non-fixed (opening) windows should operate smoothly and be equipped with screens. Wood frame windows should be checked for rot or decay, and all windows should be well caulked around their edges to prevent air leakage. Similar considerations may apply to storm windows.

The final component of exterior building data is the exterior doors. Most exterior doors for residential construction are wood or glass. Exterior wood doors should be solid (not hollow), and glass doors, whether swinging or sliding, should be made of tempered safety glass. All exterior doors should have adequate weatherstripping.

Interior Data

Most interior data concern the type and quality of interior finishes. These data not only reveal any repairs that may be necessary, but give a good indication of the overall quality of the building's construction. The quality of interior finishes has a big impact on the construction cost of a home, and has the potential for a similar impact on value.

Fig. 5.11 Building Data Form

BUILDING DATA

Address 10157 - 13th Avenue

Age 7 years

Square feet 1,350

Number of rooms 6

Construction quality very good

Style ranch

General condition very good

Feature	Good	Fair	Bad
Exterior: brick, (frame), veneer, stucco, alum	x		
Foundation: slab, bsmt, (crawl sp.)	x		
Garage: (attached), 1-car, (2-car), 3-car	x		
Patio, (deck), porch, shed, other		x	
Interior (general condition)	x		
Walls: (drywall), wood, plaster	x		
Ceilings	x		
Floors: wood, tile, (lino), concrete, (carpet)		x	
Electrical wiring	x		
Heating: (electric), gas, oil, other	x		
Air conditioning None			
Fireplace(s) None			
Kitchen	x		
Bathroom(s) 2 full	x		
Bedroom(s) 3	x		

Additional amenities Large windows in living areas

Design advantages Convenient, sunny kitchen

Design flaws Inadequate closets in the two smaller bedrooms

Energy efficiency Insulation, weatherstripping, storm windows

Location	Living Rm	Dining Rm	Kitchen	Bedrms	Baths	Family Rm
Basement						
First floor	x	x	x	3	2	None
Second floor						
Attic						

Depreciation:

Deferred maintenance Normal wear, except for deck railings

Functional obsolescence No family room

External obsolescence None

In general, the appraiser will note the materials used to cover the walls, ceilings, and floors in each room of the house. Wall and ceiling coverings are typically drywall, plaster, or wood. Floor coverings include carpet, wood, stone, and ceramic or vinyl tile, all of which can vary considerably in quality. Particular attention is paid to bathroom and kitchen finishes, as these tend to be more expensive (tiled walls, for example) and also more subject to water damage that can require costly repairs.

The quality and condition of the cabinetry, interior doors, and trim are also noted. The quality of these items, like that of all interior finishes, should be comparable to other homes in the market. Substandard quality may detract from value, and an above-normal quality may not add significantly to the home's value.

Equipment Data

The appraiser must note the specifications of the major equipment systems of the subject property, and identify any appliances that are included in the value estimate. Major equipment systems for most residences include electrical, plumbing, and heating systems; cooling systems are also standard features in many parts of the country.

Fig. 5.12 Improvements Section of the URAR

IMPROVEMENTS

General Description	Foundation	Exterior Description materials/condition	Interior materials/condition
Units ☐ One ☐ One with Accessory Unit	☐ Concrete Slab ☐ Crawl Space	Foundation Walls	Floors
# of Stories	☐ Full Basement ☐ Partial Basement	Exterior Walls	Walls
Type ☐ Det. ☐ Att. ☐ S-Det./End Unit	Basement Area sq. ft.	Roof Surface	Trim/Finish
☐ Existing ☐ Proposed ☐ Under Const.	Basement Finish %	Gutters & Downspouts	Bath Floor
Design (Style)	☐ Outside Entry/Exit ☐ Sump Pump	Window Type	Bath Wainscot
Year Built	Evidence of ☐ Infestation	Storm Sash/Insulated	Car Storage ☐ None
Effective Age (Yrs)	☐ Dampness ☐ Settlement	Screens	☐ Driveway # of Cars
Attic ☐ None	Heating ☐ FWA ☐ HWBB ☐ Radiant	Amenities ☐ Woodstove(s) #	Driveway Surface
☐ Drop Stair ☐ Stairs	☐ Other Fuel	☐ Fireplace(s) # ☐ Fence	☐ Garage # of Cars
☐ Floor ☐ Scuttle	Cooling ☐ Central Air Conditioning	☐ Patio/Deck ☐ Porch	☐ Carport # of Cars
☐ Finished ☐ Heated	☐ Individual ☐ Other	☐ Pool ☐ Other	☐ Att. ☐ Det. ☐ Built-in

Appliances ☐ Refrigerator ☐ Range/Oven ☐ Dishwasher ☐ Disposal ☐ Microwave ☐ Washer/Dryer ☐ Other (describe)

Finished area **above** grade contains: Rooms Bedrooms Bath(s) Square Feet of Gross Living Area Above Grade

Additional features (special energy efficient items, etc.)

Describe the condition of the property (including needed repairs, deterioration, renovations, remodeling, etc.).

Are there any physical deficiencies or adverse conditions that affect the livability, soundness, or structural integrity of the property? ☐ Yes ☐ No If Yes, describe

Does the property generally conform to the neighborhood (functional utility, style, condition, use, construction, etc.)? ☐ Yes ☐ No If No, describe

With regard to the electrical system, the appraiser should verify that the electrical service is adequate to supply the needs of the residence. The minimum electrical service for residences in most areas is 220-volt, 100-amp service; higher amperage service may be necessary in homes with electric-powered heating and/or cooling systems.

Important plumbing system data include the type of piping used for water supply and drain pipes, evidence of leakage or water backup, and the quality and condition of plumbing fixtures in kitchens and baths. The type, condition, and capacity of the water heater is also noted.

The appraiser should identify the type of system(s) used for heating and cooling in the house, and the type(s) of fuel (gas, oil, electricity, etc.) used to operate the system(s). The capacity of the systems should be adequate for the local climate and the size of the building. The condition of these systems should be noted as well, including any need for immediate repairs. For houses that are (or once were) heated with oil, the appraiser must note the location and condition of the oil storage tank, since this is a potential source of environmental pollution.

Finally, the appraiser will record the make and condition of any appliances included in the appraisal. Such appliances commonly include refrigerators, ovens, ranges, microwave ovens, dishwashers, disposals, kitchen exhaust fans/hoods, and washers and dryers.

Energy Efficiency Data

Energy-efficient design, construction, and equipment can improve the value of a home by reducing annual heating and cooling costs. Energy-efficient items that can influence value include above (or below) average building insulation (in ceilings, walls, and floors), insulated doors and windows, weatherstripping and caulking, and insulation of hot water systems (water heater and hot water pipes) and central heating ducts. Energy-efficient heating and cooling equipment, as well as solar design features, may also provide desirable energy cost savings.

Miscellaneous Data

Miscellaneous building data include any items that may affect value. Some common miscellaneous data are:

- size and type of car storage (attached or detached garage or carport);
- type of attic access and attic improvements (flooring, heating, finished areas);
- porches, patios, and decks;
- outbuildings (sheds, gazebos, storage buildings);
- fences and walls;
- fireplaces; and
- pools and spas.

Building Data on the Uniform Residential Appraisal Report

The Improvements section of the Uniform Residential Appraisal Report is shown in Figure 5.12. As in the case of neighborhood and site data, building data may be entered directly onto the URAR form (or other appraisal form), or may be collected on a separate building data form and later transferred to the actual appraisal form. A sample building data form is shown in Figure 5.11.

Exercise 5

Match the building characteristics on the left with the corresponding categories of building data on the right.

1. ____	floor finishes	a.	general data
2. ____	building insulation	b.	substructure data
3. ____	attic improvements	c.	exterior data
4. ____	heating system	d.	interior data
5. ____	type of foundation	e.	equipment data
6. ____	roofing material	f.	energy efficiency data
7. ____	building size	g.	miscellaneous data

Data Analysis

Once the appraiser has collected data about the community and surrounding region, identified and researched the market area, and gathered information about the property's neighborhood, site, and building characteristics, the resulting data must be analyzed. Data analysis is involved in each of the three appraisal methods: the sales comparison approach, the cost approach, and the income approach.

Comparable Properties

All of the three appraisal methods require the appraiser to gather data about **comparable properties**, which represent the kind of property that the subject property competes with in the real estate market. To reflect the subject property's value accurately, the comparables should be as similar as possible to the subject property. By collecting data and reviewing the property, the appraiser will have gathered quite a bit of information about the subject property. The appraiser needs to obtain as much of the same information about comparable properties as possible.

Some of the most reliable comparable property data are obtained from the appraiser's own files on previous appraisals. Comparable property data are also commonly gathered from secondary sources (such as multiple listing services or computer data banks). The appraiser may search public records and interview the parties to a transaction.

The appraiser often will not have the time to personally review comparable properties and verify the information as he or she does for the subject property. This makes it critical to evaluate whether the data about comparable properties are reliable. Significant errors in comparable property site or building data are likely to show up in atypical sales prices or rental incomes. When this happens, the non-conforming comparable is generally considered unreliable as a value indicator, and is either discarded from consideration, or subjected to further investigation to determine the cause of the discrepancy.

> **Example:** An appraiser identifies five properties that appear (based on secondary source data) to be comparable to the subject property in all major respects. Four of the properties sold recently for prices ranging from $640,000 to $650,000. The fifth property sold recently for $600,000. In this case, the appraiser would probably question the reliability of the value indicated by the fifth property. There may be an error in the data for the property, or the data may not include some important negative characteristic. Additional investigation to verify the data for the fifth comparable may be warranted.

Prices and Terms of Sale. One of the key pieces of data for the sales comparison approach to value (and also for the income approach) is the sales prices of comparable properties. But price alone is not a sufficient indicator of value, even for a comparable that is identical to the subject property. The appraiser must also gather data on the conditions of the sale. Of particular importance are the date of the comparable sale, its financing terms, and any special circumstances associated with the sale.

Date of sale. The date of the comparable sale is important because market values are subject to change. Just as the subject property is valued as of a specific date, the value of a comparable, as indicated by its sales price, is tied to the date of its sale. The sales dates of comparable properties should be within six months of the effective date of the appraisal. And in a rapidly changing market, the appraiser may still have to adjust the comparable sales prices for market trends.

> **Example:** A comparable property sold four months prior to the appraisal's effective date. Even though the comparable's sale date is within six months of the valuation date, the appraiser may have to adjust the comparable's sales price if neighborhood values have experienced rapid growth or decline, or if a major change (such as large layoffs at a major area employer) has occurred since the sale of the comparable.

Financing. Financing terms have a large impact on sales prices of property. When favorable financing is available, buyers are more willing, and more able, to pay higher prices for housing. Normally, financing is available on equal terms to all buyers in a market. But when a sale includes financing that is not typical of the market, the appraiser must take into account the effect of the financing terms on the price paid for the property.

Example: If average mortgage rates in the region are 7.5% for 30-year fixed-rate loans with a 20% downpayment, then a sale that is financed on those terms would ordinarily be considered equivalent to a cash sale. In this market, a buyer may be willing to pay a higher price for property with seller financing at 6%, or with no downpayment requirement. The favorable financing terms would be an added inducement to buyers to put a higher value on the property. An appraiser would rely on market data to assess the value impact of the financing terms.

Conditions of sale. Conditions of sale that affect value include special concessions by the seller, such as agreeing to pay some or all of the buyer's closing costs. Any concessions that aren't typical of the local market must be accounted for by the appraiser. The appraiser must also identify any unusual circumstances that may have applied to the comparable sale: one of the parties was under unusual pressure to sell or to buy, for example, or it wasn't an arm's length transaction (the parties were relatives, friends, or business associates). Comparable sales that did not occur under normal conditions are generally unreliable as value indicators, due to the difficulty of adjusting the sales prices to account for the circumstances of the sale.

Common sources for obtaining and/or verifying comparable price and terms data include real estate brokers, lenders, public records, and interviews with the buyer and seller themselves.

Cost Data

In the cost approach to value, cost data are used to determine the replacement or reproduction cost of the subject property. Building cost estimates can be highly complex and require considerable skill and experience to prepare. For residential appraisals, cost estimates usually use a simple cost per square foot measure. The average cost per square foot to construct a building similar to the subject property is multiplied by the gross living area of the subject to give an indication of cost.

Example: Data collected from cost manuals, cost data services, and local building contractors indicate that typical residential building costs run $80 per square foot for homes that are comparable in features to the subject property. If the subject property is a 2,500 square foot residence, its cost would be estimated as:

2,500 sq.ft. × $80/sq.ft = $200,000

The cost approach to value is discussed in detail in Chapter 8.

Income and Expense Data

If the property subject to an appraisal is (or will be) used for income production, data must be collected for the income approach to value. Income and expense data can be obtained from owners, brokers, and property managers. These data are collected for both the subject property (if available) and for comparable income properties. For the comparable properties, information on sales prices and terms is also necessary to determine the appropriate multiplier(s) to use in the income approach.

Important income and expense data include: monthly or annual rental rates; the terms of rental agreements; vacancy and bad debt rates; operating costs for salaries, utilities, repairs, maintenance, and management and professional fees; real estate taxes and insurance costs; annual replacement reserve costs for items such as roofing and mechanical systems; depreciation rates; the mortgage interest rate; and equity investment rates of return.

The income approach to value is discussed in detail in Chapter 10.

Key Terms

Building code—A system of regulations that specifies the allowable designs, materials and techniques for building construction.

Comparable—A property that has been sold in the same market that currently includes the subject property, and that appeals to the same sorts of buyers. Comparables are used in many different appraisal techniques.

Conditions of sale—An element of comparison that reflects the motivations of the buyer and seller in a real estate transaction. When conditions of sale are not typical of the market, the sales price is probably not a reliable indicator of market value.

Conventional financing—Institutional financing that is not guaranteed or insured by the government.

Cost—The actual amount of expenditure necessary to acquire or produce something.

Creative financing—Financing on terms that are not typically available in the market.

Depth—The dimension of a lot measured perpendicularly from the street on which the site address is located.

Economic base—The economic activities that support the people living in a particular area.

Environmental forces—Those aspects of the physical environment, whether natural or man-made, that influence value, including the character of the land, climate, infrastructure, and location.

Frontage—The boundary of a parcel of land that abuts a street, waterway, or other desirable feature.

General data—Data that relate to the real estate market in which a property is located, including regional, district and neighborhood data.

Governmental forces—Laws, regulations, and public services that affect the value of property in the market.

Improvement—An item of personal property that is added to the land by human effort, in such a way as to become part of the real estate. Also called a fixture.

Income—Money or other benefits that are received.

Infrastructure—Public improvements that support basic needs, such as transportation and utilities.

Location—An element of comparison that reflects the impact of neighborhood influences on value.

Market conditions—An element of comparison that reflects the state of the market on the date a property was sold. Adjustments for market conditions take into account the changes in value over time.

Neighborhood—A geographical area in which land uses are complementary and in which all properties are influenced in a similar way by the forces affecting value.

Price—The actual amount paid by a particular buyer to a particular seller in an actual transaction.

Primary data—Data that are generated by the appraiser, such as by a physical review of property or personal interviews.

Secondary data—Data generated by someone other than the appraiser, and obtained by the appraiser via a review of published materials.

Seller financing—A loan or other financial arrangement offered by a seller to a buyer in connection with the purchase of property.

Site—A parcel of land that has been prepared for use, by clearing, grading, and providing access and utilities.

Site improvement—An improvement other than a building, such as landscaping or utilities. Improvements "of" the site (such as utility access) are usually valued as part of the land. Improvements "on" the site (such as fences) are valued separately from the land.

Social forces—The numbers, lifestyles, standards, and preferences of the people in a particular market, which affect property values in that market.

Specific data—Data that relate to a specific property, such as the subject property or a comparable.

Substructure—The part of a building that is below ground level and that supports the superstructure. Substructure includes footings, foundation walls, piers, and other elements of the foundation.

Superstructure—The part of a building that is above ground and supported by the foundation.

Supply and demand—A principle of value which holds that the value of a property in a competitive market is determined by the relative levels of supply and demand. Property is worth more when demand is high compared to supply, and worth less when supply exceeds demand.

Uniform Residential Appraisal Report—A standard form report for use in appraisals of single-family residences. The URAR is approved for use in appraisals that are governed by FNMA, FHLMC, HUD, and the VA.

Value indicator—A piece of data or a derived conclusion (such as the adjusted sales price of a comparable) that is relevant to the value of the subject property in an appraisal.

Width—The dimension of a lot measured parallel to the street on which the site address is located.

Summary

I. Regional and Community Data

A. Reflect broad-scale market forces that affect value.

B. Useful as background information, and for identifying property characteristics and economic and social trends that enhance or detract from value.

C. Include data on the regional and community natural environment, economic characteristics, infrastructure, housing supply and demand, social attitudes, and political factors.

D. Important sources include publications by federal, state, and local government agencies and business trade associations.

II. Neighborhood Data

A. A neighborhood is a geographical area of complementary land uses.

1. Neighborhood boundaries are defined by changing market influences, and may or may not coincide with physical boundaries or changes in land use.

B. Neighborhood value indicators:

1. type of neighborhood
2. physical characteristics and layout
3. percent of development and evidence of change (new construction, remodeling, degree of maintenance)
4. quality, age, and condition of properties
5. traffic patterns and distances to services
6. amenities such as parks, beaches, etc.
7. negative value influences
8. overall neighborhood quality and appeal

C. Major neighborhood data sources include government agencies, trade groups, and personal review.

III. Site Data

A. Site description includes the legal description of the subject property, and information relating to zoning, land use, and property taxes and assessments.

B. Data describing the physical characteristics of the site:

1. dimensions, size, topography, soil characteristics, climate and views
2. orientation, access, distance to amenities, hazards and nuisances
3. on-site and off-site improvements

IV. Building Data

A. Building data are used to select and analyze comparable sales, and to estimate improvement costs in the cost approach to value.

B. Appraisers collect building data to describe the improvements in terms of size, style, materials and quality.

C. Building value indicators:

1. building size, quality of construction, number of living units, number of stories, architectural style, lot placement, number/size/type of rooms
2. type and condition of foundation, basement size and features
3. type and condition of roofing, gutters, exterior walls, windows and exterior doors
4. type and condition of interior wall/ceiling/floor finishes, bathroom and kitchen finishes, cabinetry and doors
5. type and condition of electrical and plumbing systems; type, age and capacity of heating and cooling systems; age and type of appliances included in appraisal
6. insulation, efficiency of heating/cooling, solar design
7. attics, car storage, patios, decks, fireplaces, outbuildings, pools, etc.

V. Data Analysis

A. Site and building data for recently sold comparable properties are necessary in order to make comparisons with the subject property.

B. Date of sale, financing terms, and sale conditions can all affect the price paid for a comparable property.

C. Building cost estimates for residential appraisals are usually made on a "per square foot" basis.

D. Comparable income and expense data must be collected when the subject property is, or will be, used for rental purposes.

Chapter Quiz

1. Which of the following types of data is most likely to be derived from secondary data sources?
   a. Building data
   b. Site data
   c. Neighborhood data
   d. Regional data

2. Which of the following is NOT a regional value indicator?
   a. Economic base
   b. Transportation systems
   c. Neighborhood boundaries
   d. Average household size

3. Data on rates of housing construction may be gathered from publications by:
   a. business trade associations
   b. the federal government
   c. city and county building departments
   d. All of the above

4. Neighborhood boundaries:
   a. are determined by market influences
   b. always correspond to physical barriers such as roads or streams
   c. never correspond to physical barriers such as roads or streams
   d. are the same as subdivision boundaries

5. Neighborhood data in an appraisal are used to:
   a. identify comparable properties for analysis in the sales comparison approach to value
   b. identify value influences that affect the subject property
   c. support the appraiser's estimate of value
   d. All of the above

6. Land that has been prepared for a particular use is known as a:
   a. lot
   b. site
   c. subdivision
   d. plat

7. Which of the following is NOT relevant to a description of the subject property site?
   a. Apparent easements or encroachments
   b. Legal description of the property
   c. Age of improvements
   d. Highest and best use

8. Which of the following dimensions would most likely be the same length?
   a. Width and depth
   b. Width and frontage
   c. Depth and frontage
   d. Frontage and setback

9. Off-site improvements that are relevant to a site description include:
   a. streets
   b. neighborhood utilities
   c. storm sewers
   d. all of the above

10. In an appraisal of residential property, building data would NOT be used to:
    a. determine highest and best use of the land as if vacant
    b. adjust the sales prices of comparable properties in the sales comparison approach
    c. estimate reproduction cost or replacement cost in the cost approach to value
    d. identify comparable properties for analysis

11. The gross living area of a residential property includes:

    a. the above grade living space
    b. all finished areas of the building
    c. finished basement space
    d. Both a) and c)

12. The most reliable building data for the subject property are acquired by:

    a. reviewing its plans and specifications
    b. interviewing the property owner
    c. personal review
    d. reviewing a previous appraisal report on the property

13. The sales price of a comparable property may need to be adjusted to account for:

    a. financing terms
    b. date of sale
    c. building size
    d. All of the above

14. If market interest rates are 8%, and a comparable property is sold with seller financing at 6%, the price paid for the comparable property is likely to be:

    a. higher than market value
    b. lower than market value
    c. the same as market value
    d. None of the above

15. In a comparable sale, the seller paid the closing costs for real estate transfer taxes. This fact would be relevant to the appraisal:

    a. only if it is not customary in the market for the seller to pay the transfer taxes
    b. only if the transfer taxes exceeded $500
    c. only if the sale was an arm's length transaction
    d. All of the above

Case Study

You have been asked to appraise the residence located at 1731 Pine Road, Oakdale, Washington 98022. Oakdale is a suburban city of approximately 40,000 people, located 15 miles from the state capital of Olympia. The subject is located in the neighborhood known locally as "Ravenswood," a five-year-old development of mostly single-family homes ranging from 2,200 to 2,600 square feet in size. The area is zoned R-1: single-family residential.

Ravenswood is bordered on the northwest by State Highway 22, beyond which rise the forested hills of Ten Oaks State Park. To the east, Maple Avenue separates the development from Oakdale's commercial district. An area of older (25-30 years old) and mostly smaller homes lies to the south across Cedar Boulevard. Cedar and Maple are both four-lane arterial streets with moderate to heavy traffic.

The terrain of Ravenswood is rolling, with elevations rising slightly to the northwest. Many properties in the neighborhood provide fine views of the hills in the state park. The majority of homes are neatly landscaped, and the neighborhood is free of litter and other eyesores. Aside from moderate traffic noise near the perimeter of the neighborhood, it is not subject to any hazards or nuisances.

About 20% of the lots remain undeveloped, but construction activity and building permit applications indicate that development of the remaining lots is proceeding at a steady pace. Virtually all homes in the neighborhood are owner-occupied.

Neighborhood utility services include municipal sewer and water service, as well as underground natural gas, electricity, phone, and TV cable. Storm runoff is channeled through open culverts. Garbage collection is available from a local private enterprise. Oakdale has its own fire department, and contracts police services from the county sheriff's office, which maintains a substation in town. Local property tax rates are $1.40 per $100 of assessed (fair market) value, which is typical of surrounding areas. There are no outstanding special assessments.

Housing supply and demand in the neighborhood appear to be in balance, although values are rising due to a strong local economy. Average marketing time for new and existing houses is between 3-4 months. Turnover is low, with only 5% of existing homes coming on the market in the past year; most sales in the neighborhood are new construction. Home prices range from $300,000 to $340,000, with an average of $325,000. Most sales are financed with conventional mortgages at rates that are currently 6.5-7%. Approximately 2% of the homes are vacant homes that have been recently completed but not yet sold.

Residents of Ravenswood are mostly white-collar professionals, with an average family income of about $85,000 per year and rising. Average family size is 4.3 people. Although most residents commute to work in Olympia, Oakdale provides a range of commercial shops, restaurants, theaters, etc., within two miles of the neighborhood, as well as Lutheran, Baptist, Methodist and Roman Catholic churches and a Jewish synagogue. There is also a small but well-staffed hospital located five miles from Ravenswood. Public elementary and high schools are located approximately ¾ of a mile south of the neighborhood.

Oakdale is served by the county bus system, which operates express service to Olympia as well as adequate local routes. Access from Ravenswood is provided by a bus stop on Cedar Boulevard. The express bus to downtown Olympia takes about 20-30 minutes, depending on traffic conditions.

The legal description of the subject property is:

Lot 17, Ravenswood Division #2, as recorded in Thurston County, Washington, plat book 34, map 19.

The assessor's tax number is 914437-13. Property taxes for the current tax year are $3,140.00. The property conforms to the local zoning, and to the deed restrictions recorded when the subdivision was platted.

The dimensions of the subject lot are 110′ × 220′. Like most of the surrounding properties, the lot is gently rolling, with a good view of the mountains. The soil is slightly rocky, but adequate to support the landscaping that consists of a well-kept lawn and evergreen shrubbery, as well as a large vegetable garden in the back yard. Drainage is excellent.

The recorded plat map shows a 10′ easement along the street frontage for installation and maintenance of the underground utilities. There are no other apparent easements or encroachments. The subject property is connected to all available neighborhood utilities.

Pine Road is a two-lane asphalt street with gravel shoulders; the road surface is in good condition. Street lighting is provided by the city, but there are no sidewalks, curbs, or gutters. The street is bordered on both sides by storm drainage culverts.

Access to the property is via an asphalt paved driveway, which also provides for adequate on-site parking. There are no apparent negative influences from hazards or nuisances.

1731 Pine Road is a two-story detached Northwest contemporary-style home. Exterior building dimensions are 30′ × 37′. The house is three years old, and in such good condition that it is the equivalent of a one-year-old home. The foundation is reinforced concrete, with a 3-4 foot crawl space. Exterior walls are of horizontal cedar siding, and the roof is cedar shakes. The house is fitted with painted metal gutters and downspouts, and the windows are wood-frame, casement type, with double-pane glass and aluminum screens. There is a solid wood-panel entry door with stained glass side-lights, and a 6′ sliding glass door off the family room.

The lower level includes a living room (15′ × 18′), dining room (13′2″ × 12′), family room (20′×12′8″), combination kitchen and breakfast room (18′6″ × 12′8″), foyer (12′ × 12′, with a 2′ × 4′ coat closet), half-bath (4′ × 5′2″), and utility room (4′ × 7′). The upstairs includes four bedrooms (13′ × 17′, 12′ × 14′6″, 10′ × 12′, and 12′ × 13′4″), two full baths (10′ × 11′6″ and 11′ × 6′) and four closets (three 2′ × 6′ and a 6′ × 6′ walk-in closet).

The walls and ceilings are finished with sheetrock and painted an off-white color. Flooring is vinyl in the kitchen, utility room, and half-bath; hardwood for the foyer; ceramic tile in the upstairs baths; and other areas of the house have wall-to-wall carpeting. The kitchen and all the baths have ceramic tile counters, and the two upstairs bathrooms have ceramic tile wainscotting as well.

The kitchen has 22′ of lower cabinets, and 16′ of uppers, as well as a refrigerator, oven/range, dishwasher, disposal, and vent fan. These kitchen appliances, along with the washer and dryer, will be sold with the house. Insulation meets local building code requirements, with R-38 in the ceiling, and R-30 in the walls and floor. There is a fireplace in the family room.

Attic access is via a drop stairs. The attic floor is sheeted with plywood to allow for storage, but the attic is not finished or heated. The electric system is 220 volts, and appears adequate for the home. Heating is central forced-air powered by a gas-fired 120,000 BTU furnace. There is no cooling system.

Attached to the house is a 2-car garage, measuring 12′ × 20′. There is a 6′ × 26′ covered entry porch, and a 20′ × 20′ concrete patio off the back of the house. The back yard is surrounded by a 5 foot high wood fence.

1. Based on the information in the case study, fill in the Neighborhood section of the Uniform Residential Appraisal Report.

NEIGHBORHOOD

Note: Race and the racial composition of the neighborhood are not appraisal factors.

Neighborhood Characteristics	**One-Unit Housing Trends**	**One-Unit Housing**	**Present Land Use %**
Location ☐ Urban ☐ Suburban ☐ Rural	Property Values ☐ Increasing ☐ Stable ☐ Declining	PRICE AGE	One-Unit %
Built-Up ☐ Over 75% ☐ 25–75% ☐ Under 25%	Demand/Supply ☐ Shortage ☐ In Balance ☐ Over Supply	$ (000) (yrs)	2-4 Unit %
Growth ☐ Rapid ☐ Stable ☐ Slow	Marketing Time ☐ Under 3 mths ☐ 3–6 mths ☐ Over 6 mths	Low	Multi-Family %
Neighborhood Boundaries		High	Commercial %
		Pred.	Other %
Neighborhood Description			
Market Conditions (including support for the above conclusions)			

2. Based on the information in the case study, fill in the Subject and Site sections of the Uniform Residential Appraisal Report.

SUBJECT

Property Address	City	State	Zip Code
Borrower	Owner of Public Record	County	
Legal Description			
Assessor's Parcel #	Tax Year	R.E. Taxes $	
Neighborhood Name	Map Reference	Census Tract	
Occupant ☐ Owner ☐ Tenant ☐ Vacant	Special Assessments $	☐ PUD HOA $	☐ per year ☐ per month
Property Rights Appraised ☐ Fee Simple ☐ Leasehold ☐ Other (describe)			
Assignment Type ☐ Purchase Transaction ☐ Refinance Transaction ☐ Other (describe)			
Lender/Client	Address		
Is the subject property currently offered for sale or has it been offered for sale in the twelve months prior to the effective date of this appraisal? ☐ Yes ☐ No			
Report data source(s) used, offering price(s), and date(s).			

SITE

Dimensions	Area	Shape	View
Specific Zoning Classification	Zoning Description		
Zoning Compliance ☐ Legal ☐ Legal Nonconforming (Grandfathered Use) ☐ No Zoning ☐ Illegal (describe)			
Is the highest and best use of the subject property as improved (or as proposed per plans and specifications) the present use? ☐ Yes ☐ No If No, describe			

Utilities	**Public**	**Other (describe)**		**Public**	**Other (describe)**	**Off-site Improvements—Type**	**Public**	**Private**
Electricity	☐	☐	Water	☐	☐	Street	☐	☐
Gas	☐	☐	Sanitary Sewer	☐	☐	Alley	☐	☐

FEMA Special Flood Hazard Area ☐ Yes ☐ No	FEMA Flood Zone	FEMA Map #	FEMA Map Date
Are the utilities and off-site improvements typical for the market area? ☐ Yes ☐ No If No, describe			
Are there any adverse site conditions or external factors (easements, encroachments, environmental conditions, land uses, etc.)? ☐ Yes ☐ No If Yes, describe			

3. Based on the information in the case study, fill in the Improvements section of the Uniform Residential Appraisal Report.

IMPROVEMENTS

General Description	Foundation	Exterior Description materials/condition	Interior materials/condition
Units ☐ One ☐ One with Accessory Unit	☐ Concrete Slab ☐ Crawl Space	Foundation Walls	Floors
# of Stories	☐ Full Basement ☐ Partial Basement	Exterior Walls	Walls
Type ☐ Det. ☐ Att. ☐ S-Det./End Unit	Basement Area sq. ft.	Roof Surface	Trim/Finish
☐ Existing ☐ Proposed ☐ Under Const.	Basement Finish %	Gutters & Downspouts	Bath Floor
Design (Style)	☐ Outside Entry/Exit ☐ Sump Pump	Window Type	Bath Wainscot
Year Built	Evidence of ☐ Infestation	Storm Sash/Insulated	Car Storage ☐ None
Effective Age (Yrs)	☐ Dampness ☐ Settlement	Screens	☐ Driveway # of Cars
Attic ☐ None	Heating ☐ FWA ☐ HWBB ☐ Radiant	Amenities ☐ Woodstove(s) #	Driveway Surface
☐ Drop Stair ☐ Stairs	☐ Other Fuel	☐ Fireplace(s) # ☐ Fence	☐ Garage # of Cars
☐ Floor ☐ Scuttle	Cooling ☐ Central Air Conditioning	☐ Patio/Deck ☐ Porch	☐ Carport # of Cars
☐ Finished ☐ Heated	☐ Individual ☐ Other	☐ Pool ☐ Other	☐ Att. ☐ Det. ☐ Built-in

Appliances ☐ Refrigerator ☐ Range/Oven ☐ Dishwasher ☐ Disposal ☐ Microwave ☐ Washer/Dryer ☐ Other (describe)

Finished area **above** grade contains: Rooms Bedrooms Bath(s) Square Feet of Gross Living Area Above Grade

Additional features (special energy efficient items, etc.)

Describe the condition of the property (including needed repairs, deterioration, renovations, remodeling, etc.).

Are there any physical deficiencies or adverse conditions that affect the livability, soundness, or structural integrity of the property? ☐ Yes ☐ No If Yes, describe

Does the property generally conform to the neighborhood (functional utility, style, condition, use, construction, etc.)? ☐ Yes ☐ No If No, describe

Quiz Answers

1. d) Regional data are most likely to be derived from secondary sources.
2. c) Neighborhood boundaries would be considered neighborhood data, rather than regional data.
3. d) Housing data may be obtained from local builders associations as well as from federal and local governments.
4. a) Neighborhood boundaries often correspond with physical barriers, but are determined by market forces.
5. d) Neighborhood data are used to identify comparable properties and to identify value influences that affect the subject property (such as nearby nuisances).
6. b) A parcel of land prepared for development is a site.
7. c) The age of the improvement has no bearing on the description of a site.
8. b) The frontage of a property is its width along a street or body of water.
9. d) Off-site improvements include streets, utilities, and storm sewers.
10. a) Building data are not relevant when determining the highest and best use of a site as if vacant.
11. a) Gross living area only includes above-grade living space. It does not include finished basement space.
12. c) The most reliable building data are obtained by personal review.
13. d) A comparable property's sales price will need to be adjusted to account for any way in which it might differ from the subject property, including the financing terms, date of sale, or size of the building.
14. a) A buyer is more likely to pay more than market value for a property in order to obtain a better-than-average financing package.
15. a) Whether the seller paid the real estate transfer taxes is relevant only if it is not customary in that market for the seller to pay the real estate transfer tax.

Exercise Answers

#1
1. a
2. b
3. a
4. b
5. b, d, e
6. d, e
7. d, e
8. c
9. d, e, f
10. f
11. c
12. d

#2
1. A neighborhood is a geographic area of complementary land uses in which all properties are influenced in a similar way by the forces affecting value.
2. Answer is "S" for all items.

#3 Refer to the list of important neighborhood characteristics.

#4 Refer to Figure 5.6 for a list of relevant physical site characteristics.

#5
1. d
2. f
3. g
4. e
5. b
6. c
7. a

Case Study Answers

1. See URAR form excerpt below.

Note: Race and the racial composition of the neighborhood are not appraisal factors.

Neighborhood Characteristics	One-Unit Housing Trends	One-Unit Housing	Present Land Use %
Location ☐ Urban ☑ Suburban ☐ Rural	Property Values ☑ Increasing ☐ Stable ☐ Declining	PRICE AGE	One-Unit 100 %
Built-Up ☑ Over 75% ☐ 25–75% ☐ Under 25%	Demand/Supply ☐ Shortage ☑ In Balance ☐ Over Supply	$ (000) (yrs)	2-4 Unit %
Growth ☑ Rapid ☐ Stable ☐ Slow	Marketing Time ☐ Under 3 mths ☑ 3–6 mths ☐ Over 6 mths	300 Low 0	Multi-Family %
Neighborhood Boundaries		340 High 5	Commercial %
To NW: SR 22; To E: Maple Avenue; To S: Cedar Boulevard		325 Pred. 5	Other %

Neighborhood Description Neighborhood is 20-30 minutes from employment opportunities downtown; Shops, restaurants, theaters, churches, schools all within several miles; Properties are well-maintained and landscaped; No negative influences from hazards or nuisances

Market Conditions (including support for the above conclusions) Most sales are arm's length transactions financed with conventional mortgages at 6.5-7% rates; Property values are increasing; Supply and demand are in balance; Turnover is low (only 5% of homes on market in past year); Few (2%) homes remain vacant

2. See URAR form excerpts below.

Property Address 1731 Pine Road	City Oakvale	State WA	Zip Code 98022
Borrower	Owner of Public Record	County Thurston	
Legal Description Lot 17, Ravenswood Division #2, plat book 34, map 19			
Assessor's Parcel # 914437-13	Tax Year [Current year]	R.E. Taxes $ 3,140	
Neighborhood Name Ravenswood	Map Reference	Census Tract	
Occupant ☐ Owner ☐ Tenant ☐ Vacant	Special Assessments $ 0	☐ PUD HOA $	☐ per year ☐ per month
Property Rights Appraised ☑ Fee Simple ☐ Leasehold ☐ Other (describe)			
Assignment Type ☐ Purchase Transaction ☐ Refinance Transaction ☐ Other (describe)			
Lender/Client	Address		
Is the subject property currently offered for sale or has it been offered for sale in the twelve months prior to the effective date of this appraisal? ☐ Yes ☐ No			
Report data source(s) used, offering price(s), and date(s).			

Dimensions 110'x 220'	Area 24,200 sq. ft.	Shape rectangular	View mountain
Specific Zoning Classification R-1	Zoning Description		
Zoning Compliance ☑ Legal ☐ Legal Nonconforming (Grandfathered Use) ☐ No Zoning ☐ Illegal (describe)			
Is the highest and best use of the subject property as improved (or as proposed per plans and specifications) the present use? ☑ Yes ☐ No If No, describe			

Utilities	Public	Other (describe)		Public	Other (describe)	Off-site Improvements—Type	Public	Private
Electricity	☑	☐	Water	☑	☐	Street	☑	☐
Gas	☑	☐	Sanitary Sewer	☑	☐	Alley	☐	☐

FEMA Special Flood Hazard Area ☐ Yes ☑ No FEMA Flood Zone FEMA Map # FEMA Map Date

Are the utilities and off-site improvements typical for the market area? ☑ Yes ☐ No If No, describe

Are there any adverse site conditions or external factors (easements, encroachments, environmental conditions, land uses, etc.)? ☑ Yes ☐ No If Yes, describe

Utility easement is 10' along frontage; no other apparent easements or encroachments

3. See URAR form excerpt below.

General Description	Foundation	Exterior Description materials/condition	Interior materials/condition
Units ☑ One ☐ One with Accessory Unit	☐ Concrete Slab ☑ Crawl Space	Foundation Walls concrete	Floors carpet, vinyl, hardwood
# of Stories 2	☐ Full Basement ☐ Partial Basement	Exterior Walls cedar siding	Walls sheetrock
Type ☑ Det. ☐ Att. ☐ S-Det./End Unit	Basement Area sq. ft.	Roof Surface cedar shakes	Trim/Finish average
☑ Existing ☐ Proposed ☐ Under Const.	Basement Finish %	Gutters & Downspouts painted metal	Bath Floor ceramic tile
Design (Style) NW contemporary	☐ Outside Entry/Exit ☐ Sump Pump	Window Type wood-frame double-pane	Bath Wainscot ceramic tile
Year Built	Evidence of ☐ Infestation	Storm Sash/Insulated	Car Storage ☐ None
Effective Age (Yrs) 1	☐ Dampness ☐ Settlement	Screens aluminum screens	☐ Driveway # of Cars
Attic ☐ None	Heating ☑ FWA ☐ HWBB ☐ Radiant	Amenities ☐ Woodstove(s) #	Driveway Surface
☑ Drop Stair ☐ Stairs	☐ Other Fuel	☑ Fireplace(s) # 1 ☑ Fence	☑ Garage # of Cars 2
☑ Floor ☐ Scuttle	Cooling ☐ Central Air Conditioning	☑ Patio/Deck ☑ Porch	☐ Carport # of Cars
☐ Finished ☐ Heated	☐ Individual ☐ Other	☐ Pool ☐ Other	☑ Att. ☐ Det. ☐ Built-in

IMPROVEMENTS

Appliances ☑ Refrigerator ☑ Range/Oven ☑ Dishwasher ☑ Disposal ☑ Microwave ☑ Washer/Dryer ☑ Other (describe) vent fan

Finished area **above** grade contains: 8 Rooms 4 Bedrooms 2½ Bath(s) 2220 Square Feet of Gross Living Area Above Grade

Additional features (special energy efficient items, etc.)

Describe the condition of the property (including needed repairs, deterioration, renovations, remodeling, etc.).

Building is recent and in good condition, with no apparent depreciation except routine physical deterioration

Are there any physical deficiencies or adverse conditions that affect the livability, soundness, or structural integrity of the property? ☐ Yes ☑ No If Yes, describe

No known conditions

Does the property generally conform to the neighborhood (functional utility, style, condition, use, construction, etc.)? ☑ Yes ☐ No If No, describe

6 Site Valuation

Overview

There are a variety of reasons for estimating the value of land or a site. It may simply be that the subject property is in fact vacant land. Or in the case of improved property, a separate valuation of the site may be required in order to apply a valuation technique (such as the cost approach to value). In this chapter, we will examine the concept of site valuation. We will begin by exploring the doctrine of highest and best use, which underlies every estimate of the market value of land. We will then review some of the more commonly used techniques for estimating land value.

After completing this chapter, you should be able to:

- define highest and best use, and understand its importance in the appraisal of real estate;
- list the four criteria for highest and best use;
- understand the distinction between the highest and best use of land as if vacant, and the highest and best use of property as improved, and the significance of each;
- understand the concepts of interim use and legal nonconforming use;
- understand the concepts of excess land and plottage;
- identify the six common methods for appraising land, and describe their basic procedures; and
- identify the critical data needed for each of the six land valuation methods.

Highest and Best Use

We have seen that real estate is not simply the land and its improvements, but the rights that go with the land, such as the right to use, subdivide, or transfer the land. The concept of highest and best use recognizes this fact—and the fact that the value of real estate depends on how it is used. For example, a particular property may be worth more for commercial development than it is worth for agricultural purposes. In real estate appraisal, the market value of property always depends on its highest and best use.

The highest and best use of property is the use that is reasonably probable and that results in the highest value. Highest and best use assumes that the market will view the value of the property in light of all its possible uses. If there is more than one possible use for the property, its value will be determined by the most productive (profitable) use.

Criteria for Highest and Best Use

To qualify as the highest and best use, the use must result in the highest value. But the use must also be reasonably probable. Uses that are not reasonably probable—due to legal, economic, or physical limitations—cannot qualify as the highest and best use.

Highest and best use analysis can be seen as a process of elimination. First, the appraiser eliminates any uses that would be illegal under existing or proposed laws, regulations, deed restrictions, or contractual agreements. Next, uses that are not possible due to the physical characteristics of the land itself are eliminated from consideration.

The remaining potential uses are then analyzed to see whether they would generate any financial return. Uses that do not generate an adequate positive return are discarded as economically unfeasible, and the others are evaluated to determine which one would generate the highest return. The result is the highest and best use.

Highest and best use is often defined as the use that is legally permitted, physically possible, economically feasible, and maximally productive. This definition reflects the process used to determine highest and best use, as described above. Keep in mind, however, that the legal, physical, and economic probabilities of a particular use are often interrelated.

Legally Permitted Use. A review of the legal restrictions that apply to the subject property is usually completed first. These restrictions include a wide variety of government regulations such as zoning, environmental, and tax regulations; and also private legal restrictions, such as easements, deed restrictions, or lease conditions.

Example: A particular site may be more valuable for commercial purposes than for residential use. But if the site's zoning allows only residential use, a commercial use would be illegal and therefore could not be the highest and best use of the land.

Fig. 6.1 Criteria for Highest and Best Use

1. Legally permitted
2. Physically possible
3. Economically feasible
4. Maximally productive

Legal restrictions affect the use of land in a variety of ways. For instance, zoning laws may limit use by such means such as setback requirements and maximum or minimum limits on lot and building size.

Example: In a residential area, the most profitable use of a 5-acre parcel may be to subdivide it into ½-acre building lots. However, this would not be considered the highest and best use of the parcel if the zoning required minimum lot sizes of one acre. In this case, subdivision into ½-acre parcels is not legally permitted, so it is not likely to occur.

Legal restrictions may also impact land use by influencing the cost of various types of development. Examples would include special property tax breaks that encourage agricultural use of property, or development fees and regulatory procedures that drive up the cost of building new housing.

Physically Possible Use. The size, shape, soil, topography, and other physical characteristics of a site are important considerations in determining its highest and best use. For example, the site must be large enough to accommodate the potential use, and the soil must be capable of supporting the necessary improvements. Water and other utilities must be available and adequate, and the climate must be suitable.

Example: A use that requires a large amount of on-site parking may be physically impossible if the site is not large enough to provide the required number of parking places.

Economically Feasible Use. The appraiser must also consider whether a given use is probable from an economic standpoint. For a use to be economically feasible, it must result in a positive economic return. If a use would result in economic loss, it is removed from consideration.

The supply of and demand for properties with a particular use is a major factor in analyzing economic feasibility. If there is already an oversupply of one type of property (such as office space or warehouses), it may not be economically feasible to develop additional property for that use, even if existing properties are profitable.

Example: An appraiser is analyzing the highest and best use of a commercial site in a small town. One of the potential uses of the site is as a gas station. The appraiser notes that the two existing gas stations in town are both profitable, but determines that there is not sufficient demand in town to support three stations. Although supply and demand are currently in balance, development of a third station would create an oversupply. In this case, the appraiser would conclude that use as a gas station could not be the highest and best use of the site, because it is not economically feasible.

Maximally Productive Use. Maximally productive use is just another way of saying "the use that results in the highest value." As discussed in Chapter 2, value can be measured in terms of productivity, meaning the ability of an asset to create wealth. The greater the productivity, the greater the value, and vice versa. If highest and best use is the use that results in the highest value, then it can also be defined as the use that is maximally productive.

Highest and Best Use and the Principle of Anticipation

The **principle of anticipation** states that the value of property is affected by the potential future benefits of its ownership. So when analyzing highest and best use, the appraiser must always consider the possible future uses of the property.

A site's legal restrictions, economic circumstances, and even physical characteristics are all subject to change. Zoning and other laws can become more restrictive, or less so. Supply and demand for particular types of properties can go up or down. Physical characteristics, such as the availability of water, can also change. Highest and best use analysis requires the appraiser to evaluate the likelihood of any changes that may affect the potential use of the property.

Example: A site is zoned for office buildings of up to three stories. The area is economically suitable for office development; thus it may appear that a three-story office building would be the highest and best use of the site. However, if the site is likely to be rezoned in the near future to allow for ten-story office buildings, it may be more profitable to wait and develop the site more intensively after the new zoning takes effect, rather than to immediately develop a three-story office building that will shortly become an underimprovement. In this case, the current highest and best use of the land may be to do nothing and simply hold it for speculation.

When conditions are such that a change in legal, economic, or physical restrictions on property use seems likely to occur, an appraiser may (and should) take this fact into consideration when determining highest and best use.

Interim Uses. When the current highest and best use of land is expected to change in the near future, the use to which the land is put while awaiting the change is called an interim use. An **interim use** is a current highest and best use that is viewed as only temporary.

A common example of an interim use is agricultural land that is currently being farmed but will soon be converted for residential or commercial development. In urban areas, parking lots are a frequent interim use of land that is not yet ready for development (due to lack of demand or some other reason). Another example of an interim use is an older building that is a candidate for replacement or extensive renovation to allow for a more productive use of the land.

Because they are expected to change in a relatively short period of time, interim uses do not usually involve expensive improvements. It does not make economic sense to put a lot of money into improvements that will have to be torn down in a few years.

Vacant and Improved Land

Highest and best use may vary, depending on whether land is vacant (or assumed to be vacant) or improved. For this reason, appraisers make a distinction between the highest and best use of land as if vacant, and the highest and best use of property as improved.

To determine the highest and best use of land as if vacant, the appraiser assumes that any existing improvements on the land do not exist. The highest and best use becomes the use that would result in the highest value if the land were vacant and ready for any kind of development. In the case of property that actually is vacant land, this assumption simply reflects the true state of affairs. But improved property may also be analyzed in this manner.

> **Example:** A property is improved with a single-family residence. If vacant, the value of the site for residential use would be $120,000. However, the zoning allows for commercial development, and the site would be worth $240,000 if vacant and available for commercial development. In this case, the highest and best use of the land as if vacant would be commercial use. The fact that the land is already improved for residential use has no effect on this determination.

The highest and best use of the property as improved takes into account the contribution of existing improvements, and also the cost of their removal (if necessary) to allow for some different use.

> **Example:** Using the facts of the example above, assume the value of the property (land and buildings), as currently improved for residential use is $360,000 ($120,000 land value plus $240,000 value contribution from the improvements). Also assume that it would cost $30,000 to remove the existing structure to allow for commercial use development.
>
> In this case, the value of the property as improved for commercial use can be calculated as follows:

$240,000	value of land if vacant and available for commercial development
– 30,000	cost to remove existing improvements
$210,000	value of property as improved for commercial use

These figures indicate that the highest and best use of the property as improved is the current residential use, since the value of the property as improved ($360,000) is higher for residential than for commercial use.

In considering the highest and best use of property as improved, keep in mind that existing improvements do not necessarily add to the value of the property, and may actually detract from it. Even when an improvement is physically sound, it may be functionally obsolete, and the necessary cost of removing it to make way for a newer structure could have a negative impact on overall property value.

> **Example:** In some areas of the country, where there is a strong demand for high-class housing, but little or no supply of vacant land for new development, existing homes in good condition may be purchased and then razed to make way for more luxurious residences. Even though the existing residences are perfectly livable, they represent a negative contribution to value, since the building lots would be worth more if they were vacant.

Legal Nonconforming Uses. When zoning laws are changed to become more restrictive, existing uses may become nonconforming. For example, an area that once allowed both commercial and residential uses may be rezoned to permit residential use only. In that case, an existing commercial building would no longer conform to the zoning laws.

Zoning laws often allow the continuation of existing uses that have become **nonconforming** due to changes in zoning regulation. Such uses are allowed to continue, but usually may not be rebuilt or expanded. A legal nonconforming use may be the highest and best use of property as improved, but generally cannot be the highest and best use of the land as if vacant, because if the land were vacant, the nonconforming use would no longer be legal.

True Highest and Best Use. For appraisal purposes, there can be only one highest and best use. When a property's highest and best use as if vacant is different from its highest and best use as improved, the appraiser must determine which one should serve as the basis of the appraisal. This is actually an easy procedure, since highest and best use is simply the use that results in the highest value.

If the highest and best use of the land as if vacant results in a higher value than the highest and best use of the property as improved, then it is the true highest and best use of the property. (Of course, the opposite is also true.)

> **Example:** In preceding examples, we looked at a property whose value for its highest and best use as improved ($360,000 for residential use) was greater than the adjusted value for its highest and best use as if vacant ($210,000 for commercial use). An appraiser in this case would conclude that the highest and best use of the subject property was residential use, since it resulted in the highest value.

Remember though, that the value indicated by the highest and best use of the land as if vacant may need to be adjusted to reflect the costs of removing existing improvements.

Comparing the highest and best use of land as if vacant to the highest and best use of property as improved helps determine whether an existing use should continue or not. If the existing use is not the true highest and best use (because the adjusted value of the land as if vacant is greater than the value of the property as improved), then a change in the use of the property is indicated.

Consistent Use. Several appraisal methods (including residual techniques and the cost approach to value) rely on the separate valuation of land and improvements. When using these techniques, the appraiser must bear in mind the **principle of consistent use**: both land and improvements must be appraised for the same use. Once the appraiser determines the true highest and best use for the property, he or she may then consider the individual values of site and improvements that are indicated by that use.

> **Example:** Returning again to the facts of our ongoing example, an appraiser would decide that the value of the subject site was $120,000, which is its value for residential purposes. Since residential use was determined to be the highest and best use of the property, both the land and the improvements must be valued on the basis of residential use. This would be the case even though the land was found to be worth more for commercial use.

Excess Land and Plottage

For any given use, there is usually an optimum amount of land associated with the use. When a parcel of land includes more land than is necessary to support its highest and best use, it is said to contain excess land. **Excess land** is land that is not needed for the highest and best use of the site.

> **Example:** The zoning in a residential neighborhood requires a minimum lot size of 5,000 square feet. Most of the lots in the neighborhood are the minimum size. In this case, a 6,000 square foot building lot located in the neighborhood would contain excess land, since the extra 1,000 square feet would not be necessary to support a house that was typical of other houses in the neighborhood (the highest and best use of the site).

On a per-square-foot basis, the value of excess land is less than the value of the portion of the site that is needed to support its highest and best use. In the example above, the 6,000 square foot lot is 20% larger than average for the neighborhood. But that 20% is excess land, so the value of the site would be less than 20% greater than the average site value.

In valuing a site, the appraiser must also consider whether any excess land is adaptable for some other use. The highest and best use of the excess land may be different from the highest and best use of the total site.

> **Example:** The highest and best use of a two-acre site is for a grocery store. However, the amount of land needed to support the grocery store use is only one acre. If the site can be subdivided, the excess one acre of land may have value for some other use, such as a strip mall.

A concept related to excess land is the concept of plottage. **Plottage** refers to the increase in value that results from combining two or more lots to allow for a more profitable highest and best use. If two lots were worth more when combined than they were separately, the added value is called the **plottage value** or **plottage increment**.

> **Example:** Two adjoining lots are each valued at $40,000. They are each too small to support a building of the size typical in the neighborhood. But if the two lots are combined, the resulting parcel is comparable in size to other neighborhood sites, and the value of the combined property is $100,000. The extra $20,000 in value is the plottage value.

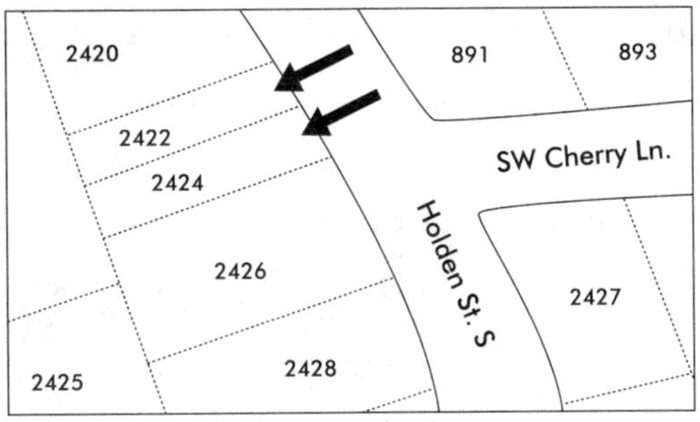

Highest and Best Use in Residential Appraisals

Strictly speaking, an analysis of highest and best use should determine the optimum use for the subject property in very specific terms. For example, a determination that residential use is the highest and best use of the subject property should also specify the characteristics of the residential improvements (optimum size, number of bedrooms, etc.).

As a practical matter, most residential appraisals do not require such a detailed analysis. Unless otherwise required, an appraiser may assume that the current use of improved residential property is its highest and best use if:

1. the value of the property as improved is higher than the value of the site as if vacant, and
2. there is adequate comparable sales data to show that the existing improvements are typical of properties for which there is demand in the local market.

Exercise 1

1. List the four criteria for highest and best use.

   1. ____________________
   2. ____________________
   3. ____________________
   4. ____________________

2. Match the concepts on the left with the corresponding statements on the right.

1. ___	interim use	a. potential future use
2. ___	consistent use	b. value increase from combining parcels
3. ___	plottage	c. land and improvements appraised for same use
4. ___	legal nonconforming use	d. downzoning
5. ___	anticipation	e. temporary highest and best use

3. In analyzing the highest and best use of land as if vacant, what does the appraiser assume?

____

Methods of Site Valuation

There are six commonly recognized methods for appraising the value of land. The **sales comparison method**, considered the most reliable, uses sales of similar vacant parcels to determine the value of the subject land or site. The **land residual** and **ground rent capitalization** methods analyze the income attributable to the land, and calculate the value of the land by capitalizing its income.

In the **subdivision development** method, the appraiser analyzes the costs of subdividing and developing land into building lots, then deducts these costs from the anticipated sales price of the lots to arrive at the value of the raw land. **Allocation** and **extraction** are used to value the land component of improved property, either by applying a ratio of land value to total property value (allocation) or deducting depreciated improvement value from total property value (extraction).

Since the sales comparison method is by far the most reliable, it is the preferred method. Generally, the other methods are used when the sales comparison method is impossible or impractical, due to a lack of adequate comparable sales data or because many properties need to be valued quickly and cheaply (such as for tax assessment purposes). Other methods may also be used to support the value estimate determined by the sales comparison method.

Residential appraisers rely primarily on the sales comparison method for site valuation, as long as adequate comparable sales data are available. Allocation and extraction are also used in residential appraisals, with extraction generally preferred over allocation. Commercial (general) appraisals may use any of the six methods for valuing land or sites.

Fig. 6.2 Methods of Land Valuation

1. Sales comparison method
2. Land residual method
3. Ground rent capitalization method
4. Subdivision development method
5. Allocation method
6. Extraction method

Sales Comparison Method

The sales comparison method relies on an analysis of actual sales in the marketplace to arrive at the value of the subject property. (According to the sales comparison method, the value of the subject land or site is indicated by the prices paid for similar parcels.)

Two factors are of critical importance in the sales comparison approach:

1. The appraiser must be able to identify a sufficient number of comparable sales in the market to serve as value indicators. (The absence of adequate comparable sales is the primary reason for resorting to one of the other methods for land valuation.)
2. The comparable sales prices must be adjusted to account for differences between the comparable sale and the subject property.

Identifying comparable properties and adjusting their sales prices are really two sides of the same coin. The sales that are the most reliable indicators of the subject property's value—those that are the most "comparable"—are the ones that require the fewest and smallest adjustments to account for differences from the subject property. On the other hand, sales that require significant adjustments may not be considered comparable at all.

Sales of Improved Property. In some cases, sales of improved property can be used as comparables for the purpose of site valuation. If a property is purchased for the purpose of demolishing the existing improvements and rebuilding new ones, the sale can serve as an indicator of site value. The appraiser would deduct the cost of demolishing the existing improvements from the sales price of the property, to arrive at an indicator for the value of the site as if vacant. This application of the sales comparison method can be quite useful in built-up areas where sales of actual vacant sites are few or nonexistent.

Elements of Comparison. An **element of comparison** is a factor that may indicate a difference in value between the subject property and a comparable. With respect to land, the most important elements of comparison include location, date of sale (market

Fig. 6.3 Elements of Comparison

1. Location
2. Date of sale
3. Financing and other terms of sale
4. Highest and best use
5. Property rights and restrictions
6. Physical characteristics
7. Degrees of site development

conditions), financing and other terms of sale, highest and best use, property rights and restrictions, physical characteristics of the land, and degree of site development (access, utilities, etc.).

Location. Ideally, comparable sales should be located in the same neighborhood as the subject property. A neighborhood can be defined as an area where market forces operate in a similar way on all properties in the area. If comparable sales from the subject property neighborhood are not available, the appraiser may consider sales from nearby neighborhoods that are subject to similar market influences. However, the appraiser will have to make adjustments for any differences in neighborhood characteristics.

> **Example:** Two neighborhoods in a city are similar in most respects, the major differences being that Neighborhood "A" is located in an area of rolling hills, while Neighborhood "B" is mostly flat in topography. An appraisal of a piece of property in Neighborhood "A" may use a comparable sale from Neighborhood "B," but the sales price of the comparable will have to be adjusted to account for any difference in desirability related to topography.

Date of sale. The date of a comparable sale is significant because market forces (and therefore values) change over time. In general, the greater the difference between the date of the comparable sale and the effective date of the subject property appraisal, the less reliable the comparable is as a value indicator. However, the rate at which market conditions are changing is a significant factor as well. A comparable sale that took place six months prior to the appraisal of the subject property is ordinarily considered fairly reliable, but might require significant adjustment in a rapidly changing market.

> **Example:** A comparable property was sold 3 months prior to the date of the subject appraisal. Since that time, however, market values have declined by an average of 10% due to an announcement of major layoffs by the town's principal employer. Even though the comparable sale is fairly recent, its price will need to be adjusted to reflect the change in market conditions.

Financing and other terms of sale. The definition of market value requires that the subject property be appraised on the basis of a cash (or cash equivalent) transaction. Otherwise, the specific financing terms must be spelled out in the appraisal. Market value also assumes that there are no undue influences or pressures on either the buyer or the seller. If a comparable sale includes financing concessions or other terms that are not typical of the market, their effect must be accounted for by adjusting the comparable's sale price.

> **Example:** A comparable property sold recently on terms which required the seller to buy down the buyer's mortgage interest rate by 1%. In this case, the appraiser must adjust the sales price of the comparable to account for any increase in price that may be attributed to the interest rate buydown.

Highest and best use. Appraisal theory assumes that the market will value property according to its highest and best use. Accordingly, comparable properties should have the same or a similar highest and best use as the subject property. In some cases, it may be possible to make an adjustment for a difference in highest and best use, particularly when the uses are similar, or when the current highest and best use is an interim use.

> **Example:** The highest and best use of the subject property is for a four-family residential use. If comparables with the identical use are not available, the appraiser may be able to use data from properties whose highest and best use is some other level of multi-family residential development (such as two-family), and make an adjustment for the difference.

Property rights and restrictions. The rights that accompany ownership of land have a large effect on value. Comparable sales must be adjusted for any differences in the property rights conveyed in the sale, and also for any differences in property restrictions such as zoning, easements, property tax rates, and private deed restrictions.

Physical characteristics. Differences in physical characteristics may include such items as size, shape, topography, and soil characteristics. When evaluating the effects of size differences between the subject and comparable properties, the appraiser must bear in mind that most land uses are associated with an optimum size. Therefore, size differences between sites with the same highest and best use do not usually result in a proportionate difference in value.

> **Example:** Two lots are each found to have a highest and best use as single-family residential properties with comparable size homes. One lot is 20,000 square feet, while the other is 22,000 square feet. All other factors being equal, the 10% greater size of the second lot is not likely to result in a 10% difference in value, because both lots are capable of supporting the same highest and best use.

Degree of development. The relative quality and availability of site improvements such as roads and utilities may also require adjustment. The availability of such improvements is one of the primary differences between raw land and a site (land that has been prepared for some use). Since the value of most site improvements is normally considered part of the value of the land, it is an important element of comparison in analyzing comparable land sales.

Comparable Sale Price Adjustments. The techniques for determining the amounts of comparable price adjustments are discussed in Chapter 9. Adjustments must be made, or at least considered, for each element of comparison (location, date of sale, etc.) that may affect the value of the subject property. The adjustment is always applied to the price of the comparable, rather than to the subject property. If the comparable is superior in some respect, its price is adjusted downward; if it is inferior to the subject property, its price is adjusted upward.

Example: A comparable lot sold recently for $90,000. Based on market analysis, you determine that the location of the lot makes it $10,000 more valuable than the subject lot. Because the comparable is superior in location, its price is adjusted downward.

$90,000 – $10,000 = $80,000

The indicated value of the subject lot is $80,000.

Depending on the data, adjustments may be in the form of a dollar amount or a percentage of the comparable sales price. When the adjustment is a percentage, the dollar amount of the percentage is calculated and then added to or subtracted from the comparable sale price.

Example: The sales price of a comparable lot is $90,000. Market data suggest that the subject is worth 10% less than the comparable, due to changes in the market since the date of the comparable sale. The amount of the adjustment is 10% of $90,000 (.10 × $90,000), or $9,000. Since the comparable is more valuable, the adjustment is made by subtracting the difference in value from the comparable sales price.

$90,000 – $9,000 = $81,000

The indicated value of subject lot is $81,000.

When calculating percentage adjustments, the order in which the adjustments are calculated can affect the results of the calculation. For this reason, adjustments are normally calculated in a particular order or sequence. The sequence used to calculate the adjustments will depend on the appraiser's analysis of the market, but in general, adjustments for property rights, financing and sale terms, and market conditions are made first, before adjustments for location and physical characteristics.

Example: An appraiser determines that a comparable sales price must be adjusted downward by 10% to account for the value of financing concessions in the comparable sale. In addition, the subject property is worth $5,000 more than the comparable due to superior utility service. The sales price of the comparable is $100,000. In this case, the amount of the adjustment for financing terms will depend on whether it is made before or after the adjustment for utilities. If the adjustment for financing terms is made first, the result is as follows.

$100,000 × 10% (.10) = $10,000 financing adjustment

$100,000 – $10,000 = $90,000 value adjusted for financing

$90,000 + $5,000 = $95,000 value adjusted for financing and utilities

If the adjustment for utilities is made first, the result is a different indicated value for the subject lot.

$100,000 + $5,000 = $105,000 value adjusted for utilities

$105,000 × 10% (.10) = $10,500 financing adjustment

$105,000 – $10,500 = $94,500 value adjusted for financing and utilities

Exercise 2

1. If a comparable property is superior to the subject property in some respect, should its sales price be adjusted upward or downward to account for the difference?

    ____

2. What is the indicated value of the subject property if a comparable property sold for $480,000 on terms that included below market financing worth $15,000?

    ____

3. List five elements of comparison that should be considered when analyzing sales of land or sites.

    1. ______________________________
    2. ______________________________
    3. ______________________________
    4. ______________________________
    5. ______________________________

Allocation Method

Allocation is a method of estimating the land value for an improved property. This method assumes that a certain percentage of a property's value is attributable to its improvements and the remaining percentage is attributable to the land. In other words, it assumes that similar properties will have similar ratios of land value to building value. For example, if a typical building value to land value ratio is 3 to 1 (i.e., buildings are typically worth three times as much as their lots), then 25% of the property's total value is allocated to the land, and 75% to the improvements. If the value of the property as a whole can be established, then determining the value of the land is simply a matter of multiplying by the appropriate percentage.

Example: An appraiser has estimated that a property is worth a total of $600,000, and that the ratio of building value to land value for similar properties is 3:2 (3 to 2). In this case, 60% of the property's value is allocated to the improvements, and 40% is allocated to the land.

$600,000 × 40% (.4) = $240,000 allocated land value

Allocation suffers from two serious drawbacks. First, in order to determine the correct ratio or percentage to apply, it is necessary to have market data: how much have builders and developers paid for land in relation to the value of the improvements that they constructed? But if reliable market data are available, there is no reason to resort to allocation; the sales comparison method is always preferable when adequate comparable sales data exist.

The second problem with allocation is that it is inherently inaccurate. At best, an allocation percentage will represent an average for a particular type of property. Lots of the same size and type (such as residential), with equal value, can be improved with buildings of different sizes, styles, and functionality. The allocation method does not take this variation in the value of improvements into consideration.

Allocation alone is not a very reliable indicator of land or site value. Accordingly, it is used only when more reliable methods are impossible (due to lack of market data) or impractical (as in the case of property tax assessment, where the values of thousands of properties must be allocated between land and improvements). Allocation is also used sometimes to check the validity of the values indicated by other methods of land valuation.

Extraction Method

Extraction is another method that is sometimes used to value land when data for comparable sales of vacant land are not available. In a sense, extraction is the cost approach to value in reverse. In the cost approach, appraisers add the value of the land to the depreciated cost of the improvements to arrive at the total value of the property. With the extraction method, the depreciated cost of improvements is subtracted from the total value of the property to arrive at the value of the land.

The extraction method is applied to comparable sales of improved property when comparable sales of vacant land are not available. By extraction, the appraiser estimates the value of the land component of the comparable sale, and then uses the data to estimate the land value of the subject property. Extraction cannot be considered reliable unless at least one of the following conditions is true:

1. the value of the comparable improvements can be reliably estimated, or
2. the value of the comparable improvements is very small in relation to the total value of the comparable property.

The most common use of extraction is probably for rural properties, where the value of land tends to represent a higher percentage of the total property value.

Example: A comparable rural property sold recently for $650,000. The appraiser estimates that the depreciated value of the comparable's improvements is between $80,000 to $100,000. By extraction, the value of the comparable's land is in the range of $550,000 to $570,000. Because the improvements represent a fairly small portion of the total value, extraction yields a range of land values that varies by less than 5%, even though the appraiser was only able to estimate improvement value to within a range of 25%.

Exercise 3

1. Calculate the indicated land value of a $240,000 property on the basis of the following building value to land value ratios.

   1.5 to 1 ______________________

   3 to 1 ______________________

   4 to 1 ______________________

2. A rural property recently sold for $990,000. If the depreciated value of the improvements is estimated at $100,000 to $150,000, what is the indicated value of the land by extraction?

   ____

Subdivision Development Method

The **subdivision development** or **land development** method is used to value vacant land when the highest and best use of the land is to be used for subdivision and development. In this method, the appraiser estimates the future value of the developed lots, and then subtracts the costs of development to arrive at the current value of the land.

Example: It is estimated that a certain property can be subdivided and developed into ten building lots at a total cost (including developer's profit) of $1,000,000. The lots are projected to sell for $200,000 apiece, or a total of $2,000,000. The value of the undeveloped land is estimated by subtracting the development costs from the anticipated sales of finished lots.

$2,000,000 – $1,000,000 = $1,000,000 land value

Because the process of developing and selling the lots may require several years to complete, the subdivision development method often requires that cash flows (projected future sales and expenses) be discounted to arrive at the present value of the land. Discounting is a means of calculating the present value of an expected future amount. Discounting takes into account the ability of money to earn interest through investment.

Example: If you place \$100 in an investment that earns 10% interest per year, your investment will pay back \$110 after one year (\$100 original investment, plus \$10 interest). The present value of \$100 is equivalent to a future value of \$110.

Discounting calculates the amount of interest that an investment could have earned, and deducts it from the amount of the future payment to arrive at the present value. Discounted present values are typically determined by using a financial calculator.

Exercise 4

1. A site can be subdivided into 100 lots, each of which is expected to sell for \$125,000. Development costs are expected to run \$40,000 per lot, and sales expenses, overhead, and profit are estimated at 25% of sales. Without allowing for discounted cash flows, what is the indicated value of the site?

____

____

Land Residual Method

The **land residual** method is typically used to estimate the land value of commercial income-producing property. It is a form of the income capitalization approach to value. (Income capitalization is discussed in detail in Chapter 10.) Income capitalization measures value as a function of income. The basic formula for income capitalization is:

Income (I) = Value (V) × Capitalization rate (R)

This formula can also be expressed as:

Value (V) = Income (I) ÷ Capitalization rate (R)

Example: A property's net annual income is \$12,000. If market data indicates a capitalization rate of 10%, then the value of the property can be estimated by income capitalization as follows.

V = I ÷ R
V = \$12,000 ÷ .10 (10%)
V = \$120,000 indicated value of property

To apply the land residual technique, the appraiser must be able to reliably determine four critical pieces of data:

1. the value (depreciated cost) of the improvements,
2. the market capitalization rates for land,
3. the market capitalization rates for buildings, and
4. the property's total net operating income.

By multiplying the building capitalization rate by the value of the improvements, the appraiser can determine the amount of the property's income that is attributable to the improvements (I = V × R). This amount is then subtracted from the total net income of the property, to find the amount of income that is attributable to the land. Finally, the land income is converted to a value figure by means of the land capitalization rate.

Example: The highest and best use of a parcel of land is determined to be a retail shopping center. The cost to construct the improvements is estimated at $1.2 million, and the property is projected to generate net annual income of $208,000. Market data indicate capitalization rates for this type of property to be 8% for land and 12% for improvements. The first step is to calculate the income attributable to the improvements, by multiplying the improvement capitalization rate times the value of the improvements.

I = V × R
I = $1,200,000 × .12 (12%)
I = $144,000 income attributable to improvements

Next, the improvement income is subtracted from the total net income to find the income attributable to the land.

$208,000 – $144,000 = $64,000 income attributable to land

Finally, the land income is capitalized by dividing it by the land capitalization rate.

V = I ÷ R
V = $64,000 ÷ .08 (8%)
V = $800,000 indicated land value

Exercise 5

1. A parcel of land is suitable for development as an apartment complex. It is estimated that the cost to build the apartments would be $2,000,000, and that annual net income would amount to $300,000. If capitalization rates for land and buildings of this type are 8% and 11%, respectively, what is the indicated value of the land by the land residual technique?

____

Ground Rent Capitalization Method

Ground rent capitalization is another means of applying the income capitalization approach to estimating the value of land. In a ground lease, the tenant leases the land from the landlord, and constructs a building on the site. Ground leases are usually long-term leases of 50 or more years, to allow the tenant to have the use of the building for the course of its useful life. The rent paid by the tenant of a ground lease is called ground rent.

When property is subject to a ground lease, its value can be estimated by capitalizing the amount of ground rent, using the formula $V = I \div R$. This is often more complicated than it sounds, however, since other factors (such as the amount of time remaining on the lease, any provisions for escalation of rent, etc.) must be taken into account. (Refer to Chapter 10 for a more detailed discussion of capitalization techniques.)

Key Terms

Adjustments—Changes in the sales price of a comparable property to account for differences between the comparable and the subject property in the sales comparison approach to value.

Allocation—A technique for valuing the land portion of improved property by deriving a ratio between the value of land and improvements for similar properties, and then applying this ratio to the total value of the subject property.

Anticipation—A principle of value which holds that value is affected by the expectations of buyers regarding the future benefits to be gained from property ownership, including the utility to be derived from ownership and the potential gain or loss on resale of the property.

Appraisal—The act or process of developing an opinion of value; an opinion of value (USPAP definition). A form of appraisal practice.

Building code—A system of regulations that specifies the allowable designs, materials, and techniques for building construction.

Capitalization rate—The percentage rate used to convert an amount of income to value in direct capitalization.

Consistent use—A rule of appraisal that requires both land and improvements to be valued for the same use.

Discounting—The process of calculating the present value of an expected future amount.

Element of comparison—A factor that may indicate a difference in value between the subject property and a comparable. Common elements of comparison include location, size, number of rooms, etc.

Excess land—Part of a parcel of land that is not necessary to support the highest and best use of the parcel, and that is adaptable for some other use.

Extraction—A technique for valuing land by deducting the depreciated value of the improvements from the total value of the property. Extraction is used most often when the value of the improvements represents a small fraction of total property value.

Ground rent capitalization—A technique for valuing land subject to a ground lease by capitalizing the amount of the ground rent.

Highest and best use—A reasonably probable use that results in the highest value for a property. The use must be legally permitted, physically possible, and economically feasible.

Improvement—An item of personal property that is added to the land by human effort, in such a way as to become part of the real estate. Also called a fixture.

Income—Money or other benefits that are received.

Interim use—A temporary use to which a property is put when its current highest and best use is expected to change in the near future. An interim use anticipates a more productive highest and best use in the foreseeable future.

Land residual technique—A technique for valuing land by capitalizing the portion of a property's income that is attributable to the land.

Legal nonconforming use—A use that would not be permitted under current zoning laws but is allowed to continue because it was permitted at the time the use was started.

Location—An element of comparison that reflects the impact of neighborhood influences on value.

Plottage—The increase in value that results from combining two or more lots under one ownership to allow for a more profitable highest and best use. If two lots are worth more when combined than they are separately, the added value is called the plottage value or plottage increment.

Price—The actual amount paid by a particular buyer to a particular seller in an actual transaction.

Private restrictions—A type of non-financial encumbrance that limits the types of uses that an owner may make of real estate. Private restrictions are most commonly created by developers at the time of subdivision, and are enforced by other property owners, often through a homeowners association. Also called deed restrictions.

Property—Anything that can be owned, including real estate and personal property.

Residential property—Property intended to be used for dwellings.

Residual—Something that is left over. Residual techniques use direct capitalization to determine the value of the left over component when the value of the other component is known (or is estimated by some other technique).

Public restrictions—Government regulations that affect land use.

Sales comparison approach—One of the three approaches to value in the appraisal process. In the sales comparison approach, the value of the subject property is indicated by the adjusted sales prices of similar properties (comparables) in the market.

Seller financing—A loan or other financial arrangement offered by a seller to a buyer in connection with the purchase of property.

Site improvement—An improvement other than a building, such as landscaping or utilities. Improvements "of" the site (such as utility access) are usually valued as part of the land. Improvements "on" the site (such as fences) are valued separately from the land.

Subdivision development method—A technique for valuing vacant land when the highest and best use of the land is for subdivision and development. The appraiser estimates the future value of the developed lots, and then subtracts the costs of development to arrive at the current value of the land. Also called the land development method.

Topography—Characteristics of the land surface.

Value—The monetary relationship between properties and those who buy, sell, or use those properties (USPAP definition). The theoretical worth of something, expressed in terms of something else, usually money.

Zoning—Government regulations that specify the allowable uses for a property. Zoning laws are an exercise of the police power and are designed to enhance property values by preventing incompatible uses.

Summary

I. Market value of a property is always determined by its highest and best use—the use that is reasonably probable and results in the highest value.

A. The highest and best use must be legally permitted, physically possible, economically feasible, and maximally productive.

B. The appraiser eliminates uses that are not likely to occur, then analyzes the remaining possible uses to determine which is the most profitable.

C. Appraisers must consider whether probable uses of the property are likely to change in the future.

1. An interim use is a temporary highest and best use that is likely to be replaced by a more profitable use in the near future.

D. In the case of improved property, the appraiser must consider both the highest and best use of the land as if vacant, and the highest and best use of the property as improved.

1. Highest and best use of land as if vacant assumes that the property is vacant and ready for development.

2. Highest and best use of property as improved takes into account the value contribution of any improvements, and also the cost that would be necessary to remove existing improvements to allow for a change in use.

3. A legal nonconforming use may be the highest and best use of property as improved, but cannot be considered as the highest and best use of the land as if vacant.

4. When the highest and best use of the land as if vacant is different from the highest and best use of the property as improved, the use that results in the highest value is the true highest and best use.

a. The cost of removing existing improvements must be taken into account when comparing the values of existing and potential uses.

E. Both land and improvements must be valued for the same use, which is the highest and best use of the property.

F. Excess land is land that is not needed for the primary highest and best use of a site.

G. Plottage is the combination of two or more parcels of land to create a larger parcel with a more profitable highest and best use. The overall value increase due to combining the parcels is called the plottage value.

II. Land or a site may be valued by several different techniques.

A. The sales comparison method is always the preferred approach to estimating market value, and should always be used when adequate comparable sales data exist.

1. Sales prices of vacant lots that are similar to the subject property indicate the value of the subject property.

2. Adjustments to the sales prices of the comparables must be made to account for differences in location, date of sale, financing and other terms of sale, highest and best use, property rights and restrictions, physical characteristics of the land, and degree of site development.

a. Comparable sales prices are adjusted upward when the subject property is superior to the comparable, and downward when the comparable has more valuable characteristics.

b. The appraiser must consider the sequence of adjustments when using percentage type adjustments.

B. Allocation assumes that there is a typical or standard ratio between the value of land and the value of improvements on the land. The land value is estimated by multiplying the total property value by the percentage allocated to land.

C. Extraction is used when the value of improvements can be reliably estimated, or when the value of the improvements is relatively insignificant in relation to the total property value. The depreciated value of the improvements is subtracted from the total value to find the value of the land.

D. The subdivision development method can be used to estimate the value of land whose highest and best use is for subdivision and development. The costs of development are subtracted from the projected sales of the finished lots, to arrive at the current value of the raw land.

1. Subdivision development analysis often requires discounting of sales and cost figures to take into account the time value of money.

E. In the land residual method, the appraiser calculates the amount of income that is attributable to a property's improvements, and then subtracts it from the total net income of the property. The result is the income that is attributable to the land, which can then be capitalized to determine land value.

F. Ground rent capitalization is another form of capitalizing land income to determine land value. The land income in this case is the rent paid by a long-term tenant under a ground lease.

Chapter Quiz

1. Which of the following is NOT a criterion for highest and best use?
   a. Maximally productive
   b. Economically feasible
   c. Practically consistent
   d. Physically possible

2. When the highest and best use of land as if vacant is different from the highest and best use of the property as improved, the true highest and best use of the property is:
   a. the highest and best use of the land as if vacant
   b. the highest and best use of the property as improved
   c. the use that results in the highest value
   d. None of the above

3. A highest and best use that is expected to change to a more profitable use in the near future is referred to as:
   a. a temporary use
   b. an interim use
   c. a nonconforming use
   d. a substandard use

4. An increase in overall value that results from combining two or more lots to create a parcel with a more profitable highest and best use is known as:
   a. plottage
   b. excess land
   c. economy of scale
   d. extraction

5. An improved residential property is valued at $300,000. If building value to land value ratios are typically 2 to 1, the land value indicated by allocation would be:
   a. $150,000
   b. $100,000
   c. $200,000
   d. $50,000

6. Extraction would be most appropriate to determine the land value of:
   a. a high-rise apartment complex
   b. a shopping center
   c. a 40-acre farm with a mobile home
   d. an older single-family residence

7. A comparable property recently sold for $450,000. Since then, average selling prices have increased by 5%. What is the comparable's adjusted price, taking into account the change in market conditions?
   a. $422,500
   b. $427,500
   c. $472,500
   d. $477,500

8. In which of the following cases would the price of the comparable property be adjusted downward?
   a. The comparable sale involved below market financing
   b. The subject property is in a superior location
   c. Market conditions have improved since the sale of the comparable
   d. None of the above

9. The use of discounting present values is a common procedure in the appraisal of land by:

   a. allocation
   b. sales comparison
   c. extraction
   d. subdivision development analysis

10. The formula used to express the relationship between income and value is:

   a. Income = Value × Capitalization rate
   b. Income = Value ÷ Capitalization rate
   c. Value = Income × Capitalization rate
   d. Value = Capitalization rate ÷ Income

Questions 11 and 12 are based on the following fact situation. Three lots were recently sold in a residential subdivision. Lot #1 is 20,000 square feet with a view, and sold recently for $200,000. Lot #2 is 15,000 square feet with no view, and sold for $135,000. Lot #3 is a 15,000 square foot view lot that sold for $175,000.

11. To account for the lack of a view, how should the price of lot #2 be adjusted?

   a. Upward by $25,000
   b. Upward by $40,000
   c. Downward by $25,000
   d. Downward by $40,000

12. To account for the extra lot size, how should the price of lot #1 be adjusted?

   a. Upward by $25,000
   b. Upward by $40,000
   c. Downward by $25,000
   d. Downward by $40,000

13. With regard to sales of vacant land, all of the following are appropriate elements of comparison, except:

   a. location
   b. financing terms
   c. zoning
   d. No exceptions exist

14. Which of the following is an example of the income approach to value?

   a. Land residual method
   b. Ground rent capitalization
   c. Both of the above
   d. Neither of the above

15. The primary reason for using a technique other than the sales comparison method in order to estimate land value is:

   a. lack of comparable sales data for sales of vacant land
   b. lack of comparable sales data for sales of improved properties
   c. lack of income data for the subject property
   d. to save time and money

Quiz Answers

1. c) A highest and best use must be legally permitted, physically possible, economically feasible, and maximally productive.

2. c) The highest and best use for a property is the use that will result in the highest value.

3. b) The current highest and best use, when the highest and best use is expected to change, is an interim use.

4. a) Plottage is the increase in value that occurs when two or more lots are combined to form a parcel that is more valuable than the sum of the individual parcels.

5. b) The value of the land would be $100,000 ($300,000 ÷ 3 = $100,000).

6. c) Extraction is a method sometimes used when most of the value in a parcel is associated with the land, rather than the building.

7. c) First, determine the amount of the adjustment ($450,000 × .05 = $22,500). Add this to the sales price, since it has gained value over time ($450,000 + $22,500 = $472,500).

8. a) The comparable property price would be adjusted downward if its sale involved below-market financing, since the buyer is likely to pay more than market value for a better financing deal.

9. d) Discounting of present values is used in the subdivision development method.

10. a) The formula for calculating value based on income is Income = Value × Rate.

11. b) The value of the view is $40,000 ($175,000 – $135,000 = $40,000). This should be added to comparable #2, since it is a feature the comparable lacks.

12. c) The value of the extra lot size is $25,000 ($200,000 – $175,000 = $25,000). This is subtracted from the comparable #1's price, since it is a feature the comparable possesses.

13. d) Location, financing terms, and zoning may all be elements of comparison among parcels of vacant land.

14. c) Both the land residual method and ground rent capitalization use the income approach to determine the value of a site.

15. a) A technique other than the sales comparison approach to value would be used primarily where there are no adequate comparable sales data.

Exercise Answers

#1

1. 1. Legally permitted
   2. Physically possible
   3. Economically feasible
   4. Maximally productive
2. 1. e
   2. c
   3. b
   4. d
   5. a
3. That the land is vacant and ready for development to any of its potential uses

#2

1. Downward
2. $465,000
3. Refer to Figure 6.3, which lists the elements of comparison.

#3

1. $96,000, $60,000, $48,000
2. Between $840,000 and $890,000

#4

1. $5,375,000

#5

1. $1,000,000

7 Residential Construction

Overview

Appraisers must have a basic understanding of residential construction for a number of reasons. To describe the building properly in the appraisal report, appraisers need to understand the terminology that is used to describe the various features of a house. Appraisers must also be familiar with the pros and cons of different building materials, techniques, and styles, in order to judge the overall quality of improvements. In addition, they must be able to identify defects or shortcomings in design, workmanship, and materials. And they need to be able to determine whether such defects can be cured and, if so, at what cost.

In this chapter, we will examine the various types and styles of homes, and the features that characterize good home design. We will also discuss the basic materials and techniques that are common in residential construction. After completing this chapter, you should be able to:

- list the five basic types of houses and describe their characteristics,
- understand the impact of architectural style on value,
- describe the factors that influence proper siting of a house on its lot,
- list the three basic activity zones of a house and describe their relationships to each other,
- describe the characteristics that affect functional utility in the various rooms of a house,
- identify the characteristics of various building components that can affect value, and
- understand the technical terminology used to describe residential construction.

Classification of Houses

Houses are generally classified on the basis of four characteristics: the number of units, whether the building is attached or detached, the number of stories, and the architectural style.

The number of **units** refers to the number of separate households that the building is designed to accommodate. Although usage may vary in different areas, the term "house" is most often used to refer to a single-family or two-family residence. If a building has three or more units that share a common access and other common areas, it is usually referred to as an apartment building.

A **detached house** is one that is not connected to any other property. **Attached houses** share one or more walls, called **party walls**, that are jointly owned by the two adjoining properties. Row houses, common in many urban areas, are an example of attached dwellings. Ownership of an attached dwelling often involves a party wall agreement, which assigns responsibility for maintenance and repair of the party wall(s).

Types of Houses

The type of a house refers to the number of stories or levels in the house, and their relationship to each other. Although modern construction methods allow for all sorts of variations, the vast majority of houses fall into five basic "types": one-story, one-and-a-half-story, two-story, split-level, and bi-level (also known as split-entry or raised ranch).

One-Story Houses. A one-story house, often called a **ranch** or **rambler**, has its entire living area on the ground floor. It may or may not have a basement as well. The advantages

Fig. 7.1 Attached and Detached Houses

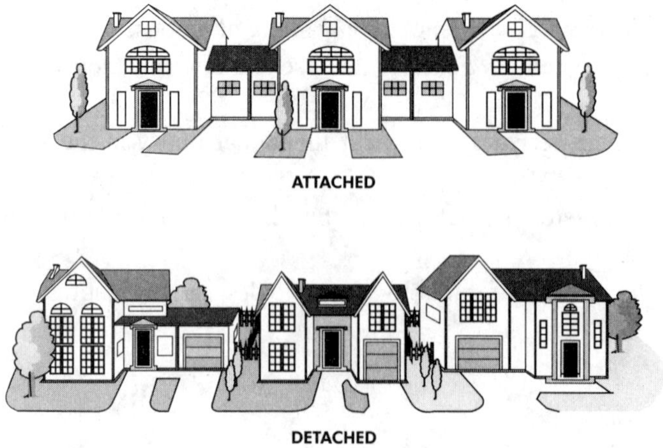

Fig. 7.2 Types of Houses

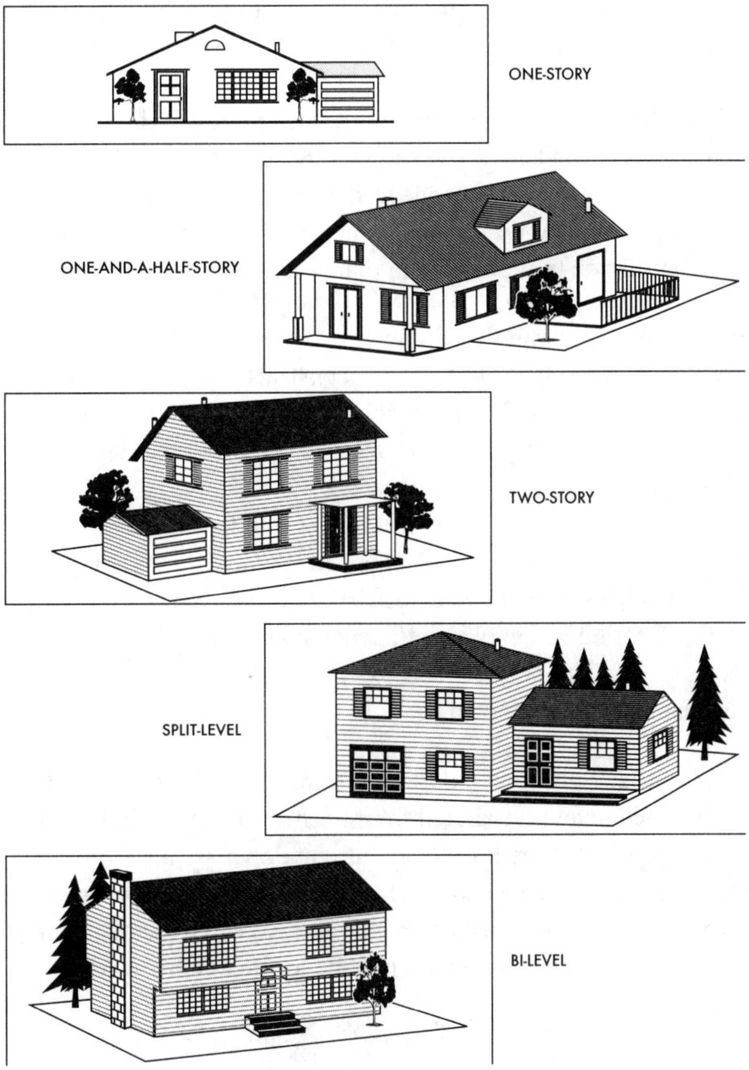

of one-story houses include ease of exterior maintenance, flexibility of floor plan design, and the fact that there are no stairs to climb.

On the downside, this type of house is relatively expensive to build; by comparison, a two-story house with the same exterior dimensions has twice the living area, with essentially no extra cost for roof or foundation. (Roof costs for a one-story house are often minimized by using a low-pitched roof line.) One-story houses also require a greater amount of lot space in relation to the amount of living area, so they may be inappropriate or impractical on small or narrow lots.

One-and-a-Half-Story Houses. Also known as a **Cape Cod**, the one-and-a-half story house has a steeply pitched roof that permits part of the attic area to be used for living space. Roof dormers, which add to the amount of usable upstairs space, are a common feature of this type of house. As in the case of one-story houses, the foundation may or may not include a basement. Construction costs per square foot tend to be lower for one-and-a-half-story houses than for one-story houses.

One-and-a-half-story houses are often built with expandability in mind. Because the ground floor normally has at least one bedroom (and sometimes two), the upstairs level can be left unfinished until the extra space is needed. However, ease of expandability will depend on the quality of the original design and construction, which should allow for adequate access (stairs), ventilation (windows), and plumbing (bathrooms) on the attic level.

Two-Story Houses. Compared to a one-story or one-and-a-half story house, the two-story house is more economical in terms of construction cost per square foot of living space. This design also allows for the most living space on a given size of lot. Bedrooms are normally located on the upper floor, providing a natural separation between the public and private areas of the house.

A concern with all multi-level houses is the design and efficiency of heating and cooling systems. Because heat rises, a poorly designed system will make it difficult to keep the lower level warm in the winter and the upstairs cool in the summer. With a well-designed system, however, heating and cooling efficiency may actually be greater than for single-story houses, since the building has less exterior surface area relative to the amount of interior space being heated or cooled.

Split-Level Houses. Split-level houses have three or four different levels, which are staggered so that each level is separated from the next by half a flight of stairs. Bedrooms and baths are located on the top level. Half a flight down are the main entry, living room, dining room and kitchen. Down another half-story, beneath the bedroom level, is space for a family room, den, or spare bedroom; the garage is often located on this level as well. A fourth level, equivalent to a basement, may be located below the living/dining/kitchen space.

The design of a split-level house lends itself to a sloped lot, where the garage and main entry can both open out at grade level. On a flat site, the main entry will be raised one-half story above the finished grade. Split-level houses have some of the same benefits as two-story houses in terms of construction cost efficiency and natural separation of the various functional areas of the home.

Bi-Level Houses. A bi-level or split-entry house has two main levels, one atop the other, with an entry or foyer located on a level halfway between. The lower level is sunk about halfway below ground, so the entry is even with the grade level. This design is sometimes called a **raised ranch**, since it is essentially a one-story house with a finished basement that has been raised partially out of the ground. The main rooms of the house are all on the upper level, with the lower story used for a family room or rec room, and perhaps a spare bedroom.

Since the lower level of a split-entry house is partly below ground, special care must be taken to provide adequate insulation and moisture-proofing. Another drawback to this design is the lack of a basement or crawl space in which to run pipes and ductwork. Nevertheless, split-entry houses are cost-effective to build, and the finished lower level space is considered part of the gross living area for appraisal purposes in many parts of the country.

Architectural Styles

Since architectural style can have a significant impact on a property's market value, it is important for appraisers to be familiar with the different styles that can be found in the United States today.

Certain architectural styles are named in reference to particular time periods or cultural groups. For example, Victorian-style houses are characterized by steeply pitched roofs and asymmetrical facades. Styles from the Romantic period borrow heavily from the designs of ancient Greece and the Italian Renaissance: Greek-Revival houses have entryway columns and simple moldings, while Italianate houses have low-pitched roofs and rectangular facades.

Architectural styles have also been influenced by local factors such as climate and the availability of different building materials. There are many examples of traditional architectural styles that are adapted to a particular location: Spanish-style houses with thick adobe walls and tile roofs in the southwest desert, Southern Colonial houses with deep shaded porches in the hot, humid south, or Cape Cod houses designed for protection from cold northern winds in New England.

Local traditional styles can still be found in many areas, but location is much less of an influence on architectural style today. Builders are no longer limited to using local materials, since modern transportation systems make different building materials widely available at a reasonable cost. The invention of central heating and cooling, as well as improved insulating materials, has broadened the range of architectural styles that can be adapted to local climates. The adoption of uniform building codes has also encouraged greater uniformity of architectural styles throughout the country.

Compatibility

In terms of value, one type or style of house is not inherently better or worse than any other. What is most important to value is the **compatibility** of the design. Compatibility has several different aspects. To maximize value, the design of a house should be compatible with:

- the designs of other houses in the area,
- the physical and environmental characteristics of the building site,
- the materials used in the construction, and
- the preferences of the local market.

Fig. 7.3 Architectural Styles

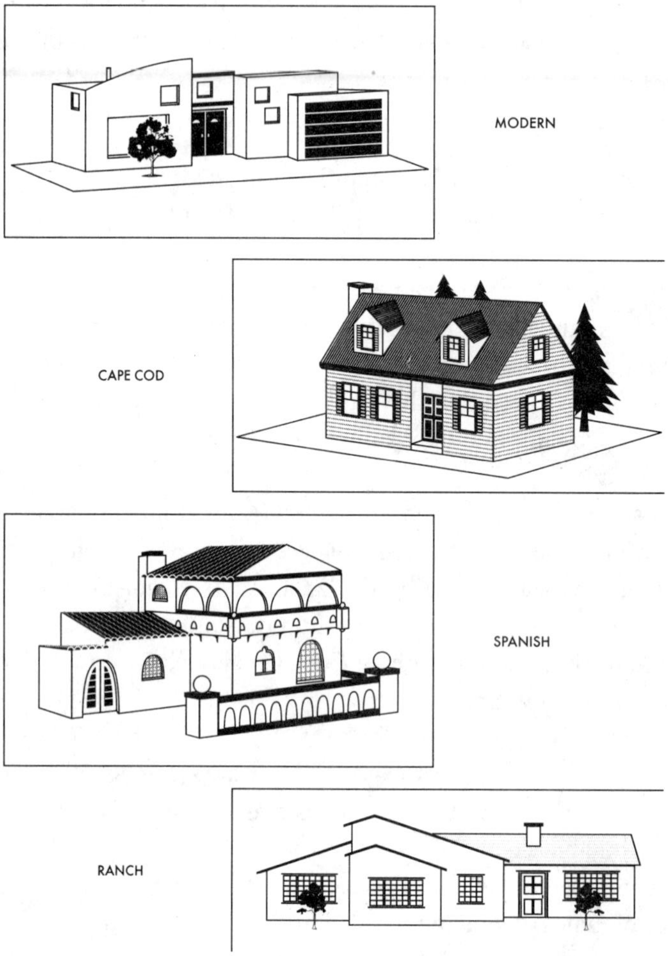

First of all, the design of a house should be compatible with the styles of other houses in the local neighborhood. The market may welcome a limited degree of uniqueness in design, but value will generally suffer if the design contrasts too radically with surrounding houses. Subdivision developers often impose design restrictions on their developments, because they know that compatibility of design will have a positive impact on property values in the subdivision.

Example: A contemporary house located in a neighborhood of other contemporary houses is likely to be viewed positively by the market. But the same house located in a neighborhood of traditional houses might seem out-of-place, and its value could suffer as a result.

Compatibility of design also refers to the suitability of the design for the particular building lot and location. Value is enhanced by a design that takes advantage of physical site characteristics, such as views. The design should also be appropriate for the topography of the site. For example, split-level designs often work well on hilly sites, while colonial-style houses do not. Finally, the design should be appropriate for the local climate. A design that is specifically adapted to a hot desert climate, for example, would be inappropriate in an area with cool, rainy weather.

A building's architectural style is often defined at least in part by the materials used in its construction. Spanish-style houses have clay tile roofs, Tudors use timber framing, and contemporary designs incorporate large areas of glass. A compatible design is one where the materials are appropriate to the style.

Example: A clay tile roof on a Cape Cod house would look ridiculous to most potential home buyers.

The final aspect of design compatibility is perhaps the most important: the design must be compatible with the demands of the market. The popularity of any given design is influenced by the economic and social forces that affect value. As lifestyles and demographics change, so does the demand for different design features in housing. Ultimately, it is the local market that determines what is a "good" design and what is a "bad" one.

Example: A development of new contemporary-style houses is built in an older community with mostly traditional housing. If the market places an emphasis on the historic character of the community, the contemporary houses will be viewed as incompatible, and their value will suffer. On the other hand, if market forces are creating a demand for more modern housing in the community, the contemporary houses may not be incompatible at all, but may simply represent a new trend in community standards.

Exercise 1

1. Match the characteristics on the right with the corresponding type or types of houses on the left. (Each characteristic may be matched with more than one type of house.)

1. ___ one-story	a. expandable living space
2. ___ one-and-a-half-story	b. natural separation of functional areas
3. ___ two-story	c. ease of maintenance
4. ___ split-level	d. finished basement
5. ___ bi-level	e. high unit cost

2. List the two factors that have traditionally influenced local architectural styles.

   a. ______________________________

   b. ______________________________

3. List three factors that have contributed to the increased uniformity of architectural styles.

   a. ______________________________

   b. ______________________________

   c. ______________________________

Elements of House Design

An appraiser must be able to identify the various elements of house design and evaluate any defects in those elements. The elements of house design include siting, interior functional zones, and room characteristics.

Siting

Siting refers to the placement of the house on the building lot. Placement is normally limited to some extent by building code setback requirements, which call for minimum distances between the house and the property's boundaries. Topographic considerations such as slopes or poor soil conditions may also limit where the house may be placed on the lot. Within these limits, however, careful placement of the house on the lot can have a significant impact on value.

There are four basic considerations in designing the placement of a house on its lot: orientation to the sun, orientation to prevailing storm winds, orientation to views, and the division of the lot into functional zones.

Orientation to the sun affects the amount of light and heat that can enter the house. In most areas, a design where the living areas of the house face south is considered optimum. This orientation takes best advantage of natural lighting in the most used areas of the home, and helps maximize solar heat gain in the winter. Excessive summer heat gain can be avoided by using wide roof overhangs, which shade the house in summer when the sun is high in the sky, but allow light and heat to penetrate in the winter when the sun's path is lower. Screening with deciduous trees is another effective way to block the summer sun, but still allow it to shine through in the winter when the trees are bare.

Fig. 7.4 Site Functional Zones

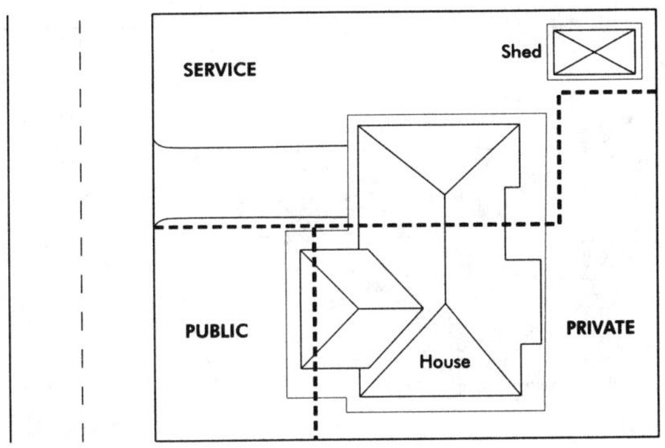

In some areas, **orientation to prevailing storm winds** is an important siting consideration. In areas that are subject to frequent or heavy storms from a particular direction, it is best to minimize the amount of window area that is directly exposed to the winds, in order to cut down on heat loss. Entries should also be sheltered from the direct path of the storms.

An **attractive view** can add significantly to the value of a house. Views should be visible from the most used areas of the house. Even if the site does not have an attractive territorial view, careful landscaping can provide a pleasant view of the lot from the living area.

The last aspect of house siting is the division of the lot into **functional zones**, the so-called public, private, and service zones. The area that can be viewed from the street frontage is the public zone. Areas shielded from the street by the house, or by fencing or other landscaping, constitute the private area. The service area includes access ways (driveway, walkways, etc.) and outdoor storage areas. Good design maximizes the amount of private area available for household activities.

Interior Functional Zones

A well-designed house should provide space for three basic activities: living, working, and sleeping. Ideally, the spaces provided for each of these activities should be separated, so that one activity does not interfere with another. For example, bedrooms should be located where they will not be disturbed by activities in the living and working areas of the house.

Figure 7.5 shows how the spaces for the three different activities can be separated into **zones**. The **living zone** includes the public areas of the house: the living room, dining room, family room, and guest bath. The **working zone** consists of the kitchen and laundry/utility room. Bedrooms and private baths are located in the **sleeping zone**.

The separate activity areas of the house are connected by hallways, stairs, and entryways, which are sometimes referred to as a fourth zone of the house, the **circulation zone**.

Fig. 7.5 House Functional Zones

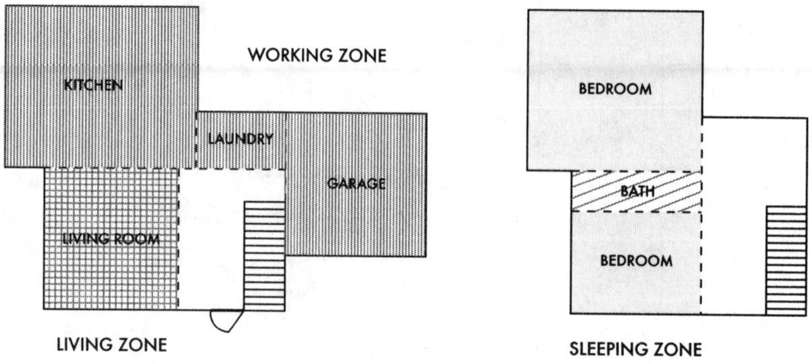

While the three activity zones should be designed to provide separation of the activities, they should also allow for easy circulation between and within zones.

Room Characteristics

Kitchens. The kitchen is commonly the most-used room in the house, so its design and location have a big impact on the functionality of the overall floorplan. The kitchens should be conveniently accessible from both the main entrance and service entrance of the house, and should be located adjacent to the dining room and family room, if these rooms are included in the design. Also, the kitchen should be designed so that it is not necessary to walk through the working area in order to reach other rooms of the house.

A critical aspect of kitchen design is the **work triangle**, which is formed by the sink, refrigerator, and range. The distances between the three points of the work triangle can make the difference between an efficient kitchen design and a poor one. If the distances are too small, the kitchen will be cramped; if they are too great, preparing a meal will seem like a five-mile hike. A distance of four to seven feet between each point of the work triangle is considered optimal.

Kitchen sizes vary considerably. Eighty square feet (8' × 10') is considered a minimum, but kitchens twice that size are common. Larger kitchens often include an eating area or family activity area. The design should include adequate counter and cabinet space, and plenty of electrical outlets for kitchen appliances.

Lighting and ventilation are important considerations in kitchen design. Overhead lights should illuminate all areas of the kitchen, and a vent or fan should be located over the cooking area to allow cooking fumes to escape. Natural lighting is desirable, but the placement of windows can be a problem. The best location for a kitchen window is over the sink. Additional windows are desirable so long as they do not take up space needed for wall cabinets. Windows should never be placed over the cooking area.

Laundry/Utility Rooms. The laundry area is best located where it will be convenient to the sleeping area of the house—off the bedroom hallway, for example. However, location of the laundry area is not as critical as most other rooms of the house, and laundries are often located in the garage or basement. The laundry area should be well ventilated, and it should be located where noise from the appliances will not disturb other activities.

Living Rooms. The living room is the main public room of the house. It should be located near the main (guest) entry, be separated from the sleeping area, and preferably be on the south side of the house. If the house has a dining room, it should be next to the living room. It should not be necessary to cross through the living room in order to reach the kitchen or bedrooms.

The size and shape of the living room should allow for easy arrangement of furniture. The minimum size is about 200 square feet, and rectangular rooms tend to work best for furniture placement.

Family Rooms. In many areas, the family room (also called a recreation room or rec room) has taken over the role of the living room as the main center of entertainment and socializing in the house. As part of the living zone, the family room should be separated from the sleeping zone; however, it is usually considered an advantage if the family room is next to (or near) the kitchen. Since the family room is a center of activity for household members, direct access to the outside is also an asset.

Dining Rooms. Dining rooms may be formal or informal. A formal dining room may be a separate room that is designed for that purpose, or it may be a part of a larger combined

Fig. 7.6 Work Triangle

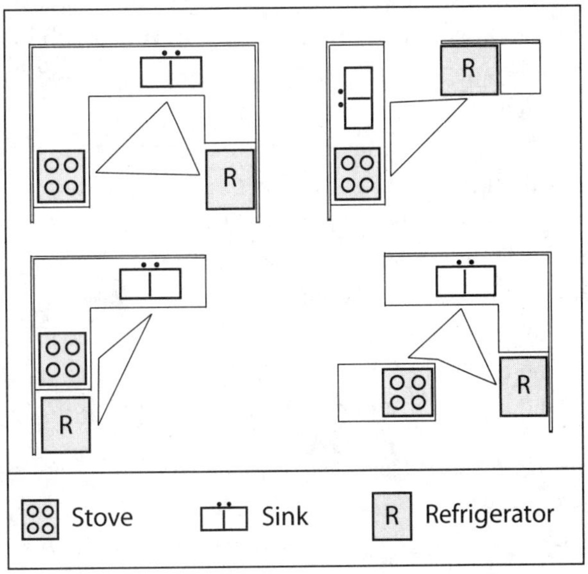

living room/dining room. An informal dining area is usually attached to or part of the kitchen itself, and it may take the form of a nook or alcove. The dining area should be large enough to accommodate a dining table and chairs (including room to get in and out from the table), and it should have easy access to the kitchen so that food does not have to be carried through other areas of the house.

Bedrooms. The number of bedrooms in a house has a major effect on value. Normally, homes with different numbers of bedrooms appeal to different segments of the market—to families of different sizes or lifestyles. The average household size in the market will have a big impact on the desirability of three- or four-bedroom homes, as opposed to two-bedroom homes.

Ideally, bedrooms should all be located in a separate sleeping zone, to provide both privacy and noise insulation. The most common arrangement is to locate the bedrooms on a separate story or wing. Each bedroom should have convenient access to a bathroom, either directly or via a private hallway. Also, it should not be necessary to go through a bedroom to reach another room (other than a private bathroom).

Depending on the room layout, a size of 9' × 10' is the minimum needed to allow for a single bed, or 10' × 12' for a double bed. Whether larger room sizes will add to value depends on local market preferences. Most homes have at least one bedroom that is larger than the others, called the master bedroom. A common trend in many areas is for larger and more luxurious master bedrooms, with walk-in closets and other amenities.

Each bedroom should have its own closet, with a minimum of four feet of closet space per occupant. More generous amounts of closet space are usually desirable, especially if the house lacks other storage areas such as a basement or attic. Locating closets along common walls (either between bedrooms, or between a bedroom and the public area of the house) can help to provide insulation from noise.

Baths. Bathrooms are classified according to the types of fixtures they include. A **full bath** includes a tub, sink, and toilet. In a **three-quarter bath**, the tub is replaced by a stand-up shower. A **half bath** has neither shower nor tub, only a sink and a toilet. A half bath may also be called a powder room, lavatory, or two-thirds bath.

As is the case with bedrooms, the number of bathrooms in a house has a significant impact on value. Although market preferences are the deciding factor, one-and-a-half to two baths is considered a minimum in most areas. There should be at least one full bath in the private area of the house, and a half bath in the public area. In a multi-story house, each story should have its own bathroom.

Bathrooms tend to be built as small as possible; 5' × 7' is the minimum needed for a full bath, and most are no larger than 6' × 8'. The exception is the private master bath, which has grown in size and amenities along with the master bedroom.

Exercise 2

1. Match each room on the left with the corresponding functional zone on the right.

   1. ___ living room
   2. ___ dining room
   3. ___ kitchen
   4. ___ family room
   5. ___ laundry
   6. ___ bedroom
   7. ___ family bath
   8. ___ guest bath

   a. working zone
   b. living zone
   c. sleeping zone

2. Match each room on the left with the room(s) or area(s) on the right that should be located near it.

   1. ___ living room
   2. ___ dining room
   3. ___ kitchen
   4. ___ family room
   5. ___ bedroom

   a. main entry
   b. service entry
   c. living room
   d. dining room
   e. kitchen
   f. family room
   g. bath

3. On the diagram below, identify the public area, private area, and service area of the lot.

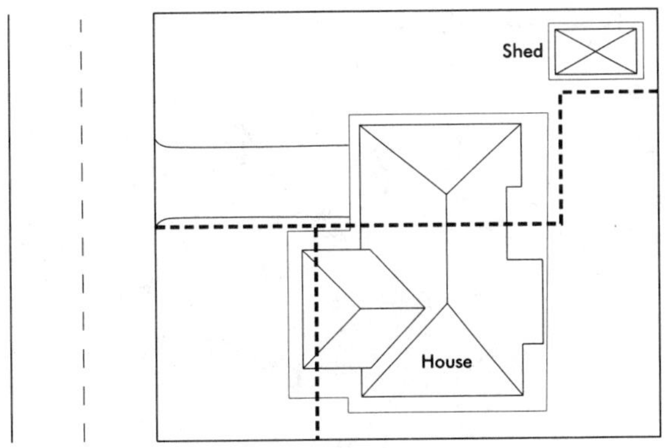

Construction Methods and Materials

Understanding construction methods and materials is important for various reasons: an appraiser must understand construction terminology to properly describe the building in the appraisal report; the appraiser must be familiar with the advantages and disadvantages of different construction methods and materials to judge the quality of the building; and the appraiser must be able to spot construction defects and wear and tear, and know whether they can be repaired and what the cost of the repairs would be.

For simplicity's sake, we will divide the various construction methods and materials used to build house into several categories:

- foundation,
- framing and sheathing,
- exterior finish,
- doors and windows,
- insulation,
- interior finishes,
- plumbing,
- heating, ventilation, and air conditioning, and
- electrical system.

Foundations

The foundation is a horizontal layer of concrete where the house is attached to the ground. Foundations perform two essential functions: they distribute the weight of the house to the subsoil, and they provide a platform to support the superstructure (the part of the house that is above ground level). In some cases, the foundation also provides usable space in the form of a basement.

Types of Foundations. There are three common types of foundations: foundation wall, pier and beam, and monolithic slab. The **monolithic slab** foundation, as the name implies,

Fig. 7.7 Types of Foundations

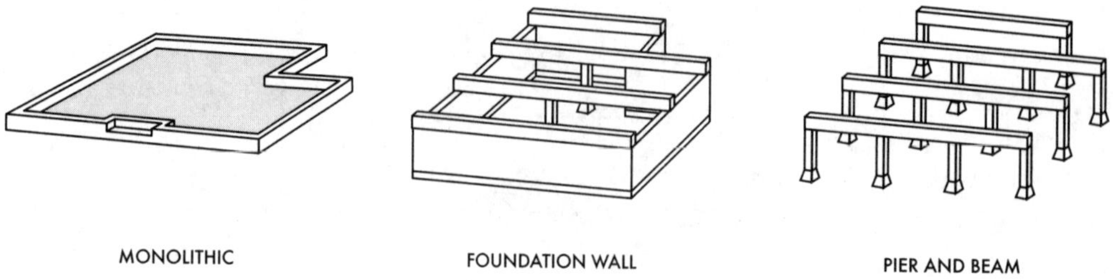

Fig. 7.8 Substructure and Superstructure

consists of a single poured concrete slab that rests directly on the soil. Certain parts of the slab, such as the perimeter, are thicker in order to provide more strength at weight bearing locations. This type of foundation is relatively inexpensive, but it has two significant drawbacks. First, there is no space under the house, so plumbing and ductwork must be routed through walls or ceilings. Secondly, the superstructure is raised only slightly above grade level, so the danger of moisture damage is high unless care is taken to provide proper drainage.

Foundation wall and **pier and beam** foundations are similar in many respects. Each uses **footings**, which are concrete pads or beams that transmit the weight of the structure to the soil. In order to distribute the weight over a larger soil surface area, footings are built wider than the foundation walls or piers that rest on them. The bottom of the footings should always extend below the ground freezing level for the area.

In a pier and beam foundation, each footing is a separate concrete pad that supports a raised block of concrete, or **pier**. The piers in turn support a network of posts and beams that form a platform for the superstructure. The superstructure is raised, so it is not susceptible to moisture damage. The space under the superstructure forms a crawl space.

The pier and beam type of foundation is distinguished from the foundation wall type primarily by the absence of a continuous perimeter foundation wall.

In a foundation wall type of foundation, the perimeter of the house is supported by a solid concrete wall which rests on a continuous footing. (Foundation wall foundations may also use piers, posts, and beams to support the central portion of the superstructure.) The foundation wall should extend far enough above grade (six inches or more) to prevent any problems with moisture damaging the superstructure.

An important benefit of foundation wall construction is that it allows for usable space below the superstructure, in the form of a **basement** or **crawl space** (depending on the depth of the excavation). Access to a basement is typically though a stairwell or an exterior door, while a crawl space is accessed through an opening called a **scuttle**.

Foundation Materials. Reinforced concrete is by far the most common material used for modern foundations. The various components of the foundation are created by digging holes or trenches in the soil (for footings), or by constructing forms (for foundation walls and columns) and then filling them with wet concrete. After the concrete has hardened, the forms (if any) are removed.

Steel rods—called **reinforcing bars**, or **rebar**—are embedded in the concrete to increase its load-bearing capacity and help resist cracking. (The reinforcement is put in place first, then the concrete is poured around it.) In the case of concrete slabs, heavy wire mesh is often used instead of rebar for reinforcement.

Framing and Sheathing

Most modern houses use **frame construction**, in which the walls, floors, ceilings, and roof are constructed as a framework that is then covered by sheathing. The framing is typically built from wooden boards, although metal framing is gaining in popularity as the price of lumber continues to rise.

Framing Lumber. Framing lumber is identified by its size in cross-section, by its moisture content, and by the species of wood from which it is made. In addition, there are various grading systems which rate the structural strength of individual boards. The most common sizes are all multiples of two inches: 2×4, 2×6, 2×8, 4×4, 4×6, etc. (The actual size of a board is usually about ½" smaller than its nominal dimensions, so a 2×4 is really 1½" × 3½".)

The moisture content of lumber is denoted by the terms **dry** or **green**. Dry lumber has a moisture content of 19% or less. Dry lumber is preferred because it is more stable; green lumber tends to shrink, and perhaps warp, as it loses its moisture content. (This shrinkage occurs mainly in cross-section, not lengthwise: boards get thinner, not shorter.)

Structural strength is most important for horizontal load-bearing elements such as beams, headers, and joists. (These terms are defined in the next section.) Building codes commonly specify the acceptable species and grades for these elements, since both wood species and grade affect structural strength.

Framing Terminology. The different elements of a house frame all have special names, depending on their position and use in the frame. In a wall frame, the vertical pieces are called **studs**, and the horizontal pieces to which the studs are attached at top and bottom are called **plates** (top plate on the top, sole plate on the bottom). A horizontal piece across the top of a door or window opening is called a **header**. A horizontal piece at the bottom of a window is a **sill**.

The boards used in floor and ceiling frames are called **joists**. Both floor and wall frames may also have **blocking**: short pieces between the studs or joists to add strength to the

Fig. 7.9 Framing Elements

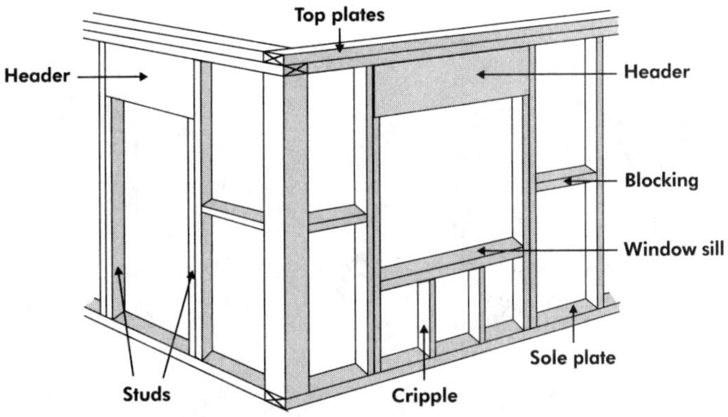

frame and to block the passage of fire through the frame. A larger horizontal piece used to support a floor or ceiling frame is called a **beam**. The vertical pieces that support a beam are called **posts**. Beams and posts are normally four inches thick or larger.

Some other common framing terms are rafter and sill plate. A **rafter** is a sloped piece of the roof frame. A **sill plate** is a horizontal board that is attached to the foundation wall (or slab) by means of anchor bolts; the first floor or wall frame is then attached to the sill plate. Because the sill plate is in contact with the foundation, it must be made of decay-resistant material, such as pressure-treated lumber.

Framing Methods. The most common styles or methods of framing are platform framing, balloon framing, and post and beam framing. In **platform framing**, the floor frame is built first, forming a platform. Then the first floor walls are framed and erected on the platform. If the building is multi-story, the process is repeated, with the second floor frame constructed on top of the first floor walls, and the second floor walls built on the platform of the second floor frame.

In **balloon framing**, the walls are built first, and they are constructed as a single frame that is the full height of the house. For a two-story house, for example, the wall frame is a single unit, two stories high. The floor frames are then attached to wall frames. This method has the advantage of leaving no breaks or irregularities on the exterior of the frame, and eliminating the effects of shrinkage of the floor frame(s). It is used most often when the exterior wall finish will be a rigid material such as stucco or brick.

Post and beam framing uses lumber with larger dimensions than the other framing methods, so the framing members can be spaced farther apart. Framing timbers are often left exposed on the interior for a dramatic effect.

Fig. 7.10 Types of Framing

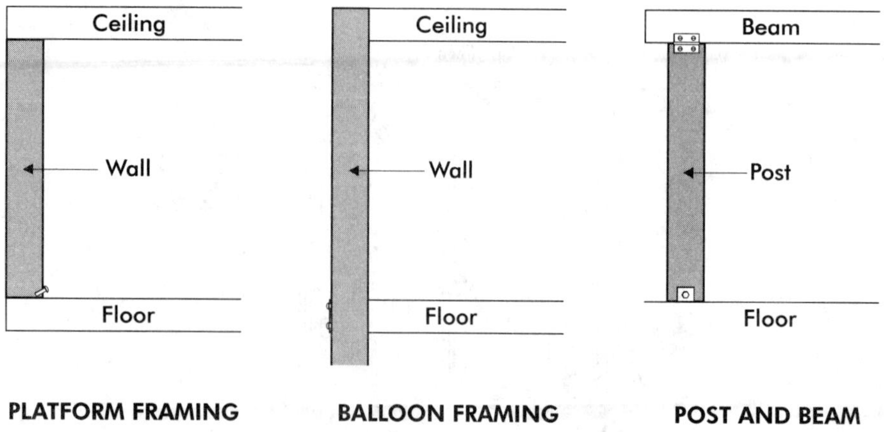

Roof Framing. The style of roof framing can add considerably to the character (and cost) of a house. There are several basic roof framing styles, and endless variations. A **flat** roof uses no rafters. It is easy to build but likely to leak. A **shed** roof consists of a single inclined surface, sloping from one side of the house to the other. **Gable** roofs have two inclined surfaces, which rise from opposite sides of the house and meet at a ridge. ("Gable" is the name for the triangular wall area formed by this type of roof.) In a **hip** roof, inclined roof surfaces rise from every wall of the house. A **mansard** roof is much like two hip roofs, with one placed on top of another. A **gambrel** (or **Dutch**) roof is like a gable roof with two sloped surfaces of different pitches.

A structure that protrudes through a roof surface is called a **dormer**. Dormers are also classified according to their roof styles: shed dormers and gable dormers (sometimes called single dormers) are the most common.

Roofs may be framed with a **joist and rafter** system, or by means of **trusses** (see Figure 7.12). Trusses have the advantage of being able to span wider distances, eliminating the need for interior bearing walls. They are also easier to install than joist and rafter roof framing. Trusses are most effective for simple roof designs.

Sheathing. Sheathing is the "skin" that is attached to the frame of the house. It is a structural component of the house, meaning that one of its functions is to add strength to the structure, and/or to carry a weight load. Sheathing gives the exterior walls added **shear strength**, which is the capacity to resist sideways wracking force. (Most of the shear strength comes from corner bracing.)

Boards may be used for sheathing in some applications, but it is more common (and often required by building codes) to use panels such as plywood, waferboard, gypsum board, etc. The sheathing applied to a floor frame is often referred to as **subflooring**.

Fig. 7.11 Roof Styles

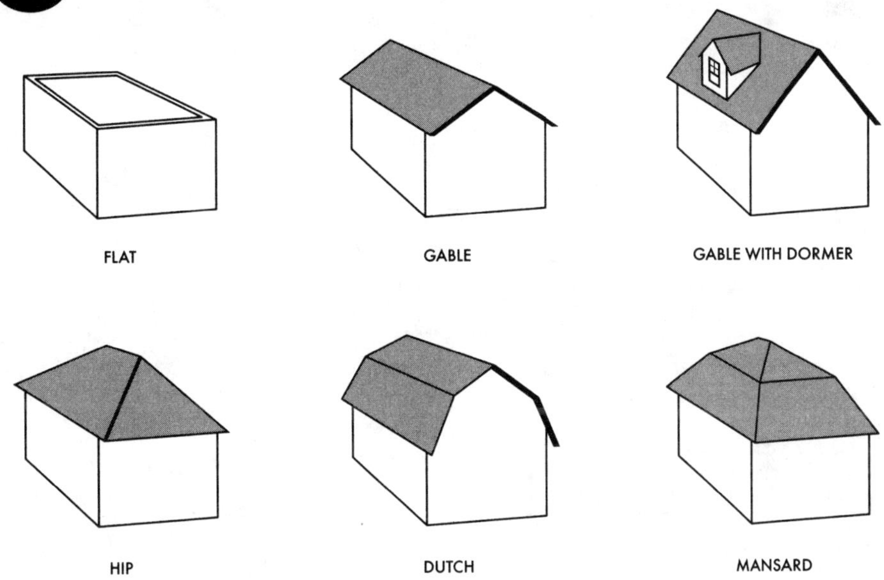

Exterior Finishes

Exterior finishes are the materials applied to the outside of the frame. Their function is to protect the structure from the elements, and to provide visual appeal. The exterior finish is attached to the sheathing, usually with a layer of waterproof paper or felt sandwiched in between. This layer, known as a **vapor barrier**, helps prevent moisture from moving into

Fig. 7.12 Roof Systems

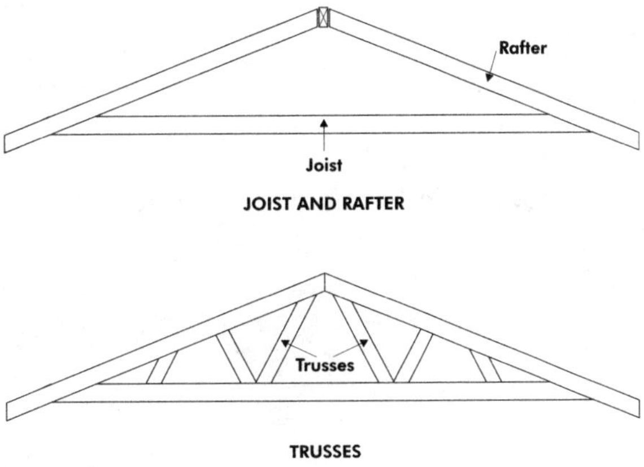

Fig. 7.13 Roof Detailing

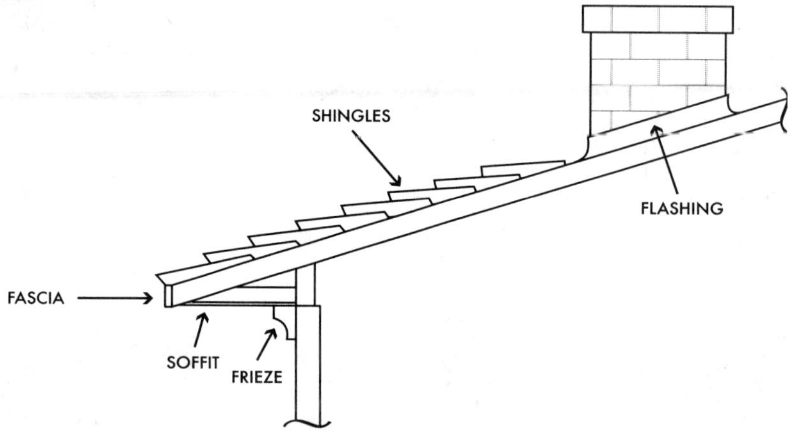

the interior of the home and condensing in the interior living areas. The exterior finish for the walls is called **siding**, and the exterior finish for the roof is called **roofing**.

Many different types of materials are used for siding, including wood, metal, vinyl, stone, brick, and stucco. Roofing materials are also quite varied; they include wood shingles, metal, tiles, slate, or composition roofing (a tar-like material in shingles or rolls). Where there are joints or gaps in the exterior finish materials, metal **flashing** is used to protect the underlying structure.

Exterior finishes also include the detailing of roof overhangs, and the trim applied around doors and windows and on the corners of the house. Roof edges are normally finished off with a **fascia** board that is attached to the ends of the rafters. The eaves of the roof may be left open (exposed), or may be enclosed by covering them with a **soffit**. Soffits are often trimmed out with a **frieze** board where they meet the wall.

Exercise 3

1. On the diagram below, fill in the names of the foundation elements that are indicated.

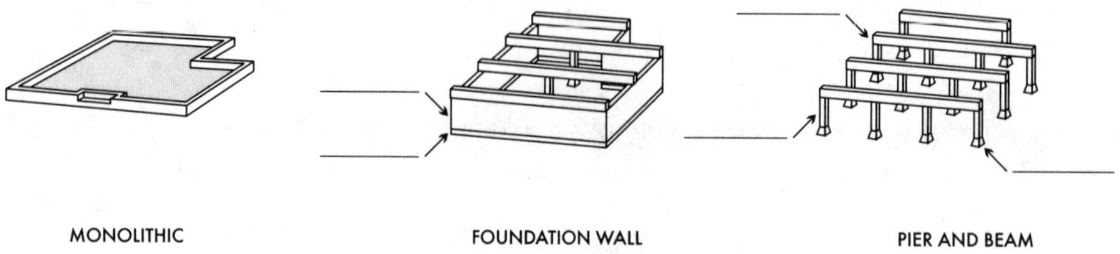

2. On the diagram below, fill in the names of the framing pieces that are indicated.

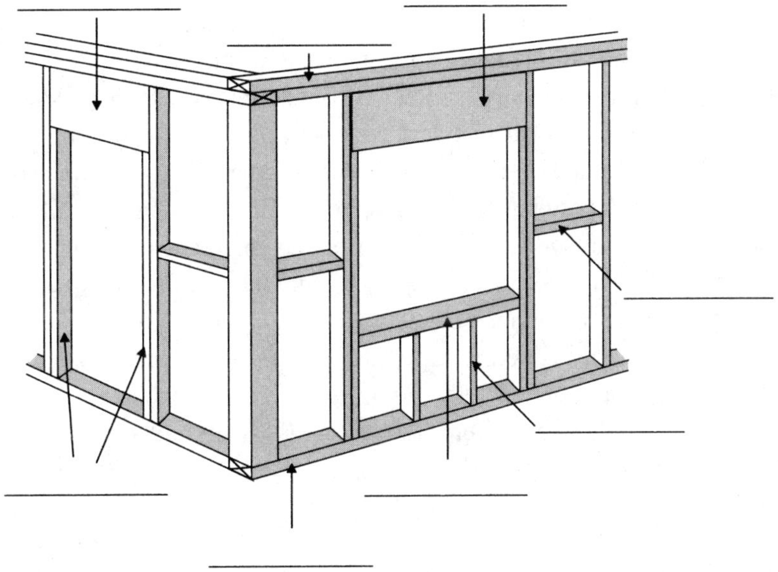

3. Identify the style of roof in each of the diagrams below.

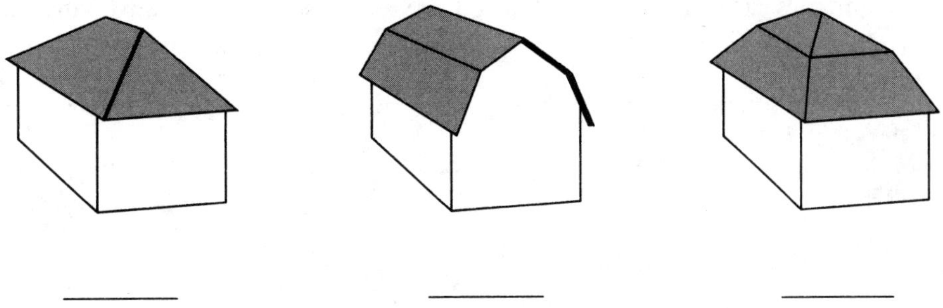

Doors and Windows

The arrangement of the windows and other openings on the walls of the house is called **fenestration**. Doors and windows can have a significant effect on construction cost. Whether the cost of the doors and windows translates into value depends mainly on whether their quality is in line with the quality of the other components of the building. Value is maximized when all aspects of the construction are compatible in quality.

Windows and doors are attached to frames called **jambs**. The horizontal piece across the top of a door or window is a **header**. The bottom of a door frame is called a **threshold**; the bottom of a window frame is a **sill**.

Doors. Doors are classified as either swinging or sliding, and are further classified by their materials and style of construction. Exterior doors are usually made of either wood, steel, or glass, while interior doors are almost always wood. Exterior doors should also be solid (not hollow), and are usually thicker (1¾") than interior doors ($1^3/_8$").

Wood doors come in two basic styles: flush and panel. A **flush** door has a hollow or solid core sandwiched between two thin sheets of veneer; the entire surface is even (flush), with no visible joints. A **panel** door has solid wood **stiles** (vertical pieces) and **rails** (horizontal pieces), that frame one or more thinner panels (made of wood, plywood, or glass). Although panel doors tend to be more expensive and more difficult to maintain than flush doors, their traditional style appeals to many people.

Sliding glass doors (patio doors) are popular in many areas of the country. These doors have one fixed panel, and one or two sliding panels, each consisting of a large sheet of glass in a metal or wooden frame. Tempered safety glass should be used in all glass doors, and insulated (double- or triple-pane) glass is important in areas with high heating and/or cooling costs.

Windows. Windows are classified by three criteria: type of glass, type of frame, and method of opening (if any). The type of glass may be regular or **safety tempered**; building codes require tempered glass for windows that are a certain distance from the floor. Glass may also be **single pane** or **multiple pane**. Multiple pane glass is more efficient in terms of insulating value.

Window frames can be made of vinyl, wood, or metal (usually aluminum). Vinyl frames are the most common type today. They provide excellent insulation and are virtually

Fig. 7.14 Elements of a Door

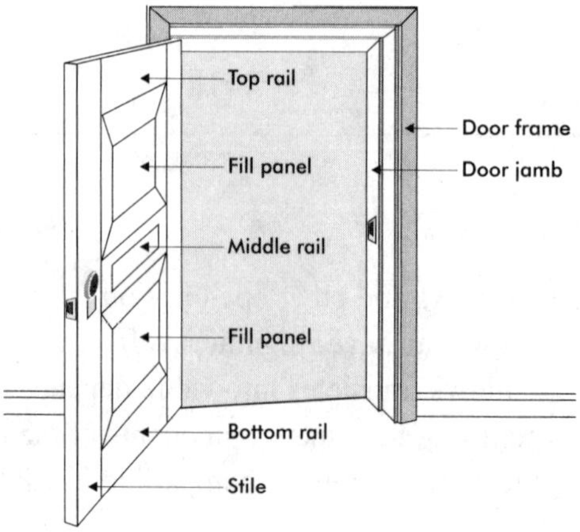

Fig. 7.15 Types of Doors

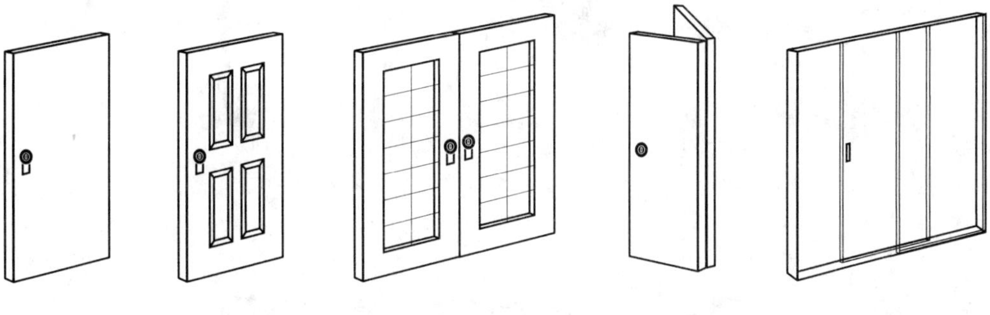

maintenance-free. Wood frames have better insulating value than metal, but are typically more expensive and require more maintenance than vinyl. Wood frames are sometimes coated with vinyl or metal to minimize maintenance requirements and increase energy efficiency.

Some of the more common styles of windows are shown in Figure 7.16. **Horizontal sliders** open by sliding back and forth. **Single-hung** or **double-hung** windows slide up and down. **Casements**, **awnings,** and **hoppers** pivot on one edge: casements at the side, awnings at the top, and hoppers at the bottom. A **jalousie** has a series of glass slats like a venetian blind that may be opened or closed with a crank or handle.

Insulation

As energy costs increase, insulation becomes an increasingly important feature of house construction. The amount of insulation required by building codes for new construction has increased steadily over the past few decades. Older homes are often retrofitted with additional insulation, as well as insulated glass and other energy-saving measures, to make them more attractive to modern energy-conscious home buyers.

Insulation is material that resists the transfer of heat. Its effectiveness is measured in terms of **R-value** (resistance to heat transfer). The higher the R-value, the better the insulation. Since most heat transfer tends to occur in the roof of a house, insulation R-value requirements for roofs are usually higher than those for walls and floors.

Common insulating materials include fiberglass, rock wool, and rigid foam. **Fiberglass** insulation comes in rolls or batts that are attached between studs, joists, or rafters. The fiberglass may be lined with building paper or foil to serve as a moisture barrier.

Rock wool is available either as loose material or in batts. Loose rock wool is sometimes called blown-in insulation, because it is installed by blowing it through a large hose.

Fig. 7.16 Types of Windows

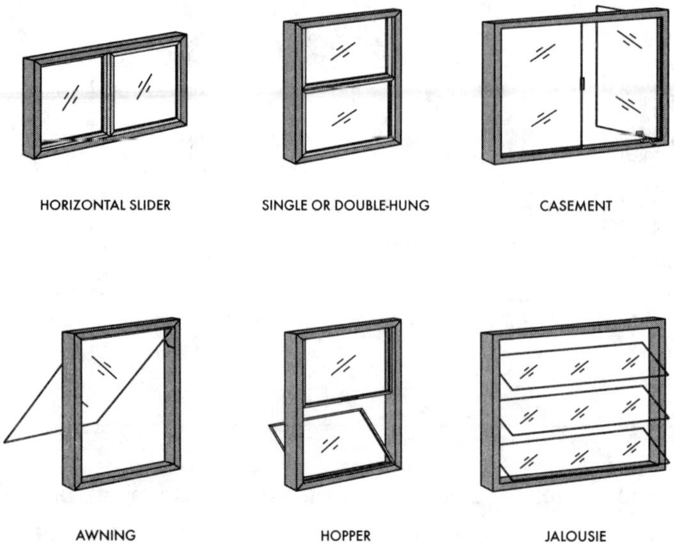

Blown-in insulation can be used to fill the space between studs in existing walls, but it will tend to settle over time, leaving the upper portion of the wall uninsulated.

Rigid foam insulation comes in large sheets similar to plywood. This type of insulation is useful when the framing is not thick enough to accommodate insulation of the desired R-value, since it can be applied on top of (instead of between) the framing studs.

Insulation can help save energy costs in other areas besides walls, floors, and ceilings. Water heaters normally have built-in insulation, which can be enhanced by wrapping the heater in an insulating blanket designed for that purpose. In addition, any hot water pipes or heating or cooling ducts that are not located within an insulated area of the house can be wrapped with insulation to reduce energy consumption and cost.

Interior Finishes

Interior finishes include floor and wall coverings, cabinets and countertops, and interior trim. Interior finishes should be comparable in quality to the other components of the house.

Wall Finishes. Lath and plaster, once the most common type of wall and ceiling finish, has been replaced in modern construction by **drywall** (also known as wallboard or plasterboard). Drywall comes in sheets (usually 4' × 8') of varying thicknesses: ½" is standard for most interior walls, but fire codes often require 5/8" in areas such as attached garages. A special type of water-resistant drywall is used for bathrooms and other areas of heavy moisture.

Drywall is nailed or screwed to the studs, and the joints and corners are then sealed with a paper or plastic tape embedded in plaster-like **joint compound**. Outside corners are protected by applying a strip of angled metal, which is also covered with joint compound. The process of sealing the joints in drywall is called **taping**.

Joint compound is also used to cover the nails and screws used to attach the drywall, and to smooth any irregularities in the wall or ceiling surface. This is known as **floating**, and it produces a **smooth-wall** finish. **Texturing** may be applied over the floated finish, either by spraying or rolling. Textured walls are normally finished with paint, while smooth walls may be painted, wall-papered, tiled, or covered with wood or synthetic paneling.

Floor Finishes. Floor finishes are applied over the subflooring of wood, plywood, or concrete. Either hardwood or carpet is an appropriate floor finish for most rooms in the house. Areas subject to drips and spills (such as kitchens, baths, and utility rooms) are often floored with ceramic or vinyl tile or rolled linoleum. Tile or stone is often used for flooring in entryways.

Cabinets and Countertops. Most modern cabinet work is prefabricated in a shop or mill and then installed on the building site. Cabinets may be solid wood or metal, or made of composite material covered with a wood or plastic veneer. Cabinets must be set true and level and securely fastened in place in order to operate properly.

Plastic laminate and ceramic tile are the most commonly used materials for countertops in kitchens and baths. Counters should have a backsplash at least four inches high, and all joints should be well sealed to prevent moisture damage.

Interior Trim. Interior trim consists of the **moldings** used around doors and windows, at the top and base of walls, and in various other areas. Moldings are usually made of wood and may be painted or stained. They come in hundreds of shapes and sizes and are often used for decorative effect. The most commonly found moldings are **casings** (used around openings) and **baseboards** (used at the base of walls).

Plumbing

The plumbing system in a house consists of hot and cold water supply lines, drain lines, plumbing fixtures, and appliances such as water heaters and water softeners.

Supply lines carry water under pressure from a well or water system. There are two sets of supply lines, one for cold water and one for hot. Galvanized steel pipe was once the standard for water supply lines, but the majority of modern construction uses copper or plastic water pipes.

Drain lines are not pressurized; water and waste flows through the drain lines under the force of gravity. For this reason, drain lines must be sloped to allow the water to drain properly. Where the drain lines connect to a fixture, a U-shaped bend is used to prevent gases from escaping into the house. The drain lines for each fixture are also connected to a system of vent pipes. Most drain lines are made from either cast iron or plastic.

The hot water supply for a house is provided by a **water heater**, which is a tank of water that is kept heated to a pre-set temperature by electricity or gas. The capacity of the water heater should be adequate to meet the needs of the occupants of the house; 40- to 50-gallon water heaters are typical for an average residence. Water heaters eventually corrode and leak, so they must be replaced periodically.

A **water softener** is a device designed to neutralize the mineral salts in water. Water with excessive mineral salts is called hard water; it can cause damage to plumbing systems by causing a mineral buildup that constricts water flow in the supply lines, and it does not dissolve soap very well. By filtering the water supply through a water softener, these problems can be eliminated.

Heating, Ventilation, and Air Conditioning

The heating, ventilation, and air conditioning system in a house is sometimes referred to the HVAC system. Most HVAC systems are central, forced-air systems. This type of system has a central heating or cooling unit connected to a series of **ducts**. Hot or cold air is blown through the ducts and out through **registers** in the different rooms of the house. Return air registers and ducts then draw the air back to the central unit, where it is reheated or recooled.

Heating and cooling systems are designed by mechanical engineers, who calculate the capacity of the heating or cooling equipment necessary to serve the house, and also design the layout and sizes of the duct work. An improperly designed system can result in some areas of the house getting too much heat or air conditioning, or in a system that is not powerful enough to provide adequate heating or cooling throughout the house.

Furnaces and air conditioners are rated according to their capacity in British Thermal Units (**BTUs**). Air conditioners are also sometimes rated in tons (one ton = 12,000 BTUs).

Electrical Systems

The electrical system in a house consists of a main panel (**breaker box** or **fuse box**), wiring, switches, lights, and outlets. The power supply is connected to the house at the main panel. Standard residential power is either 110 volts or 220 volts. 110V power is adequate for lighting and small appliances, but 220V is required for electric heating or larger electric appliances such as ranges or clothes dryers.

The breaker box or fuse box is rated as to how much current (amperage) it can distribute. Service of 100 amps is generally the minimum for a residence. A larger capacity panel is required to handle electric heating or power-hungry appliances.

At the main panel, the current is divided into circuits, each controlled by its own circuit breaker or fuse. Each major electrical appliance will normally have its own separate circuit, while several lights or outlets can be grouped together on a single circuit. The wiring of each circuit must be rated for the amount of current that the circuit breaker or fuse can carry. Too much current can cause the wiring to overheat, posing a severe fire danger.

Exercise 4

1. Identify the type of window in each of the drawings below.

2. On the diagram below, fill in the names of the door elements that are indicated.

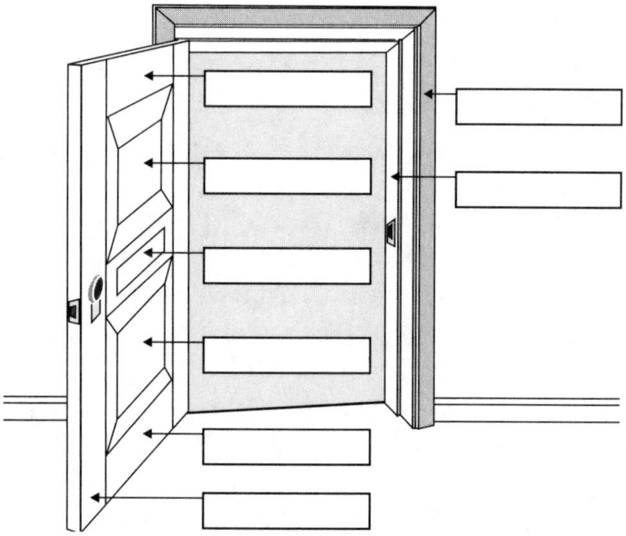

3. List three types of insulation that are commonly used in residential construction.

   a. ______________________________

   b. ______________________________

   c. ______________________________

4. Match each term on the left with the corresponding term on the right.

1. ___ furnace		a. amperage
2. ___ insulation		b. taping
3. ___ drain pipe		c. R-value
4. ___ water supply pipe		d. BTU
5. ___ circuit breaker		e. copper
6. ___ drywall		f. cast iron

Key Terms

Access—The means by which a property can be entered from a public street.

Architectural style—A recognizable category of building design.

Attached house—A house that shares one or more party walls with one or more other houses.

Attic—The area of a house between the ceiling and the rafters.

Balloon framing—A type of frame construction in which the floor frames are attached to the interior of continuous wall frames.

Baseboard—A horizontal piece of interior trim attached to the base of the walls.

Basement—A below-ground level of a house.

Bathroom—A room that has a sink, toilet, and bathtub and/or shower. A room with a sink and toilet only is called a half bath or powder room.

Beam—A large horizontal framing member used to support a floor or ceiling frame.

Bearing wall—A wall that supports the weight of some other portion of the structure, such as an upper floor or the roof.

Blocking—Short boards placed between and perpendicular to studs or joists, to provide rigidity to the frame and impede the spread of fire.

Board foot—A unit of measurement for lumber, equivalent to 144 cubic inches.

British thermal unit (BTU)—A unit of measurement for heat. HVAC equipment is commonly rated according to the number of BTUs it can produce.

Built up roof—A type of roofing consisting of alternating layers of asphalt and roofing felt.

Casing—A type of molding used around door and window openings.

Chimney—A metal or masonry structure designed to vent smoke and fumes from a fireplace.

Circulation zone—One of the four functional zones of a house; the zone that connects the separate activity areas via hallways, stairs, and entryways.

Crawl space—The space between the ground and the bottom floor of a house.

Detached house—A house that is not connected to any other property.

Dormer—A structure that projects through the roof of a building to create additional usable space on the upper floor.

Downspout—A pipe or channel used to discharge water from a gutter to the ground.

Drywall—Interior wall finish material that does not require mixing with water.

Duct—A metal passageway used to circulate or vent air in a building.

Eave—The part of a roof that overhangs the exterior walls of the building.

Flashing—Pieces of metal used to seal joints in the exterior surfaces of a building.

Flush door—A door consisting of a hollow or solid core sandwiched between two sheets of veneer.

Footing—A concrete pad or beam used to transmit the weight of a structure to the soil.

Forced-air system—A type of heating and/or cooling system that uses a fan and ducts to distribute air through the building.

Foundation wall—A part of the substructure consisting of a concrete wall that is supported by a footing.

Framing—The structural components of the superstructure, including joists, studs, headers, rafters, etc.

Frieze—An exterior trim board attached to the top of the wall below the soffit.

Gable—The triangular wall area formed by two opposing surfaces of a gable roof.

Gable roof—A style of roof with two roof surfaces rising from opposite sides of the building.

Heating, ventilating, and air conditioning (HVAC)—The equipment used to control air quality in a building.

Hip roof—A style of roof in which a separate roof surface rises from each exterior wall of the building.

Jamb—The frame in which a door or window is mounted.

Joist—The primary horizontal structural element of a floor or ceiling frame.

Living zone—One of the functional zones of a house; the zone that includes the public areas of the house: the living room, dining room, family room, and guest bathroom.

Lot—A parcel of land.

Molding—Finish material, relatively thin in cross section, used for decorative effect or to conceal joints.

Monolithic slab—A type of foundation consisting of a concrete slab resting directly on the soil.

Panel door—A door constructed of solid wood stiles and rails that frame one or more thinner panels.

Party wall—A wall that is shared by two separate properties. Houses that share party walls are referred to as attached houses.

Pier and beam—A type of foundation where each footing is a separate concrete pad that supports a raised block of concrete, or pier. The piers in turn support a network of posts and beams that form a platform for the superstructure, with the space underneath forming a crawl space.

Pitch—The angle of elevation of a roof surface, usually expressed as the number of feet of vertical rise per 12 feet of horizontal run.

Plate—A horizontal board at the top or bottom of a wall frame.

Platform framing—A system of wood-frame construction in which floor and wall frames are alternated.

Plumbing—The system of pipes and fixtures that distributes water and drains away waste in a building.

Post—A vertical structural member used to support a beam.

Post and beam framing—A system of wood-frame construction using relatively large framing members, often with exposed beams and rafters.

Private zone—The part of a residential lot that is shielded from the street.

Public zone—The part of a residential lot that can be viewed from the street frontage.

R-value—A measure of resistance to heat transfer. Insulation is rated according to its R-value.

Rafter—Any of the parallel structural members of a roof frame.

Register—An opening at the end of a duct through which warm or cold air enters a room; often controlled by a damper.

Reinforced concrete—Concrete that has been strengthened by means of embedded reinforcing steel bars (rebar) or wire mesh.

Scuttle—An opening in the floor or ceiling, giving access to a crawl space or attic.

Septic system—An on-site sewage disposal system with a tank for separation of solids and a system of pipes for distribution of liquids to a porous drain field.

Service zone—The access ways and outdoor storage areas of a residential lot.

Sewer—A underground system of pipes or channels for disposal of runoff and/or sanitary waste.

Sheathing—Structural material applied to the frame of a building to provide support for the finish materials.

Shed roof—A type of roof with a single sloped roof surface.

Slab—A horizontal concrete surface.

Sleeping zone—One of the functional zones of a house; the zone that includes the bedrooms and private bathrooms.

Sill—The bottom piece of a door or window frame.

Sill plate—A board attached to the top of a foundation wall.

Siting—The location and placement of a building on its lot.

Story—An above-ground level of a house. If a level does not have full-height walls, it is often referred to as a half-story.

Stud—Any of the vertical structural members of a wall frame.

Subflooring—Structural sheathing attached to a floor frame as a base for the finish flooring.

Substructure—The part of a building that is below ground level and supports the superstructure. Substructure includes footings, foundation walls, piers, and other elements of the foundation.

Superstructure—The part of a building that is above ground and supported by the foundation.

Threshold—A door sill.

Topography—The characteristics of the surface of the land.

Truss—A multi-piece structural framing assembly designed to span a distance between two points.

Unit—A portion of a multi-family dwelling designed to accommodate one household.

Vapor barrier—A layer of waterproof material that is placed inside exterior walls to prevent moisture from moving into the interior living areas.

Work triangle—A critical aspect of kitchen design, formed by the distances between the sink, refrigerator, and range.

Summary

I. Classification of Houses

A. A house is a single-family or two-family residence.

B. Houses may be attached or detached.

1. Attached houses share party walls.

C. Types of Houses

1. One-story, ranch or rambler: flexible design, easy maintenance, no stairs, relatively expensive.
2. One-and-a-half-story: expandable living area, lower construction costs.
3. Two-story: most cost-effective, natural separation of living zones, potential heating/cooling problems.
4. Split-level: three or four levels offset by a half story, benefits similar to two-story houses, adaptable to sloped sites.
5. Bi-level or raised ranch: similar to a one-story house with a raised basement.

D. Architectural Styles

1. Regional architectural styles were traditionally influenced by climate and local building materials.
2. Contemporary styles are more uniform, due to central heating, modern transportation, new construction techniques, and uniform building codes.
3. The effect of style on value depends on its compatibility. The most important aspect of compatibility is the demands of the market.

II. Elements of House Design

A. Siting is the location of the house on its lot.

1. Living areas should face south if possible.
2. Windows and doors should be protected from prevailing storm winds.
3. Living areas should face the view.
4. Siting should maximize the private area of the lot, and minimize public and service areas.

B. Houses have three functional zones, which should be properly located in relation to one another.

1. The public living zone includes the living room, dining room, family or rec room, and guest bathroom.

2. The working zone includes the kitchen and laundry area.
3. The private sleeping zone includes bedrooms and non-guest bathrooms.

C. Room Characteristics

1. Kitchens should have convenient access to the main and service entrances, and be located next to any dining or family rooms. The sink, range, and refrigerator form the work triangle; they should each be four to seven feet apart. Lighting and ventilation are critical.
2. Laundries require adequate ventilation, and should be located where their noise will not be a disturbance.
3. Living rooms should be near the main entry, next to any dining room, and separated from the sleeping area. Rectangular layouts are best for furniture arranging.
4. The family room should be near the kitchen and away from the sleeping zone. Direct outside access is preferable.
5. The dining area should have direct access to the kitchen. A dining area may be a separate room for formal dining and/or an area in the living room (formal) or kitchen (informal).
6. Bedrooms should be located away from the living and working areas of the house. Ample closet space is important, as is access to bathrooms. The number of bedrooms has a greater impact on value than their size. There is a trend toward larger master bedrooms.
7. Bathrooms can be half (sink and toilet), three-quarter (sink, toilet, and shower) or full (sink, toilet, and tub) bathrooms. The number of bathrooms is an important value indicator. The sleeping area should have at least one full bath, and the public area a half bath. Two-story houses should have a bathroom on each story.

III. Construction Methods and Materials

A. Foundations provide support for the superstructure.

1. A monolithic slab is a single poured concrete slab. It has no crawl space or basement.
2. Pier and beam foundations support the house on a framework of beams, which rests on raised piers set in concrete footings.
3. A foundation wall foundation is similar to a pier and beam foundation, but has a continuous concrete wall around the perimeter, resting on a continuous perimeter footing. The space enclosed by the foundation walls can be a crawl space or basement.
4. Most foundations are made from reinforced concrete.

B. Framing and sheathing provide the structural strength of the superstructure.

1. Framing lumber is identified by its cross-section dimensions, moisture content, wood species, and grade.

2. Pieces of the frame are identified by their position and use; they include studs, plates (top plate, sole plate, sill plate), headers, sills, joists, blocking, posts, beams, and rafters.

3. The three common framing systems are platform framing, balloon framing and post and beam framing.

4. Roof frames have many different styles, most of them variations or combinations of the shed, gable, and hip roof styles. The roof frame may be constructed of joists and rafters, or of roof trusses. Projecting dormers add usable space to the upper floor of the house.

5. The exterior of the wall and roof frames and the top of the floor frames are covered with sheathing, which gives more structural strength and supports the finish materials.

C. Exterior finishes provide weather protection and visual appeal. Siding and roofing are available in a wide range of materials. Exterior finishes may include flashing, soffits, fascias, and frieze boards.

D. Doors and windows are set in frames called jambs, with a header at the top and a threshold or sill at the bottom.

1. Doors are identified by thickness ($1^3/_8$", $1^3/_4$"), material (wood, steel, glass), type of construction (hollow/solid, flush/panel), and method of opening (swinging, sliding).

2. Windows are classified by type of glass (regular/tempered, single/multiple pane), frame material (wood, aluminum, vinyl), and method of opening (fixed, slider, casement, single/double hung, awning, hopper, jalousie).

E. Insulation is rated for R-value: its resistance to heat transfer. It is commonly available in fiberglass (rolls or batts), rock wool (batts or blown-in), and rigid foam (panels).

F. Interior Finishes

1. Most walls are constructed of drywall, which is taped and floated with joint compound, and may be textured, painted, papered, or paneled.

2. Floor finishes include wood, carpet, ceramic or vinyl tile, linoleum, and other materials.

3. Cabinets, countertops, and trim complete the interior finish.

G. Plumbing systems include pressurized hot and cold water supply pipes, sloping drain pipes with vents, the hot water heater, and sometimes a water softener to remove mineral salts from the water supply.

H. Modern heating and cooling systems usually have a central furnace or air conditioner that supplies hot or cold air through a system of ducts and registers. The systems are rated for capacity in BTUs or tons (one ton equals 12,000 BTUs).

I. Electrical service of 110 or 220 volts is connected to a main panel (fuse box or breaker box) that routes the power into circuits to serve appliances, lights, and outlets. The amount of current (amperage) available to a circuit is limited by the fuse or circuit breaker to prevent fire danger.

Chapter Quiz

1. A split-entry house is also known as a:
   a. split-level
   b. rambler
   c. raised ranch
   d. Cape Cod

2. Value is enhanced when the architectural style of a house is compatible with:
   a. the style of other houses in the area
   b. the materials used in the construction
   c. the characteristics of the building site
   d. All of the above

3. A house with a party wall is considered:
   a. attached
   b. detached
   c. multi-family
   d. manufactured

4. It is generally preferable for a house to be sited so that the living area faces:
   a. north
   b. south
   c. east
   d. west

5. Proper siting of a house on its lot should maximize the part of the lot devoted to:
   a. the private zone
   b. the public zone
   c. the service zone
   d. None of the above

6. The interior working zone of a house includes:
   a. the kitchen
   b. the den
   c. the laundry
   d. Both a) and c)

7. In which room would direct outside access be considered most desirable?
   a. Living room
   b. Dining room
   c. Family room
   d. Bedroom

8. Kitchens should be located with convenient access to:
   a. the service entrance
   b. the main entrance
   c. the dining room
   d. All of the above

9. The vertical pieces in a wall frame are called:
   a. studs
   b. plates
   c. headers
   d. joists

10. Which of the following would not be found in a wall frame?
    a. Stud
    b. Plate
    c. Header
    d. Joist

11. R-value is a measure of:
    a. electric current
    b. heating capacity
    c. insulation efficiency
    d. wall thickness

12. A window that opens by pivoting on one side is called a:
    a. single-hung window
    b. casement window
    c. hopper window
    d. jalousie

13. The terms stile and rail refer to parts of a:

    a. door
    b. window
    c. staircase
    d. soffit

14. The heating capacity of a furnace is measured in:

    a. volts
    b. amps
    c. BTUs
    d. kilos

15. Dry lumber is considered superior to green lumber for framing because:

    a. it is cheaper
    b. it is easier to work with
    c. it is less likely to shrink
    d. it looks better

Quiz Answers

1. c) A split-entry house is also known as a raised ranch or bi-level house.
2. d) Architectural style should be compatible with the surrounding properties, the materials used, and the nature of the site.
3. a) An attached house shares a common wall with the neighboring house. This type of wall is called a party wall.
4. b) The living area of a house should face south, so that it receives more sunlight.
5. a) A house should be placed on the site in a manner that maximizes the private area.
6. d) The interior working zone of a house includes the kitchen and the laundry room.
7. c) Direct outside access is most desirable in a family room.
8. d) A kitchen should be located in proximity to the dining room, the main entrance, and a service entrance.
9. a) Vertical members in a house frame are known as studs.
10. d) A joist is not a part of a wall frame. It is a horizontal member that supports the load of a floor or ceiling.
11. c) R-value is a measure of the efficiency of insulation.
12. b) A casement window pivots along one side of the window frame.
13. a) Rails and stiles are components of a panel door.
14. c) The heating capacity of a furnace is measured in BTUs.
15. c) Dry lumber is preferable because it is less likely to shrink.

Exercise Answers

#1 1. 1. c, e

2. a

3. b

4. b, d

5. b, d

2. a) climate; b) availability of building materials

3. Central heating; uniform building codes; modern transportation systems; improved insulating materials

#2 1. 1. b

2. b

3. a

4. b

5. a

6. c

7. c

8. b

2. 1. a, d

2. c, e

3. a, b, d, f

4. e

5. g

3. Refer to figure 7.4

#3 1. See diagram below

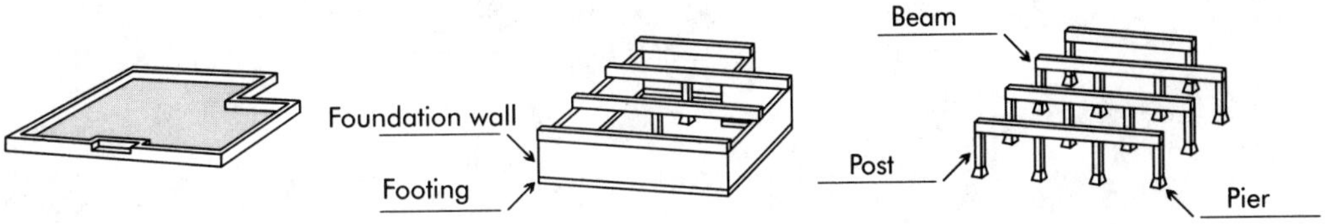

2. Refer to figure 7.9
3. Refer to figure 7.11

#4 1. Refer to figure 7.16
2. Refer to figure 7.14
3. a. fiberglass
   b. rock wool
   c. rigid foam
4. 1. d
   2. c
   3. f
   4. e
   5. a
   6. b

8 Cost Approach to Value

Overview

In Step 6 of the appraisal process, the appraiser applies the three approaches to value: the cost approach, the sales comparison approach, and the income capitalization approach. This chapter will focus on the cost approach to value. We will begin by examining the methods of estimating the cost of an improvement. We then will look at the techniques used by appraisers to calculate depreciation, which is how cost is related to value.

After completing this chapter, you should be able to:

- describe the relationship between cost, value, and depreciation;
- list the steps in the cost approach to estimating value;
- distinguish between replacement cost and reproduction cost, and understand the significance of this distinction for appraisal purposes;
- describe the types of costs that are included in an improvement cost estimate;
- describe the comparative-unit, unit-in-place, quantity survey, and cost index methods for estimating improvement costs, and list the advantages and disadvantages of each method;
- identify the sources of data for construction unit costs;
- define the term depreciation as it is used in appraisal practice;
- describe the distinctions between an improvement's physical life, useful life, and economic life, and between its actual age and its effective age;
- list the different categories of depreciation, and define the kinds of items included in each category; and
- explain how appraisers estimate depreciation using the economic age-life method, the market extraction method, and the breakdown method.

Basics of the Cost Approach

The cost approach is based on the **principle of substitution**, which states that a property's value cannot be greater than the cost of acquiring (buying or building) a substitute property of equal utility. In the cost approach, cost is related to value by the formula:

Value = Cost – Depreciation

In this formula, **cost** refers to the cost of reproducing or replacing the property's improvements. **Depreciation** is the difference between cost and value, from any cause. This basic formula applies only to the value of the improvements. The value of the land or site is determined separately (for example, by using the sales comparison method), and then added to the estimated value of the improvements to reach the total value of the property. The process of the cost approach to value can be summarized by the formula:

Property Value = Reproduction or Replacement Cost of Improvements – Depreciation of Improvements + Land Value

This formula requires three separate steps:

1. estimating the reproduction or replacement cost of the improvements,
2. estimating depreciation, and
3. estimating the value of the land.

The first part of this chapter will examine the techniques for estimating cost, and the second section will discuss depreciation. Estimation of land value is covered in Chapter 6.

Estimating Cost

Reproduction Cost and Replacement Cost

Before discussing the methods of estimating cost, it is important to distinguish reproduction cost from replacement cost. **Reproduction cost** is the cost of creating an exact replica of the improvements, using the same materials, design, layout, and level of craftsmanship. **Replacement cost** is the cost of building an improvement of equal utility, but using modern materials, techniques, layout, and design.

Replacement cost estimates are usually lower than reproduction cost estimates, because it usually costs less to build a structure using modern materials and techniques. In addition, reproduction cost must include the cost of reproducing any features that are excessive in quality or design, known as **superadequacies**. Replacement cost takes into account only the cost needed to create equal utility, so superadequacies are ignored.

Example: An older home has ¾"-thick oak plank flooring. Modern homes are using less expensive ½" planks, which the market views as comparable in terms of utility. A reproduction cost estimate would account for the cost of the more expensive ¾" flooring, while a replacement cost estimate would consider the cost of the cheaper, but functionally equivalent, ½" flooring.

The choice of either reproduction cost or replacement cost can affect the calculation of depreciation. When reproduction cost is the basis of the cost estimate, the appraiser must estimate depreciation from all causes. When replacement cost is used, some forms of depreciation (such as functional obsolescence due to superadequacies) are accounted for in the cost estimation step, and so they are not included in the depreciation estimate. This distinction is discussed in more detail in the second section of this chapter.

Types of Costs

Whether the appraiser is estimating reproduction cost or replacement cost, he or she must account for all of the types of costs necessary to construct the improvements. These include **hard costs** (also called **direct costs**), such as the cost of labor, materials, and equipment used in the construction, as well as **soft costs**, which are **indirect costs** such as architects' fees, construction loan interest, property taxes during the development period, and real estate sales commissions.

The appraiser must also account for the cost of **entrepreneurial profit**, which is the amount of profit that the owner/developer would expect to make from improving the property. Entrepreneurial profit is not the same thing as the actual profit or loss on a project. It is the amount (usually a percentage) that an investor would expect to earn when deciding to undertake a similar type of project.

Example: An appraiser estimates that total hard and soft costs for an office building at current prices would be $176,000. Developers of office property in the current market desire a 12% return on their developments. So 12% of the total cost will be allocated to entrepreneurial profit, and the remaining 88% is the hard and soft costs. The total cost can be calculated as:

$176,000 ÷ .88 (88%) = $200,000 total cost

$200,000 total cost – $176,000 hard and soft costs = $24,000 entrepreneurial profit

Cost Estimating Techniques

Cost estimating can be quite complex in practice, but in theory it is a very simple concept. The appraiser measures some feature of the improvement (such as square footage of building area, or number of doors) and multiplies it by the estimated unit cost for the feature. This procedure can be summarized with this formula:

$$Cost = Number\ of\ Units \times Cost\ per\ Unit$$

The most common cost estimating techniques all apply this same procedure. The primary difference between the techniques is in the level of detail: the simpler cost estimating techniques apply unit costs to broad-scale features such as building square footage, while the more detailed techniques apply unit costs to individual features of the construction and then add them up to find the total cost. The choice of technique is determined by the scope of the appraisal; the more detailed methods generally provide a more reliable cost estimate.

Comparative-Unit Method. In the **comparative-unit method**, cost is estimated on the basis of the square footage of building area, or the cubic footage of building volume. Residential cost estimates using this technique almost always use square footage, so it is often referred to as the **square foot method**.

Square footage is calculated by measuring and multiplying the outside dimensions of the building. The square footage is then multiplied by the estimated cost per square foot. Different costs per square foot are applied to different areas of the structure. For example, one figure is applied to the living area and another is applied to the garage. The cost of site improvements such as landscaping is also estimated separately.

Example: The drawing below shows the outline (perimeter) of a new one-story house that does not suffer from any depreciation. The living area is 1,280 square feet (32 × 40 = 1,280) and there is a 576 square foot attached garage (24 × 24 = 576). The appraiser has determined that current construction costs for similar buildings are $60 per square foot for living area and $25 per square foot for garage space. The site has been valued at $35,000, and the appraiser estimates the value of site improvements (driveway, landscaping, etc.) to be $8,500. In this case, the value of the property can be estimated by the cost approach using the square foot method as follows.

- Cost of living area = *1,280 sq.ft. × $60/sq.ft. = $76,800*
- Cost of garage = *576 sq.ft. × $25/sq.ft. = $14,400*
- Total cost of building = *$76,800 (living area) + $14,400 (garage) = $91,200*
- Total cost of improvements = *$91,200 (building) + $8,500 (other improvements) = $99,700*
- Indicated property value = *$99,700 (improvement cost) + $35,000 (site value) = $134,700*

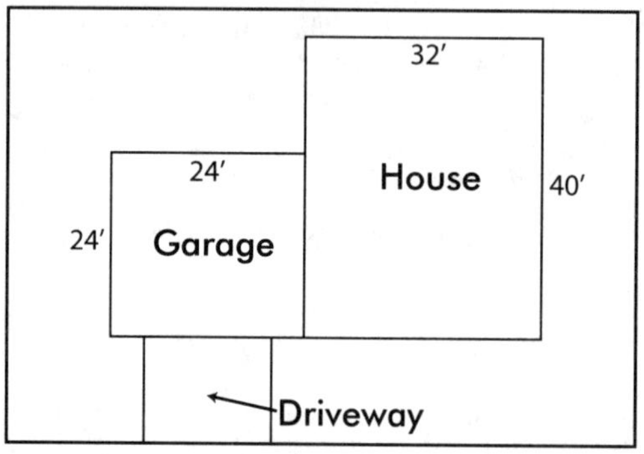

Calculating the building areas for the square foot method is a fairly simple process. The hard part is determining the appropriate unit cost per square foot. Unit costs may be derived in two ways: by market analysis, or by use of cost estimating manuals or services.

To establish unit cost by market analysis, the appraiser gathers data on sales of comparable new homes. The comparables must be similar to the subject property in both size and quality of construction, and the appraiser must be able to determine the site values for the comparables. For each comparable, the appraiser subtracts the site value from the sales price, and then divides the result by the square footage of the comparable. The result is the unit cost.

Example: A new 1,500 square foot rambler sold recently for $420,000. Market data support an estimated site value of $285,000, and the value of site improvements (landscaping, etc.) is estimated at $15,000. Accordingly, the value of the building is $120,000 ($420,000 sales price – $300,000 value of site and site improvements). Assuming the home does not suffer from any depreciation, its value should be equivalent to its cost. So the appraiser takes $120,000 (the building value or cost) and divides that by 1,500 (the size in square feet). The result, $80 per square foot, becomes the unit cost.

Choosing comparables similar in size to the subject property is important. Many types of construction costs do not vary in direct proportion to the size of the building. So, as a general rule, the unit costs per square foot will be higher for a smaller building than they will be for a larger building of the same quality and style.

Example: A 1,000 square foot house and a 1,800 square foot house each have only one kitchen. The plumbing, electrical work, cabinetry, countertops, and built-in appliances required for a kitchen are relatively expensive in relation to the rest of a house, and these costs will be about the same for both houses. Therefore, the unit cost of the 1,000 square foot house will be higher than the unit cost of the 1,800 square foot house, because the kitchen costs are divided between fewer square feet in the smaller house.

Cost per square foot is also influenced by the complexity of the building design, as illustrated in Figure 8.1. The square building with a perimeter of 20 × 20 has 80 lineal feet of perimeter wall for 400 square feet of area. The L-shaped building with the same area has a larger amount of perimeter wall, so the unit cost per square foot is higher.

Instead of estimating the unit cost, an appraiser may use local builders and developers, as well as published cost manuals and professional costing services, to find the unit cost. (Some widely used cost manuals are published by F. W. Dodge Corporation, Marshall and Swift/Boeckh Publications, and R. S. Means Company.) Cost manuals are published periodically (usually quarterly) and list the average unit costs for different sizes and styles of construction.

Fig. 8.1 Differences in Lineal Feet

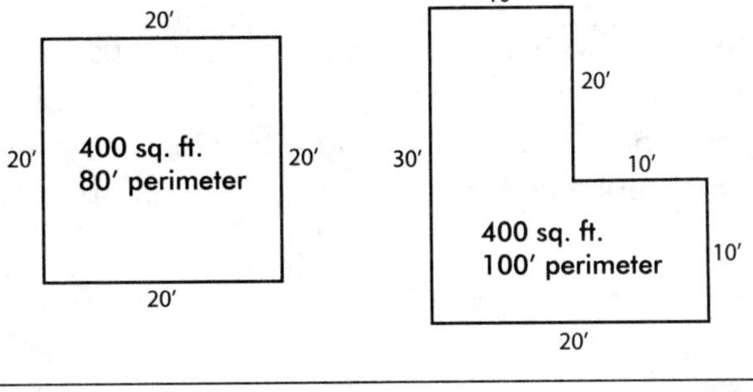

Unit cost figures must be adjusted to account for differences in construction features, size and shape, time, and location. Also, the appraiser must have a clear understanding of what the unit cost figures include, and must make additional adjustments for any cost items that are not included in the published cost figures.

Example: According to a cost manual, the average cost per square foot for an average quality one-story house of 1,500 square feet with a 160 lineal foot perimeter is $65.50. The manual also indicates that construction costs in the area where the subject property is located are 11% higher than average. The subject property has above-average exterior finishes, which add $3.50 per square foot to its cost. It also has 2,000 square feet of living area, which the appraiser estimates should reduce the unit cost by 8%. Since the date of publication of the manual, construction costs have declined by 5% due to a slowdown in the economy. A review of the cost manual indicates that its figures do not include entrepreneurial profit, which the appraiser has determined should be 10% for this type of property.

Published cost per square foot	$65.50
Adjustment for exterior finishes	+ 3.50
Subtotal	$69.00
Adjustment for larger size (100% – 8% = 92%)	× 0.92
Subtotal	$63.48
Adjustment for time (current cost) (100% – 5% = 95%)	× 0.95
Subtotal	$60.31
Adjustment for location (local cost) (100% + 11% = 111%)	× 1.11
Subtotal	$66.94
Adjustment for entrepreneurial profit	÷ 0.90
Total cost per square foot	$74.38

$74.38 × 2,000 square feet = $148,760 estimated cost of improvement (building)

Exercise 1

The drawing below shows the outline of a one-story house with an attached garage. Construction costs new for this type of house are $62.00 per square foot for living area and $26.00 per square foot for the garage. Based on this information, estimate the total cost new of the improvements.

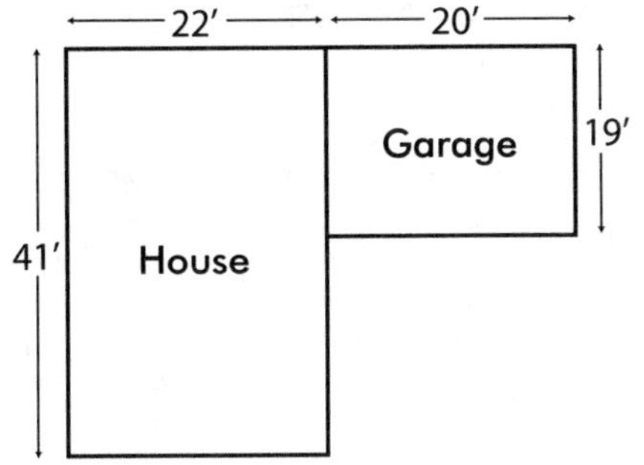

Unit-in-Place Method. The **unit-in-place method** requires the appraiser to measure the quantities of various building components, such as the foundation, floor, walls, roof, doors, windows, etc. The quantity of each item is then multiplied by its appropriate unit cost, and the subtotals for the building components are added together to get the total cost.

Unit costs for the unit-in-place method may be obtained from local builders and developers and by referring to cost manuals or costing services. The appraiser must be sure that the measurements used for the different building components are the same as the measurements for which the costs are stated.

Example: Wall framing costs may be stated as so much per lineal foot of wall, while the cost of painting the walls may be quoted as a cost per square foot of wall surface. Other costs, such as unit costs for plumbing or electrical systems, may be given as costs per square foot of building area. The appraiser must be sure to measure framing in terms of lineal foot of wall, painting in terms of square foot of wall surface, and plumbing and electrical systems in terms of square foot of building area. If the appraiser measures painting in terms of square yards of wall surface instead of square feet, he or she will not be able to apply the unit cost without making the appropriate adjustments.

As with the square foot method, the cost calculated by the unit-in-place method must be adjusted to account for differences in time (current cost) and location (local cost), and also for any cost items that are not included in the unit cost figures (such as indirect costs and entrepreneurial profit). Adjustments for differences in construction features, size, and complexity are generally not required in the unit-in-place method, since the procedure takes these differences into account.

Example: Figure 8.1 shows how the amount of exterior wall framing can vary depending on the shape of the building, even in buildings with the same square footage. The square foot method must make an adjustment to account for this variation. In the unit-in-place method, however, the actual amount of exterior wall framing is calculated (and then multiplied by its unit cost), so no adjustment is necessary.

The unit-in-place method gets its name from the fact that the unit costs for each construction item represent the total cost of installing or building the item, including the cost of materials, labor, equipment, and overhead.

Exercise 2

A one-story house measures 36′ × 40′. The house has 135 lineal feet of interior partition walls, and a roof area of 1,850 square feet. Estimate the total replacement cost of the house using the following unit-in-place costs. (For purposes of this exercise, do not deduct for door and window openings when calculating wall areas.)

Foundation:	$20.00 per lineal foot of foundation wall
Floor framing:	$4.50 per square foot of floor area
Wall framing:	$31.00 per lineal foot of exterior walls; $12.00 per lineal foot of interior partitions
Roof framing:	$3.50 per square foot of roof area
Siding:	$2.25 per square foot of exterior wall area (assume walls are 8.5′ high)
Roofing:	$2.70 per square foot of roof area
Doors and windows:	two exterior doors @ $400 each; seven interior doors @ $175 each; 240 square feet of windows @ $21.50 per square foot
Interior finishes:	walls and ceilings @ $0.75 per square foot of wall/ceiling area (assume 8′ interior wall height; interior partitions require finish on both sides); floors @ $2.00 per square foot of floor area; cabinets and fixtures @ $7,000
Mechanical systems:	$12,000 total
Electrical system:	$1.40 per square foot of living area
Indirect costs:	20% of total costs

Total Replacement Cost: ______________________________

Quantity Survey Method. The **quantity survey method** is the most detailed and most reliable method for estimating construction costs. It is similar to the unit-in-place method, in that the cost of each construction component is estimated separately, and the component costs are then added together to find the total cost. However, in the quantity survey method, the costs of labor, materials, equipment, and overhead are each calculated separately. Also, the level of detail in a quantity survey estimate is greater than in a unit-in-place estimate.

Example: In the unit-in-place method, a single unit cost is used to calculate the cost of exterior wall framing, including the cost for the framing lumber, sheathing, carpentry labor, scaffolding, etc. In the quantity survey method, the quantities of each of these items would be estimated separately, and each would be multiplied by its own unit cost (cost per board foot of framing lumber, cost per square foot of sheathing, cost per hour of carpentry labor, etc.).

Quantity survey estimates are used most often by contractors or builders. In practice, different sections of the estimate (foundation, plumbing, carpentry, electrical, etc.) are actually prepared by the different specialty subcontractors who are bidding for the job. The general contractor then combines the sub-estimates or bids into an estimate of total cost to complete the project.

Cost Index Trending. Cost index trending is a method of estimating the reproduction cost of a building whose original construction cost is known. Most people are familiar with indexes such as the cost-of-living index or the consumer price index, which track the relative change in different categories of costs. Construction cost indexes work in the same way. To find the current cost of the construction, simply divide the current index value by the index value at the time of construction, then multiply the result by the original cost.

Example: A house was built in 1980 at a cost of $100,000. The construction cost index was at 150 in 1980, and it is currently at 200. The current cost of building the house would be calculated as follows.

200 ÷ 150 = 1.33
1.33 × $100,000 (original cost) = $133,000 current cost

Cost index trending is a quick and convenient way to estimate current cost, but it is not considered very reliable. Even when the original construction cost of an improvement is known, there is no guarantee that the actual cost was typical for similar improvements that were built at the same time. This method is most appropriate for double-checking the results of some other, more reliable, cost estimating procedure.

Exercise 3

A construction cost index stood at 180 when the subject property was built for $85,000. What is the current estimated cost of the house if the index now stands at 333?

Estimating Depreciation

Estimating the replacement or reproduction cost of an improvement is only the first step in the cost approach to value. In the second step, the appraiser must estimate the amount of depreciation that the subject improvement has suffered. By deducting the total depreciation from the estimated cost, the appraiser can estimate the value of the improvement.

Terminology

For purposes of appraisal, the term **depreciation** refers to a loss in the value of an improvement (as compared to its cost) due to any reason whatsoever. Depreciation is the difference between the market value of the improvement and its cost. The amount of depreciation that has occurred between the time the improvement was built and the effective date of the appraisal is called the **accrued depreciation.**

The term depreciation is also widely used to refer to the amount of an asset's capital value that has been "written off" for accounting or tax purposes. This kind of depreciation, sometimes called **book depreciation**, has no significance from an appraisal standpoint.

Age and Economic Life. Depreciation is related to the age of an improvement. Improvements have an actual age and an effective age. **Actual age** (also called chronological or historical age) is the actual amount of time that the improvement has been in existence. For example, a house built in 1995 would have an actual age of 14 years in 2009.

Effective age is the apparent or functional age of the improvement, based on its current condition and utility and on current conditions in the market. An improvement's effective age may be the same as, greater than, or less than its actual age. Effective age is related to remaining economic life, as described below.

An improvement also has a physical life, a useful life, and an economic life. The **physical life** is the length of time the improvement can be expected to physically exist, with normal maintenance. The **useful life** is how long the improvement can be expected to perform the function it was originally designed for. The **economic life** is how long the improvement will contribute to the value of the property.

The economic life of an improvement comes to an end when it no longer represents the highest and best use of the property as improved. (Refer to the discussion of highest and best use in Chapter 6.) **Remaining economic life** is the amount of time from the effective date of the appraisal until the end of the improvement's economic life. The relation between economic life, remaining economic life, and effective age can be expressed as follows.

Economic Life = Effective Age + Remaining Economic Life

or

Effective Age = Economic Life – Remaining Economic Life

or

Remaining Economic Life = Economic Life – Effective Age

Example: A house, when built in 1995, had an estimated economic life of 50 years. The house is appraised in 2009, when its actual age is 14 years. Because the house has been well maintained, and its design and layout are still popular in the market, the appraiser estimates that it has a remaining economic life of 40 years. In this case, the effective age of the house would be 10 years (50 – 40 = 10), as compared to the actual age of 14 years.

Types of Depreciation

Depreciation is categorized according to the cause of the decrease in value, and also according to whether the decrease can be remedied. The three causes of depreciation are **physical deterioration**, **functional obsolescence**, and **external obsolescence** (which may be further categorized as either **economic obsolescence** or **locational obsolescence**). Depreciation that can be remedied is said to be **curable**; if a remedy is not possible or practical, the depreciation is **incurable**.

Physical Deterioration. Physical deterioration is depreciation that is caused by wear and tear on, or damage to, the physical components of the improvement. Broken windows, leaky roofs, peeling paint, termite damage, or worn carpeting are all examples of physical deterioration.

Physical deterioration can be curable or incurable. If the cost of correcting the deterioration is less than the added value that would result from the correction, then it is curable; otherwise, it is incurable. Curable physical deterioration is often referred to as **deferred maintenance**.

Example: Since a fresh coat of paint often adds more to the value of a house than the cost of the painting, the need for repainting is usually curable physical deterioration, or deferred maintenance. On the other hand, the cost of repairing a cracked foundation may far exceed any increase in value that would result from the repairs; in this case, the cracked foundation would be considered incurable physical deterioration.

When analyzing the physical deterioration of an improvement, a distinction is sometimes made between long-lived items and short-lived items. A **long-lived** item is a component of the improvement that is expected to last as long as the building itself does. **Short-lived** components can be expected to need replacement during the improvement's economic life. An example of a long-lived item is the foundation, which normally lasts for the life of the building. Paint and carpeting are short-lived items, which require periodic replacement.

The economic life of a short-lived improvement is normally the same as its physical life. The physical life of a long-lived improvement, on the other hand, is usually longer than its economic life: buildings are usually torn down before they fall down.

Functional Obsolescence. In addition to physical deterioration, an improvement can suffer from depreciation that is caused by design defects. This form of depreciation is called **functional obsolescence**. Whether the design is defective from the start or simply becomes outdated with the passage of time, the resulting loss in value is treated as functional obsolescence.

Fig. 8.2 Functional Obsolescence due to Poor Floor Plan

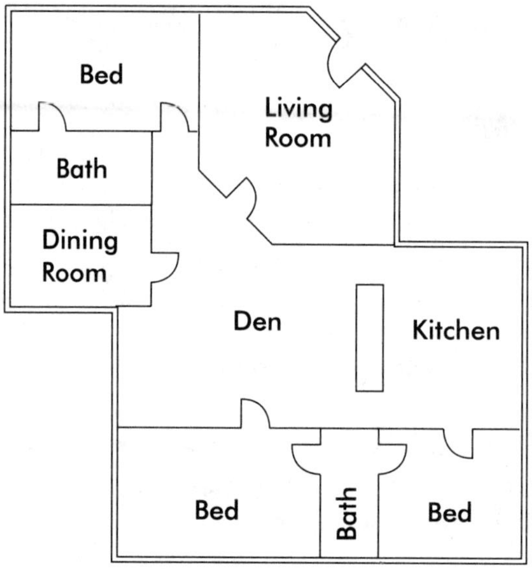

Example: Today's market prefers energy-efficient housing, which includes insulation with a high R-value. Older housing that does not meet this standard may suffer a loss in value due to functional obsolescence, even though its insulation was considered standard at the time it was built. A newer house with inadequate insulation would also suffer from functional obsolescence.

Design defects that cause functional obsolescence can be either deficiencies (such as inadequate insulation) or superadequacies. A superadequacy is a form of overimprovement; it is a design feature whose cost is greater than its contribution to value.

Example: Most modern housing uses 2×4 or 2×6 framing for wall construction. A house that was built with 2×12 wall framing would probably suffer from functional obsolescence due to a superadequacy. The cost of the superadequate wall framing would more than likely exceed any resulting value increase.

Like physical deterioration, functional obsolescence is either curable or incurable. The same test applies: if the defect can be remedied at a cost that is less than the resulting increase in value, then it is curable; otherwise, it is incurable.

Example: Inadequate insulation in the ceiling of a house is usually a curable form of functional obsolescence, because additional insulation can be installed at a reasonable cost. A house with substandard ceiling heights, on the other hand, probably suffers from incurable functional obsolescence, since it would be prohibitively expensive to increase the height of the walls.

External Obsolescence. The third form of depreciation is **external obsolescence**, which is a loss in value resulting from causes arising outside of the property itself. External obsolescence may be either economic or locational.

Economic obsolescence occurs when external factors or economic conditions cause a deterioration in the property's profitability or value. **Locational obsolescence**, on the other hand, occurs as a result of negative influences from surrounding properties.

> **Example:** A home located in an industrial area will suffer a loss in value due to its poor location; this is an example of locational obsolescence. The home will also suffer a loss in value if the community's primary employer goes out of business, devastating the local economy; this is an example of economic obsolescence.

Because it arises from causes outside the property itself, external obsolescence is almost always incurable. It may however, be temporary in nature, as in the case of a temporary slump in local market conditions.

Exercise 4

Indicate the category of depreciation that most likely corresponds to each of the items listed below. Use the following codes: curable physical deterioration (CP); incurable physical deterioration (IP); curable functional obsolescence (CF); incurable functional obsolescence (IF); economic obsolescence (E); locational obsolescence (L).

1. _____ inadequate insulation
2. _____ location near a landfill
3. _____ leaking rain gutters
4. _____ cracked concrete floor in garage
5. _____ bathroom fixtures are an unpopular color
6. _____ 12′ high ceilings in every room
7. _____ no cable TV service in neighborhood
8. _____ missing roof shingles
9. _____ entry door only 2′6″ wide
10. _____ uneven foundation settling

Methods of Estimating Depreciation

Properly estimating depreciation is the most difficult part of the cost approach. This is particularly true of older properties, which may suffer from several types and causes of

Fig. 8.3 Straight Line Depreciation

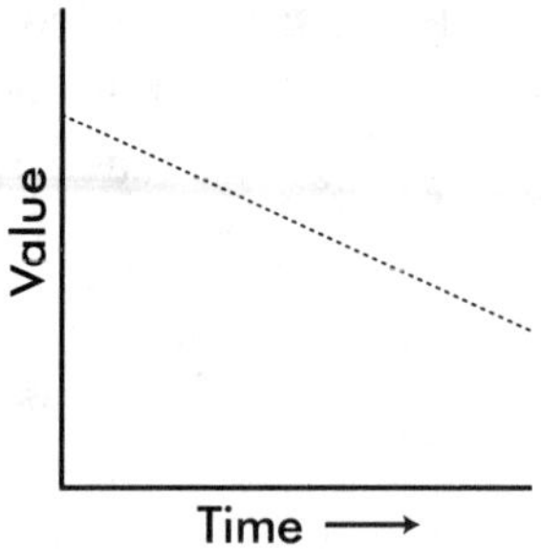

depreciation. Simpler methods of estimating depreciation tend to rely on assumptions that do not necessarily apply in every case, while more complex methods require market data that often are not available. This is one reason why the cost approach to value is considered less reliable than the sales comparison approach or the income approach.

We'll look at the three main methods appraisers use to estimate depreciation: the economic age-life method, the market extraction method, and the breakdown method.

Economic Age-Life Method. The **economic age-life method** of estimating depreciation is based on the assumption that an improvement loses value at a steady rate over the course of its economic life. According to this assumption, a graph of the depreciated value of an improvement versus its age would appear as a straight line, as shown in Figure 8.3. The economic age-life method is sometimes called the **straight line method**.

To use the economic age-life method, the appraiser must first estimate the effective age and the economic life of the improvement. (These estimates are based on data concerning similar improvements in the same market as the subject property.) The ratio of effective age to economic life—called the **economic age-life ratio** or the **accrued depreciation rate**—is then multiplied by the estimated cost* in order to determine the amount of depreciation.

Depreciation = (Effective Age ÷ Economic Life) × Cost

Example: An appraiser estimates the replacement cost of a house at $220,000. The house has an economic life of 60 years and an effective age of 15 years. Under the economic age-life method, depreciation would be calculated as follows.

15 ÷ 60 = 0.25 (25%) economic age-life ratio

0.25 × $220,000 = $55,000 accrued depreciation

$220,000 – $55,000 = $165,000 depreciated value of improvement

In an alternative version of the economic age-life method, depreciation that is caused by curable physical deterioration and curable functional obsolescence is assumed to be equal to

* For the most part, appraisers follow the same steps for estimating depreciation regardless of whether replacement cost or reproduction cost will be the basis for the value estimate. For simplicity's sake in this discussion, we usually refer to replacement cost, but keep in mind that an appraiser might use reproduction cost instead.

the cost of curing the defects. This **cost to cure** is deducted from the total estimated replacement cost, and the ratio of effective age to economic life is then applied to the remainder of the cost. When estimating effective age, the appraiser takes into account any change in effective age that would result from curing the curable physical and functional defects.

Example: Using the same figures as in the example above, assume that it would cost $5,000 to remedy the curable physical and functional defects in the house, and that curing these defects would result in the house having an effective age of only 12 years. The calculation of depreciation in this case is as follows.

$220,000 – $5,000 = $215,000 cost (adjusted for curable items)

12 ÷ 60 = 0.20 (20%) economic age-life ratio

0.20 × $215,000 = $43,000 incurable depreciation

$43,000 + $5,000 = $48,000 total depreciation

$220,000 – $48,000 = $172,000 depreciated value of improvement

The economic age-life method is the simplest method of estimating depreciation, but in many cases the other methods yield more accurate results.

Exercise 5

A house has an estimated replacement cost of $200,000. The house is 10 years old (that's its actual age), and it has an estimated economic life of 65 years. It is in need of repainting and other minor repairs, which will cost a total of $5,000. The remaining economic life of the house is currently estimated at 52 years; the remaining economic life would be 55 years if the needed repairs were completed. Estimate the depreciated value of the house under both versions of the economic age-life method.

Market Extraction Method. When adequate sales data are available, the **market extraction method** can be used to estimate depreciation. To apply the market extraction method, the appraiser begins by identifying suitable comparable sales. The comparable properties should be in the same market as the subject property, and they should be similar to the subject in terms of age, utility, and physical characteristics. They should also be affected by similar types and amounts of depreciation. The appraiser goes through the following steps for each of the chosen comparables.

1. The appraiser adjusts the comparable's sales price to reflect differences from a potential sale of the subject property in terms of financing, conditions of sale, the property interest conveyed, and other factors. The appraiser wants to estimate the comparable's replacement cost and depreciation at the time of sale, so adjustments aren't made for differences in market conditions.
2. The appraiser's next step is to subtract the estimated value of the comparable's land at the time of sale from the adjusted sales price. The remainder is the contributory value of the improvements—the portion of the adjusted price that can be attributed to the improvements.

Example: Comparable #1 sold for $579,000. The appraiser makes the appropriate adjustments and arrives at an adjusted price of $587,000. The estimated value of the comparable's land is $207,000. By subtracting the land value from the adjusted price, the appraiser calculates the contributory value of the improvements.

$587,000 – $207,000 = $380,000 contributory value of improvements

3. Next, the appraiser estimates the replacement cost of the comparable's improvements at the time of sale.
4. The appraiser subtracts the contributory value of the improvements from their replacement cost. The result is the total depreciation at the time of sale. This may be referred to as the extracted depreciation; in effect, this depreciation figure has been extracted from the comparable's sales price.

Example: Continuing with the previous example, the appraiser estimates the replacement cost of Comparable #1's improvements at $326,000. She subtracts that from the contributory value of the improvements ($380,000) to calculate the extracted depreciation.

$380,000 – $326,000 = $54,000 extracted depreciation

5. Now the appraiser divides the extracted depreciation by the comparable's replacement cost. The result shows what percentage of the cost the depreciation represents. This is called the total depreciation percentage.

Example: The appraiser divides Comparable #1's extracted depreciation ($54,000) by the replacement cost ($326,000) to find the total depreciation percentage.

$54,000 ÷ $326,000 = 16.56% total depreciation percentage for Comparable #1

After calculating a depreciation percentage for each of the comparables, the appraiser uses those percentages to decide on an appropriate depreciation percentage for the subject property. The appraiser will then multiply the subject's replacement cost by the percentage to arrive at an estimate of the subject's total depreciation from all causes.

Example: Following the same steps she used for Comparable #1, the appraiser calculates total depreciation percentages of 16.15% and 16.87% for Comparables #2 and #3. Based on the comparables' percentages, evaluated in light of all of the data, the appraiser settles on 16.42% as the total depreciation percentage for the subject property. The subject's estimated replacement cost is $339,000. The appraiser multiplies the replacement cost by the total depreciation percentage to arrive at an estimate of the total depreciation affecting the subject property's value.

$339,000 × .1642 = $55,664 estimated total depreciation for subject property

The total depreciation percentages for the comparables in the example above are quite close together, which makes it relatively easy to choose an appropriate percentage for the subject. When an appraiser's calculations result in a wider range of depreciation percentages for the comparables, it may be worthwhile to convert them to annual rates. To do this, the appraiser generally divides each comparable's depreciation percentage by its actual age.

Example: An appraiser has calculated total depreciation percentages for the comparables he's working with. Now he decides to calculate their annual depreciation rates. Comparable A is 7 years old and has a depreciation percentage of 10%. B is 18 years old and has a depreciation percentage of 31%. C is 12 years old, with a depreciation percentage of 19%.

Comparable A: 10% ÷ 7 years = 1.43% average annual depreciation rate
Comparable B: 31% ÷ 18 years = 1.72% average annual depreciation rate
Comparable C: 19% ÷ 12 years = 1.58% average annual depreciation rate

Based on these figures, the appraiser decides to use 1.65% as a depreciation rate for the subject property, which is 14 years old. By multiplying 1.65% by 14 years, the appraiser arrives at a total depreciation percentage of 23.1% for the subject property (1.65% × 14 = 23.1%). The subject's estimated replacement cost is $412,000, so the estimated total depreciation using the market extraction method is $95,172 ($412,000 × 23.1% = $95,172).

When there is plenty of good comparable data and the appraiser's cost and land value estimates are sound, the market extraction method should result in a more accurate depreciation estimate than the simpler economic age-life method. However, a limitation of both methods is that they provide only an estimate of total depreciation, as opposed to estimates for each different category of depreciation. If an appraisal assignment requires those, it's necessary to use the breakdown method of estimating depreciation.

Breakdown Method. With the breakdown method (also known as the **observed condition method**), the appraiser separately estimates the amount of each of the five types of depreciation: curable physical deterioration, incurable physical deterioration, curable functional obsolescence, incurable functional obsolescence, and external obsolescence. To do this, the appraiser may use a number of different techniques, including cost to cure, age-life ratios, and paired data analysis.

The breakdown method is seldom used in residential appraisals, but it's a good illustration of the theory of depreciation as it applies to appraisal. The process required by the breakdown method is summarized by the following outline, then explained in more detail.

1. Estimate replacement cost for each component of the improvement.
2. Estimate curable physical deterioration.
3. Estimate incurable physical deterioration.
   A. Short-lived items
   B. Long-lived items

4. Estimate curable functional obsolescence.
   A. Deficiencies
      1. Curable by addition
      2. Curable by modification
   B. Superadequacies
5. Estimate incurable functional obsolescence.
   A. Deficiencies
   B. Superadequacies
6. Estimate external obsolescence.
   A. Economic obsolescence
   B. Locational obsolescence
7. Calculate total depreciation and depreciated value of the improvement.

Step 1: The appraiser begins by estimating the replacement cost of each component of the improvement. A detailed cost estimate is required, because the amount of depreciation calculated for each item will depend on the item's estimated cost.

Step 2: The amount of curable physical deterioration (deferred maintenance) for each item in the cost estimate is estimated using the cost to cure.*

Example:

Item	*Estimated Cost*	*Cost to Cure*
Siding	$5,000	$500
Paint	$1,200	$1,200
Total curable physical deterioration		$1,700

Step 3A: Incurable physical deterioration is estimated using age-life ratios, with separate estimates for short-lived and long-lived components of the improvement. Accrued depreciation of components that don't need to be replaced immediately, but will eventually have to be, is categorized as short-lived incurable physical deterioration. An age-life ratio is calculated for each short-lived item using actual age and useful life expectancy.

Example:

Item	*Age*		*Useful Life*		*Ratio*		*Cost to Replace*		*Depreciation*
Roofing	5	÷	25	=	.20	×	$4,000	=	$800
Carpets	5	÷	10	=	.50	×	$2,000	=	$1,000
Fixtures	5	÷	20	=	.25	×	$6,000	=	$1,500
Total incurable physical deterioration for short-lived items									$3,300

Step 3B: All physical deterioration that hasn't already been dealt with in either Step 2 (curable) or Step 3 (short-lived incurable) is treated as long-lived incurable physical deterioration. To calculate this, the appraiser starts with the total cost estimate for the improvement, then subtracts the cost to cure of the items included in Step 2 and the

* In steps 2 and 4, the appraiser must first determine whether the defects are in fact curable—whether a cure is possible and whether the value added by the cure will be greater than the cost involved.

replacement cost of the short-lived items included in Step 3A. The remainder is then multiplied by the economic age-life ratio for the whole improvement.

Example:

Total estimated replacement cost of improvement	$200,000
less Replacement cost of short-lived items	– $12,000
less Cost to cure of curable items (siding and roof)	– $1,700
Subtotal	$186,300
Effective age of improvement: 5 years	
Economic life of improvement: 50 years	
Economic age-life ratio (5 ÷ 50 = .10)	× 0.10
Total incurable physical deterioration for long-lived items	$18,630

Step 4A(1): The procedure for calculating depreciation due to curable functional obsolescence depends on the nature of the particular design defect. If the defect can be cured by adding a feature to the improvement, the amount of depreciation is the difference between what it would cost to add the feature to the existing improvement and what it would have cost to include the feature in the first place.

Example: An improvement suffers from curable functional obsolescence due to the lack of a second bath. The cost of remodeling to add a second bath is $5,000. But if the house were being completely rebuilt, the cost of including a second bath in the design would be only $4,500. The depreciation due to lack of a second bath is $500 ($5,000 – $4,500).

Step 4A(2): When functional obsolescence can be cured by modifying a design deficiency, the appraiser starts with the estimated cost of the deficient item from Step 1. Any physical depreciation calculated for this item in Step 2 or 3 is subtracted from that value to avoid duplication. Then the cost of replacing the item is added. Note that this replacement cost must also include the cost of removing the deficient item. Finally, if the removed item has any salvage value, that is deducted to arrive at the functional obsolescence estimate.

Example: If the style of carpeting in the improvement is out of fashion, the depreciation due to this functional obsolescence will be calculated as follows.

Estimated cost of existing carpeting	$2,000
less Physical depreciation for existing carpeting	– 1,000
plus Cost of installing new carpeting	+ 2,600
plus Cost of removing existing carpeting	+ 100
less Salvage value of existing carpeting	– 0
Functional obsolescence for this item	$3,700

Step 4B: Curable functional obsolescence caused by superadequacies does not need to be estimated when the basis of the cost estimate is replacement cost, since replacement cost estimates don't include the costs of reproducing superadequacies. If the cost estimate is based on reproduction cost, the procedure for this step is the same as for Step 4A(2).

Step 5A: Next, the appraiser considers incurable functional obsolescence. The procedure for this step depends on whether or not the cost of the deficient item is included in the appraiser's cost estimate (in Step 1). If it is, the appraiser estimates the item's contribution to value (usually using paired data analysis, discussed below) and deducts that amount from the item's cost. (To avoid duplication, the cost is first adjusted to reflect any physical depreciation that has already been calculated for the item.)

Example: A house has outdated bathroom fixtures, which contribute only $1,500 to its value. Their cost was estimated as $3,000, and their physical depreciation as $300. The incurable functional obsolescence due to the outdated fixtures would be calculated as $3,000 (cost new) – $300 (physical depreciation) – $1,500 (value contribution of existing item) = $1,200.

If the cost of the item isn't included in the cost estimate, the appraiser must estimate its value contribution (again with paired data analysis) and subtract what it would have cost if included in the estimate of cost new.

Example: A house with 7-foot-high ceilings has a value that's $2,000 less than that of comparable houses with standard 8-foot ceilings, so adding an extra foot of wall height would add $2,000 to the value of the improvement. If it would have cost an extra $400 to build 8-foot walls in the first place, the amount of incurable depreciation for this item would be calculated as $2,000 (value contribution) – $400 (cost not included in cost estimate) = $1,600.

Step 5B: When incurable functional obsolescence is due to a superadequacy, the appraiser estimates the present value of any ongoing costs associated with the superadequacy (such as higher property taxes, insurance premiums, or utility costs). Any value contribution due to the superadequacy is then deducted. If the cost estimate (in Step 1) is for reproduction cost, the extra cost of the superadequate item (less any physical depreciation already charged) is also added to the depreciation due to incurable functional obsolescence.

Step 6: The appraiser generally uses paired data analysis (see below) to measure depreciation caused by external obsolescence (both economic and locational).

Step 7: The depreciation amounts calculated in Steps 2 through 6 are added together to find the total depreciation from all causes. This amount is then subtracted from the estimated cost (from Step 1) to find the depreciated value of the improvement.

Fig. 8.4 Calculating Depreciation

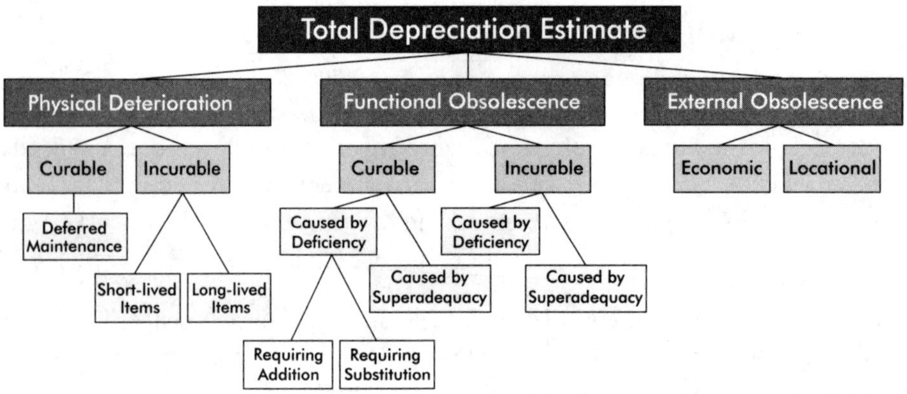

Using paired data analysis. For certain steps in the breakdown method, the appraiser often uses a technique called **paired data analysis** to estimate the depreciation caused by a particular defect. To do this, the appraiser must be able to identify comparables that have the same defect as the subject property, and other comparables that don't have that defect.

Example: The subject property suffers from functional obsolescence due to a poor floor plan. Market analysis reveals that comparable houses with similar floor plans sell for $310,000, while comparable houses with more functional floor plans sell for $330,000. This indicates that the functional obsolescence due to the poor floor plan causes $20,000 in depreciation ($330,000 – $310,000 = $20,000).

Paired data analysis is discussed in detail in Chapter 9.

Exercise 6

1. Match each form of depreciation with the technique(s) that would most likely be used to calculate it.

1.___	curable physical deterioration	a. cost to cure
2.___	incurable short-lived physical deterioration	b. age-life ratio
3.___	incurable long-lived physical deterioration	c. paired data analysis
4.___	curable functional obsolescence requiring addition	
5.___	curable functional obsolescence requiring modification	
6.___	curable functional obsolescence due to superadequacy	
7.___	incurable functional obsolescence	
8.___	external obsolescence	

2. Which form of depreciation is normally not relevant when the cost estimate is based on replacement cost? Why?

____

____

Final Value Estimate with the Cost Approach

The estimate of the depreciated cost of the improvement (the building) is the main focus of the cost approach. However, in order to obtain a value indication for the property as a whole, the appraiser must also estimate the value of the site and any site improvements. Ideally, the site value is established by the sales comparison approach (discussed in the next chapter), but a lack of data for sales of comparable vacant land may require the appraiser to determine site value by some other method. In this situation, the appraiser must rely on one of the other techniques for estimating site value, such as allocation or extraction. (Methods for estimating the value of a site are discussed in Chapter 6.)

The value of site improvements such as fences, driveways, patios, or landscaping must also be estimated, and must be included in the figure for total property value. The value of such improvements may be estimated by means of one or more of the three approaches to value: sales comparison, cost, or income capitalization. For example, the value of a fence may be estimated by calculating its depreciated cost (cost approach), or by comparing the sales prices (sales comparison approach) or net incomes (income capitalization approach) of comparable properties that have, and do not have, fencing.

The final value indication for the property is determined by adding together the depreciated cost of the building, the estimated value of the site improvements, and the estimated site value. The resulting figure indicates the value of the fee simple interest in the property. Additional adjustments are required if the property interest that is the subject of the appraisal is not the fee simple. (Appraisal of non-fee simple interests is discussed in Chapter 13.)

Key Terms

Accrued depreciation—The amount of depreciation that has occurred between the time an improvement was built and the effective date of its appraisal.

Actual age—The amount of time that an improvement has been in existence. Also called chronological age or historical age.

Book depreciation—The amount of an asset's capital value that has been written off for accounting or tax purposes. Book depreciation is not relevant to an appraisal.

Breakdown method—A method of estimating depreciation that involves separately estimating the amount of each type of depreciation. Also called the observed condition method.

Comparative-unit method—A technique for estimating the cost of improvements by multiplying the size of the improvement (square feet or cubic feet) by a unit cost figure. Also called the square foot method.

Cost—The actual amount of expenditure necessary to acquire or produce something.

Cost approach—One of the three approaches to value in the appraisal process. In the cost approach, the value of the subject property is indicated by the cost of building the subject improvements, plus the value of the site, and minus any depreciation which exists in the subject improvements.

Cost index—A statistic that tracks the relative change in construction costs over time. If the original cost of an improvement is known, its replacement cost can be estimated by dividing the current index by the index from the time of construction, and then multiplying the result by the original cost of construction.

Cost to cure—A technique for estimating depreciation by estimating how much it would cost to remedy the defects in the improvement.

Curable depreciation—Depreciation that can be remedied physically or economically.

Depreciation—The difference between cost and value, from whatever cause.

Direct costs—The costs for labor and materials used to build an improvement. Also called hard costs.

Economic age-life method—A technique for estimating depreciation, based on the assumption that an improvement loses value at a steady rate over the course of its economic life.

Economic life—The length of time during which an improvement will contribute to the value of a property. Economic life ends when the improvement no longer represents the highest and best use of the property.

Economic obsolescence—A type of external obsolescence caused by economic conditions or factors.

Effective age—The apparent or functional age of an improvement, based on its current condition and the current conditions in the market.

Entrepreneurial profit—The amount of profit that an owner/developer would expect to make from improving the property.

External obsolescence—Depreciation that results from causes arising outside of the property itself.

Functional obsolescence—Depreciation caused by defects in design.

Improvement—An item of personal property that is added to the land by human effort, in such a way as to become part of the real estate. Also called a fixture.

Income capitalization—The process of estimating value on the basis of a property's income.

Incurable depreciation—Depreciation that cannot be physically or economically remedied.

Indirect costs—Costs other than direct costs (labor and materials) that are incurred in the process of building an improvement, such as overhead, architectural fees, construction financing interest, permit fees, etc. Also called soft costs.

Locational obsolescence—External obsolescence caused by surrounding properties.

Long-lived item—A component of an improvement that is expected to last as long as the improvement itself.

Physical life—The length of time an improvement would be expected to last with normal maintenance.

Physical deterioration—Depreciation caused by wear or damage to the physical components of the improvement. Curable physical deterioration is also called deferred maintenance.

Quantity survey method—A technique for estimating the cost of an improvement by calculating the cost of labor, materials, equipment, and overhead for each item in the construction.

Remaining economic life—The amount of time from the effective date of an appraisal until the end of the appraised improvement's economic life. Remaining economic life equals economic life minus effective age.

Replacement cost—The cost of creating a substitute improvement of equivalent function and utility, using current methods, materials, and techniques.

Reproduction cost—The cost of creating an exact duplicate of an improvement, using the same design, materials, and construction methods as the original.

Short-lived item—A component of an improvement that is expected to wear out and need replacement during the economic life of the improvement.

Superadequacy—A form of functional obsolescence, consisting of a design feature whose cost is greater than its contribution to value.

Unit-in-place method—A technique for estimating the cost of an improvement by calculating the quantities of various building components and multiplying the quantity of each component by an appropriate unit cost.

Useful life—The length of time an improvement can be expected to perform its intended function.

Value—The monetary relationship between properties and those who buy, sell, or use those properties (USPAP definition). The theoretical worth of something, expressed in terms of something else, usually money.

Summary

I. In the cost approach, value is determined by adding the estimated value of the site to the depreciated cost of the improvements.

A The value of an improvement is indicated by the difference between its cost and depreciation.

II. Cost is estimated as the cost of building a new substitute improvement, at current prices as of the effective date of the appraisal.

A. Reproduction cost is the cost of creating an exact replica.

B. Replacement cost is the cost of creating an improvement of equal utility, using modern methods and materials.

C. The cost estimate must include hard (direct) costs and soft (indirect) costs, as well as entrepreneurial profit.

D. In the comparative-unit (square foot) method, cost is estimated by multiplying the amount of building area by a cost per square foot.

1. Separate unit costs are used for areas of different construction: living area, garage, etc.
2. The value of site improvements must be estimated separately.
3. Unit costs may be derived from market data, or obtained from cost manuals, local builders, and other sources.
4. Costs must be adjusted for differences in construction features, size, and complexity, as well as for differences in time (current cost) and location (local cost). An adjustment must also be made for any costs that are not included in the unit cost figure, such as indirect costs.

E. In the unit-in-place method, the appraiser applies unit costs to each of the items in a breakdown of the building's components.

1. The unit costs represent the total costs for each item, including labor, materials, equipment, etc.
2. Costs must be adjusted for current cost and local cost, and for any indirect costs that are not included.

F. A quantity survey involves a detailed estimate of the cost of each building component, including separate cost estimates for materials, labor, equipment, overhead items, and other costs of construction.

G. Cost may be estimated by means of construction cost indexes when the original construction cost is known, but this method tends to be unreliable.

III. Depreciation is the difference between value and cost. It represents the loss in value suffered by an improvement from all causes.

A. Depreciation is caused by physical deterioration, functional obsolescence, and external obsolescence. The depreciation is curable if it is possible and economically practical to fix it; otherwise it is incurable.

1. Physical deterioration is depreciation caused by physical damage or wear and tear. It may be curable (deferred maintenance) or incurable.

2. Functional obsolescence is depreciation caused by design defects. The defect may be a deficiency (something lacking) or a superadequacy (overimprovement), and may be curable or incurable.

3. External obsolescence is depreciation caused by something outside the property itself. It may be locational (from surrounding property influences) or economic (from market conditions or other economic factors). It is usually incurable, though it may be temporary in nature.

B. Methods of estimating depreciation include the economic age-life method, the market extraction method, and the breakdown method.

1. The economic age-life (straight line) method measures depreciation by applying the economic age-life ratio to the cost of the improvement. The economic age-life ratio, also called the accrued depreciation rate, is the effective age of the improvement divided by its economic life.

2. In the market extraction method, the appraiser extracts total depreciation figures from the sales prices of comparable properties, then divides extracted depreciation by estimated cost to arrive at a total depreciation percentage for each comparable. Based on those percentages, the appraiser selects an appropriate percentage for the subject property, then multiplies by the subject's estimated cost for an estimate of the total amount of depreciation.

3. The breakdown method (or observed condition method) is used to generate separate estimates for each different category of curable and incurable depreciation. Those figures are added together for an estimate of the total amount of depreciation.

IV. Final value indication is calculated by adding the depreciated value of the improvement to the site value and the estimated value of the site improvements.

Chapter Quiz

1. Which of the following cost estimating techniques would include an estimate of the labor rates and man-hours necessary to install the plumbing system in a house?
   a. Unit-in-place method
   b. Cost index trending method
   c. Quantity survey method
   d. Comparative-unit method

2. In a cost estimate using the square foot method, which of the following would not require a separate cost estimate?
   a. The second floor of a two-story house
   b. The garage
   c. The site
   d. The landscaping improvements

3. The unit costs used with the unit-in-place method include the costs of:
   a. labor
   b. materials
   c. equipment
   d. All of the above

4. Which cost estimating method requires the appraiser to adjust unit costs to account for differences in the size and complexity of the subject property?
   a. Unit-in-place method
   b. Cost index trending method
   c. Quantity survey method
   d. Comparative-unit method

5. If construction costs are 10% higher in the local market than the average costs listed in a cost manual, the appraiser should adjust the unit costs used in the cost estimate by:
   a. multiplying them by 10%
   b. multiplying them by 110%
   c. multiplying them by 90%
   d. dividing them by 90%

6. A poor floor plan is an example of:
   a. deferred maintenance
   b. a superadequacy
   c. functional obsolescence
   d. external obsolescence

7. Which of the following types of depreciation is almost always incurable?
   a. Physical deterioration
   b. Functional obsolescence
   c. External obsolescence
   d. None of the above

8. Which of the following is generally considered the most difficult part of the cost approach?
   a. Estimating depreciation
   b. Estimating reproduction cost
   c. Estimating replacement cost
   d. Applying the square foot method

9. Worn-out carpeting in a house would most likely fall into the category of:
   a. curable physical deterioration
   b. incurable physical deterioration
   c. curable functional obsolescence
   d. incurable functional obsolescence

10. In the cost approach to value, the value of the land or site is:
    a. ignored
    b. estimated separately
    c. adjusted on the basis of reproduction cost
    d. based on unit cost

11. Estimates of depreciation are generally more reliable in the case of:
    a. older homes
    b. newer homes
    c. larger homes
    d. smaller homes

12. The cost per square foot of a 2,000 square foot house is likely to be:
    a. higher than the cost per square foot of a 1,500 square foot home of comparable design
    b. lower than the cost per square foot of a 2,500 square foot home of comparable design
    c. higher than the cost per square foot of a 2,500 square foot home of comparable design
    d. None of the above

13. The effective age of an improvement:
    a. depends on the actual age of the improvement
    b. is the difference between actual age and economic life
    c. is the difference between actual age and remaining economic life
    d. is the difference between economic life and remaining economic life

14. Depreciation may be measured by the:
    a. breakdown method
    b. economic age-life method
    c. market extraction method
    d. Any of the above

15. An estimate of replacement cost would include the cost of all of the following except:
    a. entrepreneurial profit
    b. superadequacies in the subject property design
    c. construction loan interest
    d. property taxes during the construction period

Case Study

Complete the "COST APPROACH" section of the Uniform Residential Appraisal Report shown below, based on the following information. (You will need to refer to the information in the case study for Chapter 5.)

The house at 1731 Pine Road is three years old. Similar houses in the market have an economic life of 65 years. The house has been well-maintained, so you estimate that its remaining economic life is 64 years. There is no evidence of functional or external obsolescence.

Cost figures from the Marshall and Swift Residential Cost Handbook, adjusted for the local area, indicate that comparable construction has a cost in the current market of $70 per square foot for living space, $17 per square foot for covered porches, and $27 per square foot for garage space. You have estimated the "as-is" value of the other improvements on the site to be $7,500. Recent sales of vacant lots in Ravenswood support a site value estimate of $172,000.

Use this portion of the URAR to complete the case study.

COST APPROACH TO VALUE (not required by Fannie Mae)	
Provide adequate information for the lender/client to replicate the below cost figures and calculations.	
Support for the opinion of site value (summary of comparable land sales or other methods for estimating site value)	
ESTIMATED ☐ REPRODUCTION OR ☐ REPLACEMENT COST NEW	OPINION OF SITE VALUE = $
Source of cost data	Dwelling Sq. Ft. @ $ =$
Quality rating from cost service Effective date of cost data	Sq. Ft. @ $ =$
Comments on Cost Approach (gross living area calculations, depreciation, etc.)	
	Garage/Carport Sq. Ft. @ $ =$
	Total Estimate of Cost-New = $
	Less Physical Functional External
	Depreciation =$( )
	Depreciated Cost of Improvements =$
	"As-is" Value of Site Improvements =$
Estimated Remaining Economic Life (HUD and VA only) Years	Indicated Value By Cost Approach =$

Quiz Answers

1. c) The most detailed method of estimating construction costs is the quantity survey method, which includes analysis of labor rates and man-hours necessary for each component of the construction.

2. a) Only one cost per square foot is necessary for the entirety of a house, even if it has more than one story.

3. d) The unit costs in the unit-in-place method account for all labor, materials, and equipment.

4. d) The comparative-unit method (or square foot method) of estimating costs may require the appraiser to make adjustments to account for differences in the features, size, shape, and location of buildings.

5. b) To account for local construction costs that are 10% higher than average, an appraiser would multiply the costs by 110% (or 1.1).

6. c) A poor floor plan is an example of functional obsolescence.

7. c) External obsolescence may be temporary, but it is almost always incurable.

8. a) Estimating depreciation is generally considered the most difficult step in the cost approach to value.

9. a) Worn-out carpeting would most likely be considered a form of curable physical deterioration, since the cost of replacing the carpet is probably less than the value added by new carpet.

10. b) In the cost approach to value, the value of the site is determined separately and added at the end of the process.

11. b) In a newer home, less depreciation will have occurred, making depreciation estimates more reliable.

12. c) The cost per square foot of a 2,000 square foot home will be greater than the cost per square foot of a 2,500 square foot home. Smaller homes have higher costs per square foot, since both a large and small house require the same expensive components such as kitchen appliances.

13. d) Effective age is the economic life of the improvement minus the remaining economic life of the improvement.

14. d) Methods of measuring depreciation include the breakdown, economic age-life, and market extraction methods.

15. b) Superadequacies in the subject property are not considered part of the replacement cost, since replacement cost measures the cost of building an improvement with the same utility rather than an exact replica of the subject property.

Exercise Answers

#1 House: 22 ft. × 41 ft. = 902 sq. ft. area
902 sq. ft. × $62/sq. ft. = $55,924 cost of house

Garage: 20 ft. × 19 ft.= 380 sq. ft. area
380 sq. ft. × $26/sq. ft = $9,880 cost of garage

$55,924 + $9,880 = $65,804 total estimated cost new of improvements (may be rounded to $65,800)

#2 Foundation: 36 ft. + 36 ft. + 40 ft. + 40 ft. = 152 lineal ft. of perimeter
152 ft. × $20.00/ft. = $3,040

Floor framing: 36 ft. × 40 ft. = 1,440 sq. ft. of floor area
1,440 sq. ft. × $4.50/sq. ft. = $6,480

Wall framing:
Exterior: 152 ft. × $31.00/ft. = $4,712
Interior: 135 ft. × $12.00/ft. = $1,620

Roof framing: 1,850 sq. ft. × $3.50/sq. ft. = $6,475

Siding: 152 ft. × 8.5 ft. = 1,292 sq. ft. of wall area
1,292 sq. ft. × $2.25/sq. ft. = $2,907

Roofing: 1,850 sq. ft. × $2.70/sq. ft. = $4,995

Doors and windows:
Exterior doors: 2 × $400 = $800
Interior doors: 7 × $175 = $1,225
Windows: 240 sq. ft. × $21.50/sq. ft. = $5,160

Interior finishes:
Walls: 152 ft. × 8 ft. = 1,216 sq. ft. (inside of exterior walls)
135 ft. × 8 ft. × 2 ft. = 2,160 sq. ft. (interior partitions)
1,216 sq. ft. + 2,160 sq. ft. + 1,440 sq. ft. (ceilings) = 4,816 sq. ft. total area
4,816 sq. ft. × $0.75/sq. ft. = $3,612
Floors: 1,440 sq. ft. × $2/sq. ft. = $2,880
Cabinets and fixtures: $7,000

Mechanical systems: $12,000

Electrical system: 1,440 sq. ft. × $1.40/sq. ft. = $2,016

Total direct costs: $64,922

Indirect costs: 100% – 20% = 80% direct costs; 20% ÷ 80% = .25 indirect cost (25% of direct cost); .25 × $64,922 = $16,230.50

TOTAL COST: $64,922 + $16,230.50 = $81,152.50

#3 333 ÷ 180 = 1.85

1.85 × \$85,000 = \$157,250

#4
1. CF
2. L
3. CP
4. IP
5. CF
6. IF
7. E
8. CP
9. CF
10. IP

#5 Method #1: 65 – 52 = 13 years, effective age
13 ÷ 65 = 0.20 economic age-life ratio
0.20 × \$200,000 = \$40,000 accrued depreciation
\$200,000 – \$40,000 = \$160,000 depreciated value

Method #2: \$200,000 – \$5,000 (curable items) = \$195,000
65 – 55 = 10 years, effective age after repairs
10 ÷ 65 = 0.15385 economic age-life ratio
0.15385 × \$195,000 = \$30,000 accrued depreciation (incurable)
\$5,000 + \$30,000 = \$35,000 total accrued depreciation
\$200,000 – \$35,000 = \$165,000 depreciated value

#6 1.
1. a
2. b
3. b
4. a
5. a
6. a
7. c
8. c

2. Curable functional obsolescence due to superadequacies is usually not relevant when the cost is based on replacement cost, because the cost of the superadequate items is not included in the cost estimate.

Case Study Answers

See URAR form excerpt below.

COST APPROACH TO VALUE (not required by Fannie Mae)

COST APPROACH

Provide adequate information for the lender/client to replicate the below cost figures and calculations.

Support for the opinion of site value (summary of comparable land sales or other methods for estimating site value)

ESTIMATED ☑ REPRODUCTION OR ☐ REPLACEMENT COST NEW	OPINION OF SITE VALUE = $ 172,000
Source of cost data	Dwelling 2220 Sq. Ft. @ $ 70 =$ 155,400
Quality rating from cost service Effective date of cost data	Sq. Ft. @ $ =$
Comments on Cost Approach (gross living area calculations, depreciation, etc.)	Covered porch: 156 sq. ft. @ $ 17 2,652
•Site value estimated by sales comparison approach	Garage/Carport 240 Sq. Ft. @ $ 27 =$ 6,480
•Square footage obtained by exterior measurement	Total Estimate of Cost-New = $ 164,532
•Cost data obtained from Marshall & Swift	Less Physical / Functional / External
•Depreciation estimated using economic age-life method (effective age = 1 year)	Depreciation $2,532 / 0 / 0 =$(2,532)
	Depreciated Cost of Improvements =$ 162,000
	"As-is" Value of Site Improvements =$ 7,500
Estimated Remaining Economic Life (HUD and VA only) Years	Indicated Value By Cost Approach =$341,500

9 Sales Comparison Approach to Value

Overview

In the sales comparison approach, the appraiser analyzes the sales of similar properties in order to estimate the value of the subject property. In residential appraisal, more emphasis is placed on the sales comparison approach to value than on either the cost or income approaches. The sales comparison approach is preferred because it is easy for nonprofessionals to understand, and it is usually considered quite reliable.

In this chapter, we will discuss the various steps to the sales comparison approach. After completing this chapter, you should be able to:

- describe the characteristics of a real estate market, and explain the significance of real estate markets to the sales comparison approach to value;
- list the basic steps in the sales comparison approach to value;
- explain what makes a sale "comparable" for appraisal purposes;
- list the elements of comparison that are commonly used to analyze comparable sales in residential appraisals;
- understand the difference between units of comparison and elements of comparison, and describe their roles in the sales comparison approach;
- describe how adjustments are made to the prices of comparable sales;
- explain how the concept of contributory value applies to adjustments;
- understand the effect of financing terms on sales prices, and explain what is meant by cash equivalent financing terms;
- apply the techniques of paired data analysis and relative comparison analysis to obtain adjustment values for any differences in the elements of comparison;
- describe the significance of the sequence in which adjustments are made to comparable sales prices; and
- describe the process by which the value indicators from the sales comparison approach are reconciled into a single indicator of the subject property's value.

Introduction

In the sales comparison approach (also known as the **market comparison** or **market data** approach) the appraiser analyzes data from actual market transactions involving properties similar to the subject property (referred to as **comparable sales**). First, the appraiser chooses appropriate transactions, then she identifies the differences that exist between the subject property and the comparable properties, and finally, she makes price adjustments to account for those differences. The adjusted sales prices of the comparable properties then serve as the basis for an opinion about the value of the subject property.

The sales comparison approach is based on the **market theory of value**, which states that value is determined by the actions of buyers and sellers in the marketplace in response to the influences of supply and demand. Value is determined by the **principle of substitution**: a buyer will not pay more for a property than it would cost to acquire an equally desirable substitute, assuming the substitute property could be acquired within a reasonable length of time. Thus, in an active market where many equivalent properties are available, the value of any one property should be equivalent to the prices paid for similar properties. (The market theory of value and the principle of substitution are covered in greater detail in Chapter 2.)

Real Estate Markets

The concept of a real estate market is central to the sales comparison approach. A **real estate market** is a distinct group of buyers and sellers whose actions are influenced in similar ways by similar forces of supply and demand. Prices paid for properties within a given market should indicate the value of other similar properties in that market, but usually do not indicate the value of properties in a different market.

Example: Prices paid for homes in a community with a strong economic base and high wage levels are likely to be much higher than prices paid for similar homes in a depressed community.

In applying the sales comparison approach, the appraiser must be keenly aware of the subject property's market. The geographic boundaries of a market may be large or small, depending on the type of property. Markets for residential property tend to be smaller, encompassing neighborhoods or districts, while markets for large commercial properties may be national or even international.

Markets are sometimes defined by physical boundaries, but the critical factor in defining a market for appraisal purposes is similarity in the forces (economic, social, governmental, and physical/environmental) that influence value. And if these forces are rapidly changing, it becomes much more difficult to identify comparable sales, and the sales comparison approach becomes much less reliable.

Example: In a period of rapid inflation, the pool of buyers who can afford to purchase a particular size house may change almost daily, and sales of similar properties that closed a month ago may no longer be representative of the present market.

Comparable Sales

For a sale to be considered **comparable**, it must compete with the subject property. In other words, it must be in the same market as the subject property and appeal to the same sorts of buyers.

The sales comparison approach to value is the preferred approach for many appraisal purposes, including residential and vacant land appraisals. An appraiser can usually find a number of good comparables, and the values indicated by this approach are viewed as highly reliable in most cases. The strength of this approach—its reliance on market data—is also its weakness, however. If data for comparable sales is inadequate, or totally lacking, the sales comparison approach cannot be properly applied. As this is often the case for special use properties such as public buildings, the sales comparison approach is rarely used in appraising special use properties.

To use the sales comparison approach, an appraiser must have at least three comparables from the subject property's market.

Steps in the Sales Comparison Approach

The sales comparison approach involves five basic steps:

1. collecting data,
2. verifying data,
3. selecting units of comparison,
4. comparative analysis, and
5. reconciliation.

Collecting and Verifying Data. First, the appraiser must **gather data** on comparable properties in the market. In collecting the data, the appraiser needs to evaluate how similar these properties are to the subject property. The most similar comparable properties should be selected for use in the analysis.

The appraiser should collect all of the same data for the comparables that she already has for the subject property. This includes the terms and conditions of all transactions, information about the properties' physical characteristics, and information about listing prices and the prices of any pending offers, sales, or options.

In step two, the appraiser must **verify the data** that will be used. Not only does verification establish the reliability of the data, it also allows the appraiser to determine the circumstances surrounding the transaction. For example, if the buyer or seller was not typically motivated, the transaction will not be a reliable value indicator.

Interviewing a party to the transaction is considered the most reliable way to verify transaction data. Physical review is the most reliable way to verify the characteristics of the property. (Refer to Chapter 5 for more information on data collection and verification.)

Selecting Units of Comparison. When comparing different properties, it is important for the price of each property to be stated in the same unit of comparison. It would make no sense, for example, to compare one property's price per square foot of living area to another property's price per front foot of water frontage.

Therefore, the third step in the sales comparison approach is **selecting units of comparison**. That unit may be an acre, a front foot, or a square foot. For example, the price of vacant land is often stated as a price per acre, per square foot, or per front foot. In residential appraisals, the price per square foot of living area and the price for the entire property are commonly used units of comparison.

The appraiser must choose the unit or units of comparison that are most appropriate for the particular property being appraised. More than one unit may be appropriate, and the appraiser will make a comparison for each of the applicable units. If comparing several different units of comparison leads to a consistent indicator of value, that indicator of value will be more reliable. If a wide range of values results from using different units of comparison, the appraiser will want to investigate the cause of the discrepancy.

> **Example:** An analysis of comparable properties results in an indicated value for the subject property of $304,000, and an indicated value per square foot (derived separately) of $91.32. The size of the subject property is 2,000 square feet, so its indicated value based on value per square foot is $182,640 ($91.32 × 2,000). The values indicated by using different units of comparison are inconsistent, so the appraiser must investigate further to determine the reasons for the discrepancy, and make appropriate adjustments.

Analyzing and Adjusting the Comparables. The next step in the sales income approach is **comparative analysis**. The appraiser first identifies the elements of comparison that may affect the value of the subject property. For each element of comparison, the characteristics of the comparable are compared to those of the subject property; any differences are measured, and an appropriate price adjustment is made. The net total of all the adjustments for each comparable is then added to (or subtracted from) the price of the comparable to arrive at an indicator of value for the subject property.

The process of calculating and applying price adjustments is discussed in greater detail later in this chapter.

Reconciling the Value Indicators. The final step in the sales comparison approach is **reconciliation** of the value indicators provided by analysis of the comparables. Typically, the subject property's value will fall somewhere between the highest and lowest value indicator. In reconciling the different amounts, the appraiser estimates where within the range of values the subject property's value lies.

Reconciliation is not a simple averaging of the value indicators. The appraiser must evaluate the characteristics of each comparable and determine which is most reliable. Comparables that are most similar to the subject property are generally considered to be the most reliable indicators of the subject's value.

Reconciliation is discussed in greater detail at the end of this chapter.

Exercise 1

1. List the five steps in the sales comparison approach to value.

   a. ______________________________

   b. ______________________________

   c. ______________________________

   d. ______________________________

   e. ______________________________

2. List two reasons why verification of comparable data is important.

   a. ______________________________

   b. ______________________________

3. What is the most important factor in defining the boundaries of a real estate market for purposes of the sales comparison approach?

   ____

   ____

Comparative Analysis

Now let's take a more detailed look at the fourth step in the sales comparison approach, **comparative analysis**. Comparative analysis involves several steps.

Step 1: Identify the elements of comparison.

Step 2: For each element of comparison, measure the differences between the subject and each comparable, and determine an appropriate adjustment to account for each difference.

Step 3: For each comparable, find the net total adjustment and apply it to the comparable's sale price to get a value indicator for the subject property.

Identify the Elements of Comparison

The first step in the comparative analysis is to identify the elements of comparison. An **element of comparison** is any aspect of a real estate transaction that may affect the sales price, including the terms and conditions of the sale and the characteristics of the property itself.

Don't confuse elements of comparison with units of comparison. A unit of comparison is simply a unit of measurement; an element of comparison is one of the key considerations that contributes to differences in the prices paid for properties.

> **Example:** An appraiser knows that the number of baths in a house has an effect on its sales price, so the number of baths is identified as an element of comparison for the appraisal. If the subject property has two baths, but the comparable property has only one, the appraiser will adjust the sales price of the comparable property to account for the difference in this element of comparison.

The elements of comparison for a typical residential appraisal include:

- real property rights conveyed (fee simple or other interest);
- financing terms;
- conditions of sale (the motivation of the buyer and the seller);
- expenditures needed after the sale;
- market conditions (date of sale);
- location;
- physical characteristics (size, quality, etc.);
- factors affecting use (zoning, water rights, etc.); and
- non-realty items included in the sale.

Note that the first five items on this list concern the transaction, while the remaining four are property-related.

Real Property Rights Conveyed. In most residential transactions, the real property rights conveyed include the full fee simple interest in the property. Similarly, in most appraisals the property interest that is being appraised is the fee simple.

However, some appraisals may involve other types of real property rights. Two common examples of non-fee simple interests are the leasehold and the leased fee. A leasehold interest includes the rights to use property under the terms of a lease. The interest of the owner of the leased property is called the leased fee. Residential appraisals of leasehold estates usually involve long-term ground leases, where the tenant has constructed a building on the leased land. In such cases, the building belongs to the tenant (the owner of the leasehold estate), while the land belongs to the owner of the leased fee estate.

When choosing comparable properties, it's important to make sure that the real property interest involved in a comparable transaction was the same type of interest that's being appraised. For instance, if the interest being appraised is a fee simple interest in the subject property, the appraiser should not use a transaction involving a leasehold interest as a comparable.

Financing Terms. The financing used to purchase a property can affect the price paid for it. For example, if a seller financed the sale of his house at a below-market interest rate, the price paid may have been higher than the buyer would have agreed to without the seller financing.

If the financing terms do not affect the price paid for the property, the financing is referred to as **cash equivalent**. Sales that are cash equivalent do not require any price adjustment for financing terms. However, if nonstandard financing (financing terms that are not typical of those available in the market) was used, the appraiser must evaluate the impact of the financing on the transaction.

Nonstandard financing can take a wide variety of forms, from seller financing to interest rate buydowns to loan assumptions. In some cases, the monetary effect may be fairly obvious. For example, if the seller pays some or all of the points on the buyer's loan, the effect on the sales price is likely to equal the amount paid by the seller. Other cases are not so clear-cut. In a sale that involves seller financing, for instance, the buyer may benefit in any of several ways. A below-market interest rate, small downpayment, reduced (or zero) loan fees, and easier loan qualification are some of the possible benefits of seller financing.

The appraiser may be able to make an appropriate adjustment to the comparable's sales price, but if the impact on the price was too great or is too difficult to estimate, another comparable should be chosen.

Conditions of Sale. Conditions of sale are the circumstances under which a real estate transaction took place. Normal conditions of sale include a buyer and a seller who are typically motivated—whose motivations in entering into their transaction are essentially the same as those of other buyers and sellers in the real estate market.

As we discussed in Chapter 2, a sale can generally be considered to have taken place under normal conditions if:

- it was an arm's length transaction (between unrelated parties);
- neither party was subject to undue stimulus (unusual pressure to act);
- both parties acted prudently and knowledgeably, and in their own best interests; and
- the property was exposed on the open market for a reasonable length of time.

If one or more of these conditions are absent, the parties weren't typically motivated. As a result, the price paid for the property isn't necessarily a reliable indication of its market value. For instance, a seller who has been transferred to another city may accept a low offer to make a quick sale, or a developer may pay an above-market price for a property that is necessary to complete a certain project. If the buyer was a relative, friend, or business associate, the seller may have accepted a much lower price than a stranger would have been willing to pay in an arm's length transaction.

Example: The appraiser finds a comparable that is very similar to the subject property and located only two blocks away. The comparable sold for $620,000 three months ago. However, because the buyer was the seller's nephew, it wasn't an arm's length transaction, and the appraiser must assume that the motivation of the parties was not typical. The price paid may be significantly less than the property's true market value.

The appraiser must investigate the circumstances surrounding each comparable sale to make sure it took place under normal conditions. If it didn't, that usually means it should not be used as a comparable. Because the buyer and the seller were acting under the influence of forces that do not affect the market in general, the price paid is not a reliable indicator of market value. It's typically very difficult to quantify exactly how much those unusual forces affected the price.

Occasionally, however, a sale that didn't take place under normal conditions can be used as a comparable if the appraiser makes an appropriate adjustment to the price.

> **Example:** When investigating a potential comparable's conditions of sale, the appraiser learns that the seller was taking advantage of a tax break by selling the property. This wasn't a sale under entirely normal conditions, since the seller received a benefit from the transaction that isn't reflected in the price. However, in this case the seller happens to be willing to disclose exactly how much she saved as a result of the tax break. The appraiser decides to go ahead and use the sale as a comparable, adjusting the price by adding the amount of the seller's tax savings to it.

Adjustments for conditions of sale are rare and should be made with great care; the appraiser must conduct careful research to find data that support the adjustment. If sufficient supporting data are not available, the appraiser should not use the transaction as a comparable sale.

Expenditures Needed After the Sale. A property's sales price will be affected by any needed upgrading or repairs that won't be carried out before the sale closes. The buyer recognizes that she'll have to pay for the repairs soon after closing, and she'll take those anticipated expenditures into account in negotiations with the seller. Thus, if the buyer of a comparable property expected to make repairs after the sale, the appraiser should adjust the price of the comparable to reflect this.

The appraiser bases the adjustment on the amount of expenses anticipated at the time of the transaction, since the buyer and the seller determined the sales price based on what they anticipated. Even if the actual expenses turned out to be higher or lower, the anticipated expenses determine the appraiser's adjustment.

Market Conditions. The price paid for a comparable property reflects the state of the market as of the date the property was sold, but the forces that affect value are subject to constant change. If market conditions have changed between the date of the comparable sale and the effective date of the appraisal, an adjustment must be made to account for this fact. The closer a comparable sale is to the effective date of the appraisal, the more reliable it will be as a value indicator.

Comparables that sold within six months of the appraisal date do not usually require any adjustment for market conditions, unless significant change has occurred in the market since the date of the comparable sale. If the real estate market has been unusually inactive, the appraiser may have to use sales older than six months as comparables. In this case, adjustments must be made for inflation or other economic trends that have affected market prices since the date of sale.

Example: The appraiser is unable to locate three comparable properties that have sold in the past six months, so he chooses a comparable that sold ten months ago. Since then, property values have increased about 3% due to inflation. To account for the effect of inflation, the appraiser adds 3% to the comparable's sales price.

Note that comparables older than one year are usually not considered, even in the absence of any obvious change in market conditions.

Example: If the effective date of an appraisal is January 1, 2010, sales that took place prior to 2009 won't be considered as possible comparables. A sale that occurred on May 5, 2009 could be used as a comparable with an adjustment for changes in market conditions between that date and January 1, 2010. A sale that occurred on July 17, 2009 would require such an adjustment only if the market was unusually volatile during the last half of 2009.

Location. Another important element of comparison is the location of the comparable in comparison to the location of the subject property. Ideally, the comparable should be in the same neighborhood as the subject. If sufficient recent comparables are not available from the subject neighborhood, the appraiser will consider sales from nearby similar neighborhoods. However, using comparables from other neighborhoods requires the appraiser to compare the neighborhoods, as well as the individual properties. This complication should be avoided whenever possible.

Even if the comparable is located in the same neighborhood as the subject, however, the appraiser must consider any differences in value that result from location.

Example: Two identical properties located a block apart in the same neighborhood may have different values if one has a pleasant view, while the other does not. The values could also differ due to location if one is on a busy arterial, while the other is on a quiet side street.

Adjustments for locational differences normally represent differences in site value, but they may also represent differences in external obsolescence of the improvements. In the latter case, the appraiser must be careful not to make duplicate adjustments (under location and under physical characteristics) for the same item.

Physical Characteristics. Most adjustments in residential appraisals are made for differences in the physical characteristics of the site or the improvements. Comparables with differences in property rights, financing terms, conditions of sale, market conditions, or location are more likely to simply be rejected from consideration.

A wide range of physical characteristics can affect the price paid for a property. The appraiser must consider all of these potential differences, and make the appropriate adjustment for each characteristic where the subject differs from the comparable. Physical characteristics that are elements of comparison in residential appraisals include:

- size and shape of lot,
- age and condition of improvements,
- architectural style and compatibility,
- type and quality of building materials,
- square footage of living area/basement/garage,

Fig. 9.1 Houses with Different Physical Characteristics

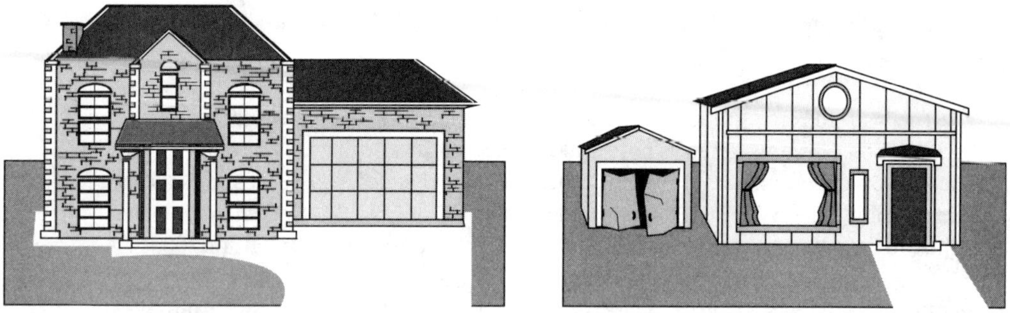

- number of rooms,
- functional utility,
- equipment and amenities, and
- site improvements.

Adjustments should always be based on an item's **contributory value**, not on its cost. According to the principle of contribution, the value of an individual component or improvement is equal to the amount of value it adds to the property as a whole. This amount, referred to as the item's contributory value, depends on market forces and is independent of the item's cost. So a second bathroom that cost $8,000 to install may add $11,000 to the home's value. Conversely, a third bathroom that also costs $8,000 to install may increase the home's value by only $5,000.

Use. Because highest and best use is central to value, comparables are usually rejected if their highest and best use does not match that of the subject property. For residential appraisals, choosing comparables with zoning restrictions similar to the subject property usually ensures that they have the same highest and best use. Other factors affecting use, such as water rights or a flood zone designation, may also be elements of comparison.

Non-Realty Items Included in Sale. An appraised value is usually the value of the subject real property only; it does not include the value of any personal property (such as non-built-in appliances) that may be sold in conjunction with the real estate. If the sales price of a comparable includes non-realty items, the appraiser must adjust the price of the comparable to account for the value of the personal property items included in the sale.

Other Elements of Comparison. The elements of comparison discussed above are the most common ones in residential appraisals. However, many other elements could conceivably influence the price paid for a particular property. The appraiser must be alert to any characteristics of the subject or a comparable that could influence value, and make whatever adjustments are necessary.

Exercise 2

1. Match the characteristic on the right with the corresponding element of comparison category on the left.

1. ___ conditions of sale	a. zoning
2. ___ financing terms	b. date of sale
3. ___ market conditions	c. personal property
4. ___ location	d. easements
5. ___ real property rights conveyed	e. lot size
6. ___ physical characteristics	f. loan assumption
7. ___ highest and best use	g. motivation
8. ___ non-realty items in sale	h. neighborhood

2. Mark each of the following that would be considered cash equivalent financing.

________ a. The seller pays points to buy down the buyer's interest rate

________ b. The buyer assumes the seller's low-interest mortgage

________ c. The buyer obtains a VA loan with no downpayment

________ d. The seller provides secondary financing to cover the buyer's large downpayment

Analyze and Adjust the Comparables

After identifying the appropriate elements of comparison, the next step in comparative analysis is to analyze the comparables. To do this, the appraiser first measures the differences between the comparables and the subject property for each element of comparison. Next, the appraiser considers how the similarities and differences affect the relative values of the properties, and adjusts the sales prices of the comparables to reflect the differences. The appraiser then uses this information to arrive at an indication of the subject property's market value, using the sales prices of the comparables as a reference point.

Measuring Differences. The differences between a comparable and the subject property can be measured in two ways:

1. qualitative (superior, inferior, or same), or
2. quantitative (dollar amount or percentage).

To analyze a difference in value based on qualitative measurement, appraisers use a technique called **relative comparison analysis**. For analyzing differences in quantitative terms, they use a technique called **paired data analysis**.

Relative comparison analysis. In relative comparison analysis, the appraiser considers the relative quality of the comparables and the subject property, without assigning a numerical value to the differences between the properties. Instead, the appraiser focuses on whether the differences make a comparable superior or inferior to the subject property.

Based on the prices of the comparables, the appraiser can develop an opinion of the subject property's value. The subject property should be worth less than comparables that are superior, and it should be worth more than comparables that are inferior.

Example: The chart below shows a market data grid for an appraisal using relative comparison analysis. The result of the analysis is an indicated range of values for the subject property. In the example, the indicated value of the subject property is greater than the prices of comparables #1 and #3, but less than the price of comparable #2, or between $274,000 and $278,000. The appraiser must still reconcile the value indicators into a single indication of value from the sales comparison approach.

Market Data Grid for Relative Comparison Analysis

Element of Comparison	Subject Property	Comparable #1	Comparable #2	Comparable #3
Sales price	--	$274,000	$278,000	$270,000
Square footage	2,000	2,000	2,100	1,900
Age	7 years	10 years	6 years	8 years
Physical condition	--	Inferior	Superior	Average
Location	--	Average	Average	Inferior
Financing terms	--	Inferior	Superior	Inferior

Relative comparison analysis provides a range of possible values for the subject property. The prices of the superior comparables define the upper end of the range, and the prices of the inferior comparables define the lower end. The appraiser can be reasonably confident that the subject property's value falls within that range, without deciding on a precise value figure.

If the comparables chosen are all superior or all inferior, only the upper or lower limit of the range can be identified. To narrow down the range of values for the subject property, the appraiser may need to look for additional comparables.

In addition to measuring the comparables against the subject property, the comparables can also be compared to each other. The appraiser can rank the comparables based on a particular characteristic and analyze where the subject property would fall in this ranking. This can help the appraiser identify trends in value related to specific elements of comparison. For example, an appraiser might rank comparables according to square footage to see where the subject property fits in. The rankings and prices of the comparables help the appraiser understand how the subject property's square footage affects its value.

Paired data analysis. In paired data analysis (also known as **matched pairs analysis**, or **paired data set analysis**), an appraiser uses data from a matched pair of properties to assign a value to an element of comparison. The appraiser first locates properties that are identical (or very similar) to each other in all aspects except one. Note that these are not the properties the appraiser has selected as comparables; they need not be similar to the subject property. By selecting two properties with only one significant difference, the appraiser isolates the effect this one characteristic has on value. This allows the appraiser to assign a value to the characteristic when it's used as an element of comparison. So when a comparable differs from the subject property as to this characteristic, the appraiser can use the value of the characteristic to adjust the price of the comparable property.

Fig. 9.2 Paired Data Analysis

Market Data Grid for Paired Data Analysis

Element of Comparison	Comparable #1	Comparable #2	Comparable #3	Comparable #4	Comparable #5
Garage size	1-car	2-car	2-car	2-car	2-car
Living area (sq. footage)	1,500	1,600	1,500	1,500	1,500
Lot size (sq. footage)	10,000	10,000	11,000	10,000	10,000
Basement	yes	no	yes	yes	no
Sales price	$250,000	$258,000	$258,000	$256,000	$250,000

Paired data analysis is best illustrated by means of an example. Figure 9.2 shows a market data grid listing several elements of comparison for five different properties. The first step is to identify pairs of properties that vary in only one characteristic. In this example, properties #1 and #4 are identical in all respects except that property #1 has a one-car garage, while property #4 has a two-car garage. Since the price paid for property #4 is $6,000 higher than the price of property #1, an appraiser would conclude that the market value of the extra garage space was $6,000.

Continuing with this example, we can see that propertics #2 and #5 are identical except for the size of the living area. Property #2 has an additional 100 square feet of living area, and sold for $8,000 more than property #5. This indicates that the market places a value of $80 per square foot on the additional living space.

Properties #3 and #4 vary only in the size of their lots. Property #3 sold for $2,000 more than property #4, so the difference in sales prices indicates a value of $2,000 for an additional 1,000 square feet of lot area. Finally, properties #4 and #5 have all the same characteristics except that property #5 is lacking a basement. Because property #4 sold for $6,000 more than property #5, the indicated value of a basement is $6,000.

The appraiser in this example has now identified adjustment values for four elements of comparison: garage size, living area, lot size, and basement. These values can then be used to make adjustments to the sales prices of comparables to account for differences between the subject property and the comparables. Figure 9.3 shows an example based on the adjustment values derived above.

Although the concept behind paired data analysis is fairly simple, the real world is more complex. Rarely will an appraiser be able to identify two properties that are identical in all characteristics except one. It is often necessary to make price adjustments for other differences first, in order to isolate the effect of the particular difference the appraiser is trying to measure.

Example: An appraiser is analyzing property data to determine the effect of different types of car storage on value. Property A has an attached garage and 1,300 square feet of living area. It sold recently for $350,000. Property B is similar, except that it has a carport instead of a garage, and contains 1,400 square feet of living area. Its sales price was $348,000.

In this case, the appraiser must first make an adjustment for the size difference between the two properties, in order to isolate the effect on value of the difference in car storage facilities. If the appraiser estimates (based on previous experience with matched pairs analysis in the subject neighborhood) that the extra 100 square feet in Property B adds $4,000 to its value, this amount would be subtracted from Property B's sales price.

The difference between the adjusted price of Property B ($344,000) and the price of Property A ($350,000) could then be used to indicate the difference in value between properties with garages and properties with carports.

The example above raises another issue that comes into play when using paired data analysis. That is, the effect of one characteristic on value can often depend on another characteristic. In the example above, the amount of the adjustment to account for the

Fig. 9.3 Adjustment Values for Paired Data Analysis

Market Data Grid for Paired Data Analysis						
Element of Comparison	Subject Property	Comp. #1	Comp. #2	Comp. #3	Comp. #4	Comp. #5
Garage size	2-car	1-car (+$6,000)	2-car	2-car	2-car	2-car
Living area (sq. footage)	1,600	1,500 (+$8,000)	1,600	1,500 (+$8,000)	1,500 (+$8,000)	1,500 (+$8,000)
Lot size (sq. footage)	10,000	10,000	10,000	11,000 (-$2,000)	10,000	10,000
Basement	yes	yes	no (+$6,000)	yes	yes	no (+$6,000)
Sales price	--	$250,000	$258,000	$258,000	$256,000	$250,000
Net adjustments	--	+$14,000	+$6,000	+$6,000	+$8,000	+$14,000
Adjusted price	--	$264,000	$264,000	$264,000	$264,000	$264,000

difference in the size of the improvements may well depend on the age of the improvements: 100 square feet of living space may add more value (in terms of dollar amount) to a ten-year-old home than it does to an 18-year-old home.

In practice, appraisers must analyze and compare hundreds of sales transactions to gain an understanding of the effects on value caused by different elements of comparison. Paired data analysis is a useful tool in this process, but more sophisticated statistical analysis is often necessary as well.

For each measured difference in an element of comparison, the appraiser must make an adjustment to account for the resulting difference in value. Adjustments are made to the prices of the comparables. If a comparable is superior to the subject in some respect, its price is adjusted downward. If the comparable is inferior to the subject, its price is adjusted upward. The appraiser makes a series of these adjustments for each significant difference between the subject property and the comparable. In this way, she arrives at an estimate of what the comparable would have sold for if it had been identical to the subject property.

Example: A comparable that sold for $440,000 has a good view, while the subject does not. The difference in value attributable to the view is $20,000. Since the comparable is superior to the subject, the $20,000 is subtracted from the comparable sales price, to give an indicated value for the subject of $420,000. If the subject had the good view and the comparable did not, the price of the comparable would be adjusted upward (comparable inferior to subject), to give an indicated value of $460,000 for the subject.

Adjustments are never made directly to the value of the subject property. This is because the subject property's value is unknown, so there is no starting point from which to make adjustments. In addition, because the appraiser is comparing several properties against the subject property, it would be easy to make mistakes such as adjusting twice for the same factor.

Typically, most of an appraiser's adjustments are made to account for differences in physical characteristics between the comparables and the subject property. Although the appraiser uses comparables that are as similar to the subject property as possible, at least some physical differences will usually exist.

Relative Comparison Analysis vs. Paired Data Analysis. At first glance, paired data analysis may appear more accurate than relative comparison analysis because it produces a precise figure instead of a range of values. However, the precision of paired data analysis can also be misleading, because the purpose of an appraisal is to evaluate the property as a whole, not just as a sum of different characteristics. Relative comparison analysis allows the appraiser to account for interrelated factors that affect value together. An appraiser should always consider both methods and choose the one that is most appropriate for the situation.

Depending on the available data, sometimes it is appropriate to use relative comparison analysis and paired data analysis together. For example, the appraiser may have paired data to support adjustments related to some elements of comparison but not others. If paired data is not available for a particular feature, the appraiser will need to use relative comparison analysis for that element of comparison instead.

When an appraisal involves both relative comparison analysis and paired data analysis, they must be used consistently. For any specific element of comparison, the appraiser should apply the same method of analysis to all of the comparables.

Exercise 3

1. Based on the data shown in the chart below, determine the adjustment amount for each characteristic listed below.

   seller financing: ______________________

   location: ______________________

   lot size: ______________________

living area: ______________________________

view: ______________________________

Market Data Grid for Paired Data Analysis						
Element of Comparison	Comp. #1	Comp. #2	Comp. #3	Comp. #4	Comp. #5	Comp. #6
Seller financing	yes	no	no	no	no	no
Location	Inside lot	Corner lot	Inside lot	Inside lot	Inside lot	Inside lot
Lot size (sq. footage)	12,000	12,000	10,000	12,000	12,000	12,000
Living area (sq. footage)	2,000	2,000	2,000	2,000	1,900	2,000
View	yes	yes	yes	yes	yes	no
Sales price	$380,000	$371,000	$369,000	$375,000	$367,000	$365,000

2. Determine the net adjustment amount and the adjusted sales price for each of the comparables shown below.

Market Data Grid for Paired Data Analysis							
Element of Comparison	Subject Property	Comp. #1	Comp. #2	Comp. #3	Comp. #4	Comp. #5	Comp. #6
Seller financing	no	yes	no	no	no	no	no
Location	Inside lot	Inside lot	Corner lot	Inside lot	Inside lot	Inside lot	Inside lot
Lot size (sq. footage)	12,000	12,000	12,000	10,000	12,000	12,000	12,000
Living area (sq. footage)	1,900	2,000	2,000	2,000	2,000	1,900	2,000
View	no	yes	yes	yes	yes	yes	no
Sales price	--	$380,000	$371,000	$369,000	$375,000	$367,000	$365,000

1. ______________________________

2. ______________________________

3. ______________________________

4. ______________________________

5. ______________________________

6. ______________________________

Adjustment Calculations. An appraiser should carefully consider the form in which adjustments to the prices of comparables are expressed, and the order in which they are applied. Although adjustments are usually expressed in terms of a dollar amount, they may also be expressed as percentages. When an adjustment is expressed as a percentage, the percentage must be converted into dollars in order to calculate the adjusted sales price.

Percentage adjustments. In converting a percentage to a dollar figure, great care must be taken to understand exactly what the percentage is referring to. Saying that Property A is worth 10% more than Property B is not the same thing as saying that Property B is worth 10% less than Property A. In the first case, the 10% is referring to the value of Property B: Property A is worth 110% (100% + 10%) of the value of Property B. In the second case, the 10% is referring to the value of Property A: Property B is worth 90% (100% – 10%) of the value of Property A. If Property A is worth $100,000, the value of Property B in the first case would be $100,000 ÷ 1.1 = $90,909. In the second case, Property B's value would be $100,000 × 0.9 = $90,000.

To determine whether a percentage applies to the value of the subject property or the value of the comparable, simply state the relationship between the values of the two properties. The statement should be in this form, with X representing the percentage amount: "Property A is worth X% more (or less) than Property B."

If your statement of the relationship has the subject property first (in other words, Property A is the subject property), the percentage applies to the value of the comparable (Property B). In that case, the adjustment calculation is simple, since it is always the comparable's value (not the subject's value) that is adjusted:

Step 1. Multiply the value of the comparable by the percentage amount to get the amount of the adjustment.

Step 2. Then add or subtract this amount from the comparable's value, depending on the relationship between the two properties.

Example: Due to changing market conditions since the date of the comparable sale, the subject should be worth 10% more than the comparable, whose price is $280,000. The relationship between the values of the properties could be stated as: "The subject property's value is 10% more than the comparable's value."

In this statement, the comparable is Property B, so the percentage applies to the comparable. In other words, the amount of the adjustment is 10% of the comparable's value. *$280,000 × .10 = $28,000.*

Since the subject property is worth more than the comparable, the price of the comparable will be adjusted upward. *$280,000 + $28,000 = $308,000.* This is the adjusted value of the comparable.

On the other hand, if the statement of the relationship says the subject property is worth more than the comparable (in other words, the comparable is Property A), then the percentage applies to the value of the subject (Property B). If the percentage applies to the value of the subject, the calculation is more difficult, since the value of the subject is not known. A four-step process is required.

Step 1: If the comparable is worth more than the subject, add the percentage to 1 (100%); if the comparable is worth less than the subject, subtract the percentage from 1 (100%).

Step 2: Divide the percentage by the number calculated in Step 1.

Step 3: Multiply the value of the comparable by the number calculated in Step 2 to get the amount of the adjustment.

Step 4: Adjust the comparable's value by the adjustment amount calculated in Step 3. Add the amount to the comparable's value if the comparable is worth less than the subject property. Subtract it if the comparable is worth more than the subject property.

Example: You've located a comparable that is nearly identical to the subject property. The comparable sold for $300,000 two weeks ago, but it's located in a different neighborhood. The comparable's neighborhood is considered a better location and its homes are generally worth about 10% more than properties in the subject property's neighborhood.

First, write out the statement of the relationship between the subject property and the comparable: *"The comparable is worth 10% more than the subject property."* The subject property is Property B, so the percentage applies to the subject property's value.

Step 1: Add the percentage (10% or 0.1) to 1. *0.1 + 1 = 1.1.*

Step 2: Divide the percentage by the result of Step 1. *0.1 ÷ 1.1 = 0.091 or 9.1% (rounded).*

Step 3: Multiply the value of the comparable by the percentage from Step 2 to find the amount of the adjustment. *$300,000 × 9.1% = $27,300.*

Step 4: Since the comparable is worth more than the subject property, adjust the comparable's value downward by the adjustment amount from Step 3. *$300,000 – $27,300 = $272,700.* This is the adjusted value of the comparable.

Sequence of Adjustments. When making adjustments for a number of different elements of comparison, the sequence in which the adjustments are made does not affect the outcome of the calculation, unless one or more of the adjustments is a percentage.

> **Example:** A comparable requires two adjustments: a 5% upward adjustment for changing market conditions, and a $10,000 downward adjustment because the comparable has an extra bathroom. The price of the comparable is $500,000.
>
> If the appraiser makes the 5% adjustment first, then the first calculation is: *5% of $500,000 = $25,000.*
>
> The two adjustment amounts are then applied to the comparable's price to get an adjusted value of $515,000 (*$500,000 + $25,000 – $10,000*).
>
> On the other hand, if the appraiser made the $10,000 adjustment first, the first calculation would be: *$500,000 – $10,000 = $490,000.*
>
> Then the percentage adjustment would be: *5% of $490,000 = $24,500.* That would mean that the adjusted value of the comparable is $514,500 (*$500,000 – $10,000 + $24,500*).
>
> Thus, in this situation, the order in which the adjustments are applied makes a $500 difference in the adjusted values.

There are no hard and fast rules for the sequence of adjustments in a sales comparison analysis. It is up to the appraiser to determine the most appropriate sequence based on the appraiser's analysis of the market. In percentage cases, however, the adjustments should be made in the following sequence: (1) real property rights conveyed, (2) financing terms, (3) conditions of sale, and (4) market conditions. These adjustments should be made first, and then adjustments concerning the comparable property (location, physical characteristics, etc.).

> **Example:** One comparable has unusual financing terms that require the appraiser to make a percentage adjustment. In addition, the comparable's price needs to be adjusted based on physical differences in the property: the comparable has a fireplace and the subject property does not.
>
> In this situation, the appraiser usually would make the adjustment for the financing first, before adjusting the value of the comparable to account for the fireplace.

Reconciliation

The final step in the sales comparison approach to value is reconciliation, in which the appraiser reviews all of the data and analysis and forms an opinion about the subject property's value. The appraiser will always analyze at least three different comparable properties, with each analysis providing a value indicator for the subject property. Even if the appraiser has chosen good comparables, it is unlikely that they will all indicate exactly the same value for the subject property. The adjusted sales prices typically present a range of values, and the appraiser must use his or her judgment and experience to select some value within this range. In addition, the appraiser may need to reconcile values based on paired data analysis with conclusions drawn from relative comparison analysis.

Choosing an appropriate value for the subject property is not a mechanical process. An appraiser should never average the values indicated by the comparables to estimate the subject property's value. Instead, in reconciling the values, the appraiser considers their relative reliability and gives more weight to the more reliable value indicators. According to the principle of substitution, a comparable that is more similar to the subject property should be a more reliable indicator of value. This is because a more similar comparable competes more directly with the subject property than less similar comparables. Other factors that may affect a value indicator's reliability might include a neighborhood's stability or a market's size: a changing neighborhood indicates unstable values, while an extremely small market can translate into less reliable indicators.

In paired data analysis, a good indicator of reliability is the extent of adjustment that is required for each comparable. Comparables requiring less adjustment are generally more reliable than those that require larger adjustments. These comparables will therefore be given more weight when the figures are reconciled.

Example: The adjusted sales prices of four comparable properties indicate the following range of values for the subject property.

Comparable	Indicated Subject Value
1	$302,300
2	$297,700
3	$305,100
4	$303,700

Comparable #1 is the most similar to the subject property and requires the fewest adjustments. Therefore, the appraiser gives the most weight to this comparable, concluding that the indicated value of the subject property is $302,000.

Fig. 9.4 Net Adjustment

Adjustment for seller financing: 5% of sales price
Adjustment for hot tub: $3,000

Element of Comparison	Subject Property	Comparable #1	Comparable #2
Seller financing	yes	yes	no
Hot tub	yes	no	yes
Sales price	--	$300,000	$290,000
Net adjustment	--	+$3,000	+$14,500 ($290,000 × .05 = $14,500)
Adjusted price	--	$303,000	$304,500

The total amount of adjustment to a comparable's sale price may be expressed as a dollar amount or a percentage, or both. A distinction is drawn between net adjustment and gross adjustment. **Net adjustment** is the net sum of positive and negative adjustments. This is the figure that is added to (or subtracted from) the sales price of the comparable, to result in the final indicator of value for the subject property.

Gross adjustment is the total dollar amount of the adjustments for the comparable, without regard to whether the adjustments are positive or negative. Appraisers use the gross adjustment figure in assessing the reliability of a comparable.

Example: An appraiser is using a comparable property that sold for $400,000. She made the following adjustments: she added $3,000 to its price because it lacks a fireplace and the subject has one, and she subtracted $6,000 from its price because it has hardwood floors and the subject doesn't.

The adjusted value of the comparable is $397,000 ($400,000 + $3,000 – $6,000). That means the net adjustment is the difference between $400,000 and $397,000, or $3,000.

The gross adjustment is the total amount of the adjustments, or $9,000 ($3,000 + $6,000). The appraiser just adds the two adjustments to calculate the gross adjustment. It doesn't matter that one of the adjustments was positive and the other was negative.

The gross adjustment figure is used in assessing a comparable's reliability because it's usually a better measure of reliability than the net adjustment. Each adjustment made to the comparable's sales price is potentially inaccurate; the more adjustments made to a comparable property, the less reliable it is as an indicator of the subject property's value. So although a comparable may appear to be reliable because it has a small net adjustment, the appraiser must also look at the gross adjustment to determine reliability.

Exercise 4

1. For each of the comparables shown below, calculate the net adjustment amount, net adjustment percent, gross adjustment amount, and gross adjustment percent.

____

____

____

____

Element of Comparison	Comparable #1	Comparable #2	Comparable #3
Garage size	+$6,000	--	--
Living area size	--	+$6,000	-$4,000
Lot size	--	+$2,000	--
Location	+$8,000	--	+$8,000
Swimming pool	-$10,000	--	-$10,000
Finished basement	+$8,000	+$8,000	--
Sale price	$420,000	$440,000	$400,000

2. Based on the information given in question 1 above, which comparable appears most reliable as an indicator of the subject property's value? Why?

____

____

____

Key Terms

Adjustments—Changes in the sales price of a comparable property to account for differences between the comparable and the subject property in the sales comparison approach to value.

Arm's length transaction—A sale between unrelated parties.

Cash equivalent—Financing on terms that are typical and commonly available in the market.

Comparable—A property that has been sold in the same market that currently includes the subject property, and that appeals to the same sorts of buyers. Comparables are used in many different appraisal techniques.

Comparable sales method—A method of deriving a direct capitalization rate by analyzing the sales prices and incomes of comparable properties in the market. The income of a comparable property is divided by its sales price to indicate the capitalization rate.

Contributory value—The amount of value contributed by an improvement to a property's total value.

Element of comparison—A factor that may indicate a difference in value between the subject property and a comparable. Common elements of comparison include location, size, number of rooms, etc.

Externalities—Factors outside of a property that influence its value.

Fee simple—A freehold estate that is the most complete and comprehensive form of real property interest, including the entire bundle of rights.

Front foot—One foot of frontage. Where the amount of frontage is an important value indicator, appraisers may analyze market prices on a per-front-foot basis.

Gross adjustment—The total of the amounts of adjustments to the sales price of a comparable, without regard to whether the adjustments are negative or positive.

Gross building area—The total area of a building, including above-grade and below-grade enclosed spaces, as calculated from the external dimensions of the building.

Gross living area—The size of the living space in a house, calculated on the basis of the outside dimensions of the structure. Gross living area includes finished areas of the house that are at or above ground level, but does not include garages, attics, or basements.

Highest and best use—The use that is reasonably probable and that results in the highest value for a property. It must be a use that is legally permitted, physically possible, and economically feasible.

Improvement—An item of personal property that is added to the land by human effort, in such a way as to become part of the real estate. Also called a fixture.

Leased fee—The real property interest of the landlord (owner) under a lease, which includes ownership but not the immediate right of possession.

Leasehold—A non-freehold estate, which includes the right of possession during the term of the lease, but not ownership or title. The real property interest held by a tenant under a lease. Also known as a tenancy. Leasehold estates include the tenancy for years (created by a term lease), the periodic tenancy (created by a period-to-period lease), and the tenancy at will (created when a tenant remains in possession with the landlord's consent after expiration of a valid lease).

Location—An element of comparison that reflects the impact of neighborhood influences on value.

Market—The interactions among a group of buyers and sellers who trade in a particular thing, such as real estate, within a particular area. The actions of the buyers and sellers in a market determine market value.

Net adjustment—The net sum of positive and negative adjustment amounts for a comparable sale.

Paired data analysis—A technique for measuring the effect on value that is caused by differences in a single element of comparison. The effect on value is estimated by comparing the prices of properties that differ in only the one element of comparison. Also called matched pairs analysis.

Personal property—All property that is not classified as real estate.

Price—The actual amount paid by a particular buyer to a particular seller in an actual transaction.

Reconciliation—The process by which an appraiser reduces two or more value indicators to a single indicator or estimate of value.

Relative comparison analysis—A technique for estimating whether a difference in a single element of comparison has a positive, negative, or neutral impact on value. Similar to paired data analysis.

Sales comparison approach—One of the three approaches to value in the appraisal process. In the sales comparison approach, the value of the subject property is indicated by the adjusted sales prices of similar properties (comparables) in the market.

Seller financing—A loan or other financial arrangement offered by a seller to a buyer in connection with the purchase of property.

Site—A parcel of land that has been prepared for use by clearing, grading, and providing access and utilities.

Site improvement—An improvement other than a building, such as landscaping or utilities. Improvements "of" the site (such as utility access) are usually valued as part of the land. Improvements "on" the site (such as fences) are valued separately from the land.

Substitution—A principle of value stating that the value of a property cannot exceed the value of equivalent substitute properties that are available in the market.

Undivided interest—A shared interest in real estate that is not limited to any physical portion of the real estate.

Unit of comparison—A unit in which price is stated for comparison purposes, such as price per square foot of living area. When comparing different properties, the price of each property must be stated in the same unit of comparison.

Value—The monetary relationship between properties and those who buy, sell, or use those properties (USPAP definition). The theoretical worth of something, expressed in terms of something else, usually money.

Value indicator—A piece of data or a derived conclusion (such as the adjusted sales price of a comparable) that is relevant to the value of the subject property in an appraisal.

Summary

I. The sales comparison approach relies on market data to indicate the value of the subject property.

A. Sales prices of comparable properties are adjusted to account for differences between the comparables and the subject.

B. The appraiser analyzes sales of properties from the same market as the subject, because properties in the same market are subject to similar value influences.

II. In the sales comparison approach, the appraiser collects and verifies data, selects units of comparison, analyzes and adjusts the comparable sales prices, and reconciles the adjusted comparable prices into a single indicator of value for the subject property.

A. Verification of data helps the appraiser form an opinion as to the reliability of the data, and may also yield additional information about the comparable sale.

B. In order to make comparisons between properties, all prices must be stated in the same unit of comparison.

1. Comparisons with several different units of comparison can add to the reliability of the final value indicator.

III. Comparative analysis is the most common procedure for analyzing differences in elements of comparison in residential appraisals.

A. For each comparable property, the appraiser measures the difference between the subject and the comparable for each element of comparison.

B. An adjustment is made to the comparable sales price for each measured difference in an element of comparison.

1. In the case of large differences, or when market data are not available to indicate the effect of the difference on value, the comparable may have to be rejected.

C. The appraiser must analyze each aspect of the comparable sales transaction and the comparable property that may affect the price paid.

1. Differences or restrictions as to the real property rights conveyed in a transaction must be accounted for.

2. If financing terms aren't typical of those available in the market, the financing isn't cash equivalent and may require an adjustment based on market data.

3. Conditions of sale should indicate an arm's length transaction with typically motivated parties.

4. Expenditures on necessary repairs made after closing that the buyer would have anticipated should be taken into account.

5. Recent sales are preferred, because changing market conditions affect values.

6. Comparables located in the same neighborhood as the subject are the most reliable.

7. The majority of adjustments in residential appraisals are for differences in physical characteristics.

8. A property whose highest and best use is not the same as the subject property's may not be a reliable comparable.

9. Non-realty components are not normally included in the value estimate.

D. Adjustments are made to the prices of the comparables.

1. Quantitative adjustments: dollar amount or percentage.

2. Qualitative adjustments: superior, inferior, equal.

E. Paired data analysis is used to derive adjustment amounts from market data.

1. Differences in the prices paid for similar properties are attributed to the value of differences in their characteristics.

2. Analysis of large numbers of transactions is often required in order to extract reliable adjustment values.

F. Relative comparison analysis is similar to paired data analysis, except that the resulting adjustment values are qualitative instead of quantitative.

G. The formula for converting percentage adjustments into dollar amounts depends on how the percentage relationship is defined.

H. The sequence of adjustments depends on the appraiser's analysis of the market, but adjustments for transactional elements of comparison are usually made before adjustments for physical elements of comparison.

I. All the individual adjustments are totaled, then added to or subtracted from the comparable sales price to give an indicator of subject property value.

1. The net adjustment is used to calculate the comparable's adjusted price.

2. The gross adjustment is an indicator of the reliability of the adjusted price as an indicator of subject property value.

J. The subject property's value should fall within the range indicated by the adjusted prices of the comparables.

1. The appraiser must reconcile the various adjusted comparable sales prices, and estimate a value or range of values for the subject that is indicated by the sales comparison approach.

Chapter Quiz

1. Which element of comparison accounts for unusual motivation on the part of the buyer or the seller?
   a. Conditions of sale
   b. Market conditions
   c. Real property rights conveyed
   d. Date of sale

2. For a sale to be considered comparable for purposes of the sales comparison approach to value:
   a. it must be located in the same neighborhood as the subject property
   b. it must be competitive with the subject property
   c. it may not include seller financing
   d. All of the above

3. Financing on terms that are typical of the market is called:
   a. conventional financing
   b. cash financing
   c. cash equivalent financing
   d. creative financing

4. An adjustment for market conditions would be indicated in the case of a comparable sale that:
   a. is located in a different neighborhood from the subject
   b. was made 1 year prior to the effective date of the appraisal
   c. includes a seller buydown of the buyer's interest rate
   d. was not an arm's length transaction

5. When the subject property is superior to a comparable in some characteristic:
   a. the subject's price is adjusted upward
   b. the subject's price is adjusted downward
   c. the comparable's price is adjusted upward
   d. the comparable's price is adjusted downward

6. Market data indicate that the subject property is worth 5% more than a comparable, due to changed market conditions since the date of the comparable sale. If the comparable sales price is $300,000, what is the adjustment for market conditions?
   a. +$15,000
   b. –$15,000
   c. +$1,500
   d. –$1,500

7. Which of the following adjustments would most likely be made first?
   a. Location
   b. Lot size
   c. Square footage
   d. Date of sale

8. A comparable is usually considered more reliable when it requires the least:
   a. net adjustment
   b. percentage adjustment
   c. gross adjustment
   d. dollar adjustment

9. The amount of the adjustment for non-standard financing is determined by:
   a. analysis of market data
   b. calculating the discounted cash value
   c. comparing the monthly payment amounts
   d. rejecting the comparable

10. Which unit of comparison would most likely be appropriate in the appraisal of a single-family residence?
    a. Total property
    b. Acre
    c. Front foot
    d. Cubic foot

Questions 11-15 are based on the following fact situation:

The subject property is a 1,700 square foot rambler, with three bedrooms, one bath, and an attached two-car garage. Comparable A has two baths and 1,800 square feet, and sold recently for $395,000. Comparable B also has 1,800 square feet, but only a one-car garage; its sales price was $384,000. Comparable C has a three-car garage and two baths, and sold for $391,000. Market data indicate the amounts of the adjustments to be $4,000 for garage space per car, $7,000 for a bath, and $8,000 for 100 square feet of living area. Other than the differences noted here, the comparables are similar to the subject property in all respects.

11. What is the total net adjustment to the price of Comparable A?
    a. +$15,000
    b. +$7,000
    c. –$1,000
    d. –$15,000

12. What is the total net adjustment to the price of Comparable B?
    a. +$4,000
    b. –$4,000
    c. –$8,000
    d. –$12,000

13. What is the total net adjustment to the price of Comparable C?
    a. +$11,000
    b. +$3,000
    c. –$3,000
    d. –$11,000

14. What is the total gross adjustment to the price of Comparable B?
    a. $4,000
    b. $8,000
    c. $12,000
    d. $16,000

15. Based only on the information given, which comparable is the most reliable indicator of the subject's value?
    a. Comparable A
    b. Comparable B
    c. Comparable C
    d. No difference

Case Study

Based on the following information, complete the "SALES COMPARISON ANALYSIS" section of the Uniform Residential Report for the property at 1731 Pine Road. (You will need to refer to the case study for Chapter 5 for additional information regarding the subject property.)

Subject: 1731 Pine Road is being appraised in connection with a sale of the property for $342,750. Data have been verified by the seller. Except for the current sale, the property has not been listed or sold within the previous 36 months. The location of the property is considered average for the neighborhood. Ravenswood has no common elements, and does not charge any HOA fee. The design and appeal of the home are good, and it is in good condition; construction quality and functional utility are average. There are no unusual energy-efficient items on the property.

Through the Oakdale Multiple Listing Service, you have identified three recent sales in the Ravenswood development. All of these sales involved transfer of a fee simple interest, as confirmed by local county records. Comparable sales data have been verified by the listing real estate brokers, and data for sales #1 and #2 were verified by the current owners of those properties as well. The MLS confirms that there were no other sales of these three properties within the past 12 months.

Except as otherwise noted, the characteristics of the comparables are equivalent to those of the subject. The estimated value differences for different elements of comparison are based on recent paired data set analyses of similar properties in the area.

Comparable 1: The property at 1947 Fir Road is approximately 2 blocks from the subject property. It was sold on June 15 of this year for $331,800, with conventional loan financing. The condition of the property is average, making it $3,000 inferior to the subject in this regard. The home is 5 years old, which you estimate should require a price adjustment of $6,000. This property has 7 total rooms, with 3 bedrooms and 2 baths and a total living area of 2,206 square feet. You have estimated an adjustment of $3,000 for the difference in number of baths, and $6,750 to account for the difference in number of bedrooms.

Comparable 2: 1702 Fir Road, located 2 blocks from the subject, is a new home that sold on August 3 of this year for $353,250. The seller paid $4,500 towards the buyer's loan discount points. The home has the same room count as the subject property, with a total of 2,432 square feet; the difference in size warrants an adjustment of $2,250. The attached garage is a 3-car, requiring an adjustment of $5,250. You estimate an adjustment of $9,000 to account for the difference in age, and $6,000 to reflect the home's superior landscaping. 1702 Fir Road is inferior to the subject in two respects: its location is next to the state highway, and the property has not been fenced. Market data indicates corresponding adjustments of $7,500 and $1,500 will be needed to account for these differences.

Comparable 3: 1616 Hemlock Way is a 2,348 square foot home that sold on April 30 of this year for $337,350. The home is 4 years old and is located one block from the subject property. The main difference between this property and the subject is that 1616 Hemlock Way has an above-average quality territorial view. The comparable's superior view of the mountains makes it worth $5,250 more. The difference in size of living area accounts for an adjustment of $750, and the difference in age for an adjustment of $3,000.

Use this portion of the URAR to complete the case study.

SALES COMPARISON APPROACH

There are comparable properties currently offered for sale in the subject neighborhood ranging in price from $ to $.

There are comparable sales in the subject neighborhood within the past twelve months ranging in sale price from $ to $.

FEATURE	SUBJECT			COMPARABLE SALE # 1				COMPARABLE SALE # 2				COMPARABLE SALE # 3			
Address															
Proximity to Subject															
Sale Price	$						$				$				$
Sale Price/Gross Liv. Area	$		sq. ft.	$		sq. ft.		$		sq. ft.		$		sq. ft.	
Data Source(s)															
Verification Source(s)															
VALUE ADJUSTMENTS	DESCRIPTION			DESCRIPTION			+(-) $ Adjustment	DESCRIPTION			+(-) $ Adjustment	DESCRIPTION			+(-) $ Adjustment
Sale or Financing Concessions															
Date of Sale/Time															
Location															
Leasehold/Fee Simple															
Site															
View															
Design (Style)															
Quality of Construction															
Actual Age															
Condition															
Above Grade	Total	Bdrms.	Baths	Total	Bdrms.	Baths		Total	Bdrms.	Baths		Total	Bdrms.	Baths	
Room Count															
Gross Living Area			sq. ft.			sq. ft.				sq. ft.				sq. ft.	
Basement & Finished Rooms Below Grade															
Functional Utility															
Heating/Cooling															
Energy Efficient Items															
Garage/Carport															
Porch/Patio/Deck															
Net Adjustment (Total)				☐ + ☐ -			$	☐ + ☐ -			$	☐ + ☐ -			$
Adjusted Sale Price of Comparables				Net Adj. % Gross Adj. %			$	Net Adj. % Gross Adj. %			$	Net Adj. % Gross Adj. %			$

I ☐ did ☐ did not research the sale or transfer history of the subject property and comparable sales. If not, explain

My research ☐ did ☐ did not reveal any prior sales or transfers of the subject property for the three years prior to the effective date of this appraisal.

Data source(s)

My research ☐ did ☐ did not reveal any prior sales or transfers of the comparable sales for the year prior to the date of sale of the comparable sale.

Data source(s)

Report the results of the research and analysis of the prior sale or transfer history of the subject property and comparable sales (report additional prior sales on page 3).

ITEM	SUBJECT	COMPARABLE SALE # 1	COMPARABLE SALE # 2	COMPARABLE SALE # 3
Date of Prior Sale/Transfer				
Price of Prior Sale/Transfer				
Data Source(s)				
Effective Date of Data Source(s)				

Analysis of prior sale or transfer history of the subject property and comparable sales

Summary of Sales Comparison Approach

Indicated Value by Sales Comparison Approach $

Quiz Answers

1. a) Conditions of sale, such as favorable financing terms, may create unusual motivation for a buyer or seller.

2. b) A comparable must be competitive with the subject property in the same market. It does not necessarily have to be in the same neighborhood or use cash equivalent financing, although in such instances adjustments may be necessary.

3. c) Financing on terms that are typical for the market is known as cash equivalent financing.

4. b) If a comparable was sold one year prior to the appraisal's effective date, an adjustment would need to be made to account for the change in value over time.

5. c) If a subject property has a feature that a comparable lacks, the comparable's price is adjusted upward in order to make the comparable more similar to the subject property.

6. a) First, determine what 5% of $300,000 is ($300,000 × .05 = $15,000). This amount should be added to the sales price of the comparable, since its value has gone up over time.

7. d) An adjustment regarding the comparable sale transaction, such as date of sale, would be made first, before adjustments concerning the comparable property.

8. c) A comparable that requires less gross adjustment (total dollar amount of adjustments, regardless of whether they are positive or negative) is more reliable.

9. a) Market data would be used to determine the amount of an adjustment made for non-traditional financing.

10. a) The total property is the usual unit of comparison in the sales comparison method.

11. d) Comparable A has one more bathroom than the subject property (so subtract $7,000) and greater square footage than the subject property (so subtract $8,000). The total net adjustment is a subtraction of $15,000.

12. b) Comparable B has a smaller garage than the subject property (so add $4,000) and greater square footage than the subject property (so subtract $8,000). The total net adjustment is a subtraction of $4,000.

13. d) Comparable C has one more bathroom than the subject property (so subtract $7,000) and a larger garage than the subject property (so subtract $4,000). The total net adjustment is a subtraction of $11,000.

14. c) Comparable B has a positive adjustment of $4,000 and a negative adjustment of $8,000, so the total gross adjustment is $12,000.

15. c) Comparable C is most reliable because it has the lowest gross adjustment: $11,000. Comparable A has a gross adjustment of $15,000 and Comparable B has a gross adjustment of $12,000.

Exercise Answers

#1 1. a. Gather comparable data

b. Verify comparable data

c. Select unit(s) of comparison

d. Analyze and adjust comparable sales prices

e. Reconcile indicated values

2. a. Verification helps the appraiser determine the reliability of the data.

b. Verification may also reveal additional details of the comparable sales transaction.

3. The forces that affect value should operate in a similar way on all properties within the boundaries of the market.

#2 1. 1. g

2. f

3. b

4. h

5. d

6. e

7. a

8. c

2. c

#3 1. See chart on following page.

Market Data Grid for Paired Data Analysis						
Element of Comparison	Comp. #1	Comp. #2	Comp. #3	Comp. #4	Comp. #5	Comp. #6
Seller financing	yes	no	no	no	no	no
Location	Inside lot	Corner lot	Inside lot	Inside lot	Inside lot	Inside lot
Lot size (sq. footage)	12,000	12,000	10,000	12,000	12,000	12,000
Living area (sq. footage)	2,000	2,000	2,000	2,000	1,900	2,000
View	yes	yes	yes	yes	yes	no
Sales price	$380,000	$371,000	$369,000	$375,000	$367,000	$365,000

Answers:

Seller financing:	+ $5,000
Corner lot:	– $4,000
Extra 2,000 sq. ft. of lot size:	+ $6,000
Extra 100 sq. ft. of living area:	+ $8,000
View:	+ $10,000

2. See chart below.

Market Data Grid for Paired Data Analysis							
Element of Comparison	Subject Property	Comp. #1	Comp. #2	Comp. #3	Comp. #4	Comp. #5	Comp. #6
Seller financing	no	yes	no	no	no	no	no
Location	Inside lot	Inside lot	Corner lot	Inside lot	Inside lot	Inside lot	Inside lot
Lot size (sq. footage)	12,000	12,000	12,000	10,000	12,000	12,000	12,000
Living area (sq. footage)	1,900	2,000	2,000	2,000	2,000	1,900	2,000
View	no	yes	yes	yes	yes	yes	no
Sales price	--	$380,000	$371,000	$369,000	$375,000	$367,000	$365,000

Answers:

Comparable #1	
Seller financing:	-$5,000
Living area:	-$8,000
View:	-$10,000
Net adjustment:	-$23,000
Adjusted price:	$357,000

Comparable #2	
Corner lot:	+$4,000
Living area:	-$8,000
View:	-$10,000
Net adjustment:	-$14,000
Adjusted price:	$357,000

Comparable #3	
Lot size:	+$6,000
Living area:	-$8,000
View:	-$10,000
Net adjustment:	-$12,000
Adjusted price:	$357,000

Comparable #4	
--	
Living area:	-$8,000
View:	-$10,000
Net adjustment:	-$18,000
Adjusted price:	$357,000

Comparable #5	
--	
--	
View:	-$10,000
Net adjustment:	-$10,000
Adjusted price:	$357,000

Comparable #6	
--	
Living area:	-$8,000
--	
Net adjustment:	-$8,000
Adjusted price:	$357,000

#4 1. See chart below.

Element of Comparison	Comparable #1	Comparable #2	Comparable #3
Garage size	+$6,000	--	--
Living area size	--	+$6,000	-$4,000
Lot size	--	+$2,000	--
Location	+$8,000	--	+$8,000
Swimming pool	-$10,000	--	-$10,000
Finished basement	+$8,000	+$8,000	--
Sale price	$420,000	$440,000	$400,000

Answers:

Net adjustment amt.	+$12,000	+$16,000	-$6,000
Net adjustment %	2.86%	3.64%	1.5%
Gross adjustment amt.	$32,000	$16,000	$22,000
Gross adjustment %	7.62%	3.64%	5.5%

2. Comparable 2 is most reliable, since it has the smallest gross adjustment.

Case Study Answers

See URAR form excerpt below.

SALES COMPARISON APPROACH

There are ____ comparable properties currently offered for sale in the subject neighborhood ranging in price from $ ____ to $ ____ .

There are 3 comparable sales in the subject neighborhood within the past twelve months ranging in sale price from $ 331,800 to $ 353,250 .

FEATURE	SUBJECT	COMPARABLE SALE # 1		COMPARABLE SALE # 2		COMPARABLE SALE # 3	
Address		1947 Fir Road		1702 Fir Road		1616 Hemlock	
Proximity to Subject		2 blks		2 blks		1 blk	
Sale Price	$ 342,750		$ 331,800		$ 353,250		$ $337,350
Sale Price/Gross Liv. Area	$ 142.81 sq. ft.	$ 150.41 sq. ft.		$ 145.25 sq. ft.		$ 143.68 sq. ft.	
Data Source(s) / Verification Source(s)	Seller	Listing broker, Current owner		Listing broker, Current owner		Listing broker	
VALUE ADJUSTMENTS	DESCRIPTION	DESCRIPTION	+(-) $ Adjustment	DESCRIPTION	+(-) $ Adjustment	DESCRIPTION	+(-) $ Adjustment
Sale or Financing Concessions		conventional		seller-paid points	-$4,500	conventional	
Date of Sale/Time		6/15		8/3		4/30	
Location	average	average		average		average	
Leasehold/Fee Simple	fee simple	fee simple		fee simple		fee simple	
Site	average	average		average		average	
View	average	average		average		above average	-$5,250
Design (Style)	average	average		average		average	
Quality of Construction	average	average		average		average	
Actual Age	3 yrs	5 yrs	+$6,000	0 yrs	-$9,000	4 yrs	+$3,000
Condition	above average	average	+$3,000	above average		above average	
Above Grade	Total / Bdrms. / Baths	Total / Bdrms. / Baths		Total / Bdrms. / Baths		Total / Bdrms. / Baths	
Room Count	8 / 4 / 2½	7 / 3 / 2	+$9,750	8 / 4 / 2½	-$5,250	8 / 4 / 2½	-$750
Gross Living Area	2,220 sq. ft.	2,206 sq. ft.		2,432 sq. ft.		2,348 sq. ft.	
Basement & Finished Rooms Below Grade	no	no		no		no	
Functional Utility	average	average		average		average	
Heating/Cooling	average	average		average		average	
Energy Efficient Items	average	average		average		average	
Garage/Carport	2-car	2-car		3-car	-$5,250	2-car	
Porch/Patio/Deck	yes	yes		yes		yes	
Landscaping	fence average	fence average		fence above average	-$6,000	fence average	
Net Adjustment (Total)		☑ + ☐ -	$ +$18,750	☐ + ☑ -	$ -$30,000	☐ + ☑ -	$ -$3,000
Adjusted Sale Price of Comparables		Net Adj. 5.7% Gross Adj. 5.7%	$ $350,550	Net Adj. 8.5% Gross Adj. 8.5%	$ $326,250	Net Adj. .9% Gross Adj. 2.7%	$ $334,350

I ☑ did ☐ did not research the sale or transfer history of the subject property and comparable sales. If not, explain

My research ☐ did ☑ did not reveal any prior sales or transfers of the subject property for the three years prior to the effective date of this appraisal.

Data source(s) Listing Broker

My research ☐ did ☑ did not reveal any prior sales or transfers of the comparable sales for the year prior to the date of sale of the comparable sale.

Data source(s) Listing Broker

Report the results of the research and analysis of the prior sale or transfer history of the subject property and comparable sales (report additional prior sales on page 3).

ITEM	SUBJECT	COMPARABLE SALE # 1	COMPARABLE SALE # 2	COMPARABLE SALE # 3
Date of Prior Sale/Transfer	none	none	none	none
Price of Prior Sale/Transfer	none	none	none	none
Data Source(s)	none	none	none	none
Effective Date of Data Source(s)				

Analysis of prior sale or transfer history of the subject property and comparable sales

No prior sales to consider

Summary of Sales Comparison Approach

Subject property is most similar to Comparable #3, which is given the most weight in the reconciliation process.

Indicated Value by Sales Comparison Approach $ $337,000

10 Income Approach to Value

Overview

The third major approach to value is the income approach: the appraiser estimates a property's value by analyzing the amount of income the property can produce. The income approach is most commonly used when appraising investment properties, such as offices, shopping centers, or apartment buildings, but it can be used for any type of property that has an active rental market. After completing this chapter, you should be able to:

- explain the relationship between income and value from an investment standpoint;
- describe the factors that determine the rate of return required by an investor;
- list the four types of income that are used to calculate value by direct capitalization, and describe how each type of income is estimated;
- explain the difference between market rent and scheduled rent, and the significance of both in the capitalization process;
- describe four common methods for deriving an overall capitalization rate;
- explain the difference between a capitalization rate and an income multiplier, and their uses in appraisal practice;
- describe the process of estimating value on the basis of residual income; and
- calculate the present value of a future income, based on specified yield requirements.

The Investor's Perception of Value

The income approach to value views real estate as an investment, just like stocks or bonds or savings accounts. It measures value through the eyes of an investor.

As we saw in Chapter 2, **production**, the ability to create wealth by generating a return in the form of income, is a measure of value. In the income approach to value, the appraiser tries to discover the specific mathematical relationship between income and value for the subject property. Once this is done, the appraiser can then convert the income of the subject property into an indicator of its value.

To determine the relationship between income and value, the appraiser estimates the rate of return that an average investor would require in order to invest in the property. The **rate of return** is the ratio between the amount of income and the amount of the investment. This rate is then applied to the property's income to indicate its value.

The rate of return on an investment is equal to the amount of income it produces divided by the amount the investor paid for the investment. Stated in mathematical terms:

Rate of Return = Amount of Income ÷ Amount of Investment

The amount paid for the investment represents the investor's idea of its value, so the formula for rate of return can also be stated as:

Rate of Return = Amount of Income ÷ Value

When this formula is rearranged, it becomes the basis for the income approach to value:

Value = Amount of Income ÷ Rate of Return

Example: If a property produces $10,000 in income per year, an investor who required a 10% rate of return would be willing to pay $100,000 for the property.

$10,000 income ÷ 0.10 rate of return = $100,000 value

An investor expects two things: repayment of the invested capital, and a reward or profit as compensation for the risk involved in making the investment. The repayment of capital—return *of* the investment—is called **recapture**, while the profit—return *on* the investment—is referred to as **interest** or **yield**. (The term yield is used to refer to the income earned by an equity investment, while interest refers to the income earned by a debt investment—a loan.)

Rate of Return

From an investor's standpoint, the rate of return is the link between value and income. For a property that produces a given amount of income, the amount an investor would be willing to pay will depend on the rate of return the investor expects. When investors expect higher rates of return, the value of property (the amount an investor is willing to pay) is less. On the other hand, lower rates of return translate into higher property values.

Example: A property produces $10,000 of annual income. An investor who required a 10% rate of return would be willing to pay $100,000 for the property.

$10,000 income ÷ $100,000 investment = 10% rate of return

But an investor who required a 20% rate of return would view the property as worth only $50,000.

$10,000 income ÷ $50,000 investment = 20% rate of return

Fig. 10.1 Investor Expectations

1. **Recapture:** Recovery of the amount paid for an investment; return of capital.
2. **Interest or Yield:** The amount earned by an investment; return on capital.

The rate of return that an investor expects depends on two factors: the risk associated with the investment, and the rates of return offered by other competing investment opportunities. These two factors determine how much an investor is willing to pay for the right to receive the income from an investment.

Risk. The **principle of anticipation**—value is based on the expectation of future benefits to be derived from ownership of property—lies at the very heart of the income approach to value. The income that an investor expects to receive from an investment is **future income**. The amount of future income can be estimated, but it cannot be guaranteed. The element of **risk**, the fact that the expected income may not be realized, is a key factor in the relationship between income and value. The greater the risk that the future income may not be realized, the higher the return an investor will require, and therefore the lower the value of the investment.

Competing Investment Opportunities. An investor who invests in a particular property gives up the opportunity to choose a different investment. Throughout the global economy, investments of all sorts (stocks, bonds, savings accounts, real estate, etc.) compete with each other for capital. The amount of capital someone is willing to invest in any particular investment is influenced by the potential return (income) and the degree of risk of that investment, in relation to competing investment alternatives.

Income Capitalization

The process of estimating value on the basis of income is called **income capitalization**. (The income approach to value is sometimes called the income capitalization approach.) There are two basic forms of income capitalization: direct capitalization and yield capitalization. In **direct capitalization**, the income from a single period (a year or month) is converted directly to value. In **yield capitalization**, the appraiser analyzes all of the anticipated cash flows over the life of the investment to determine their present value.

Exercise 1

1. What is the basic formula that describes the relationship between income and value from an investor's perspective?

____

2. What are the two key factors that influence the rate of return expected by an investor?

   a. ____

   b. ____

3. If an investment produces income of $50,000, how much will it be worth to an investor who requires a 10% rate of return? How much would the same investment be worth if the investor required a 15% rate of return?

____

____

Direct Capitalization

Direct capitalization is the simplest form of income capitalization, and it is the method most often used in residential appraisals. In direct capitalization, the estimated income for one period (usually a year) is converted directly to an indicator of value. The basic formula for direct capitalization is:

Value = Income ÷ Rate

In this formula, the income is the estimated annual or monthly income of the subject property at the time of the investment, and the rate (capitalization or "cap" rate) is a percentage rate that is used to convert the income into value.

Example: A property has an estimated annual income of $120,000. Using a capitalization rate of 12% (0.12), the value of the property would be $1 million. $120,000 ÷ 0.12 = $1 million.

Direct capitalization can also be done by multiplication, instead of division. In this case, the formula for capitalization is expressed as:

$$Value = Income \times Multiplier\ (or\ Factor)$$

In the direct capitalization process, a **factor** or **multiplier** is simply the reciprocal of the capitalization rate. To convert a multiplier to a rate (or vice versa), simply divide 1 by the multiplier or rate.

$$1 \div Multiplier = Rate$$

$$1 \div Rate = Multiplier$$

Example: A capitalization rate of 20% (0.20) is equivalent to an income multiplier of 5.0 (1 ÷ 0.20 = 5.0). So if a property's annual income is $36,000, and the investor wants a 20% rate of return, she will be willing to pay $180,000 for the property. $36,000 × 5.0 = $180,000.

To use the direct capitalization process, an appraiser must be able to determine two things:

1. the amount of income (annual or monthly) the subject property is capable of generating, and
2. the appropriate factor or rate needed to convert the income to value.

The amount of income that the subject property is capable of earning is determined by analyzing the income that is being earned by other similar properties in the market, and also by examining the terms of any existing leases on the subject property. The income multiplier or capitalization rate is determined by analyzing the rates of return that investors are willing to accept for investments with similar risks and returns.

Income

In direct capitalization, the appraiser estimates a property's income for a single period, usually a year. (Monthly income is sometimes used to capitalize income for single-family or small multi-family residential properties.) For appraisal purposes, a property's income is defined very specifically, and not necessarily in the same way that income is defined for accounting or tax purposes. Depending on the circumstances, appraisers may estimate value on the basis of:

- potential gross income,
- effective gross income,
- net operating income, or — most commonly used.
- pre-tax cash flow.

Potential Gross Income. A property's **potential gross income (PGI)** is the total amount of revenue that the property is capable of producing at full occupancy, without any deduction for expenses. For example, if rental rates for two-bedroom apartments are $1,200 per month, an apartment building with ten two-bedroom units would have a potential gross income of $12,000 per month (10 × $1,200).

The main component of potential gross income is usually **rent**, the amount paid by a tenant or lessee for the right to use property under the terms of a lease. The amount of rent that is called for under an existing lease is called **scheduled rent**, **contract rent**, or **actual rent**. In most cases, when a property is subject to an existing lease, the appraiser will determine potential gross income on the basis of the scheduled rent.

> **Example:** A certain property would rent for $50,000 per year, if it were vacant and available for leasing at current market rates. However, the property is subject to an existing long-term lease that generates $42,000 in annual rent. In this case, the appraiser would conclude that the potential gross income of the property is $42,000 per year, the amount of the scheduled rent.

For property that is not subject to an existing lease (vacant or owner-occupied property), potential gross income is determined on the basis of **market rent** (also called **economic rent**), the amount of rent a tenant would pay under current market conditions. In many cases, the appraiser must determine both the scheduled rent and the market rent for a property.

> **Example:** One unit of a triplex is owner-occupied, and the other two units are leased at $1,000 per month. Market rent for comparable units is $1,200 per month. In this case, the total potential gross income of the triplex would include $2,000 scheduled rent for the two leased units, plus $1,200 market rent for the owner-occupied unit, for a total of $3,200.

Even when a property is subject to an existing lease, market rent may be used as basis for calculating potential gross income. If an existing lease is due to expire in a short period of time, market rent is often a more realistic measure of the property's potential gross income than scheduled rent.

> **Example:** A single-family residence is currently leased on a month-to-month basis at $1,600 per month. Market rental rates for comparable properties are $1,750 per month. Since the existing lease is month-to-month, a new investor (owner) could easily raise the rent to the market rate. In this case, an appraiser would conclude that market rent is a more reliable measure of potential gross income for the property.

In addition to scheduled and/or market rent, potential gross income also includes any other income that the property is capable of generating. For example, an apartment building may have additional income from coin-operated laundry machines used by the tenants. In most small residential properties, however, the entire potential gross income will consist solely of rent.

Effective Gross Income. In contrast to potential gross income, effective gross income takes into account revenue losses that can occur as a result of vacancies and credit losses (unpaid rents). Particularly in periods of recession, it is not uncommon for rented properties to have vacancies. Even during stable periods, finding new and suitable tenants can take time, resulting in vacancies and lost revenue. Potential income is also lost when tenants fail to pay their rent.

Effective gross income (EGI) is defined as potential gross income minus an allowance for vacancies, turnover, and credit losses. This allowance, known as a **vacancy factor**, is usually expressed as a percentage of potential gross income. The vacancy factor percentage depends on local economic conditions, supply and demand for comparable rentals, and the terms of any existing leases.

Example: An apartment building has potential gross income of $15,000 per month. Vacancies and unpaid rents for the apartment typically amount to 5% of potential gross income. In this case, the monthly effective gross income would be calculated as follows.

Potential Gross Income	$15,000
less Vacancies and Bad Debts (5%)	– 750
Effective Gross Income	$14,250

A vacancy factor may not be necessary if the property is subject to a long-term lease with a high-quality tenant. In this case, an appraiser might conclude that the effective gross income is the same amount as the potential gross income.

Net Operating Income. **Net operating income (NOI)** is the form of income that is most often used in direct capitalization. Net operating income is a more reliable indicator of value than potential or effective gross income, because it represents the amount of income that is available as a return to the investor. Properties with similar gross incomes may have widely different net operating incomes, due to differences in operating expenses.

Example: Two properties each have effective gross incomes of $100,000 per year. Property A has annual operating expenses of $60,000, while Property B has annual operating expenses of $80,000. In this case, Property A has twice as much net operating income as Property B, even though their effective gross incomes are the same.

Property A: $100,000 – $60,000 = $40,000 NOI
Property B: $100,000 – $80,000 = $20,000 NOI

To determine net operating income, all the operating expenses for the property are subtracted from the effective gross income. **Operating expenses** are any ongoing expenses that are necessary to maintain the flow of income from the property. For appraisal purposes, operating expenses fall into three categories: fixed expenses, variable expenses, and reserves for replacement.

Fixed expenses are operating expenses that do not vary depending on the occupancy of the property. They must be paid regardless of whether the property is leased or vacant. The most common examples of fixed expenses are property taxes and hazard insurance premiums.

Variable expenses are operating expenses that do vary depending on occupancy. They may include a wide variety of expenses, such as utility costs, property management fees, cleaning and maintenance expenses, and leasing commissions.

Reserves for replacement are funds that are set aside for replacing short-lived components of the property: items with relatively short life spans, such as carpeting, paint, roofing, or mechanical equipment. These items routinely wear out and must be replaced. Reserves for replacement are set aside on an annual basis. The amount of the reserves is usually calculated by dividing the replacement cost of the item by its remaining useful life.

Example: The cost of replacing the roofing on a building is $12,000. If the existing roof has a remaining useful life of 10 years, the annual amount to be set aside for replacement would be $1,200.

$12,000 ÷ 10 years = $1,200

Note that some items that are often listed as expenses for accounting or tax purposes are not included as operating expenses when calculating net operating income. The most notable of these are mortgage payments (debt service), depreciation for tax purposes (book depreciation), and income taxes.

Pre-Tax Cash Flow. Pre-tax cash flow is also known as **equity dividend** or **before-tax cash flow**. It represents the amount of income that is available to the equity investor (owner), after the debt investor (mortgage lender) has been paid its portion of the net operating income. Pre-tax cash flow is calculated by subtracting mortgage debt service from net operating income. The amount of debt service that is deducted from net operating income includes both principal and interest payments on the mortgage loan(s).

Example: A property has net operating income of $45,000 per year, and annual debt service (mortgage payments for principal and interest) of $34,000. In this case, the pre-tax cash flow is $11,000 ($45,000 – $34,000).

Reconstructed Operating Statements. An **operating statement** is a financial report that lists income and expenses for a property. Owners of investment properties commonly prepare such statements for accounting and tax purposes. Although an appraiser may obtain useful information from owner-prepared operating statements, they are not used as the basis for income capitalization. A statement of income and expenses that is used for income capitalization in appraisal is known as a **reconstructed operating statement.**

There are two primary differences between a reconstructed operating statement and an owner's operating statement. First, the reconstructed statement includes all items, and only those items, that are included in the definition of income for appraisal purposes (as described above).

Example: A reconstructed operating statement would include income in the form of market rent for an owner-occupied unit in an apartment, whereas the owner's statement would not show any income for this item. On the other hand, the owner's statement would

Fig. 10.2 Reconstructed Operating Statement

Reconstructed Operating Statement for Shangri-La Apartments		
Potential gross income		
8 units @ $1,000/mo.	$96,000	
4 units @ $1,400/mo.	$67,200	
Other income	$1,500	
Total PGI (100% occupancy)	$164,700	
Less 5% for vacancy/bad debts	-$8,235	
Effective gross income		$156,465
Operating expenses		
Fixed		
Real estate taxes	$41,200	
Hazard insurance	$7,200	
Subtotal	$48,400	
Variable		
Management	$17,800	
Site maintenance	$21,700	
Utilities	$9,600	
Subtotal	$49,100	
Replacement reserves	$11,800	
Total expenses		-$109,300
Net operating income		$47,165

probably include an item for depreciation, which would not be found on the reconstructed operating statement.

The second major difference between a reconstructed operating statement and an owner's statement is that the reconstructed statement is an attempt to determine future income for the property, while the owner's statement reflects past revenues and expenses. In the income approach, it is the expected future income that is converted into value, in accordance with the principle of anticipation.

Exercise 2

Complete the reconstructed income statement below, using the following property information.

Number of units: 10

Rent per unit: $1,000 per month

Vacancy and bad debts: 5%

Property taxes: $12,000 per year

Insurance premium: $2,400 per year

Management expenses: $10,000 per year

Utilities: $30,000 per year

Maintenance expenses: $16,000 per year

Reserves for replacement: $7,000 per year

Mortgage loan payments: $2,600 per month

RECONSTRUCTED INCOME STATEMENT

Potential Gross Income	____________
less Vacancies and Bad Debts	____________
Effective Gross Income	____________
Fixed Expenses	
____________	____________
____________	____________
Variable Expenses	
____________	____________
____________	____________
____________	____________
Reserves for Replacement	____________
Total Expenses	____________
Net Operating Income	____________
Debt Service	____________
Pre-Tax Cash Flow	____________

Multipliers and Capitalization Rates

As mentioned above, income multipliers and capitalization rates are really just two different expressions of the same concept: the multiplier or the rate is the number that converts income into value. In the following discussion, we will refer primarily to capitalization rates. However, remember that any capitalization rate can be converted to a multiplier simply by dividing the number 1 by the rate.

A capitalization rate used in an appraisal of market value should reflect the rate of return that is expected by investors in the marketplace for competitive investments. Thus, capitalization rates are most reliable when they are based on an analysis of market data for comparable properties. (In an appraisal for investment value, the particular investor's required rate of return may serve as the basis for the capitalization rate.)

Appraisers use a number of techniques to estimate capitalization rates. Which technique is used depends on the availability of necessary data and the terms of the appraisal assignment. In many cases, more than one technique will be used in order to increase the reliability of the estimated rate. The most common techniques for estimating capitalization rates include:

- the comparable sales method,
- the effective gross income multiplier method,
- the band of investment method, and
- the debt coverage method.

Comparable Sales Method. The comparable sales method is considered the most reliable means of estimating a direct capitalization rate, assuming that adequate comparable sales data are available. In this method, the capitalization rate is derived by analyzing the sales prices and incomes of comparable properties that have sold recently. The appraiser divides the income of the comparable by its sales price to obtain the capitalization rate.

> **Example:** A comparable property sold recently for $240,000. The property's estimated annual income is $24,000. This comparable indicates a capitalization rate of 0.10, or 10%.
>
> *$24,000 (income) ÷ $240,000 (price) = 0.10 (rate)*

In practice, the appraiser will analyze several comparables to determine a range of capitalization rates. The capitalization rate to be used for the subject property is then determined through reconciliation. This process is virtually identical to the process of obtaining a value indicator through the sales comparison approach to value, as described in Chapter 9.

There are three important points to remember about this method of determining a capitalization rate. First, the sales price of the comparable may need to be adjusted to account for differences in market conditions or financing terms. (Differences in physical characteristics are normally accounted for by adjusting the calculated capitalization rate for the comparable in the reconciliation process.)

Example: A comparable property has a sales price of $500,000, and estimated annual income of $40,000. Due to changes in market conditions since the date of the comparable sale, an adjustment of minus 4% is indicated for the comparable's sales price.

$500,000 × 4% (0.04) = $20,000
$500,000 – $20,000 = $480,000 adjusted sales price
$40,000 (income) ÷ $480,000 (price) = 8.33% capitalization rate for comparable

The second point to keep in mind is that income must be calculated for the comparables on the same basis that it's calculated for the subject. For example, if the income calculated for the subject is the estimated net operating income for the coming year, the income calculated for each comparable must also be its estimated net operating income for the coming year. (While the comparable sales method can be used to derive a capitalization rate for any of the forms of income, net operating income is generally considered the most reliable.)

Finally, the comparables must be similar to the subject in terms of key investment criteria, including expected resale price, expected holding period for the investment, and tax consequences of the investment.

EGIM Method. It's often difficult to obtain reliable operating expense data for comparable properties. When that's the case, the appraiser can still derive a capitalization rate for net operating income by indirect means, using the effective gross income multiplier method.

The first step is to calculate an **effective gross income multiplier**, or **EGIM**, for each comparable, by dividing its sales price by its effective gross income.

EGIM = Sales Price ÷ Effective Gross Income

Next, the appraiser must determine the average ratio of operating expenses to effective gross income (the **operating expense ratio**, or **OER**) for similar properties in the market. This information may be available from published sources, or it may be determined through analysis of market data. The formula for the operating expense ratio is:

OER = Operating Expenses ÷ Effective Gross Income

The OER is subtracted from 1 to find the **net income ratio**, or **NIR** (NIR = 1 – OER). The NIR is divided by the effective gross income multiplier to arrive at a capitalization rate based on the comparable's estimated net operating income.

NOI Capitalization Rate = NIR ÷ EGIM

Example: A comparable property has effective gross income of $125,000 per year, and it sold recently for $800,000. The effective gross income multiplier (EGIM) is calculated by dividing the sales price by the effective gross income.

$800,000 (sales price) ÷ $125,000 (effective gross income) = 6.4 EGIM

The operating expense ratio for similar properties in the market is 60%. Thus, the net income ratio is 40% (1 – .60 = .40). The appraiser divides the NIR by the effective gross income multiplier to calculate a capitalization rate based on net operating income.

.40 (NIR) ÷ 6.4 (EGIM) = 0.0625, or 6.25% NOI capitalization rate for comparable

As in the comparable sales method, in the EGIM method the capitalization rates for the comparables are reconciled to determine an appropriate capitalization rate for the subject property. You'll encounter EGIMs again later in the chapter; they can be used not only to find a capitalization rate, but also to calculate value with the gross income multiplier method.

Band of Investment Method. The band of investment method recognizes that property investments are often funded in part with borrowed money, in the form of mortgage loans. The equity investor puts up only part of the purchase price of the property, with the balance supplied by the mortgage lender. With the band of investment method, the appraiser calculates separate capitalization rates for the equity investor and for the lender(s). The weighted average of these rates is then used as the **overall capitalization rate** for the property.

The capitalization rate used for the debt portion in the band of investment method is equal to the annual debt service amount (payments of principal and interest) divided by the original loan amount. This figure can be calculated mathematically, or it can be looked up in a table of mortgage constants. A **mortgage constant** is simply the annual debt service divided by the loan amount; it varies depending on the interest rate, the term of the loan, and the frequency of loan payments.

Example: A loan of $70,000 has monthly principal and interest payments of $563.24, based on monthly payments at 9% interest for 30 years. The mortgage constant for this loan is the annual total of 12 monthly payments, divided by the loan amount.

$563.24 × 12 = $6,758.88 annual debt service
$6,758.88 ÷ $70,000 = 0.0966 mortgage constant

The appraiser must also determine the capitalization rate for the equity portion of the investment. Where possible, this rate should be derived from market data, using the comparable sales approach. The rate for a comparable property can be calculated by dividing pre-tax cash flow by the amount of the equity investment. (The capitalization rate for pre-tax cash flow is sometimes referred to as the **equity dividend rate**, or **cash on cash rate**.)

Example: A comparable sold recently for $360,000, with 25% equity and a 75% loan amount. The comparable has a pre-tax cash flow of $11,000. The amount of the equity investment is 25% of the sales price, or $90,000 ($360,000 × 25%). So the equity capitalization rate (equity dividend or cash on cash rate) is 12.22%.

$11,000 ÷ $90,000 = 0.1222, or 12.22%.

The equity dividend rate is usually higher than the debt capitalization rate (mortgage constant). This is due to the fact that the equity investor has a greater degree of risk than the debt investor. The debt investor has a mortgage lien on the property, and so has first claim to the proceeds if the property is resold or foreclosed. Only the amount left over after satisfying the debt investor is available to the equity investor.

After determining the capitalization rates for debt and equity, the appraiser can calculate the overall capitalization rate to use for the subject property. This rate is the weighted average of the debt and equity rates. It is calculated by multiplying the debt and equity rates by their respective percentages of the investment, and then adding the results.

Example: The subject property's sale will be financed by a 75% loan, with a loan constant of 0.0966. The appraiser has determined that 12% is an appropriate rate for equity capitalization. The debt rate is multiplied by the debt percentage, and the equity rate is multiplied by the equity percentage. The sum of the resulting figures is the overall capitalization rate.

75% × 0.0966 = 0.0725 weighted rate for debt
25% × 0.1200 = 0.0300 weighted rate for equity
0.0725 + 0.0300 = 0.1025, or 10.25% overall cap rate

The usefulness of the band of investment method depends on the availability of market data to support the estimated debt and equity capitalization rates. In most cases, data to support the debt capitalization rate are readily available, since this rate is the mortgage constant for a loan at current market rates. Market data for equity rates can be more difficult to come by, however. When the equity rate must be derived from sources other than market data (such as published survey data), the band of investment method should be used only as a check on rates derived from another method.

Debt Coverage Method. The rationale behind the debt coverage method is that mortgage lenders will not loan money for an income property investment unless they are confident that the property's income can comfortably support the mortgage payment. With this method, the capitalization rate is calculated by dividing the debt portion of net operating income by the loan amount.

Example: A lender has determined that it is willing to make a 75% loan (a loan with a 75% loan-to-value ratio) in the amount of $150,000, secured by a property with annual net operating income of $20,000. The debt portion of NOI is $15,000 (75% loan ratio × $20,000 income), so the capitalization rate is calculated as $15,000 (debt portion of NOI) ÷ $150,000 (loan amount) = 0.10, or 10%.

The debt coverage method is a useful check for capitalization rates that are derived by other means, but it is not reliable on its own, since it is not based on market data. It merely indicates that the particular lender thinks the rate is appropriate.

Exercise 3

Calculate the overall capitalization rate for net operating income in each of the following situations.

1. A property with annual net operating income of $23,275 was recently sold for $245,000.

____

2. A property with effective gross income of $150,000 per year was sold recently for $600,000. The operating expense ratio for similar properties is 40%.

____

3. Loans available in the current market have a loan constant of 0.1162. The typical loan-to-value ratio is 75%. Market data indicate that 15% is an appropriate capitalization rate for equity investments.

____

Calculating Value by Direct Capitalization

Once the appraiser has estimated the projected income for the subject property and determined an appropriate corresponding overall capitalization rate, the calculation of value is a simple matter. The income amount is divided by the capitalization rate, and the result is the value indicator.

Example: An appraiser has estimated that a property's annual net operating income is $15,000, and that an overall capitalization rate of 10.5% is appropriate for net operating income in this case. The value of the property is then estimated as $142,900.

$15,000 ÷ 0.105 = $142,900 (rounded)

Gross Income Multipliers. As noted earlier in this chapter, the conversion of income to value is sometimes accomplished by a multiplier instead of a rate. (The result is the same in either case, since multipliers and rates are simply reciprocals of each other.) When a multiplier is used to convert income, the appraiser uses multiplication rather than division to calculate the value.

Example: The subject property has potential gross income of $120,000 per year. The appraiser has determined that the annual potential gross income multiplier for this type of property is 11. The value of the property is therefore estimated to be $1,320,000 ($120,000 × 11).

Multipliers are most often used to convert gross income to value. **Gross income multipliers (GIMs)** are derived by the comparable sales method (described above), with respect to either potential gross income (PGIMs) or effective gross income (EGIMs). The multipliers are then used to convert the corresponding category of subject property income into an indicator of value. The multipliers may be based on either annual or monthly gross incomes, as long as they are derived and applied consistently for all properties.

Example:

Comparable Sale	Adjusted Sales Price	Monthly Eff. Gross Income	EGIM (monthly)
1	$417,900	$2,100	199
2	$410,400	$1,900	216
3	$363,800	$1,700	214
4	$396,000	$2,000	198
Subject	?	$1,800	?

The comparables indicate a range of EGIMs from 198 to 216, and a corresponding range of values for the subject property between $356,400 and $388,800 ($1,800 × 198 = $356,400; $1,800 × 216 = $388,800). If comparable sales #2 and #3 were found to be the most similar to the subject, the appraiser might conclude that a reconciled EGIM of 216 is most appropriate, in which case the indicated value of the subject would be $388,800 ($1,800 × 216).

The use of gross income multipliers is limited almost exclusively to appraisals of single-family residences and small multi-family residences. In residential appraisals, a gross income multiplier is often referred to as a gross rent multiplier (GRM), since rent is usually the only form of gross income for smaller residential properties.

As discussed above, gross income is often an unreliable indicator of capitalized value, since it does not take into account operating expenses that affect the return to the investor. When using the gross income multiplier method, the appraiser simply assumes that the subject property and the comparables have similar levels of operating expenses.

Residual Techniques. A residual is something that is left over. Residual techniques use direct capitalization to determine the value of one component of a property—the "left over" component—when the value of the other component is known (or is estimated by some other technique). The process involves four steps.

Step 1: Determine the amount of income that is attributable to the known component of the property, by multiplying the value of the known component by an appropriate capitalization rate.

Step 2: Subtract the amount of income attributable to the known component from the total property income, to find the amount of income attributable to the unknown component.

Step 3: Convert the remaining income attributable to the unknown component to an indicator of value, by dividing by an appropriate capitalization rate.

Step 4: Add the estimated value of the unknown component to the value of the known component, to arrive at an indicator of total property value.

There are two basic residual techniques, each one following the four steps outlined above. In the building residual technique, the appraiser independently estimates the value of the land or site and uses the residual method to find the value of the improvements. The opposite is true of the land residual technique: building value is estimated independently, and the residual method is applied to determine the land or site value.

Example (building residual): An appraiser has determined by the sales comparison method that the site value of the subject property is $500,000. Market data indicate that appropriate capitalization rates for land and improvements are 9.75% and 12.00%, respectively. Total annual net operating income for the property has been estimated at $170,000.

Step 1: $500,000 (land value) × 0.0975 (land capitalization rate) = $48,750 income attributable to land

Step 2: $170,000 (total income) – $48,750 (land income) = $121,250 income attributable to building

Step 3: $121,250 (building income) ÷ 0.12 (building capitalization rate) = $1,010,000 indicated building value (rounded)

Step 4: $500,000 (land value) + $1,010,000 (building value) = $1,510,000 indicated total property value

Example (land residual): In a feasibility study, an appraiser has estimated that the cost of constructing a new office building would be $1,200,000, and that the expected net operating income is $197,000. The appraiser has derived capitalization rates of 10% for land and 13.5% for the building.

Step 1: $1,200,000 (building value) × 0.135 (building capitalization rate) = $162,000 income attributable to building

Step 2: $197,000 (total income) – $162,000 (building income) = $35,000 income attributable to land

Step 3: $35,000 (land income) ÷ 0.10 (land capitalization rate) = $350,000 indicated land value

Step 4: $1,200,000 (building value) + $350,000 (land value) = $1,550,000 indicated total property value

Some authorities refer to a third type of residual technique, the property residual technique. However, this is not a true residual method. In the property residual technique, total property value is estimated by dividing total property income by the overall capitalization rate for the property. This is nothing more than the basic direct capitalization procedure (Value = Income ÷ Capitalization Rate); there is no "residual" involved.

Exercise 4

1. Calculate the effective gross income multiplier for each of the properties below.

Property	Sales Price	Annual Effective Gross Income	Annual EGIM
1	$187,400	$9,200	_______
2	$184,600	$9,400	_______
3	$180,100	$8,900	_______
4	$181,600	$9,600	_______

2. Use the residual technique to calculate the total property value on the basis of the following information.

   Land value: $50,000 (estimated by sales comparison)
   Land capitalization rate: 8.5%
   Building capitalization rate: 12.0%
   Total property income: $22,250

   ____

   ____

Yield Capitalization

In direct capitalization, the appraiser estimates the value of a property on the basis of its projected income for one period, usually a year. With yield capitalization, on the other hand, property value is derived from an analysis of all the income payments that will be received over the life of the investment. The basic process of yield capitalization has four steps.

Step 1: Select an appropriate holding period for the investment. The **holding period** is the life span of the investment; it is usually the length of time from the date the property is purchased by the investor until the date the property is resold.

Step 2: Estimate the amounts of all payments to the investor (cash flows) during the holding period of the investment. This includes all income from the investment, as well as the **reversion**, the amount received by the investor when the property is sold at the conclusion of the holding period.

Step 3: Select an appropriate **yield rate** (or rates) to apply to each of the cash flows.

Step 4: Using the selected yield rate(s), convert each cash flow from the property into its **present value**. The sum of the present values of all the cash flows is the indicated value of the investment.

Once we have explained some important terminology, we will look at an example that goes through all of these steps.

Discounting

The process of converting the amount of a future payment into its present value is called **discounting**, or **discounted cash flow analysis**. This process assumes that payment of a given amount is worth less in the future than it is today, for two reasons. First of all, prices will go up because of inflation; an amount of money will have less purchasing power in the future than it does in the present. And second, by waiting until sometime in the future to receive the payment, the investor loses the opportunity to use the funds for some other purpose in the meantime.

The relationship between present value and future value can be illustrated by the example of a savings account. Assume that a savings account pays 10% interest per year. If you put $100 into the account today, you will have $110 in the account after one year—the original $100 plus $10 interest. In this case, the present value of $100 is equivalent to a future value of $110.

To calculate future value from a known present value, you multiply the present amount by 1 plus the interest rate. In the example of the savings account, we multiplied $100 by 1 plus 10%, or 1.10, to get the future value of $110. With discounting, the calculation is simply reversed. You start with the known (or assumed) amount of the future payment, and divide by 1 plus the interest (yield) rate, to get the present value.

Example:

$110 (future value) ÷ 1.10 (1 plus yield rate) = $100 present value

Compounding. A yield rate (or interest rate) is an amount per period (for example, 10% per year). In discounting, the yield rate must be expressed as a rate per compounding period.

The **compounding period** is the time interval after which interest is actually paid. (For example, compounded monthly means the accrued interest is actually paid at the end of each month.) At the end of each compounding period, the amount of the principal grows by the amount of paid interest. The rate per compounding period is known as the **effective interest rate**, or **effective yield rate**.

Example: An investment pays 12% per year, compounded monthly. In this case, the effective yield rate of the investment is actually 1% per month. The effect of monthly compounding is shown in the chart below.

Month	Starting Balance	Interest	Ending Balance
1	$1,000.00	$10.00	$1,010.00
2	1,010.00	10.10	1,020.10
3	1,020.10	10.20	1,030.30
4	1,030.30	10.30	1,040.60
5	1,040.60	10.41	1,051.01
6	1,051.01	10.51	1,061.52
7	1,061.52	10.62	1,072.14
8	1,072.14	10.72	1,082.86
9	1,082.86	10.83	1,093.69
10	1,093.69	10.94	1,104.63
11	1,104.63	11.05	1,115.68
12	1,115.68	11.16	1,126.84

In this example, a present value of $1,000.00 is equal to a future value after one year of $1,126.84, at an effective yield rate of 1% per month (12% per year compounded monthly).

Reversion Factors. When calculating the present value of a future payment, it is customary to use financial tables or a financial calculator, rather than manually calculating the discount amount. Tables of **reversion factors** allow the appraiser to calculate present value by simple multiplication.

Example: To manually calculate the present value of a payment of $1,000 that will be made in ten years, at an effective yield rate of 10% per year, an appraiser would have to divide $1,000 by 1.10 (1 plus the yield rate) ten times, once for each year (compounding period). Using a table of reversion factors, however, the appraiser can see that the reversion factor for ten years at 10% annual effective interest is .385543 per $1 of income. So the present value of the future $1,000 payment is $385.54 ($1,000 × .385543). The same result could be obtained by entering the payment amount, effective yield rate, and number of compounding periods into a financial calculator.

Annuities. In discounted cash flow analysis, the term **annuity** refers to a series of regular payments, such as regular monthly rental payments under the terms of a lease. The critical characteristic of an annuity is that each payment is made at the same periodic interval. The interval can be monthly or yearly or some other regular period, but it must be the same for each payment.

When the payments under an annuity are all the same amount (level annuity), or when they increase or decrease at a steady rate (increasing or decreasing annuity), the process of discounting the payments to their present value is simplified. The appraiser can use published financial tables or a financial calculator to determine the present value of the entire annuity.

Example: An investment is projected to produce income of $1,000 per month, for a term of five years. Using a yield rate of 10% per year, the appraiser can look up the corresponding present value factor (called the Inwood coefficient) in a level annuity table. In this case, the factor is 47.065369 per $1 of income, so the present value of the annuity is $47,065.37 (47.065369 × $1,000). The same result could be determined by entering the term, yield rate, compounding period, and periodic income amount into a financial calculator.

When the payments under an annuity vary without any regular pattern (**irregular annuity**), each payment must be discounted separately. The individual present values of all the payments are then added together to find the present value of the annuity.

Example: An investment is projected to yield payments of $5,000 after one year, $12,000 after two years, and $7,000 after three years. Because the payment amounts are irregular, the appraiser would have to discount each of the three payments separately, then add the discounted values together to find the present value of the income stream.

Yield Rates

As is the case with overall capitalization rates, yield rates must be selected on the basis of market data when estimating market value. (An investor's required yield rate may be used when estimating investment value.) In some cases, different yield rates may be applied to different parts of the income stream. For example, one yield rate may be applied to calculate the present value of property's income payments, and a separate rate in order to find the present value of the reversion payment that comes when the property is sold. In general, the yield rate is a function of the amount of risk that is associated with a particular payment.

It should be apparent that yield capitalization is much more involved than direct capitalization, since the appraiser must estimate income amounts and yield rates for each income payment that is projected to occur during the life of the investment. This approach is most appropriate when it reflects the thinking of the average investor for the type of property being appraised. For this reason, and also because of the cost involved in such detailed analysis, yield capitalization is rarely used in the appraisal of residential real estate.

Appraisal using yield capitalization can be very complicated, but it is always done using the four steps discussed above. Most appraisers will perform yield capitalization using a financial calculator or specially created software, but in order to help you better understand the yield capitalization process, the following example will work through all of the steps.

Example: An appraiser is given the problem of appraising a 1,000 square foot one-unit retail space for an investor. The investor expects to hold the property for ten years. The appraiser finds out the following information by researching the local market.

- Rent will be $20 per square foot per month in the first year
- Market rents will increase 5% per year
- Vacancies and bad debts will be 5% per year
- Operating expenses will be $100,000 in the first year
- Operating expenses will increase 5% per year
- A 13% rate of return is appropriate for both the rental income and the resale of the building
- To calculate the resale value of the building, the appraiser will apply a 10% capitalization rate to the eleventh year net operating income, and then subtract 2.5% of the resale price for sales expenses

Step 1: The appraiser must choose a holding period. In this case, the appropriate holding period is ten years, the length of time the investor expects to hold the property.

Step 2: The appraiser must estimate the amount of all payments to the investor during the holding period. There are two different cash flows in this problem: the cash flow from monthly rental income, and the cash flow from the reversion received when the property is resold.

The appraiser will calculate the cash flow from rental income first. This will require calculating the cash flow for each year. To calculate each year's cash flow, the appraiser will need to:

1. increase the previous year's market rent by 5%,
2. subtract 5% for bad debts and vacancies,
3. calculate operating expenses (which increase 5% per year), and
4. subtract operating expenses to find each year's net operating income.

For instance, the first year's potential gross income would be $240,000.

$20 per square foot × 1,000 square feet = $20,000 monthly rent

$20,000 monthly rent × 12 months = $240,000 annual rent

There would be a $12,000 deduction for vacancies and bad debts, leaving an effective gross income of $228,000.

$240,000 potential gross income × .05 = $12,000 vacancies and bad debts

$240,000 potential gross income – $12,000 vacancies and bad debts = $228,000 effective gross income

Operating expenses would be $100,000, leaving a net operating income of $128,000 for the first year.

$228,000 effective gross income – $100,000 operating expenses = $128,000 net operating income

In the second year, market rents will go up 5%, so the potential gross income will be $252,000.

$240,000 1st year potential gross income × .05 = $12,000 increase

$240,000 1st year potential gross income + $12,000 increase = $252,000 2nd year potential gross income

Vacancies and bad debts will be $12,600, leaving an effective gross income of $239,400.

$252,000 potential gross income × .05 = $12,600 vacancies and bad debts

$252,000 potential gross income – $12,600 vacancies and bad debts = $239,400 effective gross income

Operating expenses will increase to $105,000, leaving a net operating income of $134,400.

$100,000 1st year operating expenses × .05 = $5,000 increase

$100,000 1st year operating expenses + $5,000 increase = $105,000 2nd year operating expenses

$239,400 effective gross income – $105,000 operating expenses = $134,400 net operating income

The appraiser will repeat this process until she has calculated net operating income for each of the eleven years. (The eleventh year is not relevant for income purposes, but it will be used to calculate the subject property's resale value.)

Year	PGI	V/BD	EGI	OE	NOI
1	$240,000.00	$12,000.00	$228,000.00	$100,000.00	$128,000.00
2	$252,000.00	$12,600.00	$239,400.00	$105,000.00	$134,400.00
3	$264,600.00	$13,230.00	$251,370.00	$110,250.00	$141,120.00
4	$277,830.00	$13,891.50	$263,938.50	$115,762.50	$148,176.00
5	$291,721.50	$14,586.08	$277,135.42	$121,550.63	$155,584.79
6	$306,307.58	$15,315.38	$290,992.20	$127,628.16	$163,364.04
7	$321,622.96	$16,081.15	$305,541.81	$134,009.57	$171,532.24
8	$337,704.11	$16,885.21	$320,818.90	$140,710.05	$180,108.85
9	$354,589.32	$17,729.47	$336,859.85	$147,745.55	$189,114.30
10	$372,318.79	$18,615.94	$353,702.85	$155,132.83	$198,570.02
11	$390,934.73	$19,546.74	$371,387.99	$162,889.47	$208,498.52

Step 3: The appraiser must choose an appropriate yield rate for each cash flow. Based on market data and the investor's needs, 13% is an appropriate rate for both the rental income and the resale value.

Step 4: The appraiser must apply the appropriate yield rate to each component of the cash flow. For each year's cash flow, the appraiser will need to apply the appropriate reversion factor. These factors can be obtained from a table of reversion factors for a 13% rate over ten years. For instance, the first year's operating income is multiplied by the appropriate reversion factor, indicating that the discounted value of the first year's income is $113,274.37.

$128,000 net operating income × 0.884956 = $113,274.37 discounted income

The appraiser will repeat this process for each of the ten years of the holding period, and then add the discounted value of each year to find the discounted value of the total cash flow from rental income.

Year	NOI	Factor	Discounted Value
1	$128,000.00	0.884956	$113,274.37
2	$134,400.00	0.783147	$105,254.96
3	$141,120.00	0.693050	$97,803.22
4	$148,176.00	0.613319	$90,879.16
5	$155,584.79	0.542760	$84,445.20
6	$163,364.04	0.480319	$78,466.85
7	$171,532.24	0.425061	$72,911.67
8	$180,108.85	0.376160	$67,749.75
9	$189,114.30	0.332885	$62,953.31
10	$198,570.02	0.294588	$58,496.35
Total			$832,234.84

Now the appraiser must calculate the reversion, which is the amount the investor receives when the building is sold. The appraiser will divide the subject property's eleventh year income by a 10% capitalization rate, to find that the property's resale value in ten years is $2,084,985.20. (Remember that this step in the process uses a 10% capitalization rate, rather than the 13% rate applied to the rental income.)

$208,498.52 11th year net operating income ÷ .1 = $2,084,985.20

The appraiser must subtract 2.5% of the sales price to account for selling expenses, resulting in a total of $2,032,860.57.

$2,084,985.20 sales price × .025 = $52,124.63 selling expenses

$2,084,985.20 sales price – $52,124.63 selling expenses = $2,032,860.57 received by investor

The appraiser must now calculate the discounted value of the proceeds from the sale, using the same 13% rate of return that applied to the rental income. The appraiser will apply the reversion factor obtained from the same ten-year, 13% table.

$2,032,860.57 future value × 0.294588 = $598,856.33 present value

Finally, the appraiser will add the present value of the reversion and the present value of the future income, to determine the present value of the subject property.

$598,856.33 present value of reversion + $832,234.84 present value of rental income = $1,431,091.17 present value of property

Key Terms

Annuity—A series of regular periodic payments, such as regular monthly rental payments under the terms of a lease.

Anticipation—A principle of value which holds that value is affected by the expectations of buyers regarding the future benefits to be gained from property ownership, including the utility to be derived from ownership and the potential gain or loss on resale of the property.

Band of investment technique—A method of deriving a direct capitalization rate by combining separate capitalization rates for the equity (investor) and debt (lender) portions of a property's income.

Building residual technique—A technique for valuing improvements by capitalizing the portion of a property's income that is attributable to the improvements.

Cash flow—Payments made to an investor in connection with an investment.

Compound interest—Interest that is calculated on both principal and accrued interest.

Contract rent—The amount of rent that is called for under an existing lease. Also called scheduled rent.

Contribution—The increase in overall property value that results from the presence of one component of the property. The principle of contribution holds that the value of a component of a property is equivalent to the amount by which it increases the value of the property as a whole.

Debt coverage method—A method of deriving an overall capitalization rate for a property, by dividing the debt portion of net operating income by the loan amount.

Debt coverage ratio—A property's annual net operating income divided by its annual mortgage debt service.

Debt financing—Borrowed funds that are used to finance an investment.

Depreciation—The difference between cost and value, from whatever cause.

Direct capitalization—The process of estimating value on the basis of income from a single period, usually one year. The formula for direct capitalization is Value = Income ÷ Capitalization Rate, or Value = Income × Multiplier.

Discounted cash flow analysis—The process of converting the expected cash flows of an investment to present value.

Discounting—The process of calculating the present value of an expected future amount.

Effective gross income—Potential gross income minus an allowance for vacancies and bad debt losses.

Effective gross income multiplier—Sales price divided by effective gross income. A factor that can be used either to find a capitalization rate or to convert effective gross income to value using direct capitalization.

Effective gross income multiplier method—A method of deriving a capitalization rate using operating expense and net income ratios. A property's net income ratio is divided by its effective gross income multiplier to find the capitalization rate.

Equity dividend rate—A rate used to convert pre-tax cash flow to value, using direct capitalization. Also called the cash on cash rate.

Fixed expense—An operating expense that does not vary depending on the occupancy of a property.

Future value—The value of something as of some future date.

Holding period—The life span of an investment; the length of time from the date a property is purchased until the date the property is resold.

Income—Money or other benefits that are received.

Income approach—One of the three approaches to value in the appraisal process. In the income approach, the value of the subject property is indicated by the amount of net income that the property can generate. Also called the income capitalization approach.

Income capitalization—The process of estimating value on the basis of a property's income.

Income property—Property used for the production of income.

Investment value—The value of a property to a particular investor with specific investment goals. Investment value is inherently subjective.

Land residual technique—A technique for valuing land by capitalizing the portion of a property's income that is attributable to the land.

Market rent—The amount of rent that a property should be able to command under current market conditions.

Market value—In general, the amount of cash (or cash equivalent) that is most likely to be paid for a property on a given date in a fair and reasonable open market transaction. Specific (but varied) definitions of market value can be found in the USPAP and in many state laws. Also called exchange value or value in exchange.

Mortgage constant—The amount of annual mortgage debt service for a loan divided by the loan amount. The mortgage constant depends on the interest rate of the loan, the loan term, and the frequency at which loan payments are due. Also called a loan constant.

Mortgage debt service—The periodic amount due under the terms of a mortgage loan, including payments of both principal and interest.

Net income ratio—Net income divided by effective gross income; the complement of the operating expense ratio (1 – OER = NIR).

Net operating income—Effective gross income, minus all operating expenses.

Operating expense ratio—Operating expenses divided by effective gross income; the complement of the net income ratio (1 – NIR = OER).

Operating expenses—The expenses associated with an income-producing property, including fixed expenses, variable expenses, and reserves for replacement.

Operating statement—A financial report listing income and expenses for a property.

Overall capitalization rate—A capitalization rate used to convert a property's total net operating income to value using direct capitalization.

Potential gross income—The total periodic amount of revenue that a property is capable of producing at full occupancy, without any deduction for expenses; usually an annual amount. Potential gross income includes rent and any other income that the property is capable of generating.

Potential gross income multiplier—A factor used to convert potential gross income to value using direct capitalization.

Present value—The value of something as of the present time. Expected future payments or benefits may be converted to their present value by discounting.

Pre-tax cash flow—Net operating income minus mortgage debt service costs. Also called equity dividend.

Rate of return—The amount of income produced by an investment, divided by the amount the investor paid for the investment, usually expressed as a percentage. Also called an interest rate.

Recapture—Recovery of the amount paid for an investment; return of capital.

Reconstructed operating statement—A projected (future) operating statement that includes only those items that are included in the appraisal definitions of potential gross income, effective gross income, net operating income, and pre-tax cash flow.

Rent—The amount paid by a tenant or lessee for the right to use property under the terms of a lease.

Reserves for replacement—Amounts set aside to cover the cost of replacing short-lived items for an income property; a form of operating expense. The amount of reserves is usually calculated by dividing the replacement costs of the items by their remaining useful lives.

Residual—Something that is left over. Residual techniques use direct capitalization to determine the value of the leftover component, when the value of the other component is known (or is estimated by some other technique).

Reversion factor—A factor used in financial calculations to calculate the present value of a future amount.

Vacancy factor—An amount (usually a percentage) deducted from a property's potential gross income to account for vacancies and unpaid rents.

Variable expense—An operating expense that varies depending on the level of occupancy of a property.

Yield—1. Interest. 2. The amount earned by an equity investment, as compared to the amount earned by a debt investment (loan).

Yield capitalization—The process of estimating value on the basis of all the anticipated cash flows (the total income) over the life of an investment.

Summary

I. The income approach views property as an investment whose value depends on the amount of income it produces.

A. The amount of income, in relation to the amount of the investment, is the rate of return.

1. An investor who expects a higher rate of return will pay less for a property than an investor who will accept a lower rate of return.

B. The rate of return required by the average market investor depends on the degree of risk of the investment, and also on the rates of return available on other competing investments.

1. According to the principle of anticipation, investors consider the potential future income from an investment. The fact that the anticipated income cannot be guaranteed is the source of risk in the investment.

2. The higher the degree of risk, the higher the rate of return an investor will require.

3. An investment must offer a rate of return that is comparable to rates on competing investment alternatives with similar degrees of risk.

II. Direct capitalization converts the income from a single period, usually a year, into an indicator of property value.

A. To calculate value, the property's income is either divided by a capitalization rate or multiplied by an income multiplier.

B. An appraiser may capitalize potential gross income, effective gross income, net operating income, or pre-tax cash flow.

1. Potential gross income is the total amount of income the property is capable of producing at full occupancy.

a. For properties subject to long-term leases, potential gross income may be estimated on the basis of scheduled rent, the rent called for in the lease.

b. For owner-occupied or vacant properties, potential gross income is based on market rent, the rent the property could produce at current market rates.

c. Potential gross income also includes any incidental income the property may produce, in addition to the rent.

2. Effective gross income is equal to potential gross income minus a vacancy factor (usually a percentage) for expected vacancies and bad debt losses.

3. Net operating income is equal to effective gross income minus expenses of operating the property. It represents the amount of income that is available to the investor, so it is a more reliable measure of value than gross income.
   a. Fixed expenses are expenses that do not depend on the amount of income produced by the property (the level of occupancy).
   b. Variable expenses may change depending on the amount of income.
   c. Replacement reserves are amounts set aside to cover the cost of replacing short-lived components of the building. They may be calculated by dividing the replacement cost of an item by its remaining useful life.
4. Pre-tax cash flow (equity dividend) is equal to net operating income minus debt service costs. It is the amount of income that is available to the equity investor after the debt investor has been paid.
5. The estimate of income is commonly prepared in the form of a reconstructed operating statement.

C. In direct capitalization, the capitalization rate (or income multiplier) represents the relationship between income and value.
   1. In market value appraisals, the capitalization rate must be derived from analysis of market data, such as incomes and sales prices of comparables.
   2. In the comparable sales method, the incomes of comparable properties are divided by their sales prices, to yield a range of capitalization rates for the subject property.
      a. The sales prices of the comparables must be adjusted to account for differences in market conditions or financing terms. Differences in physical characteristics are accounted for in the reconciliation phase.
      b. Income for the subject property and for the comparables must be estimated on a consistent basis.
      c. The comparables must be similar to the subject in terms of key investment criteria, such as expected resale price, holding period, and tax benefits of ownership.
   3. When operating expenses for comparables can't be reliably estimated, the appraiser may use the effective gross income multiplier (EGIM) method to derive a capitalization rate for net operating income.
      a. EGIM = Sales Price ÷ Effective Gross Income
      b. The operating expense ratio is the average ratio of operating expenses to effective gross income for similar properties in the market.
      c. The net income ratio is the complement of the operating expense ratio: NIR = 1 – OER.
      d. To calculate the capitalization rate for net operating income, a comparable property's NIR is divided by its EGIM.

4. The band of investment technique derives the overall capitalization rate for a property by using the weighted average of separate rates for different components of the investment.

    a. The rate for the debt component is equal to the mortgage constant, which is the amount of annual debt service cost divided by the loan amount.

    b. The rate for the equity component is derived from market data for comparable sales. It is usually higher than the debt rate, due to the higher degree of risk for the equity investor.

5. The debt coverage method derives the capitalization rate by dividing the debt portion of net operating income by the loan amount.

D. The basic formula for direct capitalization is Value = Income ÷ Overall Capitalization Rate.

1. In residential appraisals, gross income is often capitalized by means of a factor instead of a rate, using multiplication instead of division. The factor may be a potential gross income multiplier (PGIM) or an effective gross income multiplier (EGIM).

2. When the value of one component of the property (land or building) can be estimated independently, the value of the remaining component can be estimated by capitalizing the residual income attributable to it.

III. Yield capitalization involves an analysis of all cash flows that will be generated by the property during the term of the investment (the holding period).

A. Each cash flow (including the expected proceeds from resale at the end of the investment) is discounted to its present value at a selected yield rate. The sum of the present values represents the indicator of subject property value.

B. Discounting calculations are simplified by use of financial tables and/or financial calculators.

C. An entire series of cash flows can be discounted in a single calculation under certain circumstances. The cash flows must occur on a regular periodic basis (annuity payments), and they must be either equal (level) amounts or amounts that change (increase or decrease) in a regular pattern.

D. For appraisals of market value, the yield rate(s) used in discounting the cash flows must be derived from market data.

Chapter Quiz

1. The process of estimating value by capitalizing the total income from a single time period is called:
   a. direct capitalization
   b. indirect capitalization
   c. yield capitalization
   d. equity capitalization

2. A property's equity dividend is also called:
   a. potential gross income
   b. effective gross income
   c. net operating income
   d. pre-tax cash flow

3. To determine net operating income, which of the following would be deducted from effective gross income?
   a. Mortgage debt service costs
   b. Income taxes
   c. Property taxes
   d. Depreciation

4. Expenses that depend on the amount of income generated by the property are known as:
   a. rent expenses
   b. pre-tax expenses
   c. variable expenses
   d. maintenance expenses

5. Which of the following types of income would give the most reliable value indicator in the income approach to value?
   a. Potential gross income
   b. Effective gross income
   c. Net operating income
   d. No difference

Questions 6 through 8 are based on the following facts:

A property consists of six apartment units, with a market rent of $1,000 per month per unit. One of the units is occupied by the apartment manager, who receives free rent in return for managing the complex. Average bad debt and vacancies account for 10% of total rental income, and annual operating expenses are $30,000.

6. What is the property's annual potential gross income?
   a. $54,000
   b. $60,000
   c. $64,800
   d. $72,000

7. What is the property's annual net operating income?
   a. $24,000
   b. $30,000
   c. $34,800
   d. $42,000

8. If the monthly effective gross rent multiplier is 55.56, what is the indicated value of the property (rounded to the nearest $100)?
   a. $250,000
   b. $277,800
   c. $300,000
   d. $333,400

9. Using an overall capitalization rate of 8%, what is the indicated value of a property with net operating income of $35,000 per year?

   a. $280,000
   b. $437,500
   c. $560,000
   d. Cannot be determined from the information given

10. The process of converting the amount of a future payment to its present value is known as:

    a. discounting
    b. reduction
    c. reversion
    d. recapture

11. When capitalizing the portion of income that goes to satisfy the debt investor (lender), the capitalization rate used in the band of investment technique is equivalent to:

    a. the mortgage interest rate
    b. the mortgage constant
    c. the equity capitalization rate
    d. the Inwood coefficient

12. For a property that is subject to a long-term lease, an appraiser would most likely estimate potential gross income on the basis of:

    a. market rent
    b. historical rent
    c. effective rent
    d. scheduled rent

13. From an investor's point of view, the value of a property depends primarily on:

    a. the recapture rate
    b. the rate of return
    c. the amount of equity
    d. the rate of inflation

14. When deriving a capitalization rate by analyzing the sales prices and incomes of comparable properties in the market, an appraiser may need to adjust the sales price of a comparable to account for differences in:

    a. market conditions
    b. operating expenses
    c. location
    d. vacancy rates

15. When estimating the potential gross income of a four-plex in which one unit is owner-occupied, the appraiser would:

    a. estimate the market rent of the owner-occupied unit
    b. assume the owner-occupied unit would rent for the same amount as the other units
    c. exclude any potential income from the owner-occupied unit
    d. exclude income and expenses related to the owner-occupied unit

Case Study

Based on the following information, determine the value of the subject property using the income approach. Enter the indicated value on the line in the Uniform Residential Appraisal Report labeled "INDICATED VALUE BY INCOME APPROACH." Attach an additional page describing the comparables and the method used to indicate the value. You may use a gross income multiplier in order to determine the subject property's value.

SUBJECT: 1731 Pine Road is being appraised in connection with a sale of the property for $342,750. Prior to its sale, it was rented at a monthly rate of $1,900. Through the Oakdale Multiple Listing Service, you have located three recent sales in the Ravenswood development of single-family properties that were occupied by renters rather than by the owners. The comparables were similar to the subject property in terms of expected holding period of the investment.

COMPARABLE 1: 1433 Poplar Street is approximately four blocks from the subject property. It was sold three months ago for $345,000 with conventional loan financing. The monthly potential gross income from this property was $1,950.

COMPARABLE 2: 1322 Cottonwood Street is approximately five blocks from the subject property. It was sold four months ago for $348,000 with conventional loan financing. The monthly potential gross income from this property was $1,900.

COMPARABLE 3: 905 Locust Street is approximately eight blocks from the subject property. It was sold six months ago for $325,000 with conventional loan financing. The monthly potential gross income from this property was $1,750.

Use this portion of the URAR to complete the case study.

INCOME	INCOME APPROACH TO VALUE (not required by Fannie Mae)			
	Estimated Monthly Market Rent $	X Gross Rent Multiplier	= $	Indicated Value by Income Approach
	Summary of Income Approach (including support for market rent and GRM)			

Quiz Answers

1. a) The process of capitalizing total income from a single time period is known as direct capitalization.

2. d) Pre-tax cash flow is also known as the equity dividend or before-tax cash flow.

3. c) Net operating income is determined by subtracting operating expenses, such as property taxes, from effective gross income.

4. c) Expenses that vary depending on income generated are variable expenses.

5. c) Net operating income gives the most reliable value indicator, since it accounts for operating expenses.

6. d) The property's potential gross income is $72,000 (6 units × 12 months × $1,000 rent = $72,000).

7. c) The property's net operating income is $34,800 ($72,000 potential gross income – 10% bad debts and vacancies = $64,800 effective gross income – $30,000 operating expenses = $34,800).

8. c) First, determine the monthly effective gross income ($6,000 potential gross income – 10% bad debts and vacancies = $5,400). Then multiply the monthly effective gross income by the multiplier ($5,400 × 55.56 = $300,024) and round to the nearest $100 ($300,000).

9. b) The indicated value is $437,500 ($35,000 ÷ .08 = $437,500).

10. a) The process of converting a future payment into its present value is discounting.

11. b) In the band of investment method of estimating a capitalization rate, the mortgage constant (i.e., the annual debt service divided by the loan amount) is equivalent to the capitalization rate.

12. d) For an existing long-term lease, an appraiser will estimate income based on scheduled rent (unless the lease is set to expire in a short period of time).

13. b) To an investor, the rate of return is the most important factor in determining value.

14. a) An appraiser may need to make adjustments for market conditions when using the comparable sales method to estimate a capitalization rate.

15. a) If a unit is owner-occupied, an appraiser will use the market rent for that unit to determine the property's value.

Exercise Answers

#1 1. Value = Amount of Income ÷ Rate of Return

2. a. Risk

b. The rates of return on competing investments

3. \$50,000 ÷ 0.10 = \$500,000
\$50,000 ÷ 0.15 = \$333,333

#2

Potential Gross Income	\$120,000
Vacancies and Bad Debts	\$6,000
Effective Gross Income	\$114,000
Fixed Expenses	
property taxes	\$12,000
insurance	\$2,400
Variable Expenses	
management	\$10,000
utilities	\$30,000
maintenance	\$16,000
Reserves for Replacement	\$7,000
Total Expenses	\$77,400
Net Operating Income	\$36,600
Debt Service	\$31,200
Pre-Tax Cash Flow	\$5,400

#3 1. \$23,275 ÷ \$245,000 = 0.095, or 9.5% NOI capitalization rate

2. \$600,000 ÷ \$150,000 = 4 EGIM

1 – 0.40 OER = .60 net income ratio

.60 NIR ÷ 4 EGIM = .15, or 15% NOI capitalization rate

3. 0.1162 × 0.75 = 0.087, or 8.7% weighted debt rate

0.15 × 0.25 = 0.038, or 3.8% weighted equity rate

8.7% + 3.8% = 12.5% overall NOI capitalization rate

#4 1. 20.4; 19.6; 20.2; 18.9

2. \$50,000 × 0.085 = \$4,250 income attributable to land

\$22,250 – \$4,250 = \$18,000 income attributable to building

\$18,000 ÷ 0.12 = \$150,000 indicated building value

\$50,000 + \$150,000 = \$200,000 indicated total property value

Case Study Answers

ADDENDUM TO URAR, REGARDING INCOME APPROACH

Since comparable data were available, determination of an appropriate multiplier is best made through the comparable sales method. All comparables were similar to the subject property in financing terms and were sold within the six months prior to the sale of the subject property, so no adjustments are necessary.

Comparable 1 gross rent multiplier: $345,000 ÷ $1,950 = 176.9

Comparable 2 gross rent multiplier: $348,000 ÷ $1,900 = 183.2

Comparable 3 gross rent multiplier: $325,000 ÷ $1,750 = 185.7

Reconciled gross rent multiplier to be applied to subject property: 182

Value indicated by income approach: $1,900 × 182 = $345,800

[The gross rent multiplier chosen through reconciliation is a subjective choice made according to an individual appraiser's best judgment, and your answer may legitimately differ. Since no comparable is significantly different in terms of date of sale, financing terms, or physical condition, all three comparables should be given approximately equal weight in this example.]

Income Approach Addendum

	Price	Monthly rent	PGRM
Comparable 1 (1433 Poplar Street)	$345,000	$1,950	176.9
Comparable 2 (1322 Cottonwood Street)	$348,000	$1,900	183.2
Comparable 3 (905 Locust Street)	$325,000	$1,750	185.7

The comparables are all very similar to the subject property, so no comparable receives particular weight.

The reconciled potential gross rent multiplier chosen is 182.

Here's the appropriate URAR section.

INCOME	INCOME APPROACH TO VALUE (not required by Fannie Mae)
	Estimated Monthly Market Rent $ 1,900 X Gross Rent Multiplier 182 = $ 345,800 Indicated Value by Income Approach
	Summary of Income Approach (including support for market rent and GRM)

11 Reconciliation and Final Value Estimate

Overview

After applying the three approaches to value, an appraiser will have more than one indicator of the subject property's value. To arrive at a final estimate of value, the appraiser must consider all of the evidence supporting the different value indicators, as well as the relevance of the different appraisal techniques to the particular appraisal problem at hand. This process is called reconciliation, and it is the focus of this chapter. After completing this chapter, you should be able to:

- define the term "reconciliation" as it applies to appraisal practice,
- describe the kinds of situations in which reconciliation is used in an appraisal,
- describe the characteristics of a "credible" appraisal,
- identify the factors that affect the reliability of a value indicator,
- name the two main types of final value estimates and list their advantages and disadvantages, and
- explain how and why rounding is used to express value estimates.

Reconciliation

In the course of the appraisal process, an appraiser develops several different indicators of the subject property's value. Those indicators may be derived by analyzing data from different comparable properties, or by using different units of comparison or different appraisal techniques.

Different value indicators serve as cross-checks against each other. Large discrepancies between different value indicators tell the appraiser that he or she has failed to consider some important value influence, or perhaps made an error in a mathematical calculation. The greater the number of value indicators, the greater the understanding of the market forces affecting the subject property's value, and the more reliable the final value estimate.

But even when the value indicators all fall within a narrow range, they will rarely (if ever) be exactly the same. In the reconciliation step of the appraisal process, the appraiser analyzes the data and reasoning that went into the value indicators in order to arrive at a single indication of value.

Definition of Reconciliation

In appraisal practice, the term **reconciliation** has two similar but slightly different meanings. In its more limited sense, reconciliation refers to the particular step in the appraisal process when the appraiser arrives at a final value estimate. In this step, the appraiser analyzes the value indicators that were derived using the different approaches to value, assigns different weights to the indicators based on their reliability and relevance, and then uses his or her judgment to make a final estimate of the subject property's value.

In a more general sense, reconciliation refers to the process of analyzing two or more different value indicators, weighting them according to reliability and relevance, and determining a single value (or range of values) that the appraiser feels is most appropriate based on all the evidence. This can occur at any point in the appraisal process when the appraiser needs to derive a single value from a number of value indicators, not just when making a final value estimate.

Use of Reconciliation in Appraisals

Reconciliation (in the general sense) may be required for three different appraisal purposes:

1. to reconcile values indicated by different comparable properties,
2. to reconcile values indicated by different units of comparison, or
3. to reconcile values indicated by different appraisal techniques.

Reconciling Values From Different Comparables. Reconciling values indicated by different comparable properties is very common in appraisals. The sales comparison method is considered reliable only if data are available from several comparable properties. Consequently, reconciliation is required virtually every time an appraisal uses comparable sales data.

Appraisers may reconcile comparable property values in order to derive:

- an indicator of unit price (price per total property, price per square foot, etc.) for the subject property in the sales comparison approach,
- an indicator of land or site value in the cost approach,
- an indicator of unit cost (such as cost per square foot) in the cost approach, or
- an income multiplier or capitalization rate for the subject property in the income approach.

Example: Using the sales comparison approach to value, an appraiser analyzed three comparable sales. The resulting adjusted sales prices of the three comparables were:

Comparable #1: $285,200
Comparable #2: $281,500
Comparable #3: $287,300

To obtain a single indicator of value from the sales comparison approach, the appraiser must reconcile the three different values indicated by the comparables.

Reconciling Values From Different Units of Comparison. Reconciliation may also be required when different units of comparison are used. This occurs most often in the sales comparison approach.

Example: In appraising an apartment building, an appraiser used the sales comparison approach to derive the following value indicators for the subject property.

Price per square foot of gross building area: $43.50
Price per dwelling unit: $52,000
Price per square foot of net leasable area: $49.00

The subject property has 11,000 square feet of gross building area, 10 units, and a net leasable area of 10,000 square feet, resulting in three different indications of value.

Value indicator based on gross building area: $43.50 × 11,000 = $478,500
Value indicator based on number of units: $52,000 × 10 = $520,000
Value indicator based on net leasable area: $49.00 × 10,000 = $490,000

The appraiser must reconcile the values indicated by the three different units of comparison to reach a single indicator of subject property value.

Reconciling Values From Different Appraisal Techniques. The third situation that may require reconciliation occurs when different appraisal techniques generate different value indicators. An obvious example of this situation is the final value estimate, where the appraiser must reconcile the value indicators from the different approaches to value. But reconciling values from different techniques can also occur within a single approach to value. In the income approach, for example, an appraiser may need to reconcile values obtained by direct capitalization and yield capitalization (discounting).

Fig. 11.1 Situations Requiring Reconciliation

1. Different comparable properties
2. Different units of comparison
3. Different appraisal techniques

Exercise 1

1. What are the two definitions of "reconciliation," as used in appraisal?

   a. ______________________________

   b. ______________________________

2. List the three types of situations in which reconciliation may be necessary in an appraisal.

   a. ______________________________

   b. ______________________________

   c. ______________________________

The Reconciliation Process

Reconciliation is not a mathematical process. No formulas are involved, and appraisers should never attempt to reconcile value indicators by averaging or by using other similar mathematical techniques. Rather, reconciliation calls for judgment and experience on the part of the appraiser. The appraiser must evaluate all of the evidence supporting the different value indicators, giving weight to the indicators that, based on the evidence, are the most reliable and relevant.

Reconciliation involves two steps:

1. reviewing the processes that led to the different value indicators, and
2. making the reconciliation judgment.

Reviewing the Appraisal

In the first step in the reconciliation process, the appraiser reviews all of the data, calculations, and reasoning that led to the various value indicators. This review helps to ensure that no mistakes were made. Each mathematical calculation is double-checked for accuracy, preferably by someone other than the appraiser who made the original calculations. Having a second person check the math can help turn up mistakes that would otherwise be overlooked.

The appraiser makes sure that all appraisal techniques have been applied consistently and that any assumptions were used consistently. The appraiser also checks to see that:

- all value indicators were derived on the basis of the same definition of value,
- all properties were evaluated on the basis of the same highest and best use,
- all properties were evaluated on the basis of the same real property interest, and
- the characteristics of the subject property were defined consistently in the various approaches and techniques.

Example: In the sales comparison approach, differences between the age and condition of the improvements of the subject property and a comparable property require an adjustment to the comparable's sales price. In the cost approach, the effective age of the subject property's improvements is a factor in calculating straight-line depreciation. For the purposes of both appraisal methods, the age and condition of the subject property's improvements should be the same.

Another purpose of reviewing the appraisal is to assess the relative reliability of the different value indicators. Reliability is a crucial factor in judging the significance of a given value indicator. The more reliable a particular indicator, the more weight it will be given in the reconciliation process. (Assessing the reliability of value indicators is discussed in more detail below.)

The appraiser must also check to see that the information used to arrive at the value indicators is thorough and complete. To reach a credible value estimate, all relevant data must be considered, and all pertinent appraisal techniques must be applied.

Finally, the appraiser must review the appraisal to ensure that the value indicators have been derived in accordance with the terms of the appraisal assignment, including the definition of value, the purpose and use of the appraisal, and any other terms that may affect the value estimate. The appraiser's job is to answer the client's specific question concerning the value of a property. The data selected for the appraisal, and the appraisal techniques employed, should all be suited to answering the client's question, as defined by the terms of the appraisal assignment.

Example: Appraisals for mortgage loan underwriting purposes are often subject to regulations from a secondary market agency such as the Federal National Mortgage Association (Fannie Mae) or the Federal Home Loan Mortgage Corporation (Freddie Mac). In that case, the appraiser must be sure that the data and techniques used conform to the agency's guidelines.

Assessing the Reliability of Value Indicators

As discussed in the previous section, the reliability of a particular value indicator is a critical factor in the reconciliation process. The greater the reliability, the more weight that indicator receives. The reliability of a value indicator depends on three factors:

1. the amount of data supporting the indicator,
2. the level of accuracy of the indicator, and
3. the relevance of the indicator to the appraisal problem.

Fig. 11.2 Value Indicator Criteria

1. Amount of data
2. Level of accuracy
3. Relevance

Amount of Data. All other things being equal, a value indicator is considered more reliable when it is supported by more data. For example, in the sales comparison approach to value, a value indicator supported by data from sales of twenty comparable properties is more reliable than a value indicator that is based on only three comparables. In this case, the greater amount of data represents a larger slice or "sampling" of the market. According to statistical theory, a larger sampling results in a lower margin of error; in other words, it is more reliable.

The amount of data supporting the value indicators is relevant on three levels. First, as noted in the previous paragraph, value indicators are more reliable when they are supported by data that represent a larger sampling of the market. Second, a value indicator's reliability depends on the level of detail of the data supporting it.

> **Example:** In the cost approach to value, a building cost estimate derived by the unit-in-place method is generally considered more reliable than an estimate based on cost per square foot of building area, due to the relatively higher level of detail required by the unit-in-place method. An even more detailed cost estimate, using the quantity survey method, would be considered even more reliable.

Finally, a value indicator is considered more reliable when it is supported by several different independent sources, as compared to an indicator derived from a single source.

> **Example:** An appraiser who has estimated the value of a site by the sales comparison approach may also employ allocation or extraction to obtain a second, independent indicator of site value. If the two separate value indicators are reasonably similar, the reliability of the site value estimate is enhanced.

Level of Accuracy. The reliability of a value indicator also depends on its accuracy. In assessing the level of accuracy, the appraiser must consider both:

- the accuracy of the original data, and
- the accuracy of the resulting value indicator.

The accuracy of the original data used in an appraisal is critical. If the data are inaccurate, the value conclusions drawn from them cannot possibly be reliable, regardless of the amount of data or the techniques used by the appraiser. This fundamental principle is summarized neatly by the phrase, "garbage in, garbage out."

In appraisal, the accuracy of data is measured by how well they have been verified. For some types of data, such as the physical characteristics of the subject property, personal review by the appraiser is the most reliable form of verification. Other data, such as details of a sales transaction, are often verified by interviewing one of the parties to the transaction (the buyer or seller). If particular data are especially important to a transaction, it is especially important to verify the data using the most reliable source available.

Example: An error in the data concerning the physical characteristics of the subject property (such as square footage of building area) could easily lead to a significant miscalculation of value. A similar error in the data concerning a comparable property is somewhat less critical, since more than one comparable will be analyzed. Any error in the comparable property data is likely to show up as a discrepancy in the adjusted sales price, in comparison to the adjusted sales prices of the other comparables. Since the subject property data are more critical to the outcome of the valuation process, they require a higher level of verification.

In addition to confirming the accuracy of the original data, the appraiser must consider the level of accuracy of the resulting value indicator. Even if the original data are completely accurate, the resulting value indicator may still be considered more or less reliable, depending on the nature of the appraisal technique used.

Example: In the sales comparison approach, the sales prices of comparable properties are adjusted to account for the differences between each comparable and the subject property. Assuming that the comparable sales data are completely accurate, the resulting value indicators (the adjusted sales prices of the comparables) may still not be 100% reliable, especially if significant adjustments were required. Each time an adjustment is made to a comparable's sales price, the appraiser must determine the dollar amount of the adjustment. Since each adjustment amount is itself an estimate of value (the value of the characteristic for which the adjustment is being made), each adjustment introduces a level of uncertainty into the value indicator. The greater the number of adjustments, and the greater their dollar amounts, the greater the uncertainty in the resulting value indicator.

Relevance. The third factor that influences the reliability of a value indicator is its relevance to the particular appraisal problem. In assessing the relevance of a value indicator, the appraiser first checks to see that the indicator itself is consistent with the terms of the appraisal assignment, including the definition of value used and the intended use of the appraisal.

Example: In an appraisal assignment that seeks the investment value of a property, a value indicator calculated by means of a market-derived capitalization rate would not be particularly relevant. When estimating investment value, it is the client investor's required rate of return that relates income to value, not the rate of return expected by a typical market investor.

The second consideration in assessing the relevance of a value indicator is the appropriateness of the appraisal technique used to derive the indicator. A technique is appropriate if it reflects the way the market (or the appraisal client) views the value of the subject property. Often, the relevance of an appraisal technique depends on the type of property being appraised.

Example: In appraisals of single-family residences, the value indicated by the sales comparison approach is usually given the most weight, since it most accurately reflects the way the market views the value of this type of property. Most home buyers value property on the basis of what it would cost to purchase a substitute home of comparable utility.

On the other hand, an appraisal of office property would probably give much more weight to the value indicated by the income approach, since this approach mirrors the thinking of investors who look at value in terms of the amount of income that a property is capable of producing.

Making the Reconciliation Judgment

After reviewing the data, calculations, and reasoning that support the different value indicators, and correcting any errors or deficiencies that may have been discovered, the appraiser can determine a reconciled value. As noted earlier, this process relies heavily on the appraiser's experience and judgment. There is no "formula" for reconciliation.

The choice of a reconciled value should be supported—but not determined—by the evidence in the appraisal. In the end, the appraiser's judgment must be the deciding factor. As long as the appraiser has considered all the relevant evidence and used sound logical reasoning in arriving at a value conclusion, the figure chosen by the appraiser will be a credible estimate of value.

Exercise 2

1. In the review step of reconciliation, what five things does the appraiser look for?

    a. ____________________

    b. ____________________

    c. ____________________

    d. ____________________

    e. ____________________

2. What are the three criteria for judging the reliability of a value indicator in an appraisal?

a. ______________________________

b. ______________________________

c. ______________________________

Final Value Estimate

The process of reaching a final value estimate is essentially the same as the reconciliation process described above. The appraiser reviews all of the data, calculations, and reasoning contained in the entire appraisal and considers them in light of the terms of the specific appraisal assignment. The reliability of each value indicator is assessed, based on the amount of data supporting the value indicator and on the data's level of accuracy and relevance to the appraisal problem. The more reliable an indicator is, the more weight it is given by the appraiser. If necessary, additional data are collected and additional analysis is performed in order to reach a defensible estimate of value.

USPAP Standards for Credible Appraisal

In reviewing the appraisal for the final estimate of value, the appraiser must consider whether the appraisal satisfies all the requirements of a "credible appraisal" as defined in Standard 1 of the Uniform Standards of Professional Appraisal Practice.

Standards Rule 1-1 states:

In developing a real property appraisal, an appraiser must:

(a) be aware of, understand, and correctly employ those recognized methods and techniques that are necessary to produce a credible appraisal;

(b) not commit a substantial error of omission or commission that significantly affects an appraisal; and

(c) not render appraisal services in a careless or negligent manner, such as by making a series of errors that, although individually might not significantly affect the results of an appraisal, in the aggregate affects the credibility of those results.

If the appraisal does not meet the standards for a credible appraisal, additional data collection, verification, and/or analysis will be required before a final value estimate can be made.

The answers to the following questions will indicate whether the appraisal has been completed in a credible and professional manner.

- Have sufficient general and specific data been collected and verified in order to support the value conclusion?
- Have any critical data (general or specific) been overlooked or omitted?
- Have the data been described and analyzed consistently throughout the appraisal?
- Have all relevant appraisal techniques been applied?
- Is the derivation of all value indicators free from errors in calculation or logic?
- Does the value conclusion reflect all the terms of the appraisal assignment, including the definition of value, the real property interest subject to the appraisal, the effective date of the appraisal, the purpose and use of the appraisal, and any other terms and limiting conditions?

Point Estimates and Range Values

An appraisal is an estimate or opinion of value and thus is inherently uncertain. Nevertheless, the majority of appraisals state the final value estimate as a single dollar amount, known as a **point estimate**. In many cases, a point estimate is required by the terms of the appraisal assignment, either for legal reasons or because of client preference.

Alternatively, a value estimate may be stated as a **range value**. For example, an appraiser may estimate that a property's value falls in the range of $200,000 to $220,000, and report this as the final value estimate. Range values reflect the inherent uncertainty of appraisal estimates, but they can present problems of their own. If the stated range is too broad, it can be essentially meaningless and of no use to the client. On the other hand, a narrow range may imply a level of certainty that does not exist.

Many people misinterpret a range value as a guarantee that the property's value is no lower than the bottom of the range, and no higher than the top, when in fact a range value is simply the appraiser's estimate of the range in which the property's value is most likely to fall. For this reason, many appraisers prefer to use point estimates instead of range values, even when this is not required by the terms of the appraisal assignment.

Rounding. Whether a final value estimate is stated as a point estimate or a range value, it is customary to round the figures to reflect the degree of certainty that the appraiser has in the value estimate. In general, the figure(s) for the final value estimate will contain no more than three significant digits (numbers other than zero), followed by the appropriate number of zeros. A higher number of significant digits would imply a level of certainty that is unrealistic in most appraisals.

Example: An estimated value of $343,800 (four significant digits) would normally be rounded, perhaps to $344,000 (three significant digits).

The degree of rounding is a reflection of the appraiser's degree of confidence in the value estimate. Lower degrees of rounding reflect higher degrees of confidence, and vice versa.

Example: In the example above, the estimated value was rounded to the nearest $1,000, reflecting a high degree of confidence. If the appraiser had a lower degree of confidence in the estimate, the figure might have been rounded to the nearest $5,000 ($345,000), or even to the nearest $10,000 ($340,000).

Exercise 3

1. Describe the potential drawbacks to using a range value as opposed to a point estimate.

 ____

 ____

 ____

2. List two reasons for rounding the final value estimate in an appraisal.

 a. ______________________________

 b. ______________________________

Key Terms

Appraisal—The act or process of developing an opinion of value; an opinion of value (USPAP definition). A form of appraisal practice.

Capitalization rate—The percentage rate used to convert an amount of income to value in direct capitalization.

Comparable—A property that has been sold in the same market that currently includes the subject property, and that appeals to the same sorts of buyers. Comparables are used in many different appraisal techniques.

Cost—The actual amount of expenditure necessary to acquire or produce something.

Cost approach—One of the three approaches to value in the appraisal process. In the cost approach, the value of the subject property is indicated by the cost of building the subject improvements, plus the value of the site, and minus any depreciation that exists in the subject improvements.

Direct capitalization—The process of estimating value on the basis of income from a single period, usually one year. The formula for direct capitalization is Value = Income ÷ Capitalization Rate, or Value = Income × Multiplier.

Discounting—The process of calculating the present value of an expected future amount.

Income approach—One of the three approaches to value in the appraisal process. In the income approach, the value of the subject property is indicated by the amount of net income that the property can generate. Also called the income capitalization approach.

Reconciliation—The process by which an appraiser reduces two or more value indicators to a single indicator or estimate of value.

Sales comparison approach—One of the three approaches to value in the appraisal process. In the sales comparison approach, the value of the subject property is indicated by the adjusted sales prices of similar properties (comparables) in the market.

Uniform Standards of Professional Appraisal Practice—Appraisal standards issued by the Appraisal Standards Board of the Appraisal Foundation and adopted as minimum standards by Title XI of FIRREA.

Unit of comparison—A unit in which price is stated for comparison purposes, such as price per square foot of living area. When comparing different properties, the price of each property must be stated in the same unit of comparison.

Value—The monetary relationship between properties and those who buy, sell, or use those properties (USPAP definition). The theoretical worth of something, expressed in terms of something else, usually money.

Value indicator—A piece of data or a derived conclusion (such as the adjusted sales price of a comparable) that is relevant to the value of the subject property in an appraisal.

Yield capitalization—The process of estimating value on the basis of all the anticipated cash flows (the total income) over the life of an investment.

Summary

I. Reconciliation is the process of analyzing two or more different value indicators to reach a single estimate of value.

A. Reconciliation can also specifically refer to the step in the appraisal process where the appraiser reaches a final value estimate.

B. An appraiser may have to reconcile values that are indicated by different comparable properties, different units of comparison, and/or different appraisal techniques.

II. Reconciliation depends on the appraiser's judgment and experience.

A. Mathematical formulas or techniques (such as averaging) are not used.

B. The process of reconciliation begins with a review of all the data, calculations, and reasoning that have led to the different value indicators.

1. All calculations must be checked for accuracy, and any mistakes must be corrected.
2. The different appraisal techniques must be applied consistently to the subject property and to all comparables.
3. The appraiser must assess the reliability of each value indicator. The reliability of a value indicator depends on the amount of data, the level of accuracy, and the relevance to the appraisal problem. The more reliable an indicator is, the more weight it is given.
4. All pertinent data must be included and analyzed.
5. The value indicators must be derived in accordance with the terms of the appraisal assignment.

C. The appraiser uses his or her judgment and experience to reconcile the value indicators, giving the most weight to the most reliable and relevant indicators.

III. The final value estimate must meet the USPAP requirements for a "credible appraisal":

A. Sufficient general and specific data were collected and verified;

B. No critical data were overlooked or omitted;

C. Data description and analysis were consistent throughout the appraisal;

D. All relevant techniques were applied;

E. No errors in calculations or logic were made; and

F. Value conclusion reflects all of the appraisal assignment's terms.

IV. The final value estimate is stated either as a point estimate or as a range value.

A. Range values reflect the inherent uncertainty of appraisal estimates, but are still open to misinterpretation.

B. Most appraisers prefer to use point estimates.

C. Final value estimates are typically rounded to three significant figures (numbers other than zeros), followed by the appropriate number of zeros.

Chapter Quiz

1. The most important factor in the reconciliation process is the:
   a. amount of data
   b. accuracy of the value indicators
   c. relevance of the appraisal techniques
   d. appraiser's judgment and experience

2. An appraiser may have to reconcile values indicated by different:
   a. units of comparison
   b. appraisal techniques
   c. comparable properties
   d. All of the above

3. To reconcile different value indicators into a final estimate of value, the appraiser:
   a. calculates the average of all the different indicators
   b. chooses the indicator that is most relevant to the appraisal problem
   c. evaluates the reliability of the different indicators
   d. gives the most weight to the value indicated by the sales comparison approach

4. When appraising single-family residences, an appraiser is likely to rely most on the value indicated by the:
   a. sales comparison approach
   b. cost approach
   c. income approach
   d. None of the above

5. When reconciling value indicators, the appraiser will review the data and procedures used to derive the indicators in order to:
   a. correct any errors in computation
   b. assess the value indicators' reliability
   c. ensure that all appraisal techniques have been applied consistently
   d. All of the above

6. Which of the following is NOT a factor in the reconciliation process?
   a. The definition of value
   b. The date of the appraisal report
   c. The effective date of the appraisal
   d. The purpose and use of the appraisal

7. The final value estimate in an appraisal is normally rounded:
   a. in order to reflect the inherent uncertainty of the appraisal process
   b. because it is required by the terms of the appraisal assignment
   c. to the nearest $1,000
   d. All of the above

8. Which of the following is NOT a factor influencing a value indicator's reliability?
   a. The amount of data supporting the indicator
   b. The verification of the data supporting the indicator
   c. The sophistication of the appraisal technique used
   d. The relevance of the appraisal technique used

9. The reliability of a value indicator derived by the sales comparison approach depends on:
   a. the number of adjustments made to the comparable's sales price
   b. the amount of the adjustments made to the comparable's sales price
   c. the manner in which the comparable sales data were verified
   d. All of the above

10. The amount of data supporting a value indicator is significant because:
    a. it indicates whether the appraiser has done a thorough job
    b. a larger amount of data always leads to a more reliable value estimate
    c. a value conclusion is more reliable when it is supported by independent sources
    d. All of the above

11. A value indicator derived by the income capitalization approach would be least relevant in an appraisal of:
    a. an office building
    b. vacant land
    c. a single-family residence
    d. a shopping center

12. For a final value estimate of $216,700, the highest level of appraiser confidence in the estimated value would be indicated by rounding to:
    a. $210,000
    b. $215,000
    c. $217,000
    d. $220,000

13. The relevance of an appraisal technique to a particular appraisal problem would most likely depend on:
    a. the type of property being appraised
    b. the effective date of the appraisal
    c. the identity of the appraisal client
    d. the size of the subject improvements

14. A final value estimate that is stated as a single dollar amount is known as a:
    a. range value
    b. single value
    c. dollar estimate
    d. point estimate

15. In the process of reconciliation, the appraiser must choose a value that is:
    a. supported by the evidence
    b. higher than the lowest value indicator
    c. lower than the highest value indicator
    d. All of the above

Case Study

Complete the RECONCILIATION section of the Uniform Residential Appraisal Report, based on the following information. (If necessary, refer back to the information in the case studies from earlier chapters.)

1731 Pine Road was reviewed on September 1 of this year, which is the effective date of the appraisal. Since the home is relatively new and in good condition, the appraisal is made "as is," with no required repairs or other conditions.

Based on all the evidence used in the appraisal, you have estimated the value of the property to be $337,000. This figure is within the range of values indicated by the sales comparison approach, and it is consistent with the value derived in the cost approach as well. It is also supported by the fact that Comparable #3, with an adjusted sales price of $334,350, was the most similar to the subject property of all the available comparables, requiring gross adjustments of only 2% of the original sales price.

The income approach and the cost approach were used as guides. The greatest weight was given to the sales comparison approach, since the subject property is an owner-occupied single-family residence.

Use this portion of the URAR to complete the case study.

RECONCILIATION

Indicated Value by: Sales Comparison Approach $ Cost Approach (if developed) $ Income Approach (if developed) $

This appraisal is made ☐ "as is", ☐ subject to completion per plans and specifications on the basis of a hypothetical condition that the improvements have been completed, ☐ subject to the following repairs or alterations on the basis of a hypothetical condition that the repairs or alterations have been completed, or ☐ subject to the following required inspection based on the extraordinary assumption that the condition or deficiency does not require alteration or repair:

Based on a complete visual inspection of the interior and exterior areas of the subject property, defined scope of work, statement of assumptions and limiting conditions, and appraiser's certification, my (our) opinion of the market value, as defined, of the real property that is the subject of this report is $, as of , which is the date of inspection and the effective date of this appraisal.

Quiz Answers

1. d) Reconciliation is a largely subjective process, so the most important factor is the appraiser's judgment and experience.

2. d) An appraiser may have to reconcile values indicated by different units of comparison, appraisal techniques, or comparable properties.

3. c) An appraiser will give more weight to a value indicator that is more reliable.

4. a) When appraising a single-family residence, an appraiser will give more weight to a value indicator obtained using the sales comparison approach.

5. d) During the reconciliation process, an appraiser must look for any errors or inconsistencies and also assess the reliability of the value indicators.

6. b) The date of the appraisal report is not a consideration in the reconciliation process.

7. a) The final value estimate is rounded to reflect the uncertainty of the appraisal process. The more uncertain an appraiser is, the fewer significant digits he or she will use.

8. c) The sophistication of the appraisal technique has no bearing on how reliable the resulting value indicator is.

9. d) The reliability of a value indicator depends on the number and amount of adjustments made, as well as the manner in which the data were verified.

10. c) While mere quantity of data does not necessarily reflect reliability, the verification of data with independent sources indicates greater reliability.

11. b) A value indicator derived by income capitalization would be least relevant in determining the value of vacant land.

12. c) The highest level of confidence would be expressed by rounding a value indicator of $216,700 to the nearest $1,000, or $217,000.

13. a) The relevance of a particular appraisal technique depends on the type of property being appraised.

14. d) A final value estimate stated as a single dollar amount is a point estimate.

15. a) Under any circumstances, the final value estimate must be supported by the evidence.

Exercise Answers

#1 1. a. The step in the appraisal process in which the appraiser arrives at a final value estimate.

b. The general process of analyzing two or more different value indicators and determining a single value the appraiser feels is most appropriate.

2. a. to reconcile value indicators derived from different comparables

b. to reconcile indicators derived from different units of comparison

c. to reconcile indicators derived from different appraisal techniques

#2 1. a. accuracy of mathematical calculations

b. consistent application of appraisal techniques and assumptions

c. reliability of value indicators

d. completeness of data collection and analysis

e. compliance with the terms of the appraisal assignment

2. a. quantity of data supporting the indicator

b. accuracy of the indicator and its supporting data

c. relevance to the appraisal problem of the data and techniques used to derive the indicator

#3 1. If the value range is too broad, it may be useless to the client; if it is too narrow, it may mislead the client by implying a level of precision that is not present in the appraisal.

2. a. to reflect the uncertainty inherent in the appraisal process

b. to indicate the appraiser's level of confidence in the accuracy of the value estimate

Case Study Answer

See URAR form excerpt below.

RECONCILIATION

Indicated Value by: Sales Comparison Approach $ 337,000 Cost Approach (if developed) $ 341,500 Income Approach (if developed) $ 345,800

The greatest weight is given to the sales comparison approach, since the subject property
is an owner-occupied single-family residence with numerous comparables available.
The cost approach and income approach are used as guides.

This appraisal is made ☑ "as is", ☐ subject to completion per plans and specifications on the basis of a hypothetical condition that the improvements have been completed, ☐ subject to the following repairs or alterations on the basis of a hypothetical condition that the repairs or alterations have been completed, or ☐ subject to the following required inspection based on the extraordinary assumption that the condition or deficiency does not require alteration or repair:

Based on a complete visual inspection of the interior and exterior areas of the subject property, defined scope of work, statement of assumptions and limiting conditions, and appraiser's certification, my (our) opinion of the market value, as defined, of the real property that is the subject of this report is $ $337,000 , as of 9/1 , which is the date of inspection and the effective date of this appraisal.

12 The Appraisal Report

Overview

The appraisal report is the final step in the appraisal process. In the report, the appraiser communicates his or her opinions, analyses, and conclusions to the client. In the case of a written report, other people besides the client may read and rely on the report as well. It is important that the appraiser present the contents of the appraisal report in a manner that is meaningful to the client and not misleading to any parties. After completing this chapter, you should be able to:

- distinguish between the various types of appraisal reports and explain their uses;
- list the essential elements that must be included in every professional appraisal report and understand the significance of each element; and
- identify the various sections of the Uniform Residential Appraisal Report (URAR) and describe how an appraisal is communicated on this form.

The Appraisal Report

It is important to note that an appraisal report is *not* the same thing as an appraisal. An **appraisal** is an estimate of value, based on professional experience and recognized valuation techniques. An **appraisal report** is simply the means by which the appraiser's value conclusions are communicated to the client and to other users of the report.

The type of report used to communicate the appraisal does not dictate or limit the appraisal process. Regardless of the type of report used, the appraisal itself must be conducted in accordance with the "recognized methods and techniques that are necessary to produce a credible appraisal" (USPAP Standards Rule 1-1(a)). In addition, the appraiser must maintain a work file for the appraisal that is sufficient to document compliance with Standards Rule 1-1.

The form and content of real property appraisal reports are governed by Standard 2 of the USPAP, which requires the appraiser to communicate the report in a manner that is not misleading. This guiding principle is described in more detail in Standards Rule 2-1.

Each written or oral real property appraisal report must:

1. *clearly and accurately set forth the appraisal in a manner that will not be misleading;*
2. *contain sufficient information to enable the intended users of the appraisal to understand the report properly; and*
3. *clearly and accurately disclose all assumptions, extraordinary assumptions, hypothetical conditions, or limiting conditions used in the assignment.*

Standards Rule 2-1 applies to all real property appraisal reports, without exception. To comply with this rule, an appraiser must present a report's information in a manner that is easy to understand. If any technical terms are used, they should be clearly defined. The report must also provide enough information for the client to understand how the appraiser reached an opinion of value.

Appraisals typically involve a number of general assumptions and conditions. For example, the appraiser will usually assume that the property complies with all applicable zoning and environmental regulations. The general assumptions and conditions must be disclosed in the appraisal report. The appraiser will usually keep a list of standard assumptions and conditions and select those that apply to the appraisal in question.

Example: An appraisal assumes that title to the subject property is good and marketable, that the use of the subject property is in accordance with applicable zoning laws, and that there are no hidden conditions that affect the value of the property. However, the appraiser does not independently verify these facts.

When describing the assumption that the use of the property is in conformity with current zoning restrictions, an appraiser might use the following language: "It is assumed that all applicable zoning and use regulations and restrictions have been complied with, unless a nonconformity has been stated, defined, and considered in the appraisal report." (Appraisal Institute)

In addition to the general assumptions and conditions, the appraiser must be sure to mention any extraordinary assumptions and hypothetical or limiting conditions that apply to the current situation and affect the opinion of value. As we discussed in Chapter 3, an **extraordinary assumption** is something the appraiser assumes to be true for that particular property, even though it is not yet certain.

Example: Adam completes an appraisal of an office building in downtown Spokane. The building is currently unoccupied, but the owner is in the final stages of negotiating a lease agreement with a prospective tenant. Adam's opinion of value is based on the assumption that the lease agreement will be executed. In the appraisal report, Adam must disclose this assumption and explain its effect on his opinion of value.

For **hypothetical conditions**, the appraiser analyzes the property as if some specified condition were true, even though in reality it is not.

> **Example:** ABC Investments is buying a property that was formerly used as a dry cleaning business. The soil is contaminated with solvents that will be removed before the sale closes. ABC therefore asks the appraiser to evaluate the property as if the contamination does not exist.

A **limiting condition** exists when the appraisal does not cover an issue that may affect the property's value. The appraiser should address these limitations at the outset of the appraisal assignment and make sure the client understands and agrees to them.

Among the many limiting conditions that may be found in appraisals, some of the more common are statements to the effect that:

- the sole purpose of the appraisal is to estimate value;
- the appraisal does not constitute a survey;
- the appraisal does not constitute a legal opinion regarding title or other legal matters;
- the appraisal does not constitute an engineering report or property inspection report;
- the appraisal is made under conditions of uncertainty and is based on a limited amount of data; and
- the appraisal is made with certain assumptions regarding the needs and expertise of the client.

Assumptions and conditions have two primary purposes. First, they help the client and other readers of the appraisal report to understand its meaning and avoid drawing unwarranted conclusions. This is an increasingly important issue, since many states require lenders to provide copies of appraisal reports to their borrowers. While a lender may understand the assumptions and limitations of an appraisal report without having them spelled out, an unsophisticated borrower is not likely to have the same level of understanding.

> **Example:** John applies for a loan from ABC Bank to purchase a house. ABC Bank gives John a copy of the appraisal report that was made in connection with John's loan application. John may assume that the appraiser has verified the boundaries of the property and the condition of the title.
>
> However, this is not normally the case in an appraisal. By clearly stating (in the limiting conditions) that the appraisal does not constitute a survey or a legal opinion of the condition of the title, the appraisal report can prevent John from assuming that the boundaries and title to the property are okay.

The second purpose of assumptions and limiting conditions is to limit the liability of the appraiser. This does not mean that limiting conditions can be used as an excuse for an incompetent appraisal. But limiting conditions can and do limit the circumstances under which an appraiser may be held liable for the results of any actions that are taken based on an appraisal report. For example (as mentioned in the discussion of use of the appraisal), the appraisal may state that its conclusions are valid only for the particular client, and only for the use stated in the report.

Exercise 1

1. Give the two main reasons for using limiting conditions in an appraisal.

   a. ______________________________

   b. ______________________________

2. List three limiting conditions commonly found in an appraisal.

   a. ______________________________

   b. ______________________________

   c. ______________________________

Types of Appraisal Reports

Appraisal reports may be broadly categorized as either oral reports or written reports. An oral report is communicated in speech, either in person or by phone; written appraisal reports are communicated in writing. Written reports may be further classified according to their content and format, as illustrated in Figure 12.1.

Oral Reports

The type of report used to communicate an appraisal depends on the needs of the client. An oral report is used when the needs of the client would not be served by a written report. Oral reports include expert testimony given by an appraiser in a deposition or court of law.

The fact that a report is made orally does not necessarily affect the contents of the report. The appraiser must still describe and explain the relevant data and analysis that went into the opinion of value. Like written reports, oral reports must adhere to the requirements of Standards Rule 2-1: the report must be clear and not misleading, contain sufficient information, and disclose any assumptions and limitations that affect the appraisal.

An oral report must include all of the information that would be contained in a comparable written report. We will look at the requirements for written reports later in this chapter.

The appraiser must maintain written records of all oral reports, including a summary or transcript of the report itself, and any notes or other documentation necessary to show compliance with the USPAP and to support the conclusions contained in the report.

Fig. 12.1 Types of Appraisal Reports

Oral Reports (communicated in speech)

Written Reports (communicated in writing)

- Classified by content:
  - Self-contained report
  - Summary report
  - Restricted use report
- Classified by format:
  - Narrative report
  - Form report

Written Report Content

As noted above, written appraisal reports may be classified by both content and format. The content of an appraisal report must satisfy the requirements of one of the three reporting options described in USPAP Standards Rule 2-2:

- Self-Contained Appraisal Report,
- Summary Appraisal Report, or
- Restricted Use Appraisal Report.

The primary differences between these three types of written appraisal reports relate to the level of detail included in the report. The self-contained appraisal report contains the most comprehensive level of detail, while the restricted use appraisal report is the most abbreviated. The summary appraisal report falls somewhere in between.

Example: In a self-contained report, the appraiser must describe the property using any combination of property sketch, photograph, and written comments.

In a summary report, the appraiser is simply required to provide a summary description of the property, using the same methods.

In a restricted use report, the appraiser need only identify the property, using a legal description, address, copy of a survey, or property sketch.

The appraiser and the client should decide in advance which reporting option to use. In choosing between reporting options, the appraiser should consider the complexity of the appraisal problem. The intended use of the appraisal report may determine whether the report needs to be extremely detailed or more concise.

Self-Contained Appraisal Report. As its name implies, a self-contained appraisal report contains all of the information necessary to understand the appraisal. The report should contain a full description of the subject real estate, including any of the property's physical and economic characteristics that are relevant to the assignment. In addition to a written description and comments, many appraisers include photographs and a sketch of the property.

A self-contained report must describe the scope of work used to develop the appraisal, including the research and analyses performed and (if appropriate) the research and analyses not performed. The report must describe the information analyzed, the appraisal methods and techniques employed, and the reasoning supporting the appraiser's analyses, opinions, and conclusions. If any of the major approaches to appraisal (the sales comparison, cost, or income approach) was not used, that must be explained. If the purpose of the appraisal is to determine the property's market value, the appraiser must describe how he arrived at his opinion of the property's highest and best use. Since most residential appraisals focus on market value, this requirement almost always applies.

If a self-contained appraisal report has other intended users in addition to the client, these intended users must be identified in the report.

Summary Appraisal Report. In a summary appraisal report, certain information that would be described in more detail in a self-contained appraisal report is presented in a summarized format. This includes, for example, the description of the real estate, the scope of work, the information analyzed, the appraisal methods and techniques employed, the reasoning that supports the opinions and conclusions, and the rationale for the appraiser's opinion of highest and best use.

Other information must be presented in essentially the same way it would be in a self-contained appraisal report, such as the identity of any intended users other than the client, the intended use of the appraisal, the use of the property, and the reasons why any of the major approaches to appraisal was not applied.

Restricted Use Appraisal Report. A restricted use appraisal report must include the basic information required for all written reports. However, instead of describing or summarizing how the appraisal was conducted, the report simply states the extent of the appraisal process and the results—beyond that, the report refers to the appraiser's work file.

A restricted use report must identify the subject real estate and state the scope of work used to develop the appraisal, the appraisal methods and techniques employed, and the appraiser's value opinions and conclusions. It does not need to describe, summarize, or state the information analyzed.

Because a restricted use report contains limited information, it's especially important to make sure that the information presented is not misinterpreted or relied on inappropriately. The report must include a prominent warning that the appraiser's opinions and conclusions may not be understood properly without additional information from the appraiser's work file.

A restricted use report is designed to be used only by the appraiser's client, and it must prominently state this limitation. If parties other than the client will use the report, the appraiser should prepare a self-contained report or a summary report instead.

Certification. Regardless of the reporting format chosen, all written appraisal reports must contain a certification signed by the appraiser. The certification should be similar in content to the form provided in USPAP Standards Rule 2-3, which states:

Each written real property appraisal report must contain a certification that is similar in content to the following form:

I certify that, to the best of my knowledge and belief:

- *The statements of fact contained in this report are true and correct.*
- *The reported analyses, opinions, and conclusions are limited only by the reported assumptions and limiting conditions and are my personal, impartial, and unbiased professional analyses, opinions, and conclusions.*
- *I have no (or the specified) present or prospective interest in the property that is the subject of this report and no (or the specified) personal interest with respect to the parties involved.*
- *I have no bias with respect to the property that is the subject of this report or to the parties involved with this assignment.*
- *My engagement in this assignment was not contingent upon developing or reporting predetermined results.*
- *My compensation for completing this assignment is not contingent upon the development or reporting of a predetermined value or direction in value that favors the cause of the client, the amount of the value opinion, the attainment of a stipulated result, or the occurrence of a subsequent event directly related to the intended use of this appraisal.*
- *My analyses, opinions, and conclusions were developed, and this report has been prepared, in conformity with the Uniform Standards of Professional Appraisal Practice.*
- *I have (or have not) made a personal inspection of the property that is the subject of this report. (If more than one person signs this certification, the certification must clearly specify which individuals did and which individuals did not make a personal inspection of the appraised property.)*
- *No one provided significant real property appraisal assistance to the person signing this certification. (If there are exceptions, the name of each individual providing significant real property appraisal assistance must be stated.)*

In the certification, the appraiser accepts responsibility for the contents of the appraisal report, and discloses any personal interest or bias with respect to the subject property or the client. The appraiser also certifies that the appraisal work and report conform to professional standards and that his or her compensation is not contingent on the appraisal results.

Addenda

It is common for appraisal reports to include a final section for addenda and exhibits. These additional documents might include the appraiser's qualifications, plat maps, zoning maps, soils maps, photographs of the subject property, copies of the deed and any applicable leases, and anything else the appraiser believes necessary.

Written Report Format

The preceding section described the classification of appraisal reports according to their content (level of detail), as set out in the USPAP. Traditionally, written appraisal reports have also been classified according to their format: narrative, form, or letter.

Narrative Reports. The word "narrative" means "story." In essence, a narrative report is a "story" that tells the reader how and why the appraiser reached a final value conclusion. The advantage of the narrative report is that it allows the appraiser to present the material in such a way as to guide the reader through the entire appraisal process. The appraiser can explain the relevance of the selected data and the significance of the valuation techniques that were employed.

No hard and fast rules exist for organizing the material in a narrative report, but the narrative should be clearly understandable and not misleading. The structure of narrative reports may vary from appraiser to appraiser, and from one appraisal assignment to the next. However, most narrative reports contain similar types of information, which may be grouped into four categories: summary information, definitions and terms, subject property data, and valuation analysis.

Summary information. Summary information is often presented at the beginning of the narrative report, to allow the reader to quickly identify the subject of the report and the appraiser's conclusions. Most reports begin with a **title page**, listing the address of the subject property, the names and addresses of the appraiser and the client, and the effective date of the appraisal. The title page is followed by a **table of contents** which guides the reader to the different sections and subsections of the report.

A **summary of important facts and conclusions** is often presented near the beginning of the report as well. This summary may include such information as the appraiser's opinion of the highest and best use of the property, the estimated site value, the values derived from the three value approaches, and the final value estimate. The information presented in this summary is explained in greater detail in the data and analysis sections of the narrative report.

Definitions and terms. Important definitions and terms that should be discussed in the report include:

- definition of value used in the appraisal;
- definition of property rights appraised;
- effective date of the appraisal;

- purpose and intended use of the appraisal;
- scope of work; and
- assumptions and limiting conditions.

Definitions and terms may be presented in a single section of the report, or in two or more different sections. For example, the assumptions and limiting conditions are often presented in a separate section at the end of the report, while the definitions of value and property rights appraised are commonly stated in the introductory materials.

Subject property data. In narrative reports, it is common practice to present the subject property data in a separate section, before the section containing the valuation analysis. This practice is consistent with the appraisal process, in which the appraiser collects and verifies the relevant data before proceeding with the application of the various analytical techniques.

All significant data relied on by the appraiser in performing the appraisal should be presented, so that the reader will be able to understand the appraiser's reasoning in analyzing the data and reaching a final value conclusion. Subject property data that are typically provided in a narrative report include:

- general data relating to the region, city, and neighborhood;
- the legal description of the subject property;
- a description of the subject site and improvements;
- a description of the subject property's zoning, real estate taxes, and assessments; and
- the sales history of the subject property, including the terms of any pending sale or current listing.

When the data are extremely detailed but still significant to the appraisal, they may be included as an **addendum** to the appraisal report, rather than in the body of the report itself. For example, if the property is subject to a commercial lease, the lease documents may be attached as an addendum to the report. In this case, the section of the report describing the subject property would contain a summary of the important lease terms, and refer the reader to the addendum for additional information.

Valuation analysis. In the valuation analysis section of the narrative report, the appraiser describes the appraisal methods that were used and the reasoning that led to the final value conclusion. Market data that were used in the analysis (comparable sales data, construction cost estimates, etc.) are also described.

Specifically, the report should include the data, techniques, and reasoning that were used to determine:

- the highest and best use of the land as if vacant;
- the highest and best use of the property as improved;
- the value of the subject property site;
- the value of the subject property under each of the three approaches to value; and
- the final reconciled estimate of subject property value.

Fig. 12.2 Format for Narrative Appraisal Report

Summary information
- title page
- letter of transmittal
- table of contents
- summary of key facts and conclusions

Definitions and terms

Subject property data
- general data
- legal description of subject property
- description of site and improvements
- zoning, taxes, assessments
- sales history of subject property

Valuation analysis
- data
- techniques
- reasoning

Certification

Addenda

Certification. As with all written appraisal reports, a narrative report must include a certification that meets the requirement of USPAP Standards Rule 2-3. If the appraiser belongs to a specific professional appraisal association, that association may require additional certifications or a statement of the appraiser's professional qualifications.

Letter of transmittal. Narrative appraisal reports are usually accompanied by a letter of transmittal. A letter of transmittal is simply a brief letter addressed to the appraisal client and signed by the appraiser. It identifies the subject property, the real property interest that was appraised, the effective date of the appraisal, and the appraiser's final estimate of value. The letter of transmittal should also include a statement to the effect that the appraiser has performed all appropriate steps to complete the appraisal assignment (including a personal review of the subject property), and should identify any extraordinary assumptions or limiting conditions that apply to the value estimate.

A letter of transmittal may be a separate cover letter that accompanies the appraisal report, or it may be included as part of the report itself. If it is included as part of the report, it is usually placed at the beginning of the report, immediately following the title page.

Form Reports. Form reports, the most common type of appraisal report, are used to communicate appraisals in a standardized format. Form reports help ensure that all information required by the client is included, and make it easier for the client to locate and review specific items. However, they reduce the appraiser's ability to tailor the report to the circumstances of the specific appraisal problem. Therefore, the choice between a form report and a narrative report always depends on the needs of the client.

When preparing an appraisal that will be communicated with a form report, the appraiser must keep in mind that the structure and content of the particular report form are not a substitute for—or a guide to—a competent appraisal. The appraiser must still be guided by the USPAP and the steps in the appraisal process. All relevant data must be collected and analyzed, and all appropriate appraisal techniques must be applied, in order to make a competent value judgment. In addition, the appraisal must be communicated in a manner that will not be misleading.

> **Example:** The space for reporting the appraiser's analysis of data is often limited on a form report. If necessary, the appraiser should attach an addendum to the form, in order to adequately communicate any additional analysis that is essential to understanding the value conclusions contained in the report.

Form reports are usually summary appraisal reports. However, depending on the amount of detail required by the form and the amount of supporting documentation, a form report could be classified as a self-contained or restricted use appraisal report instead.

Some of the most common form reports are those used in the appraisal of residential property for real estate lending purposes. Appraisal clients who deal with large numbers of appraisals, such as lenders, insurers, and government agencies, often require appraisers to use standard forms designed to satisfy their particular appraisal requirements. These typically include the following forms:

- the Uniform Residential Appraisal Report (Fannie Mae Form 1004/ Freddie Mac Form 70), for appraisals of single-family residences;
- the Small Residential Income Property Appraisal Report (Fannie Mae Form 1025/ Freddie Mac Form 72), for appraisals of two- to four-unit income properties; and
- the Individual Condominium Unit Appraisal Report (Fannie Mae Form 1073/ Freddie Mac Form 465), for appraisals of single condominium units.

The Uniform Residential Appraisal Report form is shown in Figure 12.3.

Letter Reports. In the past, appraisal reports often took the form of a single-page letter, which simply stated the appraiser's value conclusion and referred to additional information in the appraiser's file. Letter reports are no longer in general use, since they don't conform to the requirements of USPAP Standard 2.

Exercise 2

1. The type of report used to communicate an appraisal is determined by

   ____.

2. What are the three appraisal reporting options authorized by USPAP?

   a. ____

   b. ____

   c. ____

3. What is the main difference between the three reporting options?

   ____

   ____

4. Match each item on the left with the corresponding category of information on the right.

1._____	table of contents	a.	summary information
2._____	cost estimate	b.	definitions and terms
3._____	limiting conditions	c.	subject property data
4._____	legal description	d.	valuation analysis
5._____	title page		
6._____	purpose and intended use of appraisal		
7._____	zoning and taxes		
8._____	reconciliation		

Uniform Residential Appraisal Report (URAR)

The Uniform Residential Appraisal Report form is one of the most commonly used form reports in the appraisal industry. This form is used in the vast majority of single family residential appraisals made for mortgage lending purposes, and is required by most secondary market agencies, including the Federal National Mortgage Association (Fannie Mae) and the Federal Home Loan Mortgage Corporation (Freddie Mac).

The URAR has six pages. The first page is used to describe the subject property, and the second page contains the appraiser's sales comparison data and analysis. The third page has room for the cost approach and income approach data and analyses, and any PUD project information. The fourth, fifth, and sixth pages contain general information that applies to all appraisals reported using the form, as well as room for the appraiser's certification.

Statement of Purpose

The URAR form begins by stating: "The purpose of this summary appraisal report is to provide the lender/client with an accurate, and adequately supported, opinion of the market value of the subject property." This statement clarifies the appraisal's purpose: to provide the client with an opinion of the property's market value.

Subject Section

The first section of the URAR form, the SUBJECT section, is used to identify the subject property. On the first line, the appraiser enters the property's common street address (city, state, and zip code). The address should correspond to the physical location of the property; a post office box or similar non-physical address is not acceptable.

Line 2 of the SUBJECT section has spaces for the name of the borrower (whose loan application is the reason for the appraisal), the name of the current owner of record, and the county in which the property is located.

The property's legal description is included on line 3. If the legal description will not fit in the space provided, it may be attached as an addendum to the report. The appraiser should use line 3 to reference the addendum.

Property tax information for the subject property is filled in on line 4. The tax assessor's parcel number is the tax identification number used by the local assessor to identify the property for tax purposes. The appraiser enters the amount of property taxes (ad valorem taxes) that are currently assessed against the subject property. The appraiser also identifies the tax year that corresponds to the listed tax figures.

If the neighborhood or development in which the subject is located has a commonly accepted name (such as "River Heights" or "Parkview Estates"), the appraiser enters the name on line 5. If there is no common name for the neighborhood, the appraiser enters "N/A" (not applicable) or "None." This is followed by a Map Reference, which should correspond to whatever map system is most commonly used by local appraisers and lenders. The last item on line 5 is the number of the U.S. government census tract in which the

Fig. 12.3 Uniform Residential Appraisal Report form

Uniform Residential Appraisal Report

File #

The purpose of this summary appraisal report is to provide the lender/client with an accurate, and adequately supported, opinion of the market value of the subject property.

SUBJECT

Property Address | City | State | Zip Code
Borrower | Owner of Public Record | County
Legal Description
Assessor's Parcel # | Tax Year | R.E. Taxes $
Neighborhood Name | Map Reference | Census Tract
Occupant ☐ Owner ☐ Tenant ☐ Vacant | Special Assessments $ | ☐ PUD | HOA $ | ☐ per year ☐ per month
Property Rights Appraised ☐ Fee Simple ☐ Leasehold ☐ Other (describe)
Assignment Type ☐ Purchase Transaction ☐ Refinance Transaction ☐ Other (describe)
Lender/Client | Address
Is the subject property currently offered for sale or has it been offered for sale in the twelve months prior to the effective date of this appraisal? ☐ Yes ☐ No
Report data source(s) used, offering price(s), and date(s).

CONTRACT

I ☐ did ☐ did not analyze the contract for sale for the subject purchase transaction. Explain the results of the analysis of the contract for sale or why the analysis was not performed.

Contract Price $ | Date of Contract | Is the property seller the owner of public record? ☐ Yes ☐ No | Data Source(s)
Is there any financial assistance (loan charges, sale concessions, gift or downpayment assistance, etc.) to be paid by any party on behalf of the borrower? ☐ Yes ☐ No
If Yes, report the total dollar amount and describe the items to be paid.

NEIGHBORHOOD

Note: Race and the racial composition of the neighborhood are not appraisal factors.

Neighborhood Characteristics	One-Unit Housing Trends	One-Unit Housing	Present Land Use %
Location ☐ Urban ☐ Suburban ☐ Rural	Property Values ☐ Increasing ☐ Stable ☐ Declining	PRICE AGE	One-Unit %
Built-Up ☐ Over 75% ☐ 25–75% ☐ Under 25%	Demand/Supply ☐ Shortage ☐ In Balance ☐ Over Supply	$ (000) (yrs)	2-4 Unit %
Growth ☐ Rapid ☐ Stable ☐ Slow	Marketing Time ☐ Under 3 mths ☐ 3–6 mths ☐ Over 6 mths	Low	Multi-Family %
Neighborhood Boundaries		High	Commercial %
		Pred.	Other %

Neighborhood Description

Market Conditions (including support for the above conclusions)

SITE

Dimensions | Area | Shape | View
Specific Zoning Classification | Zoning Description
Zoning Compliance ☐ Legal ☐ Legal Nonconforming (Grandfathered Use) ☐ No Zoning ☐ Illegal (describe)
Is the highest and best use of the subject property as improved (or as proposed per plans and specifications) the present use? ☐ Yes ☐ No If No, describe

Utilities	Public	Other (describe)		Public	Other (describe)	Off-site Improvements—Type	Public	Private
Electricity	☐	☐	Water	☐	☐	Street	☐	☐
Gas	☐	☐	Sanitary Sewer	☐	☐	Alley	☐	☐

FEMA Special Flood Hazard Area ☐ Yes ☐ No | FEMA Flood Zone | FEMA Map # | FEMA Map Date
Are the utilities and off-site improvements typical for the market area? ☐ Yes ☐ No If No, describe
Are there any adverse site conditions or external factors (easements, encroachments, environmental conditions, land uses, etc.)? ☐ Yes ☐ No If Yes, describe

IMPROVEMENTS

General Description	Foundation	Exterior Description materials/condition	Interior materials/condition
Units ☐ One ☐ One with Accessory Unit	☐ Concrete Slab ☐ Crawl Space	Foundation Walls	Floors
# of Stories	☐ Full Basement ☐ Partial Basement	Exterior Walls	Walls
Type ☐ Det. ☐ Att. ☐ S-Det./End Unit	Basement Area sq. ft.	Roof Surface	Trim/Finish
☐ Existing ☐ Proposed ☐ Under Const.	Basement Finish %	Gutters & Downspouts	Bath Floor
Design (Style)	☐ Outside Entry/Exit ☐ Sump Pump	Window Type	Bath Wainscot
Year Built	Evidence of ☐ Infestation	Storm Sash/Insulated	Car Storage ☐ None
Effective Age (Yrs)	☐ Dampness ☐ Settlement	Screens	☐ Driveway # of Cars
Attic ☐ None	Heating ☐ FWA ☐ HWBB ☐ Radiant	Amenities ☐ Woodstove(s) #	Driveway Surface
☐ Drop Stair ☐ Stairs	☐ Other Fuel	☐ Fireplace(s) # ☐ Fence	☐ Garage # of Cars
☐ Floor ☐ Scuttle	Cooling ☐ Central Air Conditioning	☐ Patio/Deck ☐ Porch	☐ Carport # of Cars
☐ Finished ☐ Heated	☐ Individual ☐ Other	☐ Pool ☐ Other	☐ Att. ☐ Det. ☐ Built-in

Appliances ☐ Refrigerator ☐ Range/Oven ☐ Dishwasher ☐ Disposal ☐ Microwave ☐ Washer/Dryer ☐ Other (describe)
Finished area **above** grade contains: | Rooms | Bedrooms | Bath(s) | Square Feet of Gross Living Area Above Grade
Additional features (special energy efficient items, etc.)

Describe the condition of the property (including needed repairs, deterioration, renovations, remodeling, etc.).

Are there any physical deficiencies or adverse conditions that affect the livability, soundness, or structural integrity of the property? ☐ Yes ☐ No If Yes, describe

Does the property generally conform to the neighborhood (functional utility, style, condition, use, construction, etc.)? ☐ Yes ☐ No If No, describe

Freddie Mac Form 70 March 2005 | Page 1 of 6 | Fannie Mae Form 1004 March 2005

Uniform Residential Appraisal Report

File #

SALES COMPARISON APPROACH

There are comparable properties currently offered for sale in the subject neighborhood ranging in price from $ to $.

There are comparable sales in the subject neighborhood within the past twelve months ranging in sale price from $ to $.

FEATURE	SUBJECT	COMPARABLE SALE # 1		COMPARABLE SALE # 2		COMPARABLE SALE # 3	
Address							
Proximity to Subject							
Sale Price	$		$		$		$
Sale Price/Gross Liv. Area	$ sq. ft.	$ sq. ft.		$ sq. ft.		$ sq. ft.	
Data Source(s)							
Verification Source(s)							
VALUE ADJUSTMENTS	DESCRIPTION	DESCRIPTION	+(-) $ Adjustment	DESCRIPTION	+(-) $ Adjustment	DESCRIPTION	+(-) $ Adjustment
Sale or Financing Concessions							
Date of Sale/Time							
Location							
Leasehold/Fee Simple							
Site							
View							
Design (Style)							
Quality of Construction							
Actual Age							
Condition							
Above Grade Room Count	Total / Bdrms. / Baths	Total / Bdrms. / Baths		Total / Bdrms. / Baths		Total / Bdrms. / Baths	
Gross Living Area	sq. ft.	sq. ft.		sq. ft.		sq. ft.	
Basement & Finished Rooms Below Grade							
Functional Utility							
Heating/Cooling							
Energy Efficient Items							
Garage/Carport							
Porch/Patio/Deck							
Net Adjustment (Total)		☐ + ☐ -	$	☐ + ☐ -	$	☐ + ☐ -	$
Adjusted Sale Price of Comparables		Net Adj. % Gross Adj. %	$	Net Adj. % Gross Adj. %	$	Net Adj. % Gross Adj. %	$

I ☐ did ☐ did not research the sale or transfer history of the subject property and comparable sales. If not, explain

My research ☐ did ☐ did not reveal any prior sales or transfers of the subject property for the three years prior to the effective date of this appraisal.

Data source(s)

My research ☐ did ☐ did not reveal any prior sales or transfers of the comparable sales for the year prior to the date of sale of the comparable sale.

Data source(s)

Report the results of the research and analysis of the prior sale or transfer history of the subject property and comparable sales (report additional prior sales on page 3).

ITEM	SUBJECT	COMPARABLE SALE # 1	COMPARABLE SALE # 2	COMPARABLE SALE # 3
Date of Prior Sale/Transfer				
Price of Prior Sale/Transfer				
Data Source(s)				
Effective Date of Data Source(s)				

Analysis of prior sale or transfer history of the subject property and comparable sales

Summary of Sales Comparison Approach

Indicated Value by Sales Comparison Approach $

RECONCILIATION

Indicated Value by: Sales Comparison Approach $ Cost Approach (if developed) $ Income Approach (if developed) $

This appraisal is made ☐ "as is", ☐ subject to completion per plans and specifications on the basis of a hypothetical condition that the improvements have been completed, ☐ subject to the following repairs or alterations on the basis of a hypothetical condition that the repairs or alterations have been completed, or ☐ subject to the following required inspection based on the extraordinary assumption that the condition or deficiency does not require alteration or repair:

Based on a complete visual inspection of the interior and exterior areas of the subject property, defined scope of work, statement of assumptions and limiting conditions, and appraiser's certification, my (our) opinion of the market value, as defined, of the real property that is the subject of this report is $, as of , which is the date of inspection and the effective date of this appraisal.

Freddie Mac Form 70 March 2005 Page 2 of 6 Fannie Mae Form 1004 March 2005

Uniform Residential Appraisal Report

File #

ADDITIONAL COMMENTS

COST APPROACH

COST APPROACH TO VALUE (not required by Fannie Mae)

Provide adequate information for the lender/client to replicate the below cost figures and calculations.

Support for the opinion of site value (summary of comparable land sales or other methods for estimating site value)

ESTIMATED ☐ REPRODUCTION OR ☐ REPLACEMENT COST NEW	OPINION OF SITE VALUE .... = $
Source of cost data	Dwelling Sq. Ft. @ $ .... =$
Quality rating from cost service Effective date of cost data	Sq. Ft. @ $ .... =$
Comments on Cost Approach (gross living area calculations, depreciation, etc.)	
	Garage/Carport Sq. Ft. @ $ .... =$
	Total Estimate of Cost-New .... = $
	Less Physical | Functional | External
	Depreciation =$( )
	Depreciated Cost of Improvements........ =$
	"As-is" Value of Site Improvements........ =$
Estimated Remaining Economic Life (HUD and VA only) Years	Indicated Value By Cost Approach .... =$

INCOME

INCOME APPROACH TO VALUE (not required by Fannie Mae)

Estimated Monthly Market Rent $ X Gross Rent Multiplier = $ Indicated Value by Income Approach

Summary of Income Approach (including support for market rent and GRM)

PUD INFORMATION

PROJECT INFORMATION FOR PUDs (if applicable)

Is the developer/builder in control of the Homeowners' Association (HOA)? ☐ Yes ☐ No Unit type(s) ☐ Detached ☐ Attached

Provide the following information for PUDs ONLY if the developer/builder is in control of the HOA and the subject property is an attached dwelling unit.

Legal name of project

Total number of phases Total number of units Total number of units sold

Total number of units rented Total number of units for sale Data source(s)

Was the project created by the conversion of an existing building(s) into a PUD? ☐ Yes ☐ No If Yes, date of conversion

Does the project contain any multi-dwelling units? ☐ Yes ☐ No Data source(s)

Are the units, common elements, and recreation facilities complete? ☐ Yes ☐ No If No, describe the status of completion.

Are the common elements leased to or by the Homeowners' Association? ☐ Yes ☐ No If Yes, describe the rental terms and options.

Describe common elements and recreational facilities

Freddie Mac Form 70 March 2005 Page 3 of 6 Fannie Mae Form 1004 March 2005

Uniform Residential Appraisal Report

File #

This report form is designed to report an appraisal of a one-unit property or a one-unit property with an accessory unit; including a unit in a planned unit development (PUD). This report form is not designed to report an appraisal of a manufactured home or a unit in a condominium or cooperative project.

This appraisal report is subject to the following scope of work, intended use, intended user, definition of market value, statement of assumptions and limiting conditions, and certifications. Modifications, additions, or deletions to the intended use, intended user, definition of market value, or assumptions and limiting conditions are not permitted. The appraiser may expand the scope of work to include any additional research or analysis necessary based on the complexity of this appraisal assignment. Modifications or deletions to the certifications are also not permitted. However, additional certifications that do not constitute material alterations to this appraisal report, such as those required by law or those related to the appraiser's continuing education or membership in an appraisal organization, are permitted.

SCOPE OF WORK: The scope of work for this appraisal is defined by the complexity of this appraisal assignment and the reporting requirements of this appraisal report form, including the following definition of market value, statement of assumptions and limiting conditions, and certifications. The appraiser must, at a minimum: (1) perform a complete visual inspection of the interior and exterior areas of the subject property, (2) inspect the neighborhood, (3) inspect each of the comparable sales from at least the street, (4) research, verify, and analyze data from reliable public and/or private sources, and (5) report his or her analysis, opinions, and conclusions in this appraisal report.

INTENDED USE: The intended use of this appraisal report is for the lender/client to evaluate the property that is the subject of this appraisal for a mortgage finance transaction.

INTENDED USER: The intended user of this appraisal report is the lender/client.

DEFINITION OF MARKET VALUE: The most probable price which a property should bring in a competitive and open market under all conditions requisite to a fair sale, the buyer and seller, each acting prudently, knowledgeably and assuming the price is not affected by undue stimulus. Implicit in this definition is the consummation of a sale as of a specified date and the passing of title from seller to buyer under conditions whereby: (1) buyer and seller are typically motivated; (2) both parties are well informed or well advised, and each acting in what he or she considers his or her own best interest; (3) a reasonable time is allowed for exposure in the open market; (4) payment is made in terms of cash in U. S. dollars or in terms of financial arrangements comparable thereto; and (5) the price represents the normal consideration for the property sold unaffected by special or creative financing or sales concessions* granted by anyone associated with the sale.

*Adjustments to the comparables must be made for special or creative financing or sales concessions. No adjustments are necessary for those costs which are normally paid by sellers as a result of tradition or law in a market area; these costs are readily identifiable since the seller pays these costs in virtually all sales transactions. Special or creative financing adjustments can be made to the comparable property by comparisons to financing terms offered by a third party institutional lender that is not already involved in the property or transaction. Any adjustment should not be calculated on a mechanical dollar for dollar cost of the financing or concession but the dollar amount of any adjustment should approximate the market's reaction to the financing or concessions based on the appraiser's judgment.

STATEMENT OF ASSUMPTIONS AND LIMITING CONDITIONS: The appraiser's certification in this report is subject to the following assumptions and limiting conditions:

1. The appraiser will not be responsible for matters of a legal nature that affect either the property being appraised or the title to it, except for information that he or she became aware of during the research involved in performing this appraisal. The appraiser assumes that the title is good and marketable and will not render any opinions about the title.

2. The appraiser has provided a sketch in this appraisal report to show the approximate dimensions of the improvements. The sketch is included only to assist the reader in visualizing the property and understanding the appraiser's determination of its size.

3. The appraiser has examined the available flood maps that are provided by the Federal Emergency Management Agency (or other data sources) and has noted in this appraisal report whether any portion of the subject site is located in an identified Special Flood Hazard Area. Because the appraiser is not a surveyor, he or she makes no guarantees, express or implied, regarding this determination.

4. The appraiser will not give testimony or appear in court because he or she made an appraisal of the property in question, unless specific arrangements to do so have been made beforehand, or as otherwise required by law.

5. The appraiser has noted in this appraisal report any adverse conditions (such as needed repairs, deterioration, the presence of hazardous wastes, toxic substances, etc.) observed during the inspection of the subject property or that he or she became aware of during the research involved in performing this appraisal. Unless otherwise stated in this appraisal report, the appraiser has no knowledge of any hidden or unapparent physical deficiencies or adverse conditions of the property (such as, but not limited to, needed repairs, deterioration, the presence of hazardous wastes, toxic substances, adverse environmental conditions, etc.) that would make the property less valuable, and has assumed that there are no such conditions and makes no guarantees or warranties, express or implied. The appraiser will not be responsible for any such conditions that do exist or for any engineering or testing that might be required to discover whether such conditions exist. Because the appraiser is not an expert in the field of environmental hazards, this appraisal report must not be considered as an environmental assessment of the property.

6. The appraiser has based his or her appraisal report and valuation conclusion for an appraisal that is subject to satisfactory completion, repairs, or alterations on the assumption that the completion, repairs, or alterations of the subject property will be performed in a professional manner.

Freddie Mac Form 70 March 2005 Page 4 of 6 Fannie Mae Form 1004 March 2005

Uniform Residential Appraisal Report

File #

APPRAISER'S CERTIFICATION: The Appraiser certifies and agrees that:

1. I have, at a minimum, developed and reported this appraisal in accordance with the scope of work requirements stated in this appraisal report.

2. I performed a complete visual inspection of the interior and exterior areas of the subject property. I reported the condition of the improvements in factual, specific terms. I identified and reported the physical deficiencies that could affect the livability, soundness, or structural integrity of the property.

3. I performed this appraisal in accordance with the requirements of the Uniform Standards of Professional Appraisal Practice that were adopted and promulgated by the Appraisal Standards Board of The Appraisal Foundation and that were in place at the time this appraisal report was prepared.

4. I developed my opinion of the market value of the real property that is the subject of this report based on the sales comparison approach to value. I have adequate comparable market data to develop a reliable sales comparison approach for this appraisal assignment. I further certify that I considered the cost and income approaches to value but did not develop them, unless otherwise indicated in this report.

5. I researched, verified, analyzed, and reported on any current agreement for sale for the subject property, any offering for sale of the subject property in the twelve months prior to the effective date of this appraisal, and the prior sales of the subject property for a minimum of three years prior to the effective date of this appraisal, unless otherwise indicated in this report.

6. I researched, verified, analyzed, and reported on the prior sales of the comparable sales for a minimum of one year prior to the date of sale of the comparable sale, unless otherwise indicated in this report.

7. I selected and used comparable sales that are locationally, physically, and functionally the most similar to the subject property.

8. I have not used comparable sales that were the result of combining a land sale with the contract purchase price of a home that has been built or will be built on the land.

9. I have reported adjustments to the comparable sales that reflect the market's reaction to the differences between the subject property and the comparable sales.

10. I verified, from a disinterested source, all information in this report that was provided by parties who have a financial interest in the sale or financing of the subject property.

11. I have knowledge and experience in appraising this type of property in this market area.

12. I am aware of, and have access to, the necessary and appropriate public and private data sources, such as multiple listing services, tax assessment records, public land records and other such data sources for the area in which the property is located.

13. I obtained the information, estimates, and opinions furnished by other parties and expressed in this appraisal report from reliable sources that I believe to be true and correct.

14. I have taken into consideration the factors that have an impact on value with respect to the subject neighborhood, subject property, and the proximity of the subject property to adverse influences in the development of my opinion of market value. I have noted in this appraisal report any adverse conditions (such as, but not limited to, needed repairs, deterioration, the presence of hazardous wastes, toxic substances, adverse environmental conditions, etc.) observed during the inspection of the subject property or that I became aware of during the research involved in performing this appraisal. I have considered these adverse conditions in my analysis of the property value, and have reported on the effect of the conditions on the value and marketability of the subject property.

15. I have not knowingly withheld any significant information from this appraisal report and, to the best of my knowledge, all statements and information in this appraisal report are true and correct.

16. I stated in this appraisal report my own personal, unbiased, and professional analysis, opinions, and conclusions, which are subject only to the assumptions and limiting conditions in this appraisal report.

17. I have no present or prospective interest in the property that is the subject of this report, and I have no present or prospective personal interest or bias with respect to the participants in the transaction. I did not base, either partially or completely, my analysis and/or opinion of market value in this appraisal report on the race, color, religion, sex, age, marital status, handicap, familial status, or national origin of either the prospective owners or occupants of the subject property or of the present owners or occupants of the properties in the vicinity of the subject property or on any other basis prohibited by law.

18. My employment and/or compensation for performing this appraisal or any future or anticipated appraisals was not conditioned on any agreement or understanding, written or otherwise, that I would report (or present analysis supporting) a predetermined specific value, a predetermined minimum value, a range or direction in value, a value that favors the cause of any party, or the attainment of a specific result or occurrence of a specific subsequent event (such as approval of a pending mortgage loan application).

19. I personally prepared all conclusions and opinions about the real estate that were set forth in this appraisal report. If I relied on significant real property appraisal assistance from any individual or individuals in the performance of this appraisal or the preparation of this appraisal report, I have named such individual(s) and disclosed the specific tasks performed in this appraisal report. I certify that any individual so named is qualified to perform the tasks. I have not authorized anyone to make a change to any item in this appraisal report; therefore, any change made to this appraisal is unauthorized and I will take no responsibility for it.

20. I identified the lender/client in this appraisal report who is the individual, organization, or agent for the organization that ordered and will receive this appraisal report.

Freddie Mac Form 70 March 2005 Page 5 of 6 Fannie Mae Form 1004 March 2005

Uniform Residential Appraisal Report

File #

21. The lender/client may disclose or distribute this appraisal report to: the borrower; another lender at the request of the borrower; the mortgagee or its successors and assigns; mortgage insurers; government sponsored enterprises; other secondary market participants; data collection or reporting services; professional appraisal organizations; any department, agency, or instrumentality of the United States; and any state, the District of Columbia, or other jurisdictions; without having to obtain the appraiser's or supervisory appraiser's (if applicable) consent. Such consent must be obtained before this appraisal report may be disclosed or distributed to any other party (including, but not limited to, the public through advertising, public relations, news, sales, or other media).

22. I am aware that any disclosure or distribution of this appraisal report by me or the lender/client may be subject to certain laws and regulations. Further, I am also subject to the provisions of the Uniform Standards of Professional Appraisal Practice that pertain to disclosure or distribution by me.

23. The borrower, another lender at the request of the borrower, the mortgagee or its successors and assigns, mortgage insurers, government sponsored enterprises, and other secondary market participants may rely on this appraisal report as part of any mortgage finance transaction that involves any one or more of these parties.

24. If this appraisal report was transmitted as an "electronic record" containing my "electronic signature," as those terms are defined in applicable federal and/or state laws (excluding audio and video recordings), or a facsimile transmission of this appraisal report containing a copy or representation of my signature, the appraisal report shall be as effective, enforceable and valid as if a paper version of this appraisal report were delivered containing my original hand written signature.

25. Any intentional or negligent misrepresentation(s) contained in this appraisal report may result in civil liability and/or criminal penalties including, but not limited to, fine or imprisonment or both under the provisions of Title 18, United States Code, Section 1001, et seq., or similar state laws.

SUPERVISORY APPRAISER'S CERTIFICATION: The Supervisory Appraiser certifies and agrees that:

1. I directly supervised the appraiser for this appraisal assignment, have read the appraisal report, and agree with the appraiser's analysis, opinions, statements, conclusions, and the appraiser's certification.

2. I accept full responsibility for the contents of this appraisal report including, but not limited to, the appraiser's analysis, opinions, statements, conclusions, and the appraiser's certification.

3. The appraiser identified in this appraisal report is either a sub-contractor or an employee of the supervisory appraiser (or the appraisal firm), is qualified to perform this appraisal, and is acceptable to perform this appraisal under the applicable state law.

4. This appraisal report complies with the Uniform Standards of Professional Appraisal Practice that were adopted and promulgated by the Appraisal Standards Board of The Appraisal Foundation and that were in place at the time this appraisal report was prepared.

5. If this appraisal report was transmitted as an "electronic record" containing my "electronic signature," as those terms are defined in applicable federal and/or state laws (excluding audio and video recordings), or a facsimile transmission of this appraisal report containing a copy or representation of my signature, the appraisal report shall be as effective, enforceable and valid as if a paper version of this appraisal report were delivered containing my original hand written signature.

APPRAISER

Signature ____________
Name ____________
Company Name ____________
Company Address ____________
____
Telephone Number ____________
Email Address ____________
Date of Signature and Report ____________
Effective Date of Appraisal ____________
State Certification # ____________
or State License # ____________
or Other (describe) ____________ State # ____________
State ____________
Expiration Date of Certification or License ____________

ADDRESS OF PROPERTY APPRAISED
____
____

APPRAISED VALUE OF SUBJECT PROPERTY $ ____________

LENDER/CLIENT
Name ____________
Company Name ____________
Company Address ____________
____
Email Address ____________

SUPERVISORY APPRAISER (ONLY IF REQUIRED)

Signature ____________
Name ____________
Company Name ____________
Company Address ____________
____
Telephone Number ____________
Email Address ____________
Date of Signature ____________
State Certification # ____________
or State License # ____________
State ____________
Expiration Date of Certification or License ____________

SUBJECT PROPERTY

☐ Did not inspect subject property
☐ Did inspect exterior of subject property from street
Date of Inspection ____________
☐ Did inspect interior and exterior of subject property
Date of Inspection ____________

COMPARABLE SALES

☐ Did not inspect exterior of comparable sales from street
☐ Did inspect exterior of comparable sales from street
Date of Inspection ____________

subject is located. If the property is not located within a census tract, the appraiser enters "None" or "N/A."

Line 6 is used to indicate whether the property is owner-occupied, tenant-occupied, or vacant. If the property is currently subject to any special assessments, these are noted here. If the subject is located in a PUD, the corresponding box is also checked, and the appraiser fills in the annual or monthly amount of any homeowners association dues. (Note that the URAR is not used for condominium units; there is a standard form specifically intended for condominium units.)

On line 7, the appraiser checks the appropriate box to indicate whether the real property interest being appraised is the fee simple or a leasehold. The appraiser then indicates whether the appraisal is being made in connection with a purchase or refinance transaction, and space is provided for the client's name and address.

Finally, the appraiser indicates whether the property is currently on the market (or has been on the market within the last twelve months), and includes any relevant listing information.

Contract Section

The CONTRACT section of the URAR contains information about the terms of sale for the subject property. (If the appraisal is not being made in connection with a sale of the property, the items on this line should be marked "N/A.") The appraiser first indicates whether he or she has analyzed the sales contract and includes the results of the analysis. The appraiser then enters the total amount of the sales price and the sale date, and indicates whether the seller is the owner of public record (as well as the source of this information).

Next, the appraiser fills in the amounts of any loan charges, concessions, or other financial assistance paid by the seller or another party. Examples of such items include payment of loan discounts or other closing costs, interest rate buydowns, loan assumptions, gift funds, downpayment assistance, or any other special arrangements that may have affected the sales price. Items of personal property included in the sale must be noted here as well.

Neighborhood Section

In the third section of the URAR report, the appraiser describes the neighborhood in which the subject property is located. The first part of this section contains a series of boxes relating to the density and development of the neighborhood, and trends in property values and marketability. The appraiser should check one box on each line.

Next, the appraiser indicates the range of prices and ages of single-family housing units in the neighborhood, and the predominant (most frequently occurring) sales price for single-family residences. When specifying the age and price ranges, the appraiser may ignore isolated cases of properties that fall well outside the normal ranges.

The last block at the top of the NEIGHBORHOOD section relates to land use, with the appraiser providing a percentage breakdown of various land uses in the neighborhood. The total of reported percentages should add up to 100%.

The rest of the NEIGHBORHOOD section provides three spaces for the appraiser's comments and analysis. First, the appraiser must specify the physical boundaries of the neighborhood. The boundaries should be marked or easily identifiable on an attached location map. Next, the appraiser must describe the neighborhood's defining characteristics.

Finally, the appraiser must provide an analysis of market conditions in the subject neighborhood. This analysis should include data to support the appraiser's judgments regarding market trends, as reported above under Property Values, Demand/Supply, and Marketing Time. Analysis of typical sales and financing terms in the neighborhood is also important, both as an indicator of neighborhood market trends and for purposes of comparison between the subject property and comparable properties in the sales comparison approach.

Site Section

In the fourth section of the URAR form, the appraiser describes the subject property site. The appraiser enters the dimensions of the site and the calculated square footage (or acreage) of the land, and then describes the shape of the site and the view, if any. The zoning (if any) that applies to the site is noted, along with the conformity of the current use to the zoning regulations. If the present use does not conform to current zoning regulations, the appraiser should explain the resulting effect, if any, on the subject property value.

The appraiser must then indicate whether the property's highest and best use as improved is also the property's present use. Typically, the answer is yes. If the present use does not represent the highest and best use as improved, the appraiser must include an explanation of the analysis leading to that conclusion.

The SITE section includes spaces to describe the utilities and off-site improvements that serve the subject site. Available public utilities are indicated by checking the corresponding boxes. If the site is served by non-public utilities (private wells, septic systems, etc.), the appraiser must comment as to the effect on marketability. Off-site improvements are similarly identified as either public or private.

If any part of the property lies within an area that has been designated as a Special Flood Hazard Area by the Federal Emergency Management Agency (FEMA), the appraiser checks the Yes box and indicates the FEMA zone number, map number, and effective map date. A copy of the flood zone map, showing the location of the subject property, should also be attached to the report.

Next, the appraiser indicates whether the property's utilities and off-site improvements are typical for the market area. If not, the appraiser must include a brief explanation.

The final part of the SITE section asks whether any adverse site conditions or factors (such as easements, encroachments, etc.) exist; if any do, the appraiser must include a description.

Improvements Section

The DESCRIPTION OF IMPROVEMENTS section begins with nine labeled subsections, each relating to a different aspect or characteristic of the improvements.

General Description. General characteristics that the appraiser must describe include whether an accessory unit exists, the number of above-grade stories in the building, and whether the building is attached or detached. The architectural style is described in accordance with local custom and terminology, and it is noted whether the improvements are existing or proposed. The age of the house is its actual or chronological age stated in years, while the effective age reflects the appraiser's judgment as to the building's remaining economic life.

Foundation. Here, the appraiser indicates whether the foundation is a concrete slab or has a crawl space or basement (partial or full). If a basement exists, the appraiser notes the total square footage of basement area, and the percentage of the basement that has been finished. Checkmarks may be used to indicate the presence of an outdoor entry/exit to the basement, a sump pump, and any evidence of pest infestation, dampness, or settlement in the foundation. If further explanation is necessary, it should be provided in the COMMENTS section or in an addendum to the report.

Exterior Description. The exterior is described by noting the types of materials used for the different components. For example, a building might be described on the form as having a concrete foundation, brick veneer exterior walls, cedar shake roof surface, aluminum gutters, etc. The appraiser also reports the condition of each of the components.

Interior. As with the exterior description, the interior of the house is described according to the materials used for the various components of the construction, and the condition of those materials.

Attic. If the house has an attic, the appraiser checks the Stairs, Drop Stair, or Scuttle box to indicate the type of access to the attic space. The form also has boxes to indicate whether the attic is floored, heated, and/or finished. —IF NO Attick - ☑ NONE.

Heating. Here, the appraiser records the type of heating system (forced air, baseboard, etc.) and the type of fuel used by the system (oil, gas, coal, etc.). "Yes" or "No" is entered to indicate whether the house has central air conditioning or an individual cooling unit. If there is a cooling system other than central air, its type is noted in the blank for Other.

Amenities. Any amenities on the subject property are indicated by checking the corresponding box in this area. Such amenities include patios, decks, pools, fences, and porches. The number of fireplaces and wood-burning stoves, if any, is noted. If appropriate, amenities may be described in greater detail in the COMMENTS section, and their sizes and locations should be indicated on the plot plan or floor plan attached to the report.

Driveway Surface. The existence of a garage or carport is noted by checking the appropriate box. The appraiser also indicates the number of parking spaces, and whether the garage or carport is attached, detached, or built-in.

Appliances. Any appliances that are considered part of the real estate (i.e., not personal property) and that are included in the appraiser's valuation of the property are indicated here by checking the appropriate box.

In the second half of the IMPROVEMENTS section, the appraiser enters the total number of rooms, bedrooms, and baths, and the total square footage of gross living area. These totals should include finished, above-grade living areas only. When counting the total number of rooms, it is common practice to exclude certain types of rooms (such as foyers, baths, and laundry rooms) from the total room count. Exactly which types of rooms are included or excluded from the room count depends on local customs. It is critical, however, that the same rules be applied to both the subject property and to all comparable properties when determining total room counts.

Next, the IMPROVEMENTS section contains a series of spaces for the appraiser to discuss additional features or characteristics of the subject property that are not covered in the sections above. First, any special features that may affect the value of the property are noted. Examples of such features include energy-efficient items such as solar heating or insulated glass, as well as other unusual features of the building or site such as skylights, outbuildings, or landscaping.

The second section is for comments relating to the quality and condition of the improvements. The appraiser should report any items of depreciation that will affect the valuation of the property, including physical deterioration, and items of functional or external obsolescence.

The appraiser uses the third comments section to describe any conditions or deficiencies that adversely affect the property's livability, soundness, or structural integrity. This includes any known environmental hazards that exist on the property or in the vicinity of the property.

In the last comments section, the appraiser indicates whether the property conforms to its neighborhood in terms of style, condition, use, etc. If the answer is "No," the appraiser uses the space to elaborate further.

Sales Comparison Analysis Section

The main section of the second page of the URAR presents the appraiser's sales comparison analysis, which is the heart of a residential appraisal. At the top of the page, the appraiser indicates the number of comparable homes in the subject property's neighborhood that are currently on the market or that have sold in the past twelve months, along with their prices or price ranges. This section provides a quick synopsis of the comparables used in the appraisal.

Basic Property Data. The first part of the SALES COMPARISON ANALYSIS section consists of a comparison grid, with spaces to list the characteristics of the subject property and three comparables. At the top of the grid, the appraiser lists information about the locations and sales prices of the properties, and the sources of data. The street address (including the city or town) of each property is listed first, followed by the distance from the subject to each comparable (Proximity to Subject). The distances may be stated in miles, fractions of miles, or blocks. To aid the reader in locating the comparables on a map, the direction (north, south, etc.) from the subject to each comparable should be given as well.

The data and/or verification sources should be clearly identified. If the source is a person (buyer, seller, broker, etc.), the identification should include the person's name and phone number. For other types of data sources (such as a multiple listing service), the identification should contain the specific file number or listing number from which the data were obtained or verified.

Value Adjustments: Description Columns. The lower portion of the sales comparison grid is used to show the value adjustments that were made to the prices of the comparables. The appraiser must fill in each line of the DESCRIPTION column for the subject property and each comparable.

Sales or Financing Concessions are described for the comparables only, not for the subject. For each comparable, the appraiser notes the type and amount of financing, the interest rate, and any concessions that may have affected the sales price. If necessary due to the limited space on the form, the description of the sales and financing concessions may be attached as an addendum.

Date of Sale/Time is also shown only for the comparables. In most cases, only the month and year of the sale are reported. Unless otherwise indicated by the appraiser, it is assumed that the date reported here is the date of closing or settlement for the sale. If another date (such as the contract date) is used, the appraiser must report this fact in a comment or addendum.

Many of the items of comparison on the grid can be described by rating each property as "good," "average," "fair," or "poor" with respect to the particular item. These items include Location, Site, View, Design (Style), Quality of Construction, Condition, and Functional Utility. As an alternative, the descriptions of these items for the comparables can be stated in terms of comparison to the subject, as "superior," "same," or "inferior." The appraiser may also include additional descriptive information for these items, such as the size of the site or the type of view.

Example: If the subject property has a sweeping view of the mountains, this might be described on the View line as "Mountain/Good." A comparable property with a less dramatic view could be described as "Mountain/Average," or "Mountain/Inferior."

The line item for Leasehold/Fee Simple is described by simply stating whether the real property interest is a leasehold or a fee. Actual age is the actual or chronological age of the property, stated in years. The appraiser may also report the effective age in parentheses to the right of the actual age, if this factor is significant.

The figures reported for Above Grade Room Count and Gross Living Area for the subject property should be identical to the figures used in the description of the improvements on the first page of the form. Figures for the comparables must be derived in a manner that is consistent with the approach used for the subject.

Example: If a combination living/dining area in the subject was reported as two separate rooms, a similar area in a comparable must also be considered as two rooms in the "Total" room count.

Value Adjustments: Adjustment Columns. In the Adjustment columns, the appraiser fills in only those items where adjustments were actually made. If no adjustment is made for a particular line item, the Adjustment column is simply left blank for that item. For each adjustment shown on the grid, the appraiser must indicate whether the amount of the adjustment is positive or negative (plus or minus).

Totals. The last two lines of the sales comparison grid show the net total of adjustments for each comparable and the resulting adjusted sales prices. The appraiser indicates whether the net total adjustment is positive (+) or negative (–) by checking the appropriate box for each comparable. The Adjusted Sales Price should be equal to the Sales Price on line three of the grid, plus or minus the net total adjustment.

Prior Sales History. Below the sales comparison grid is a space for the appraiser to discuss the prior sales and transfer histories of the subject property and the comparables. First, the appraiser indicates whether he or she researched the prior sales and transfer history of the properties. The appraiser then explains whether this research revealed any sales or transfers of the subject property during the three years prior to the appraisal, or any sales or transfers of any comparable within one year of the comparable's sale date. For each such sale, the appraiser should report the sales price, the date of settlement or closing for the sale, and the source from which these data were obtained.

The appraiser must comment on the consideration given to prior sales history data in arriving at the reconciled value indicator for the sales comparison approach. With respect to the subject property, the terms of any current listing agreement, option, or sales contract should also be discussed. If there were no prior sales in the past year to consider, the appraiser should report this fact as well.

Summary of Sales Comparison Approach and Indicated Value. Below the sales comparison grid is space for the appraiser's discussion of the sales comparison analysis. Here, the appraiser must explain how the values indicated by the comparables were reconciled into a single indicator of value from the sales comparison approach. Since reconciliation is not a simple averaging of the three adjusted comparable prices, the appraiser should state which comparable(s) was (or were) given the most weight in the reconciliation process, and explain the reasons why.

The last line of the SALES COMPARISON APPROACH section is used by the appraiser to report the calculated value indicator for the subject property, based on the sales comparison approach.

Reconciliation Section

In the bottom section of the second page of the URAR form, the appraiser reports his or her final reconciliation and estimate of value for the subject property. First, the appraiser fills in the value indicators reached from the different appraisal approaches. Note that the cost approach and income approach are optional, while the sales comparison approach is not.

The appraiser must then explain how the value indicators from the different approaches to value were reconciled to reach a final value estimate. This explanation must be sufficient to allow the reader to follow and understand the appraiser's reasoning.

Next, the appropriate box is checked to indicate whether the property is appraised:

- "as is,"
- subject to completion of planned improvements on the basis of a hypothetical condition that specific improvements have been completed, or
- subject to repairs or alterations on the basis of a hypothetical condition that the repairs or alterations have been completed, or
- subject to a required inspection based on an extraordinary assumption that the condition or deficiency does not require alteration or repair.

Space is provided to fill in the referenced repairs, alterations, or inspection.

Finally, the appraiser specifies the final estimate of value and the effective date of the appraisal, in a statement that specifically references the report form's defined scope of work, statement of assumptions and limiting conditions, and the appraiser's certification. (We'll discuss these generic form items later in our discussion of the URAR form.)

Additional Comments Section

The third page of the URAR form begins with the ADDITIONAL COMMENTS section, a large area provided for the appraiser to include any observations, analysis, and other comments that did not fit into the appropriate sections above.

Cost Approach Section

Further down on the page, the appraiser reports his or her cost approach to value analysis. At the top of the COST APPROACH section is space for the appraiser to include information necessary for the client to replicate the appraiser's figures and calculations. Space is also provided for the appraiser to provide a summary of the data and methods used to estimate the site value.

Below and on the left hand side of the section, the appraiser indicates whether the value estimate is based on reproduction cost or replacement cost, and provides the source of the cost data. The appraiser also fills in the quality rating from the cost service, as well as the cost data's effective date. The appraiser then explains how the figures used in the cost approach were derived. The appraiser should describe how site value was determined, show the calculations used to find the square footage of building area, and list the source that was used for the per-square-foot construction cost figures. The analysis and calculation of depreciation must also be explained here. If necessary, an addendum should be attached to provide full documentation of the cost approach analysis.

If the appraisal is for a HUD or VA loan, the appraiser should include an estimate of the improvements' remaining economic life.

On the right hand side of the COST APPROACH section, the appraiser enters the figures for site value, improvement costs, and depreciation, and shows the calculations that result in the indicated value from the cost approach. The figures used here for building size (square footage) and depreciation should be consistent with the corresponding figures and analysis in the DESCRIPTION OF IMPROVEMENTS section and the SALES COMPARISON ANALYSIS section.

Income Approach Section

The INCOME APPROACH section of the URAR form simply consists of two lines where the appraiser reports the calculation of the value indicator from this approach. For purposes of the URAR, value from the income approach is calculated by multiplying the subject property's estimated monthly market rent by a derived monthly gross rent multiplier. There is a small amount of room for the appraiser to report the data and analysis used to derive these figures, but this information would ordinarily be reported in an addendum. The income approach is normally used for single-family residences only if the subject property is located in an area of rental housing.

PUD Section

If the subject property is located in a PUD (planned unit development), the appraiser must fill out this section of the URAR form. A PUD is a group of individually owned properties that share common ownership or use of certain areas or facilities within the development. The common areas are administered by a homeowners association (HOA), and the individual properties are subject to annual or monthly dues to support the maintenance of the common areas.

If the homeowners association is controlled by the developer or builder, this fact must be noted by checking the appropriate box, and additional information concerning the arrangement should also be provided as an addendum. Control of the HOA by the developer has led to abusive practices in the past, and may make the property ineligible for certain financing programs. The appraiser should also indicate the type of dwelling unit being appraised, and whether it is attached or detached.

If the developer or builder does control the homeowners association and the subject property is an attached unit, then the rest of the PUD section must be filled out. First, the appraiser lists the project's legal name and the total number of its development phases. The appraiser also lists the total number of units in the PUD, the number of units that are for sale, and the number of units that have already been sold or rented. If the project is currently under development, these numbers should include both existing and planned units, with a further descriptive analysis of construction status provided as an addendum.

The appraiser must also indicate whether the property was created by converting an existing building or development into a PUD and, if so, the date of the conversion. If the PUD contains any multi-dwelling units, this should be indicated and the data source stated. Finally, the appraiser must describe the quantity, type, and size of the common elements of the project. If any common elements are leased to or by the homeowners association, this fact must be indicated and the rental terms described.

If a supervisory appraiser is involved in the appraisal, she signs the form as well, and checks the box to indicate whether or not she personally reviewed the property.

Exercise 3

1. Match each item on the left with the section or sections of the URAR in which it is reported. More than one choice may be appropriate.

1. ___	subject property address	a.	SUBJECT
2. ___	prior sales of subject	b.	NEIGHBORHOOD
3. ___	final value estimate	c.	PUD
4. ___	subject square footage	d.	SITE
5. ___	site value	e.	DESCRIPTION OF IMPROVEMENTS
6. ___	energy-efficient items	f.	COMMENTS
7. ___	market conditions	g.	COST APPROACH
8. ___	HOA dues	h.	SALES COMPARISON APPROACH
9. ___	common elements	i.	RECONCILIATION
10. ___	property rights appraised		
11. ___	adverse easements		
12. ___	condition of improvements		
13. ___	conditions of appraisal		
14. ___	effective date of appraisal		
15. ___	housing supply and demand		

Pg.5+6

Statements, Definitions, and Appraiser's Certification

The remainder of the URAR form consists of three pre-printed pages containing definitions, a statement of assumptions and limiting conditions, and the appraiser's certification.

The section begins by stating that the URAR form should be used only to report the appraisal of a one-unit property (or a one-unit property with an accessory unit). The form should not be used to report the appraisal of a manufactured home or condominium unit; independent report forms exist for those purposes.

The next paragraph states that the appraisal report is subject to the scope of work, intended use, intended user, definition of market value, statement of assumptions and limiting conditions, and certifications set forth in this section of the URAR form. The appraiser cannot modify, add, or delete any of these items, except to:

- expand the scope of work to include additional research or analysis due to the appraisal assignment's complexity; or
- include additional certifications that do not materially alter the appraisal report.

According to the URAR form, the scope of work is defined by the complexity of the appraisal assignment and the reporting requirements of the URAR appraisal form. At a minimum, the appraiser must:

1. perform a complete visual inspection of the property's interior and exterior;
2. inspect the neighborhood;
3. perform at least a drive-by inspection of each of the three comparables;
4. research, verify, and analyze data from reliable sources; and
5. report the analysis, opinions, and conclusions in the appraisal report.

The URAR form further specifies that the appraisal report's intended user is the lender/client, and the report's intended use is to evaluate the subject property for a mortgage finance transaction. The form also contains the definition of market value adopted by Fannie Mae and Freddie Mac (see Chapter 2).

Next, the URAR form contains a statement of assumptions and limiting conditions to which the appraiser's certification is subject:

1. Title is assumed to be good and marketable.
2. The sketch included in appraisal report is only an approximation.
3. The appraiser has reviewed the appropriate map sources and noted whether the property is located in an identified flood hazard area, but is not a surveyor and makes no guarantees as to the flood zone determination.
4. The appraiser will not give testimony or appear in court in connection with the appraisal, unless arrangements have been made in advance (or as otherwise required by law).

5. The appraiser has noted any adverse physical conditions he is aware of, and assumes that there are no other adverse property conditions. The appraiser is not responsible for any such conditions that do exist. The appraisal should not be considered an environmental assessment of the property.
6. For an appraisal that is subject to repairs or alterations, the appraiser has based the appraisal on the assumption that the repairs and alterations will be completed in a professional manner.

The next part of the URAR form contains the appraiser's certification, which consists of a list of statements regarding the appraiser's qualifications, compliance with the Uniform Standards of Professional Appraisal Practice, and the work performed in the appraisal. At the bottom of the certification section, the appraiser signs the form, indicating that he or she certifies and agrees with the statements contained in the certification. The appraiser should also fill in his contact information and certification or license information, the appraisal's effective date, the subject property's address and appraised value, and the lender/client's contact information.

If a supervisory appraiser was involved with the appraisal, he or she must sign the supervisory appraiser's certification section, and fill in his or her contact and certification/license information below. The supervisory appraiser must also note whether he or she personally inspected the subject property or the comparable properties.

Addenda to the URAR Form

An appraiser must also be familiar with the addenda used with the URAR. One of the standard addendum forms is described below. Of course, a standard addendum form won't always exist for every situation in which the appraiser needs to add information to the URAR. When necessary, the appraiser should supplement the URAR by creating addenda and attaching other documents as appropriate.

Energy Addendum. The Energy Addendum is an optional two-page report used when appraising properties with special energy-efficient features. This form was designed to help lenders who are underwriting energy-efficient properties. It is divided into two parts (one for each page) that can be used separately, and each should be treated as a separate report.

The first part of the addendum is used for rating the energy efficiency of the subject property. The second part is used to estimate the value of energy-efficient items when adequate comparable data are not available.

Key Terms

Adjustments—Changes in the sales price of a comparable property to account for differences between the comparable and the subject property in the sales comparison approach to value.

Amenities—Things that make a property more desirable.

Appraisal—The act or process of developing an opinion of value; an opinion of value (USPAP definition). A form of appraisal practice.

Assumptions—Facts that an appraisal assumes are true, but that the appraiser does not independently verify. All assumptions should be specified in the appraisal report. (Assumptions may be general or extraordinary.)

Attic—The area of a house between the ceiling and the rafters.

Basement—A below-ground level of a house.

Condominium—A type of property ownership that combines fee simple ownership of an individual unit (and the airspace it occupies) with shared ownership of common areas.

Form report—A written appraisal report prepared on a standardized form, usually with addenda.

Heating, ventilating, and air conditioning (HVAC)—The equipment used to control air quality in a building.

Highest and best use—The use that is reasonably probable and that results in the highest value for a property. It must be a use that is legally permitted, physically possible, and economically feasible.

Homeowners association (HOA)—A nonprofit organization designed to manage the common areas of a development and to enforce the covenants of the development.

Insulation—Material used in construction to reduce the transfer of heat.

Letter report—A written appraisal report in the form of a letter to the client.

Limiting conditions—A statement or explanation in an appraisal report that limits the application of the conclusions contained in the report.

Manufactured housing—Housing that is not constructed on the building site.

Narrative report—A written appraisal report in narrative format; the most complete form of appraisal report, setting forth all the data relied on by the appraiser, and fully describing the appraiser's analysis and conclusions.

Neighborhood—A geographical area where land uses are complementary, and all properties are influenced similarly by the forces affecting value.

Oral report—An appraisal report that is communicated in speech, including a deposition or oral testimony.

Planned unit development (PUD)—A subdivision where fee simple ownership of a unit or lot is combined with common ownership of open space, recreational facilities, or other common elements.

Reconciliation—The process by which an appraiser reduces two or more value indicators to a single indicator or estimate of value.

Report—Any communication (written or oral) of an appraisal, appraisal review, or appraisal consulting service that is transmitted to the client upon completion of an assignment (USPAP definition). The means by which an appraiser's value conclusions are communicated to the client.

Restricted use appraisal report—A written appraisal report that is prepared in accordance with USPAP Standards Rule 2-2(c).

Sales comparison approach—One of the three approaches to value in the appraisal process. In the sales comparison approach, the value of the subject property is indicated by the adjusted sales prices of similar properties (comparables) in the market.

Self-contained appraisal report—A written appraisal report that is prepared in accordance with USPAP Standards Rule 2-2(a).

Site—A parcel of land that has been prepared for use by clearing, grading, and providing access and utilities.

Substructure—The part of a building that is below ground level and that supports the superstructure. Substructure includes footings, foundation walls, piers, and other elements of the foundation.

Summary appraisal report—A written appraisal report that is prepared in accordance with USPAP Standards Rule 2-2(b).

Superstructure—The part of a building that is above ground and supported by the foundation.

Uniform Residential Appraisal Report (URAR)—A standard form report for use in appraisals of single-family residences. The URAR is approved for use in appraisals that are governed by Fannie Mae, Freddie Mac, the FHA (HUD), and the VA.

Uniform Standards of Professional Appraisal Practice (USPAP)—Appraisal standards issued by the Appraisal Standards Board of the Appraisal Foundation, and adopted as minimum standards by Title XI of FIRREA.

Summary

I. Real property appraisal reports are governed by Standard 2 of the USPAP and the corresponding Standards Rules.

A. General requirements are set forth for all types of appraisal reports.

B. Minimum standards apply to oral appraisal reports; more specific requirements are mandatory for written appraisal reports.

C. All written appraisal reports must include a signed appraiser certification.

II. Appraisal reports may be oral or written.

A. The type of report used does not affect the appraisal process required to prepare a competent and credible appraisal.

B. Oral reports include expert testimony given in a deposition or court of law.

III. The USPAP classify written appraisal reports according to their level of detail.

A. Self-contained reports contain comprehensive detail.

B. Summary reports are more concise.

C. Restricted use reports contain the least detail. Use of a restricted use report is limited to the client only.

IV. Written appraisal reports may also be classified by their format.

A. Narrative reports take the form of a story and are usually quite detailed.

1. Narrative reports are usually broken down into subsections covering summary matters, definitions and terms, subject property data, and valuation analysis.

2. A narrative report is usually accompanied by a letter of transmittal.

B. Form reports are made on standardized forms and are used by many appraisal clients such as lenders and insurers.

C. Letter reports, which traditionally took the form of a one-page letter, are no longer widely used, because they do not meet USPAP requirements.

V. The Uniform Residential Appraisal Report (URAR) is used in most appraisals of single-family residences that are made for lending purposes.

A. The URAR form is six pages. The first page contains data describing the subject property; the second and third pages contains the appraiser's valuation analysis;

and the remaining pages contain definitions, a statement of assumptions and limiting conditions, and the appraiser's certification.

B. Standard addenda to the URAR exist, such as the Energy Addendum. An appraiser may create additional addenda for situations not addressed by the standard form addenda.

Chapter Quiz

1. According to USPAP Standard 2, an appraisal must be communicated in a manner that is not:
   a. confusing
   b. misleading
   c. ineffective
   d. difficult to understand

2. Which of the following types of appraisal reports is/are subject to the certification requirement in USPAP Standards Rule 2-3?
   a. Narrative report
   b. Form report
   c. Neither of the above
   d. Both of the above

3. Standardized appraisal reports used by lenders, insurers, and similar high-volume appraisal clients are known as:
   a. uniform reports
   b. letter reports
   c. form reports
   d. national reports

4. Which type of appraisal report would be most likely to include a table of contents?
   a. Narrative report
   b. Form report
   c. Letter report
   d. Letter of transmittal

5. The most detailed type of appraisal report is the:
   a. Self-Contained Appraisal Report
   b. Summary Appraisal Report
   c. Restricted Use Appraisal Report
   d. Standard Appraisal Report

6. Use of the Uniform Residential Appraisal Report is required for single-family residential appraisals that will be used by:
   a. Fannie Mae
   b. Freddie Mac
   c. Ginnie Mae
   d. All of the above

7. On the URAR form, the gross living area of the subject property improvements is reported in the:
   a. SUBJECT section
   b. DESCRIPTION OF IMPROVEMENTS section
   c. SALES COMPARISON ANALYSIS section
   d. Both b) and c)

8. In determining the total room count for a residence, the appraiser would normally include all of the following except:
   a. bedrooms
   b. bathrooms
   c. living rooms
   d. dining rooms

9. Information that will not fit in the space provided for it on a form appraisal report should be:
   a. written in the margins of the report
   b. included in a different section of the report
   c. omitted from the report, but kept in the appraiser's files
   d. attached to the report as an addendum

10. In the SALES COMPARISON ANALYSIS section of the URAR form, the appraiser must report all sales of the subject property and the comparables that occurred within the previous:
    a. six months
    b. one year
    c. two years
    d. three years

11. In a written appraisal report, the appraiser must certify all of the following except:
    a. that the statements of fact contained in the report are true
    b. that the appraiser's compensation is not contingent on reporting a predetermined value
    c. that the appraiser has (or has not) personally reviewed the subject property
    d. that the report is valid for up to 90 days from the effective date of the appraisal

12. According to Standards Rule 2-2, a written appraisal report must always include:
    a. the identification of the real property rights appraised
    b. the appraiser's opinion of the highest and best use of the property
    c. Both of the above
    d. Neither of the above

13. Which of the following statements is/are true?
    a. The process used by an appraiser to estimate value depends on the type of report required by the client.
    b. An appraisal report may omit items that are required by Standards Rule 2-2 if the client gives the appraiser written permission to do so.
    c. Both of the above
    d. Neither of the above

14. On the URAR form, the estimated site value of the subject property is reported in the:
    a. SUBJECT section
    b. SITE section
    c. COMMENTS section
    d. COST APPROACH section

15. A restricted use appraisal report:
    a. is intended for use only by the appraiser's client
    b. describes the information analyzed in much greater detail than a summary appraisal report
    c. isn't required to state the scope of work or the appraisal methods used
    d. is no longer considered acceptable, since it doesn't comply with USPAP standards

Quiz Answers

1. b) An appraisal should never be communicated in a misleading manner.

2. d) All written appraisal reports, regardless of format, must conform to the certification requirements of Standards Rule 2-3.

3. c) A standardized report made for a client such as a lender is known as a form report.

4. a) A narrative report is the most thorough and detailed report, and therefore is most likely to contain a table of contents.

5. a) The type of report with the most detailed content is the Self-Contained Appraisal Report.

6. d) Appraisals that will be used by Fannie Mae, Freddie Mac, or Ginnie Mae all must use a Uniform Residential Appraisal Report form.

7. d) Gross living area would be reported in both the DESCRIPTION OF IMPROVEMENTS and SALES COMPARISON ANALYSIS sections of the URAR form.

8. b) Bathrooms are typically not considered part of the room count for a house.

9. d) Any relevant information for which there is not an appropriate space on an appraisal report form should be included as an addendum.

10. b) In the sales comparison section, the appraiser must list any sales of the subject property and the comparables that took place within one year prior to the valuation date.

11. d) The appraiser's certification does not include a certification that the appraisal is valid for 90 days following the effective date of the appraisal.

12. a) A written appraisal report must always include a description of the real property interest being appraised. An opinion of the highest and best use of the property should be included if appropriate.

13. d) The process used to determine value may depend on the purpose and use of the appraisal, but not on the type of appraisal report. An appraiser may not omit items required by Standards Rule 2-2.

14. d) The estimated value of the site is reported in the COST APPROACH section. (The SITE section merely describes the improvements, size, shape, and topography of the site.)

15. a) A restricted use appraisal report must state the scope of work and the appraisal methods used, but (unlike a summary report) it doesn't state the information analyzed. It is intended for use only by the appraiser's client.

Exercise Answers

#1

1. a. To assist the client and other readers of the appraisal to understand its content and meaning

   b. To limit the appraiser's liability

2. Some common limiting conditions are:
   - the sole purpose of the appraisal is to estimate value;
   - the appraisal does not constitute a survey;
   - the appraisal does not constitute a legal opinion regarding title or other legal matters;
   - the appraisal does not constitute an engineering report or property inspection report;
   - the appraisal is made under conditions of uncertainty and is based on a limited amount of data; and
   - the appraisal is made with certain assumptions regarding the needs and expertise of the client.

#2.

1. The needs of the client
2. Self-contained, summary, and restricted use
3. The level of detail
4. 1. a
   2. d
   3. b
   4. c
   5. a
   6. b
   7. c
   8. d

#3.

1. a, h
2. h
3. i
4. e, g, h
5. g

6. f, h
7. b
8. a
9. c
10. a
11. d
12. e, h
13. i
14. i
15. b

13 Appraising Special Interests

Overview

One of the fundamental factors influencing an appraisal is the nature of the real property rights that are being appraised. Although appraisers usually are asked to estimate the value of fee simple estates, they are sometimes assigned the task of valuing partial interests in residential properties. After completing this chapter, you should be able to:

- describe the ways of dividing property ownership between two or more individuals or entities, including horizontal and vertical subdivision, transfers of limited real property rights, and methods of shared ownership;
- identify the appraisal techniques and considerations that are applicable to appraisals involving leaseholds, leased fees, easements, liens, and fractional interests in real estate; and
- describe the characteristics of condominiums, PUDs, cooperatives, and timeshare interests, and identify the appraisal techniques that are used when appraising these types of interests.

Partial Interests in Real Estate

The complete ownership interest in real estate is called the **fee simple**. The holder of a fee simple interest, or fee simple estate, has complete control over the ownership and use of the property, subject only to governmental limitations (i.e., property taxes, land use regulations, and the power of eminent domain). A fee simple interest in property can be divided between two or more individuals; when this occurs, each individual has a **partial interest** in the property. For example, if a husband and wife share ownership of their family home, each has a partial interest in the home. The total of all partial interests in a property is equivalent to the fee simple interest.

Fig 13.1 Ways to Divide the Fee Simple

Ways to Divide the Fee Simple

The fee simple interest in a piece of property can be divided in three ways:

1. the real property may be physically divided,
2. the bundle of rights that constitutes real property ownership may be divided, and
3. ownership of the property as a whole may be shared.

Physical Division of Real Property. One of the most common ways to divide the fee simple interest in a property is to divide the property itself into smaller units. This process is known as **subdivision**. The fee simple ownership of the original undivided property is divided into two or more separate fee simple interests, one for each parcel in the subdivision.

Example: The owner of a five-acre tract of land may subdivide it into five one-acre parcels, each of which can then be sold separately. The original fee simple interest in the five acres is divided into five different fee simple estates, one for each of the one-acre parcels.

The familiar process of subdividing land into separate lots or parcels is called **horizontal subdivision**. But real estate can also be divided vertically. In **vertical subdivision**, the

Fig 13.2 Vertical vs. Horizontal Subdivision

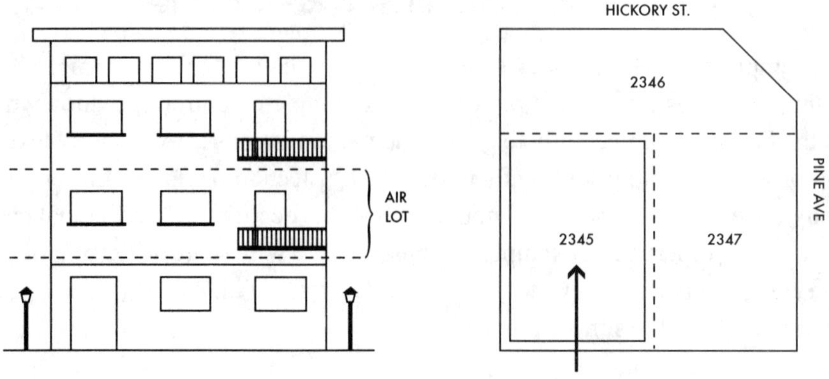

ownership of the subsurface, surface, or air space associated with a property is separated from the ownership of the rest of the property.

Example: The owner of a condominium unit has a fee simple interest in the airspace that is occupied by the unit, but does not have fee simple ownership of the land or subsurface beneath the unit.

Division of the Bundle of Rights. Fee simple ownership of real estate is often described as a **bundle of rights**, including the rights to sell, will, encumber, lease, occupy, and use the property. The second way of dividing a fee simple is to transfer some of the rights that go with fee simple ownership. Three ways of relinquishing part of the bundle of ownership rights are leases, easements, and liens.

Leases. A **lease** is a temporary transfer of the rights to occupy and to use a property. It divides a fee simple into a **leasehold estate**, which is held by the lessee (the tenant), and a **leased fee**, which is held by the lessor (the landlord). The leasehold estate gives the tenant the right to occupy and use the property for the term of the lease, subject to the conditions of the lease agreement. The leased fee consists of all the remaining rights in the property, including the right to receive the rental payments and the right to recover the use and possession of the property at the expiration of the lease term.

Easements. The right to use property or a portion of a property for a particular purpose can also be transferred for an indefinite period of time, which results in an **easement**. The holder of the easement has the right to use the property for a specific purpose as defined in the easement grant. The fee simple owner retains all other rights to the property, including the right to use the property in any manner, as long as that use does not interfere with the easement. Most residential properties are subject to easements of one sort or another, such as easements for the maintenance of roadways or utilities.

Example: Figure 13.3 illustrates a right-of-way easement that allows the owner of Parcel B to cross a portion of Parcel A. The owner of Parcel A is free to make any legal use of her land, provided that the use does not interfere with B's right of access across A's property.

Fig 13.3 Easement Appurtenant

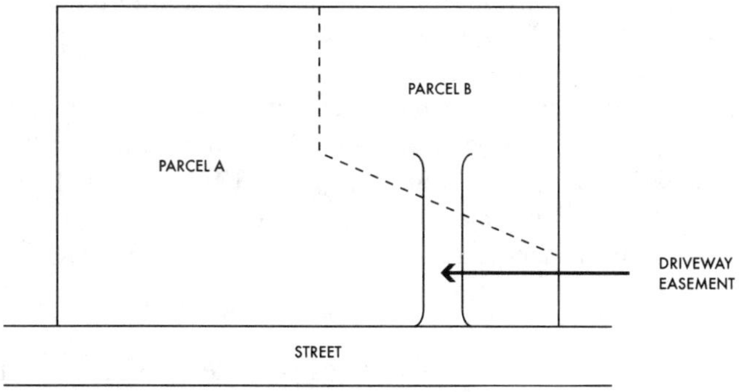

There are two types of easements: easements appurtenant and easements in gross. An **easement appurtenant** benefits a parcel of land; ownership of the easement rights is attached to (or "runs with") ownership of the benefited parcel. In the example above, the right-of-way is an easement appurtenant to Parcel B. If the owner of Parcel B were to sell his land, the right-of-way easement would be transferred to the new owner along with the land.

In contrast to an easement appurtenant, an **easement in gross** benefits only a person or other legal entity, rather than a parcel of land. A common example of an easement in gross is a utility easement, which benefits the utility company that owns the easement rights. An easement in gross does not run with the land. In other words, the ownership of an easement in gross is not transferred along with the ownership of any parcel of property.

Liens. A security interest, or **lien**, gives the lienholder the right to sell the liened property under certain conditions, and to use the proceeds of the sale to satisfy a debt. Liens are frequently used to secure a debt of the property owner. Mortgages and deeds of trust are the most common examples of agreements that create liens against property.

Sharing Ownership of the Entire Property. The third way to divide the fee simple interest is to share it among two or more individuals or entities. Depending on the type of co-ownership, the individual rights and responsibilities of the co-owners are defined by law and/or by the terms of contractual agreements. Common forms of co-ownership include joint tenancy, tenancy in common, and marital co-ownership. Co-ownership can also occur indirectly, as when property is owned by a corporation, partnership, or trust.

Joint tenancy. In a joint tenancy, each of the joint tenants has an equal, undivided interest in the entire property. A property owned by joint tenants cannot be transferred without the agreement of all of the joint tenants. Most joint tenancies include a **right of survivorship**, which means that if one joint tenant dies, ownership of the property automatically vests in the surviving joint tenant(s).

Tenancy in common. A tenancy in common is similar to a joint tenancy, with a few exceptions. As is the case with joint tenants, tenants in common each own an undivided interest in the entire property. However, a tenant in common is free to transfer his or her interest by will. There is no right of survivorship as there is in a joint tenancy. Another distinction between joint tenancy and tenancy in common is that tenants in common do not necessarily have equal ownership shares. While joint tenants always have equal shares proportionate to the number of joint tenants, tenants in common may own the property in unequal shares.

> **Example:** If a property is owned by three people in joint tenancy, each of the three has an undivided ⅓ interest in the property. But if they owned the property as tenants in common, the percentages of ownership would be specified either in the deed by which they took title or in a co-tenancy agreement. The co-tenants might each have a ⅓ share, or one of them might have (for instance) a 50% share, another a 30% share, and the third the remaining 20% share.

Marital property. The laws of most states provide for special forms of shared ownership between husbands and wives. A **tenancy by the entireties** is one type of marital

Fig 13.4 Tenancy in Common vs. Joint Tenancy

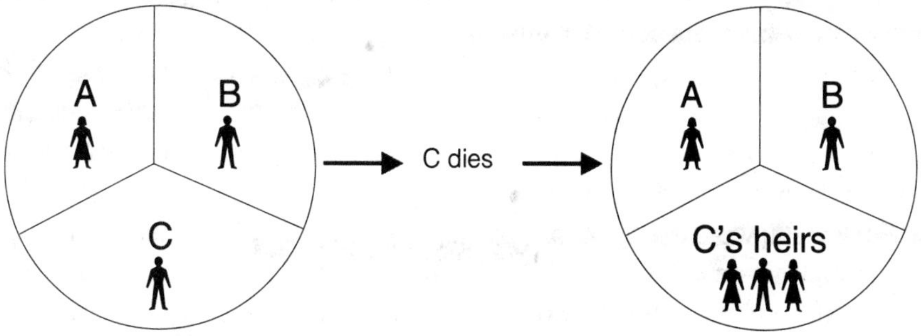

A, B, and C owned property as tenants in common, each with an undivided 1/3 interest. Then C died, and his heirs inherited his share of the property. Now the property is owned by A, B, and C's heirs as tenants in common. C's heirs share C's 1/3 interest.

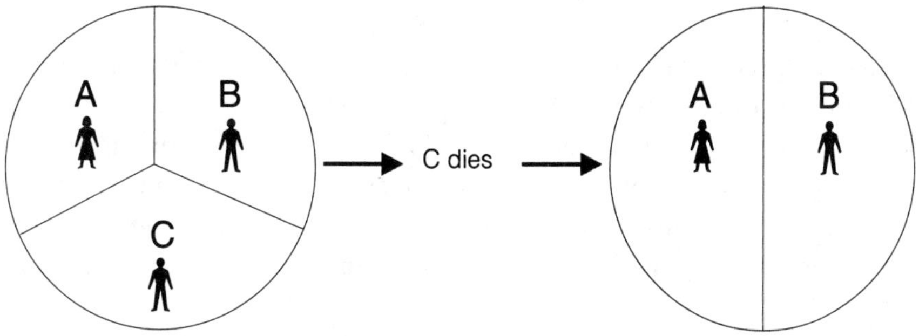

A, B, and C owned property as joint tenants, each with an undivided 1/3 interest. Then C died. Now, by the right of survivorship, A and B own the property as joint tenants, each with an undivided 1/2 interest.

ownership. It is very similar to a joint tenancy, except that the co-tenants must be husband and wife. Real property owned "by the entireties" cannot be disposed of by either spouse without the consent of the other, and passes to the surviving spouse automatically if one of them dies.

Community property is another form of co-ownership between husband and wife. Community property is established and defined by law in a number of states, primarily in the western part of the country. The husband and wife each have an undivided one-half interest in all community property, and the right of survivorship applies.

Artificial entities. Corporations, partnerships, and trusts are artificial legal entities, with characteristics, rights, and liabilities that are defined by law. These entities are capable of owning property, just as an individual person is, and they are often created for the express purpose of owning, leasing, or developing real estate.

The owners of a **corporation** are called **shareholders**. Although the shareholders own the corporation, they do not directly own the property of the corporation. Corporate property is owned by the corporation itself as a separate, independent legal entity. Control over corporate property (such as the power to sell, lease, or mortgage the property) is vested in the **officers** of the corporation. The officers are appointed (and removed) by the **board of directors**, who are in turn subject to periodic election by the shareholders.

A **partnership** is a legal arrangement by which two or more persons or entities share rights and responsibilities with respect to a business. The rights and obligations of the partners are spelled out in a partnership agreement. In most states, real property may be owned in a partnership's name. The partnership agreement defines the percentage share of each partner's ownership, and also defines the extent of each partner's right to transfer, use, or encumber partnership property.

There are two types of partnerships: general and limited. Each partner in a **general partnership** may act on behalf of the partnership, and each is also fully liable for any responsibilities of the partnership. A **limited partnership** is made up of at least one general partner and at least one limited partner. While the rights and liabilities of limited partners are restricted by individual partnership agreements and applicable state laws, limited partners are generally prohibited from any active participation in the partnership business. The rights and liabilities of the general partners are generally the same as those of a partner in a general partnership.

Some states also recognize a relatively new type of business entity known as a **limited liability company** (LLC). The LLC combines attributes of a corporation and a partnership. The management structure of an LLC is more flexible than a corporation's, and LLC members can manage the business in the same manner as partners in a partnership. At the same time, an LLC limits the personal liability of individual members for company obligations, in much the same way that liability is limited for limited partners and for corporate shareholders.

A **trust** is a legal arrangement in which title to property is passed to a **trustee**, who manages the property for the benefit of a **beneficiary**. The beneficiary may be the original (pre-trust) owner of the property, or some other person designated to receive the income from the trust property.

Exercise 1

1. Match each term on the left with the corresponding term on the right.

1. ___	leasehold	a.	director
2. ___	vertical subdivision	b.	transferable undivided interest
3. ___	joint tenancy	c.	lessee
4. ___	leased fee	d.	burdened parcel
5. ___	easement	e.	beneficiary
6. ___	tenancy in common	f.	right of survivorship
7. ___	lien	g.	air lot
8. ___	corporation	h.	security interest
9. ___	trust	i.	lessor

2. List three types of property interests that may include a right of survivorship.

   a. ______________________________

   b. ______________________________

   c. ______________________________

3. An easement that benefits a person or legal entity, as opposed to benefiting a parcel of land, is called a/an:

   ____

4. The authority to transfer property owned by a corporation is held by:

   ____

5. Match each of the interests or types of ownership on the left with the corresponding category on the right.

1. ___ easement		a. division of physical real estate
2. ___ partnership		b. division of bundle of rights
3. ___ leased fee		c. shared ownership
4. ___ horizontal subdivision		
5. ___ lien		
6. ___ community property		
7. ___ joint tenancy		

Appraising Partial Interests

In the previous section of this chapter, we examined the ways in which ownership of the fee simple interest can be divided among two or more persons or entities. Now we will take a look at the impact of partial ownership on value, and the appraisal techniques used to value partial interests.

Leasehold and Leased Fee Interests

A lease divides the ownership of property into two interests: the landlord's leased fee interest and the tenant's leasehold interest. Assuming that both interests are freely transferable, the combined values of these two estates should be equal to the total value of the fee simple.

When valuing either the leased fee interest or the leasehold interest, the appraiser must carefully consider the terms of the lease agreement itself. Standards Rule 1-4(d) of the USPAP recognizes the importance of the lease terms in appraisals of leasehold and leased fee estates:

> *When developing an opinion of the value of a leased fee estate or a leasehold estate, an appraiser must analyze the effect on value, if any, of the terms and conditions of the lease(s).*

To appraise a leasehold or leased fee interest, the appraiser compares the terms of the subject property lease's agreement with the terms of similar leases that are currently available in the market. If the subject property's lease terms are equivalent to current market terms, then the value of the leased fee is equivalent to the value of the entire fee simple, and the value of the leasehold is zero. The landlord (the owner of the leased fee) is receiving the full market rate of income from the property, so the value of her fee interest is not affected by the lease. Similarly, the tenant is obligated to pay the current market rate for the right to use the property, so his leasehold does not have any inherent value.

However, if the subject property's lease terms (in comparison to market terms) favor the landlord or the tenant, then the values of both estates are affected. Terms favoring the landlord increase the value of the leased fee and decrease the value of the leasehold. Conversely, if the terms favor the tenant, the value of the leasehold is enhanced, and the value of the leased fee suffers.

In valuing a leasehold or leased fee, the appraiser must consider all the terms of the subject property lease, to determine whether they convey an advantage to the landlord or tenant. Terms that are most likely to have an effect on value include:

- the amount of rent, including any scheduled changes in the rent;
- the allocation of property expenses, such as taxes, hazard insurance premiums, and maintenance expenses; and
- the remaining unexpired term of the lease, including any renewal options.

Rent. One of the most important terms in a lease is the amount of rent the tenant is required to pay to the landlord. The amount of rent that is specified in the lease is called **scheduled rent** or **contract rent**. The appraiser compares the scheduled rent for the property with its **market rent**, which is the amount of rent the property could command if it were available for lease in the current market (as of the effective date of appraisal).

> **Example:** A three-bedroom, one-bath house is subject to a one-year lease that calls for monthly rent payments of $1,625. Similar houses in the market are currently renting for $1,650 per month. In this case, the house's contract rent is $1,625 per month, but its market rent is $1,650 per month.

Scheduled or contract rent may differ from market rent for a number of reasons. For example, the original lease agreement may have favored one of the parties over the other, due to a superior bargaining position. Above- or below-market rent may also reflect concessions on the part of the tenant or landlord with respect to other conditions of the lease, such as higher rent payments in exchange for improvements provided by the landlord. And even if the contract rent is equivalent to the market rent at the outset of the lease, changing market conditions over time can result in the scheduled rent becoming higher or lower than market rent.

Example: A house was rented on January 1, with a one-year lease at $1,500 per month. The $1,500 monthly rent was equivalent to the market rent as of the first of the year. Six months later, on July 1, market rents for this type of housing have fallen to $1,475 per month, due to a decrease in demand. So as of July 1, the market rent for the property is $1,475 per month, but its contract rent is still $1,500, and will remain so until the lease expires at the end of the year.

If the scheduled rent is higher than current market rent, the difference is referred to as **excess rent**. Excess rent increases the value of the leased fee, and decreases the value of the leasehold, because the tenant is paying (and the landlord is receiving) higher-than-market rent for the use of the property. Below-market rent has the opposite effect. When market rent exceeds contract rent, it is the leased fee that suffers in value, and the value of the leasehold estate is enhanced.

Example: Two similar properties are subject to long-term leases, one with rent of $2,500 per month, the other with rent of $2,700 per month. According to the principle of substitution, a buyer should be willing to pay more for the property (the leased fee) with the higher income. On the other hand, the tenant of the $2,500 per month property is in a better (more valuable) position than the tenant of the $2,700 per month property, since he is receiving similar benefits (the right to use the property) at a lower cost.

When the amount of rent is a fixed amount over the entire lease term, the lease is said to be a **level payment** or **flat lease**. However, many leases call for rent payments to be adjusted during the lease term. When adjustments are called for at specific times and in specific amounts, the lease is called a **step-up** or **step-down lease**, depending on whether the adjustments are increases or decreases in the amount of rent.

Example: A five-year lease may call for payments of $1,400 per month in the first year, with annual rent increases of 5%. Since the rent increases will occur at specific times (annually) and in specific amounts (5%), the lease is a step-up lease.

Periodic rent adjustments may also be tied to market conditions, such as changes in the market value of the leased property (**reevaluation leases**) or changes in the Consumer Price Index or some other economic index (**index leases**). When appraising leasehold or leased fee interests, the appraiser must consider not only the current amount of contract rent, but also the effect on value of any scheduled or potential changes.

Other Lease Charges. A lease in which the tenant is responsible only for rent payments is called a **gross lease**. In a gross lease, the landlord pays for the expenses of maintaining the property, such as real estate taxes and assessments, hazard insurance premiums, and improvement maintenance expenses. If the tenant is obligated to pay some or all of the maintenance expenses, the lease is called a **net lease**. (A lease in which the tenant pays all three categories of expenses—taxes, insurance and maintenance—is sometimes called a **triple net lease** or **net, net, net lease**.)

The allocation of property expenses affects the appraiser's determination of market rent. For a given property, the amount of market rent will be higher for a gross lease, and lower if the tenant is responsible for expenses in addition to rent. For example, a property may have market rent of $2,000 per month under a gross lease, or $1,700 per month (plus expenses) under a triple net lease.

The allocation of expenses under a lease also allocates the risk that these expenses may increase during the term of the lease. For example, the party (the landlord or tenant) who is responsible for paying the real estate taxes bears the risk that the tax rate or assessed value will go up during the term of the lease, resulting in a higher property tax expense. The appraiser must consider the likelihood of such increases (or decreases) when estimating the effect on value of expense allocation provisions.

Lease Term. The third aspect of a lease that is most likely to affect the value of a leasehold or leased fee estate is the length of the remaining (unexpired) lease term. This is a major factor in this type of valuation, because the longer the lease will remain in force, the greater the effect that favorable or unfavorable lease conditions will have on value.

> **Example:** A property is currently rented for $1,000 per month, in a market where similar properties rent for $2,000 per month. Ordinarily, such a large difference between contract rent and market rent would have a significant impact on the values of the leasehold and leased fee interests. However, if the lease is due to expire after one month, its effect on value will be minimal. Once the lease expires, the property can be rented out at current market levels.

In a periodic lease (such as a month-to-month lease), either party can terminate the agreement with minimum notice, so any favorable or unfavorable lease conditions have a minimal effect on value. With a fixed term lease, however, both parties are bound for a specific period of time. When valuing a leasehold or leased fee, the appraiser is not concerned with the length of the lease term itself, but rather with the length of time from the effective date of the appraisal to the conclusion of the lease term. This is the period during which any favorable or unfavorable lease conditions will affect the value of the leasehold and leased fee estates.

> **Example:** A ten-year term lease was signed five years ago. If the property (leased fee) is appraised this year, the appraiser will be concerned only with the remaining term (five years). The length of the original lease term is irrelevant to the appraisal.

Renewal Options. Many long-term leases include renewal options, which allow the tenant to renew the lease on specified terms after the conclusion of the original lease term. If the renewal terms are favorable to the tenant, the appraiser will take them into account when valuing the leasehold or leased fee. If the renewal terms favor the landlord, however, they are usually ignored by the appraiser. Since the tenant is the one who chooses whether or not to exercise the renewal option, it is unlikely that the lease will be renewed if the terms favor the landlord.

Appraisal Techniques. The most effective technique for appraising leasehold and leased fee interests is usually the income capitalization approach. When appraising a leased fee, the appraiser can use residual techniques or discounting to estimate the value of the leased fee estate. To appraise a leasehold, the appraiser would capitalize or discount the difference between contract rent and market rent. In either case, the capitalized income amounts and the choice of capitalization or discount rates would be affected by such factors as the amount of the contract rent, the allocation of property expenses, the length of the remaining lease term, and the terms of any renewal options.

Easements

Easements may enhance or detract from value, or they may have no effect at all. An easement that is typical of most properties in an area or neighborhood, such as a utility maintenance easement, generally has little if any effect on value. Atypical easements, on the other hand, may have a substantial effect on value. The sales comparison approach is usually the most effective means for estimating the effect of an easement.

It should be noted that an easement's effect on value is not necessarily equivalent for both the benefited and the burdened properties. For example, an access or right-of-way easement may substantially enhance the value of the benefited parcel, without causing a corresponding decline in the value of the property that is crossed by the easement.

Liens

Most appraisals estimate the value of property on the assumption that title is free and clear of any liens or other similar encumbrances. However, an appraiser may be called upon to estimate the value of property subject to a specific lien or liens. Sales comparison and income capitalization techniques are the most appropriate methods for valuing such interests. The terms of the underlying obligation (the amount, interest rate, repayment schedule, prepayment penalties, and assumability of the debt secured by the lien) are critical factors in estimating the effect on value.

Example: A property with a fee simple value of $200,000 is subject to a mortgage lien in the amount of $80,000. The value of the property subject to the mortgage would depend on the terms of the mortgage note. If the note has standard market terms and no prepayment penalty, the value of the owner's mortgaged interest may be equivalent to the value of the fee simple minus the amount of the mortgage. However, the value could be greater if, for example, the mortgage loan were freely assumable and had a below-market interest rate. In either case, the appraiser's estimate of value should be supported by adequate market evidence.

Shared Ownership Interests

It might seem that the valuation of a shared ownership interest, such as a 50% partnership share, would be a simple matter of applying a percentage to the total value of the property. However, this is not always the case. Shared ownership frequently entails some form of limitation on the rights of a partial owner to control the use and transfer of the property, and these limitations can in turn affect the value of the partial interest.

Example: The interest of a majority shareholder in a corporation is generally worth more than his or her proportionate share of the corporate assets, since the majority interest conveys the ability to control the use and disposition of the assets.

Conversely, stock shares in a corporation typically sell for less than their pro rata value, since they represent minority holdings without any control over the corporation.

USPAP Standards Rule 1-2(e)(v) addresses the appraisal of shared interests:

In developing a real property appraisal, an appraiser must:

(e) identify the characteristics of the property that are relevant to the type and definition of value and intended use of the appraisal, including:

(v) whether the subject property is a fractional interest, physical segment, or partial holding;

Comment: ...An appraiser is not required to value the whole when the subject of the appraisal is a fractional interest, a physical segment, or a partial holding.

As indicated by the comment to Standards Rule 1-2(e)(v), appraisal of a shared interest does not require appraisal of the entire property. Even so, under some circumstances an appraiser may consider it appropriate to appraise the entire property in order to value a shared interest. In any case, the appraiser should always consider those factors (such as issues of control over use and disposition of the property) that may make a fractional interest worth more or less than its proportionate share of total property value.

Exercise 2

1. Which appraisal approach is usually the most appropriate for valuing leasehold or leased fee estates?

____

2. A renewal option in a lease can normally be ignored for appraisal purposes if the terms of the option favor the:

____

3. If market rent exceeds contract rent, which estate is enhanced in value?

____

4. If property is leased on terms that are equivalent to terms currently available for similar properties in the market, the value of the leased fee should be equivalent to:

____

5. The effect on value caused by an existing lien depends on:

____

Other Forms of Ownership

In the preceding sections of this chapter, we have examined various types of partial ownership interests in real estate, and some of the important considerations involved in appraising such interests. In the remainder of this chapter, we will look at more complex types of real estate interests, involving combinations of fee simple interests and partial interests.

Condominiums and PUDs

Condominiums and PUDs (planned unit developments) are very similar types of ownership. Each combines fee simple ownership of an individual unit with shared ownership of common areas. An owner has full title to his or her unit in a condominium or PUD, and the individual units may be sold, mortgaged, or leased. Ownership of the common areas in the project, as well as the cost of maintaining the common areas, is shared among all the individual unit owners. The common areas are managed by a homeowners association under the terms of established bylaws, and periodic charges or dues are levied on each unit in the project to cover the cost of common area maintenance.

Condominiums. A condominium project is basically an apartment complex where each unit is owned separately in fee simple. The owner of a condominium unit has fee simple title to the three-dimensional airspace (air lot) that is occupied by the unit. All of the land in the project is owned jointly, along with common elements of the building(s) such as the exterior walls, roofs, foundations, and common stairs and hallways. Jointly owned recreational facilities, such as swimming pools or tennis courts, are often present as well.

The most reliable method for appraising condominium units is the sales comparison method. If adequate rental data are available, the income approach may also be used to support the value indicated by the sales comparison method. The comparables used for the sales comparison method must themselves be condominium properties, preferably from within the same project as the subject.

If units from other projects are used as comparables in the sales comparison method, the appraiser must make adjustments to those properties to account for differences in project amenities and common area management. A significant element of comparison in this regard is the amount of charges or dues that are levied on the unit for common area maintenance. These charges can vary widely from one project to another, even when the projects offer similar amenities.

Differences between condominium projects can be very difficult to account for in terms of their effects on value. For this reason, comparables are best chosen from projects that are similar in overall layout, total number of units, and recreational facilities.

PUDs. In a planned unit development, which is a special type of subdivision, the developer is allowed to exceed the normal zoning density in exchange for setting aside part of the development as open space. The individual units or lots in a PUD are owned in fee simple and may be detached homes, townhouses, or condominiums. The open space areas are owned in common through a homeowners association, or sometimes are deeded to the local community. Like condominium projects, PUDs often include jointly owned recreational facilities or other amenities.

Appraisal considerations for PUD units are similar to those for condominiums. The most reliable comparable sales will be found within the same development as the subject, and should be similar in type (detached, townhouse, or condominium) to the subject. Important elements of comparison are the extent of common areas and amenities, the quality of common area management, and the level of dues or charges levied for common area maintenance.

Cooperatives

In a cooperative, real estate (usually an apartment building) is owned by a corporation. Each shareholder of the corporation receives a proprietary lease on one of the apartments. (The number of required shares may vary from unit to unit within the project.) Thus, "ownership" of a cooperative apartment unit actually consists of ownership of shares in the cooperative corporation, plus a leasehold interest in a particular unit.

The cooperative shareholder-tenants make monthly payments to the corporation to cover the costs of managing and maintaining the property and to make the payments on any corporate debt service. The total cost of keeping the cooperative afloat is prorated among the total number of shares. Each tenant then pays a monthly figure based on the number of shares he or she owns.

Control over the project is vested in the corporation's board of directors, which is elected by the shareholders. The board operates the project in accordance with corporate bylaws.

Like condominium and PUD units, cooperative units are best appraised using the sales comparison approach, and the best comparables are units from within the same cooperative apartment building as the subject property. The appraiser may use comparables from other similar cooperatives, but must be careful to make adjustments to account for differences in corporate assets and liabilities. Many cooperative corporations carry mortgage debt that is secured by the project real estate, and the amount of that debt can have a significant impact on the value of the corporate shares.

> **Example:** A cooperative with 20 units has mortgage debt of $400,000. Assuming each unit requires the purchase of 5% (one twentieth) of the corporate shares, each shareholder would be responsible for 5% of the corporate debt, or $20,000. If a comparable unit in a different cooperative was subject to only $10,000 worth of debt, an adjustment to the comparable sales price would be required to account for this difference.

If adequate rental data are available, the income approach may also be applied in the appraisal of cooperatives. However, many cooperatives prohibit their shareholder-tenants from subletting their units, in which case the income approach would not be applicable.

Timeshares

In a timeshare, the rights to use a property (usually a recreational property) are divided according to time segments. Each timeshare interest conveys the right to use the property during a specific time period each year, such as June 1 through June 14. Ownership rights (as opposed to use rights) may or may not be included in the timeshare interest. If the timeshare includes a proportionate share of ownership, it is called a **timeshare estate**; if not, the interest is called a **timeshare use**.

The sales comparison approach is usually the most reliable method for appraising timeshares, but the income and cost approaches also may be applicable in particular cases. Important elements of comparison for timeshares include the type of interest (estate or use) and the desirability of the time period covered by the interest in relation to the location of the property. For example, a timeshare interest in a beach property in the Northeast would be more valuable in June than in December, while the opposite would be true for a timeshare in a ski resort.

New timeshare projects are often heavily promoted by the developer. The appraiser should take into account the effect of the promotion on the sales prices of units in a new project. Resale prices are often a more reliable indicator of value than original sale prices of timeshare units. An analysis of marketing time for resales will alert the appraiser to any weakness in market demand.

Exercise 3

1. What are the two types of interests that constitute "ownership" of a cooperative unit?

   a. ______________________________

   b. ______________________________

2. Resale prices of timeshare units are often more reliable indicators of value than original sales prices, because they are not affected by:

   ____

3. The most reliable comparables for an appraisal of a condominium are:

   ____

4. List two important elements of comparison for condominiums and PUDs that are not applicable to most other types of properties.

   a. ______________________________

   b. ______________________________

5. The amount of corporate debt is an important element of comparison in the appraisal of:

   ____

Key Terms

Air rights—Rights of ownership or use with respect to air space.

Appurtenance—Something that goes along with ownership of real estate, such as mineral rights or an easement.

Bundle of rights—A description of property ownership in terms of the various rights that ownership conveys.

Collateral—Property that serves as security for a debt.

Commercial property—Property that is used for trade or business.

Community property—A form of common ownership by a husband and wife in states that recognize this type of ownership. Each spouse holds an undivided one-half interest in all community property, and the right of survivorship applies.

Conditions of sale—An element of comparison that reflects the motivations of the buyer and seller in a real estate transaction. When conditions of sale are not typical of the market, the sales price is probably not a reliable indicator of market value.

Condominium—A type of ownership that combines fee simple ownership of an individual unit (and the airspace it occupies) with shared ownership of common areas.

Contract rent—The amount of rent that is called for under an existing lease. Also called scheduled rent.

Cooperative—A form of ownership in which property is owned by a corporation and individual units are leased to the shareholders.

Deed—An instrument used to convey title to real estate.

Deed of trust—A type of specific, voluntary lien that is similar in most respects to a mortgage, but with different rules of foreclosure.

Dominant tenement—A parcel of land that has the benefit of an easement.

Easement—A non-exclusive right to use someone else's property for a particular purpose. A type of non-financial encumbrance. Appurtenant easements benefit a particular piece of real estate. Easements in gross benefit individuals or organizations.

Encumbrance—A real property interest that does not include the present or future right of possession. Financial encumbrances (such as mortgages) affect title to the real estate. Non-financial encumbrances (such as easements) affect the use of the real estate.

Estate—A real property interest that includes the right of possession, i.e., the exclusive right to occupy and use the real estate. Estates may be freehold estates (ownership) or leasehold estates (tenancy).

Excess rent—The amount by which a property's contract rent exceeds its market rent.

Fee simple—A freehold estate that is the most complete and comprehensive form of real property interest, including the entire bundle of rights.

Flat lease—A lease in which the amount of rent does not change during the entire lease term. Also known as a level payment lease.

Freehold—An estate that includes the rights of ownership or title, either presently or in the future. Freehold estates include the fee simple, the life estate, the estate in remainder, and the estate in reversion.

General partnership—A partnership in which each partner is fully entitled to act on behalf of the partnership.

Gross lease—A lease in which the tenant is responsible only for rent payments, and not for payment of any expenses.

Ground lease—A long-term lease of vacant land on which the tenant constructs a building.

Ground rent—The rent paid under the terms of a ground lease.

Homeowners association (HOA)—A nonprofit organization designed to manage the common areas of a development and to enforce the covenants of the development.

Index lease—A lease that calls for periodic adjustment of the rent amount, based on changes in an economic index.

Joint tenancy—A form of common ownership in which each owner (joint tenant) has an undivided interest in the entire property and cannot transfer his or her interest without the consent of the other joint tenant(s). Most joint tenancies include a right of survivorship, which means that if one joint tenant dies, ownership of the property automatically vests in the surviving joint tenant(s).

Landlord—The holder of a leased fee interest. Also called the lessor.

Lease—A contract between a landlord and a tenant, which temporarily separates the ownership of real estate from the right of possession. The interest of the owner/landlord is called a leased fee, and the tenant's interest is called a leasehold.

Leased fee—The real property interest of the landlord (owner) under a lease, which includes ownership but not the immediate right of possession.

Leasehold—A non-freehold estate, which includes the right of possession during the term of the lease, but not ownership or title; the real property interest held by a tenant under a lease. Also known as a tenancy. Leasehold estates include the tenancy for years (created by a term lease), the periodic tenancy (created by a period-to-period lease), and the tenancy at will (created when a tenant remains in possession with the landlord's consent after expiration of a valid lease).

Lien—A financial encumbrance. The holder of a lien has the right to force the sale (foreclosure) of the liened property and use the proceeds of the sale to satisfy a debt in the event that the debt is not paid according to its terms. Specific liens (such as mortgages) apply only to a particular piece of real estate, while general liens (such as judgment liens) apply to all real estate owned by the debtor.

Life estate—A freehold estate that terminates automatically upon the death of the person designated as the measuring life.

Limited partnership—A form of partnership that includes general partners who have authority to act on behalf of the partnership, and limited partners who share financial risks and rewards but do not control the partnership assets.

Market rent—The amount of rent that a property should be able to command under current market conditions.

Mineral rights—The right to extract minerals from a property.

Net lease—A lease in which the tenant is responsible for payment of some property expenses (taxes, insurance, and/or maintenance) in addition to the rent.

Net, net, net lease—A lease in which the tenant is responsible for payment of all property expenses (taxes, insurance, and maintenance) in addition to the rent. Also called a triple net lease.

Off-site improvement—An improvement that benefits a property but is not located on the property, such as a street or alley.

On-site improvement—An improvement that is located on the property in question.

Option—The right to do something (such as purchase a property for a set price or renew a lease on specified terms) at a future date.

Partial interest—Any real property interest other than the fee simple. Usually refers to a shared common ownership in real estate.

Partnership—A legal arrangement by which two or more persons or entities share rights and responsibilities with respect to property used in a business.

Periodic lease—A lease that has no fixed expiration date, but continues in effect until terminated by one of the parties.

Periodic tenancy—The tenant's estate created by a periodic lease.

Planned unit development—A subdivision where fee simple ownership of a unit or lot is combined with common ownership of open space, recreational facilities, or other common elements.

Rent—The amount paid by a tenant or lessee for the right to use property under the terms of a lease.

Residential property—Property intended to be used for dwellings.

Servient tenement—A parcel of land that is subject to an easement.

Step-up lease—A lease that calls for specific rent increases at specific times during the lease term. Also called a graduated lease.

Subdivision—(1) The division of one parcel of real estate into two or more separate parcels. (2) A group of properties that have been developed for a particular use.

Sublease—A lease of property from one tenant to another.

Tenancy by the entireties—A form of common ownership in which the co-tenants are husband and wife.

Tenancy in common—A form of common ownership in which each owner (co-tenant) has an undivided interest in the entire property and can freely transfer his or her interest without the consent of the other co-tenant(s).

Tenant—The holder of a leasehold estate. Also called a lessee.

Tenant improvement—An improvement of leased property made by the tenant.

Term—A length of time, such as the duration of a lease agreement (lease term), or the time for repayment of a loan (loan term).

Timeshare—A shared ownership interest that includes the right to use the property only during a specified time of the year.

Title—An ownership (freehold) interest in real estate.

Trade fixture—A fixture installed by a tenant in connection with the operation of a business on leased property. Usually considered to be the personal property of the tenant, not part of the real estate.

Uniform Standards of Professional Appraisal Practice (USPAP)—Appraisal standards issued by the Appraisal Standards Board of the Appraisal Foundation and adopted as minimum standards by Title XI of FIRREA.

Summary

I. The fee simple interest in real estate may be divided to create smaller or partial interests.

A. Subdivision splits a single fee simple interest into two or more smaller fee simple estates.

1. Horizontal subdivision: land divided into parcels.
2. Vertical subdivision: air lots, as in a condominium.

B. The bundle of ownership rights may be divided by means such as leases, easements, and liens.

C. Ownership of a property may be shared by two or more individuals or entities.

1. Ownership is shared directly in joint tenancies, tenancies in common, and marital communities.
2. Ownership can also be shared indirectly when property is owned by an artificial entity such as a partnership, corporation, or trust.

II. The characteristics of a real property interest influence the appraiser's selection and analysis of data, and the choice of appraisal techniques.

A. In appraisals of leaseholds and leased fee interests, the appraiser must consider the effects on value caused by the terms of the lease agreement.

1. Rent

   a. If contract rent is higher than market rent, the value of the leased fee is enhanced and the value of the leasehold is diminished. These value effects are reversed if market rent exceeds contract rent.

   b. The amount of contract rent may be stable over the term of the lease, or it may be subject to change.

2. Allocation of property expenses affects the appraiser's estimate of market rent. Similar properties will command higher rents if the landlord pays these expenses, and lower rents if the tenant pays them.

3. The significance of the lease depends on how much longer it will be in effect: the remaining unexpired term of the lease.

   a. Renewal options may increase the length of time that the lease remains in effect, but renewals are usually exercised only if the lease terms are favorable to the tenant.

4. The income approach is usually the most reliable indicator of value for leasehold and leased fee interests.

B. Easements are usually appraised by the sales comparison method.

   1. An easement may have value to the person or parcel that receives the benefit of the easement, and it may also affect the value of the burdened parcel of land.

   2. However, the effects on the values of the benefited and burdened estates are not necessarily equivalent.

C. Liens

   1. The effect on value caused by a lien depends on the terms of the underlying obligation secured by the lien.

   2. This effect is most reliably determined by the sales comparison method.

D. Shared interests

   1. The value of a shared interest in real estate does not necessarily correspond to the pro rata share of ownership, due to limitations on the ability of a partial owner to control the use and transfer of the property.

   2. The sales comparison method is the best one for estimating the value of fractional interests.

III. Condominiums, PUDs, cooperatives, and timeshares all have unique characteristics that may affect their values. Each of these types of properties is best appraised through the sales comparison method, using sales of similar properties in the same development or a similar development.

A. Condominiums and PUDs include fee simple ownership of individual units or lots, plus shared ownership of common areas.

   1. The lots in a condominium are air lots. PUD lots may be conventional detached lots, townhouses, and/or condominiums.

   2. Important elements of comparison include:

      a. the types of amenities that are part of the common ownership, and

      b. the fees or dues levied on each unit to support management and maintenance of the common areas.

B. Cooperatives

   1. "Ownership" of a cooperative unit includes:

      a. ownership of shares in the cooperative corporation that holds fee title to the project, plus

      b. a proprietary lease for the unit.

   2. Each owner pays a pro rata share of maintenance costs and corporate debt service. The amount of these costs is an important element of comparison for cooperative properties.

C. Timeshares allocate the use of property on the basis of specified time periods. A timeshare estate also includes a share of the fee ownership, while a timeshare use does not.

1. In making a sales comparison, the appraiser should consider the nature of the interest (estate or use), as well as the desirability of the particular time of year covered by the interest.
2. Aggressive marketing by developers may distort original sales prices of timeshares. Resale prices are usually more reliable indicators of value.

Chapter Quiz

1. Which of the following interests in real estate represents the most complete form of ownership?
   a. Leasehold
   b. Leased fee
   c. Fee simple
   d. Tenancy in common

2. Which of the following interests in real estate would normally include a right of survivorship?
   a. Fee simple
   b. Joint tenancy
   c. Tenancy in common
   d. Tenancy for years

3. A real property interest that includes fee simple ownership of an air lot and shared ownership of common areas is called a:
   a. leasehold
   b. cooperative
   c. tenancy in common
   d. condominium

4. The cost of managing and maintaining the common areas of a development is an important consideration in the appraisal of:
   a. condominiums
   b. cooperatives
   c. PUDs
   d. All of the above

5. If a lease calls for rental payments that are higher than current rents for comparable properties:
   a. the value of the leased fee estate is enhanced
   b. the value of the leasehold estate is enhanced
   c. the effect on value depends on the original lease term
   d. Both a) and c)

6. In a tenancy in common:
   a. each owner has the undivided right to use the entire property
   b. each owner has an equal share in the ownership of the property
   c. an owner may not transfer his or her interest without the consent of all the other co-owners
   d. All of the above

7. When appraising a leasehold or leased fee interest, an appraiser must:
   a. determine the value of the fee simple
   b. consider the effect on value of the lease terms
   c. give the most weight to the value indicated by the income approach
   d. All of the above

8. The amount of mortgage debt carried by the project is a significant consideration in the appraisal of units in a:
   a. planned unit development
   b. condominium project
   c. cooperative apartment building
   d. timeshare development

9. In order to appraise the interest of a joint tenant, an appraiser should:
   a. multiply the total property value by the pro rata share of ownership of the joint tenant
   b. divide the total property value by the pro rata share of ownership of the joint tenant
   c. subtract the values of the interest(s) of the other joint tenant(s) from the total property value
   d. consider whether the value of the interest of the joint tenant contributes pro rata to the value of the total property

10. Ownership of a unit in a cooperative project includes:
    a. ownership of corporate shares
    b. a leasehold interest in the cooperative unit
    c. responsibility for a pro rata share of corporate debt
    d. All of the above

11. In a corporation:
    a. the directors are elected by the shareholders
    b. the directors are appointed by the officers
    c. the officers are elected by the shareholders
    d. None of the above

12. Which of the following is NOT an important consideration in the appraisal of a leased fee estate?
    a. The amount of rent
    b. The allocation of property expenses
    c. A renewal option on terms favorable to the landlord
    d. The length of the unexpired lease term

13. When the amount of rent required by a lease is higher than rents being charged for similar properties in the market, the difference is referred to as:
    a. scheduled rent
    b. contract rent
    c. excess rent
    d. market rent

14. A lease calling for specific increases in the rental amount at specific times during the lease term is called a:
    a. step-up lease
    b. reevaluation lease
    c. index lease
    d. periodic lease

15. An appraiser would be most likely to use the income approach when appraising a:
    a. condominium unit
    b. leased fee
    c. cooperative unit
    d. tenancy in common

Quiz Answers

1. c) A fee simple interest is the most complete form of ownership.

2. b) Joint tenancy is distinguished by the right of survivorship.

3. d) The owner of a condominium unit owns the air rights to a unit in fee simple and a partial interest in common areas as a tenant in common.

4. d) The costs associated with management and maintenance of common areas are an important consideration when appraising condominiums, cooperatives, and PUDs.

5. a) Above-market rents would be more attractive to a potential buyer of the leased fee, increasing the value of the leased fee. When valuing a leased fee, the appraiser is not concerned with the length of the lease term itself, but with the length of time remaining in the lease.

6. a) In a tenancy in common, each owner has the right to use the entire property. Shares of ownership may be unequal, and an owner may transfer her share without the consent of the other parties.

7. b) An appraiser appraising a leasehold or leased fee interest must determine whether the terms of the lease affect the value.

8. c) The amount of mortgage debt carried by the corporation is an important consideration when appraising a unit in a cooperative.

9. d) In appraising a partial interest in a property, the appraiser must consider how the amount of the ownership share affects the value. (For instance, a majority stake in a company might be worth more than its pro rata value because of the benefits associated with majority ownership.)

10. d) Ownership of a cooperative unit involves ownership of shares in the corporation that owns the building, including liability for the corporate debt, and a long-term proprietary lease on a unit in the building.

11. a) In a corporation, directors are elected by shareholders. The directors, in turn, appoint officers, who are responsible for overseeing day-to-day operations.

12. c) An appraiser will not consider a renewal option favorable to the landlord to be a factor in determining the value of a leased fee, since the tenant is unlikely to renew.

13. c) The difference between an unusually high scheduled rent and market rent is known as excess rent.

14. a) A lease where the rental amount increases at specific intervals in the lease term is a step-up lease.

15. b) An appraiser is most likely to use the income approach in estimating the value of a leased fee.

Exercise Answers

#1

1.
   1. c
   2. g
   3. f
   4. i
   5. d
   6. b
   7. h
   8. a
   9. e
2.
   a. Joint tenancy
   b. Tenancy by the entireties
   c. Community property
3. Easement in gross
4. The officers of the corporation
5.
   1. b
   2. c
   3. b
   4. a
   5. b
   6. c
   7. c

#2

1. The income capitalization approach
2. Landlord (lessor)
3. The leasehold
4. The value of the fee simple
5. The terms of the underlying obligation secured by the lien

#3 1. a. Ownership of shares in the cooperative corporation

b. A proprietary leasehold interest in one of the cooperative units

2. Aggressive marketing on the part of the timeshare developer

3. Other condominium units in the same project as the subject

4. The nature of the commonly owned amenities; the quality of common area management; the dues or fees charged to the individual units to cover the cost of maintaining common areas

5. Cooperative units

14 The Appraisal Profession

Overview

Like all professions, appraisal is governed by widely accepted standards of practice and rules of ethical conduct. At one time, the standards were unofficial, established by and enforced through various private professional associations, in the form of membership rules and codes of ethics. In the late 1980s, professional associations worked together to develop the Uniform Standards of Professional Appraisal Practice, which eventually were adopted as official guidelines for measuring the professionalism of an appraiser. In the same period, the practice of appraisal became subject to increased governmental regulation, including government licensing and certification requirements.

After completing this chapter, you should be able to:

- explain how a profession is distinguished from other types of occupations;
- identify the major professional appraisal associations as well as their membership designations;
- describe the licensing and certification requirements of the Financial Institutions Reform, Recovery and Enforcement Act of 1989 (FIRREA);
- define the term "federally related transaction" as it applies to appraisals under Title XI of FIRREA;
- list the types of federally related transactions that require the services of a state-certified or state-licensed appraiser;
- identify the five federal financial institutions regulatory agencies (FFIRAs);
- understand the minimum appraisal standards established by the five federal financial regulatory agencies;
- understand the appraisal requirements of the major secondary market organizations (Fannie Mae and Freddie Mac);
- explain the significance of the Uniform Standards of Professional Appraisal Practice (USPAP); and
- understand the general principles contained in the USPAP Introduction section.

Professional Associations

A profession can be broadly defined as a calling that requires specialized knowledge. But what really distinguishes a profession from other types of occupations is the existence of self-imposed standards of professional conduct and competence. These standards are developed by **professional associations**, and enforced by the associations through their membership requirements.

Membership in a professional association usually has two basic requirements. First, prospective members must demonstrate their competence through some combination of education, experience, and/or testing. A minimum level of continuing education is often a requirement for maintaining or renewing membership. Many professional organizations support the education of their members (and of others in the profession) by offering seminars and courses, and also by publishing textbooks, reports, and professional journals.

The second basic requirement of membership in most professional organizations is that a member must agree to be bound by the association's standards of professional conduct (standards of practice, code of ethics, etc.). The association itself decides whether its members have lived up to those standards, through the process of peer review.

Membership in a professional association is indicated by a professional designation (see Figure 14.1). Some organizations have more than one designation, to indicate different levels or types of professional expertise. From the point of view of the general public, the significance of such designations depends on two things: the standards of competence and conduct that the association requires of its members, and the reliability of the association in enforcing those standards. The more rigorous the standards and the more vigilant the association is in maintaining them, the more the public will trust in the professionalism of the association's members.

Exercise 1

1. List two ways in which professional appraisal associations contribute to the education of their members (and of others in the industry).

   a. ______________________________

   b. ______________________________

2. What are the two basic requirements for membership in most professional appraisal associations?

   a. ______________________________

   b. ______________________________

Fig. 14.1 Professional Appraiser Designations

Accredited Review Appraisers Council (founded 1987)
- AAR (Accredited in Appraisal Review)

American Association of Certified Appraisers (founded 1977)
- CA-R (Certified Appraiser - Residential)
- CA-S (Certified Appraiser - Senior)
- CA-C (Certified Appraiser - Consultant)

American Society of Appraisers (founded 1936)
- ASA (Accredited Senior Appraiser)
- ASR (Accredited Senior Residential Appraiser)

American Society of Farm Managers and Rural Appraisers (founded 1929)
- ARA (Accredited Rural Appraiser)

American Society of Professional Appraisers (founded 1984)
- CRRA (Certified Residential Real Estate Appraiser)
- CCRA (Certified Commercial Real Estate Appraiser)

Appraisal Institute (founded 1990, by the merger of the American Institute of Real Estate Appraisers and the Society of Real Estate Appraisers)
- MAI (Member of the Appraisal Institute)
- SRA (Senior Residential Appraiser)

Appraisal Institute of Canada
- CRA (Canadian Residential Appraiser)
- AACI (Accredited Appraiser, Canadian Institute)

International Association of Assessing Officers (founded 1934)
- AAE (Accredited Assessment Evaluator)
- CAE (Certified Assessment Evaluator)
- RES (Residential Evaluation Specialist)
- CPE (Certified Personalty Evaluator)

International Right of Way Association (founded 1934)
- SR/WA (Senior Member)

National Association of Independent Fee Appraisers (founded 1961)
- IFA (Member)
- IFAS (Senior Member)
- IFAC (Appraiser - Counselor)

National Association of Master Appraisers (founded 1982)
- MRA (Master Residential Appraiser)
- MFLA (Master Farm and Land Appraiser)
- MSA (Master Senior Appraiser)
- CAO (Certified Appraisal Organization)

National Association of Real Estate Appraisers (founded 1966)
- CREA (Certified Real Estate Appraiser)

National Association of Review Appraisers and Mortgage Underwriters (founded 1975)
- CRA (Certified Review Appraiser)
- RRA (Registered Review Appraiser, Canada)

National Residential Appraisers Institute (founded 1977)
- CMDA (Certified Market Data Analyst)
- GSA (Graduate Senior Appraiser)
- SCA (Senior Certified Appraiser)

National Society of Real Estate Appraisers (founded 1956)
- RA (Residential Appraiser)
- CRA (Certified Real Estate Appraiser)
- MREA (Master Real Estate Appraiser)

3. What two factors influence the general public's perception of the significance of membership in a professional appraisal association?

   a. ______________________________

   b. ______________________________

Standards of Professional Competence and Conduct

Prior to the 1980s, appraisers were subject to little, if any, government regulation. Most states had no licensing or certification requirements for appraisers, and the standards of the professional associations applied only to their own members. With the collapse of the savings and loan industry in the 1980s, however, the appraisal profession began to undergo a profound change. Questionable appraisal practices and a lack of industry standards for competence and professional conduct were considered contributing factors in the S&L failures. In response to this crisis, the appraisal industry (and the federal government) began to take the first steps towards industry-wide standards for appraisers.

The USPAP and FIRREA

In 1985, nine professional appraisal associations (the American Institute of Real Estate Appraisers, the American Society of Appraisers, the American Society of Farm Managers and Rural Appraisers, the Appraisal Institute of Canada, the International Association of Assessing Officers, the International Right-of-Way Association, the National Association of Independent Fee Appraisers, the National Society of Real Estate Appraisers, and the Society of Real Estate Appraisers) joined together to form the **Appraisal Foundation,** a nonprofit corporation based in Washington, D.C. The Appraisal Foundation created the **Uniform Standards of Professional Appraisal Practice (USPAP).** The original USPAP took effect in 1987.

In 1989, the USPAP were incorporated into law through the **Financial Institutions Reform, Recovery and Enforcement Act of 1989 (FIRREA),** commonly known as "the S&L bail-out bill." The primary effects of this bill were to close down insolvent savings institutions and reorganize the federal agencies that regulated the savings and loan industry, but it also extended federal oversight to the appraisal industry for the first time. In addition to enacting the USPAP into law, this bill also required states to certify and license appraisers on the basis of recognized standards of competence.

At about the same time that FIRREA took effect, the Appraisal Foundation set up two new boards: the **Appraisal Standards Board (ASB)** and the **Appraiser Qualifications Board (AQB).** The Appraisal Standards Board is charged with promoting the acceptance of the USPAP, and also with updating the standards on an ongoing basis to reflect new developments in appraisal practice. The Appraiser Qualifications Board establishes educational, experience, and examination requirements for state certification of appraisers.

Real Estate Appraisal Reform Amendments

From the standpoint of the appraisal industry, the most significant part of FIRREA is **Title XI**, also known as the **Real Estate Appraisal Reform Amendments**. The purpose of Title XI is to "provide that federal financial and public policy interests in real estate related transactions will be protected by requiring that real estate appraisals utilized in connection with federally related transactions are performed in writing in accordance with uniform standards by individuals whose competency has been demonstrated and whose professional conduct will be subject to effective supervision." In other words, Title XI is designed to promote uniform standards for appraisal practice, set up appraiser qualifications, and establish regulatory power over the appraisal industry.

Every appraisal that falls within the scope of Title XI must satisfy these three basic requirements:

1. it must be performed by a state-certified or state-licensed appraiser;
2. it must be performed in accordance with specified appraisal standards; and
3. it must be a written appraisal.

Appraiser Licensing and Certification. The first basic requirement of Title XI is that all covered appraisals must be performed by state-certified or state-licensed appraisers. To implement this requirement, Title XI authorizes individual states to establish appraiser certification and licensing agencies. Title XI also provides for a national registry of certified and licensed appraisers.

The distinction between state certification and state licensing involves the nature of the qualifying standards imposed by the appraiser certification and licensing agencies. To be state-certified, an appraiser must satisfy requirements that measure up to the minimum qualifications established by the Appraiser Qualifications Board (AQB) of the Appraisal Foundation, and must also pass an examination that is equivalent to the Uniform State Certification Examination approved by the AQB. Individual states may impose stricter requirements for state certification, as long as the minimum AQB standards are met.

In contrast, the qualifications for state-licensed appraisers are established by the individual states. The AQB has issued recommended qualification standards for state licensing, but these are not strictly mandatory. Although no minimum qualification standards exist

Fig. 14.2 Title XI Real Estate Appraisal Reform Amendments

1. Appraiser licensing/certification
2. Uniform standards of practice
3. Uniform qualification standards
4. Regulation of appraisers

for state licensing, the standards established by a state must be consistent with the purpose of Title XI. A federal governmental body known as the Appraisal Subcommittee of the Federal Financial Institutions Examinations Council (FFIEC) has the authority to decide whether a state's licensing criteria are adequate or not.

AQB guidelines call for states to offer four real property appraiser classifications:

- certified general appraiser,
- certified residential appraiser,
- licensed appraiser, and
- trainee appraiser.

A certified general appraiser is qualified to appraise all types of properties. A certified residential appraiser is qualified to appraise only one- to four-unit residential properties.

A licensed appraiser may perform appraisals involving either residential or non-residential property, but only in transactions where a state-certified appraiser is not required by law. (A state-certified appraiser is required in complex transactions and in transactions where the property value exceeds certain limits. We'll discuss these rules shortly.)

A trainee appraiser works under the supervision of a certified or licensed appraiser, and is allowed to perform whatever types of appraisals the supervising appraiser is authorized to perform. Throughout the training period, the supervising appraiser must review and accept responsibility for all appraisal reports prepared by the trainee. In addition, until the trainee reaches a certain level of competence, the supervising appraiser must personally inspect the appraised properties with the trainee.

The AQB publishes educational guidelines for each classification, including outlines of required course content. For all classifications, there are prerequisite course requirements (courses that must be taken before certification, licensing, or authorization as a trainee) and also continuing education requirements.

Since 2008, college-level education has been required for certified appraisers. A certified general appraiser must have at least a bachelor's degree, or in lieu of a degree, a minimum of 30 college semester hours in specified courses. A certified residential appraiser must have at least an associate degree, or in lieu of a degree, 21 college semester hours in specified courses.

Appraisal Standards. The second basic requirement of Title XI is that appraisals must be performed in accordance with specified standards of appraisal practice. Title XI specifically recognizes the Uniform Standards of Professional Appraisal Practice (USPAP) as the minimum standards for appraisals covered by FIRREA. It also directs the federal financial institutions regulatory agencies (FFIRAs) to establish minimum standards for appraisals that fall under their jurisdiction. FFIRA appraisal standards include the USPAP, plus additional standards issued by each agency. (FFIRA appraisal standards are described in more detail below.)

Written Appraisals. The third requirement of Title XI is that all appraisals under FIRREA must be written appraisals. The term "written appraisal" is defined to mean an appraisal "that is independently and impartially prepared by a licensed or certified appraiser, setting forth an opinion of defined value of an adequately described property, as of a specific date, supported by presentation and analysis of relevant market information."

Exercise 2

1. What crisis led to adoption of uniform standards for appraisers?

   ____

2. What organization was formed in 1987 to promote the USPAP and to help ensure that appraisers are qualified to offer their services?

   ____

   Within this organization, who has responsibility for promoting and maintaining the USPAP?

   ____

   And within the organization, who is responsible for developing and promoting standards of competence for appraiser certification and licensing?

   ____

3. What federal law was passed in 1989 that requires state licensing and certification of appraisers?

   ____

4. List another name for Title XI of FIRREA:

   ____

5. What federal agency is responsible for ensuring that state appraisal licensure requirements are adequate?

____

6. Who establishes the minimum qualifying standards for state-certification of appraisers under Title XI?

____

7. Name the type of state certification that qualifies an appraiser to perform appraisals of all types of properties.

____

8. List the three basic requirements for appraisals that fall within the scope of Title XI:

   a. ____

   b. ____

   c. ____

Appraisals Covered by FIRREA

Whether or not an appraisal is subject to the requirements of Title XI depends on whether it is made in connection with a federally related transaction. A federally related transaction is defined as:

> *...any real estate-related financial transaction which (a) a federal financial institutions regulatory agency engages in, contracts for, or regulates; and (b) requires the services of an appraiser.*

For purposes of this definition, real estate related financial transactions include any transaction involving:

> *...(a) the sale, lease, purchase, investment in or exchange of real property, including interests in real property, or the financing thereof; (b) the refinancing of real property or interests in real property; and (c) the use of real property or interests in property as security for a loan or investment, including mortgage-backed securities.*

The concept of a "federally related transaction" is significant because it defines the scope of the application of Title XI. The appraisal regulations of Title XI apply to all federally related transactions. That means they apply to most appraisals performed for financial institutions in connection with the transfer or financing of real estate.

De Minimis Value. One of the characteristics of a federally related transaction is that it "requires the services of an appraiser." According to regulations issued by the federal financial institutions regulatory agencies, transactions with a value that is less than a certain minimum amount (referred to as the **de minimis value**) do not require the services of an appraiser. As a result, they are not federally related transactions, and Title XI doesn't apply to them. The de minimis value currently set by each FFIRA is $250,000.

When a Certified Appraiser is Required

As we said, one of Title XI's requirements is that the appraisal for a federally related transaction must be performed by either a state-licensed or a state-certified appraiser. Relatively simple appraisals may be performed by a licensed appraiser, but more complex appraisals require a certified appraiser.

Specifically, Title XI requires the use of state-certified appraisers in federally related transactions with a value of $1 million or more. However, there's an exception for transactions involving residential property with up to four dwelling units; appraisals in those transactions can be performed by state-licensed appraisers, unless either the value or the complexity is too great. To implement these rules, each FFIRA has issued additional regulations specifying the types of transactions that require a state-certified appraiser. These regulations focus on three factors:

1. the value of the transaction;
2. whether or not the subject property is residential (with up to four units); and
3. whether or not the transaction is "complex"—that is, the property, the form of ownership, or the market conditions are unusual.

Current FFIRA regulations require state-certified appraisers in the following types of federally related transactions:

- all transactions with a value of $1 million or more;
- all nonresidential transactions with a value of $250,000 or more; and
- all complex residential transactions with a value of $250,000 or more.

The appraisals for all other federally related transactions may be performed by a state-licensed appraiser.

Legislation passed by Congress in 2008 to address the nationwide mortgage foreclosure crisis included a provision concerning the appraisals used for FHA loans. Now those must be performed by appraisers who have been educated in FHA appraisal requirements and certified either by the state where the property is located or by a generally recognized professional appraisal organization.

Exercise 3

1. The two requirements for a transaction to be considered federally related are:

   a. ______________________________

   b. ______________________________

2. What is the de minimis transaction amount below which a transaction will not be considered federally related?

   ____

3. List three types of federally related transactions that require a state-certified appraiser:

   a. ______________________________

   b. ______________________________

   c. ______________________________

FFIRA Appraisal Regulations

Federal Financial Institutions Regulatory Agencies

In order to understand the effect of FIRREA on the appraisal industry, it is important to know what is meant by the term "federal financial institutions regulatory agencies" (FFIRAs). For the purposes of FIRREA, the FFIRAs are five government agencies that have various regulatory powers over financial institutions such as banks, savings and loans, and credit unions. These five agencies are:

- the Board of Governors of the Federal Reserve System, - Fed. monetary policy
- the Federal Deposit Insurance Corporation, - Deposits in Banks
- the Office of the Comptroller of the Currency, - Commercial Banks
- the Office of Thrift Supervision, and - Savings + Loans
- the National Credit Union Administration. - Credit Unions

Federal Reserve System. The Federal Reserve System, commonly referred to as "the Fed," is the central banking system of the United States. It is an independent agency that is responsible for national monetary policy. It also has regulatory authority over commercial banks that are members of the Federal Reserve System. The Fed is controlled by a seven-member Board of Governors.

Federal Deposit Insurance Corporation. The FDIC manages the system of national deposit insurance for participating banks and savings institutions. It also has conservator and receiver powers with respect to insolvent commercial banks, and with respect to thrifts that became insolvent after August 9, 1992. The FDIC is an independent agency.

Office of the Comptroller of the Currency. The Office of the Comptroller of the Currency (OCC) is a division of the Treasury Department. It regulates federally chartered commercial banks.

Office of Thrift Supervision. The OTS was created by FIRREA to take over the responsibilities of the disbanded Federal Home Loan Bank Board, with respect to regulating savings and loan institutions. Like the OCC, it is part of the Treasury Department.

National Credit Union Administration. This independent agency, commonly known as NCUA, has regulatory authority over nationally chartered credit unions.

FFIRA Appraisal Standards

Title XI of FIRREA requires the five FFIRAs to establish standards for appraisals in connection with federally related transactions. These agencies have issued regulations adopting the following minimum standards, which apply to all appraisals in connection with federally related transactions.

The regulations state that in federally related transactions, all appraisals shall, at a minimum:

(a) conform to generally accepted appraisal standards as evidenced by the Uniform Standards of Professional Appraisal Practice (USPAP) promulgated by the Appraisal Standards Board of the Appraisal Foundation unless principles of safe and sound banking require compliance with stricter standards;
(b) be written and contain sufficient information and analysis to support the institution's decision to engage in the transaction;
(c) analyze and report appropriate deductions and discounts for proposed construction or renovation, partially leased buildings, non-market lease terms, and tract developments with unsold units;
(d) be based upon the definition of market value set forth in the USPAP; and
(e) be performed by state-licensed or state-certified appraisers in accordance with USPAP requirements.

The FFIRAs have also issued regulations concerning the independence of appraisers. A **staff appraiser**—such as an appraiser employed by a lender—must work independently from the institution's lending, investment, and collection functions. A staff appraiser cannot have a financial interest in the property being appraised. And an **independent fee appraiser**—in other words, a self-employed appraiser who takes appraisal clients—should be hired directly by the financial institution using the appraisal. A lender may use an appraisal prepared by an appraiser engaged by another financial institution only if the appraiser has no financial interest in the property and the appraisal otherwise meets all FFIRA standards.

Secondary Market Appraisal Guidelines

Primary lenders such as banks and savings institutions operate in local markets. Their loan officers are familiar with the local trends that may affect the value of the real estate that is the collateral for their loans. Investors in the secondary market, however, do not have this advantage. They may be purchasing securities that are backed by mortgages from all over the country.

In essence, the secondary market investors must rely on the primary market lenders to properly qualify their loans. Loan qualifying means investigating the creditworthiness of borrowers to verify that the real estate collateral holds sufficient value to ensure recovery of the loan funds in the event of borrower default. Because of this reliance, the secondary market organizations that purchase and package loans demand that those loans meet specific criteria.

Loans meeting all of the standards of the secondary market are called **conforming loans** and are eligible to be sold to organizations such as the Federal National Mortgage Association (Fannie Mae) and the Federal Home Loan Mortgage Corporation (Freddie Mac). These secondary market organizations will not purchase **nonconforming loans**—loans that do not meet their standards. Secondary market loan standards include specific requirements for appraisals performed in connection with loans, and most primary lenders adhere to these standards.

The following sections describe the appraisal rules of Fannie Mae and Freddie Mac, the two most important secondary market organizations with respect to residential real estate. These rules apply to all appraisals of one- to four-unit residential properties in connection with loans that will be sold to Fannie Mae or Freddie Mac.

Appraiser Qualifications

Fannie Mae and Freddie Mac require that all appraisals be performed by appraisers who are state-licensed or state-certified in accordance with the procedures established in Title XI of FIRREA. To ensure the objectivity of an appraisal, the appraiser must be selected and hired directly by the lender, not by one of the parties to the real estate transaction. The lender is required to verify that the appraiser has the knowledge and experience required for the type of property being appraised, and that the appraiser is actively engaged in appraisal work on a regular basis.

Unacceptable Appraisal Practices

The following practices are prohibited by Fannie Mae and Freddie Mac's rules:

- use of inaccurate data regarding the subject property, the neighborhood, or a comparable property;
- failure to report and comment on any factor that may have a negative value influence on the subject property;
- use of a comparable property (in the sales comparison approach) that has not been personally reviewed by the appraiser by, at a minimum, driving by and reviewing the exterior;
- use of comparables that are not as similar as possible to the subject property, or use of inappropriate comparables;
- use of comparable sales data that are provided by a party to the transaction (such as the buyer, seller, or real estate broker) without independent verification of the data;
- making sales comparison adjustments that do not reflect market reactions, or failing to make adjustments that do reflect market reactions;
- consideration of discriminatory factors (race, color, sex, religion, handicap, national origin, or family status) in the valuation analysis; or
- developing a conclusion that is not supported by market data.

Reporting Requirements

Report Forms. Fannie Mae and Freddie Mac require appraisals to be made on approved forms. The forms for one- to four-unit residential properties include the Uniform Residential Appraisal Report Form, the Small Residential Income Property Appraisal Report, and the Individual Condominium Unit Appraisal Report. (Form reports are discussed in more detail in Chapter 12.)

Age of Appraisal Report. Appraisals must be dated within one year prior to the date of the loan made by the primary lender. In addition, if the appraisal is dated more than four months prior to the loan date, the appraiser must certify that the property has not declined in value since the date of the report. If the property has in fact declined in value during that period, the appraiser must perform a new appraisal.

Completion Certificates. When an appraisal has been made subject to the completion of repairs or improvements to the subject property, the appraiser must issue a certificate of completion once the repairs or improvements have been completed. This certificate verifies that the conditions stated in the original appraisal have been satisfied. If necessary (as, for example, in the case of new construction that was appraised on the basis of plans and specifications), new photographs of the completed improvements must accompany the certification.

In general, property must be appraised subject to completion of repairs or improvements if conditions exist that affect the livability of the property. Property with structural defects that do not affect livability may be appraised on an "as is" basis, in which case a completion certificate is not necessary.

Selection of Comparable Properties. A valuation based on the sales comparison approach must be included in the appraisal report. The sales comparison analysis must be based on at least three completed (closed or settled) comparable sales, although the appraiser may use additional comparable sales (including prior sales of the subject property), contracts, or listings if appropriate to support the sales comparison analysis. Comparable sales should be no older than one year prior to the appraisal date, and the appraiser must comment on the reasons for using any comparables that are older than six months.

In the case of properties in established neighborhoods or projects, the best comparables are those in the same neighborhood or project as the subject. However, in the case of new developments (new subdivisions, condominiums, or PUD projects), at least one comparable should be outside the control of the developer/builder. This could be a comparable from a similar neighborhood or project outside the new development, or a resale within the development that did not involve the developer/builder.

Financing Data. The appraiser must also include financial data relating to the transaction, including any information regarding sales concessions that might affect the sales price of the property. Ordinarily, the appraiser may simply include a copy of the sales contract. Other items that may need to be disclosed include loan fees or charges, discounts to the sales price, interest rate buydowns or other forms of below-market-rate financing, credits or refunds of borrower expenses, or personal property included in the sale.

Exercise 4

1. List the five federal financial institutions regulatory agencies:

   a. ______________________________

   b. ______________________________

   c. ______________________________

   d. ______________________________

   e. ______________________________

2. Which of the following would be considered unacceptable appraisal practices under Fannie Mae/Freddie Mac rules?

   a. Failure to report and comment on any factor that may have a negative value influence on the subject property

   b. Use of comparables that are not as similar as possible to the subject property, or use of inappropriate comparables

   c. Making sales comparison adjustments that do not reflect market reactions, or failing to make adjustments that do reflect market reactions

3. Fannie Mae/Freddie Mac appraisals must be dated within one year prior to:

   ____

4. What is the minimum number of comparable sales for the sales comparison approach in a Fannie Mae/Freddie Mac appraisal?

   ____

   The comparable sales must be no older than:

   ______________________________ prior to the appraisal date.

The Uniform Standards of Professional Appraisal Practice

The Uniform Standards of Professional Appraisal Practice represent a major step toward self-regulation in the appraisal industry. These standards have been widely adopted by professional appraisal associations, and by government regulatory agencies as well.

The USPAP consist of:

- an introductory section on general principles,
- ten Standards, with associated Standards Rules, and
- clarifying Statements on Appraisal Standards.

In addition, the Appraisal Standards Board (ASB) has issued a number of **Advisory Opinions**, which give advice from the ASB on the application of the standards to specific appraisal situations.

Fig. 14.3 USPAP Standards

Standard 1 – Real Property Appraisal, Development
Standard 2 – Real Property Appraisal, Reporting
Standard 3 – Appraisal Review, Development and Reporting
Standard 4 – Real Property Appraisal Consulting, Development
Standard 5 – Real Property Appraisal Consulting, Reporting
Standard 6 – Mass Appraisal, Development and Reporting
Standard 7 – Personal Property Appraisal, Development
Standard 8 – Personal Property Appraisal, Reporting
Standard 9 – Business Appraisal, Development
Standard 10 – Business Appraisal, Reporting

General Principles. The first section of the USPAP consists of a preamble, four general provisions (covering ethics, competency, scope of work, and jurisdictional exception), and a list of definitions. This introductory section is discussed in greater detail in the final section of this chapter.

Standards and Standards Rules. There are ten Standards in the USPAP, as shown in Figure 14.3. Each Standard consists of a generalized statement (the standard itself) followed by more detailed and specific Standards Rules. The Standards that are relevant to residential real estate appraisal (Standards 1 and 2), along with their Standards Rules, are discussed in the chapters of this text that cover the corresponding topics.

Statements on Appraisal Standards. In addition to modifying existing Standards Rules, the ASB has the authority (under the bylaws of the Appraisal Foundation) to issue formal **Statements on Appraisal Standards**, which clarify, interpret, explain, or elaborate on the Standards. These Statements have the same binding force as the other provisions of the USPAP. Statements relevant to residential appraisal include:

Statement 3 – Retrospective Value Opinions
Statement 4 – Prospective Value Opinions
Statement 6 – Reasonable Exposure Time in Real Property and Personal Property Market Value Opinions

Advisory Opinions. Advisory Opinions illustrate the application of the USPAP in particular situations. However, advisory opinions do not have the binding effect of the USPAP. They neither establish new standards nor interpret existing ones; they merely indicate the advice and opinion of the Appraisal Standards Board. The following Advisory Opinions are relevant to residential appraisals:

Advisory Opinion O-1 – Sales History
Advisory Opinion O-2 – Inspection of Subject Property Real Estate
Advisory Opinion O-4 – Standards Rule 1-5(b)

Modifications of USPAP. The ASB has the authority to amend or modify the USPAP, as well as to issue Statements on Appraisal Standards and Advisory Opinions. A revised edition of the USPAP is issued every two years. Appraisers should always be aware of the latest standards, in order to ensure that their actions conform to the requirements of the USPAP.

Introductory Provisions of the USPAP

The introductory provisions of the USPAP are general rules that apply to all types of appraisals. There are six introductory provisions:

1. Definitions,
2. Preamble,
3. Ethics Rule,
4. Competency Rule,
5. Scope of Work Rule, and
6. Jurisdictional Exception Rule.

Definitions

The first provision of the introductory section of the USPAP clarifies the meaning of specific terms as they are used in the standards. (Many of these definitions are cited throughout this book.)

Preamble

The Preamble provides an overview of the USPAP. The Preamble states the underlying rationale for the standards and sets forth certain basic guidelines.

The purpose of the Uniform Standards of Professional Appraisal Practice is to promote and maintain a high level of public trust in appraisal practice by establishing requirements for appraisers.

It is essential that appraisers develop and communicate their analyses, opinions, and conclusions to intended users of their services in a manner that is meaningful and not misleading.

The Preamble also explains how the USPAP documentation is organized. Standards 1 and 2 address the development and communication of a real property appraisal, while

Standard 3 establishes guidelines for reviewing an appraisal and reporting that review. Standards 4 and 5 cover the development and communication of appraisal consulting assignments. Standard 6 addresses developing and reporting mass appraisals. Standards 7 and 8 contain requirements for personal property appraisals, and Standards 9 and 10 contain requirements for business appraisals.

Ethics Rule

The first substantive provision of the USPAP is the Ethics Rule, which requires an appraiser to observe the highest standards of professional ethics in regard to conduct, management, confidentiality, and record keeping.

The Conduct section of the Ethics Rule requires the appraiser to perform assignments ethically and competently, in accordance with the USPAP. The appraiser must perform with impartiality, objectivity, and independence, and without accommodation of personal interests. An appraiser may not act as an advocate for any party or issue, accept an assignment predicated on reporting a predetermined opinion or conclusion, or communicate assignment results in a misleading or fraudulent manner. In addition, an appraiser may not use or rely on unsupported conclusions relating to characteristics such as race, color, religion, national origin, gender, marital status, familial status, age, receipt of public assistance income, or handicap.

The Management section concerns the ethics of appraisal business practices, particularly compensation arrangements and advertising. Practices specifically identified as unethical include compensation arrangements contingent on reporting a predetermined result or favorable direction in value, undisclosed fees or procurement payments, and false or misleading advertising.

The Confidentiality section requires the appraiser to protect the confidentiality of information obtained from a client or results produced for a client. Disclosure of such information is limited to the client, to persons authorized by the client or by law, and to members of an authorized peer review committee.

The final section of the Ethics Rule is the Record Keeping section. This part sets forth the record keeping requirements for all appraisals, including the types of records that must be kept and how long they must be maintained. It specifies the information and documentation that must be included in the appraiser's workfile, and requires the workfile to be retained for at least five years after preparation, or two years after the final disposition in any judicial proceeding in which the appraiser testified, whichever period expires later.

Competency Rule

The Competency Rule prohibits appraisers from accepting appraisal assignments for which they are not qualified by both knowledge and experience. An exception is allowed only if the appraiser informs the client in advance of the lack of appropriate qualifications, takes the necessary steps to ensure that the appraisal is performed competently, and fully describes these facts in the appraisal report.

Prior to accepting an assignment or entering into an agreement to perform any assignment, an appraiser must properly identify the problem to be addressed and have the knowledge and experience to complete the assignment competently; or alternatively, must:

1. *disclose the lack of knowledge and/or experience to the client before accepting the assignment;*
2. *take all steps necessary or appropriate to complete the assignment competently; and*
3. *describe the lack of knowledge and/or experience and the steps taken to complete the assignment competently in the report.*

Scope of Work Rule

As we discussed in Chapter 3, the scope of work involved in an appraisal is the type and extent of research and analyses that the appraiser performs to fulfill the assignment. Among other things, it includes the extent to which the property is inspected. The Scope of Work Rule requires the appraiser to perform the scope of work necessary to produce credible results for the assignment.

For each appraisal, appraisal review, and appraisal consulting assignment, an appraiser must:

1. *identify the problem to be solved;*
2. *determine and perform the scope of work necessary to develop credible assignment results; and*
3. *disclose the scope of work in the report.*

An appraiser must properly identify the problem to be solved in order to determine the appropriate scope of work. The appraiser must be prepared to demonstrate that the scope of work is sufficient to produce credible assignment results.

The official comments on this rule state that appraisers have "broad flexibility and significant responsibility" in determining the appropriate scope of work for an assignment. The appraiser may consult with the client in determining the appropriate scope of work, but responsibility for the determination is the appraiser's alone. To be credible, the assignment results must be supported by the relevant evidence and logic, in the context of the intended use of the appraisal.

The Scope of Work Rule has three subsections: Problem Identification, Scope of Work Acceptability, and Disclosure Obligations.

The Problem Identification section states that the appraiser must gather and analyze information about the assignment elements that are necessary to properly identify the appraisal problem to be solved. These elements include the client and any other intended users, the intended use of the appraisal, the type and definition of value, the effective date of the appraisal, the subject of the assignment and its relevant characteristics, and the assignment conditions (assumptions, extraordinary assumptions, hypothetical conditions, jurisdictional exceptions, and other conditions that affect the scope of work). This information serves as the basis for deciding what research and analysis is needed.

The Acceptability section reiterates that the scope of work must include the research and analyses that are necessary to develop credible assignment results. Assignment conditions must not limit the scope of work to such a degree that the results aren't credible in the context of the intended use. And neither the intended use nor the client's objectives must be allowed to lead to biased results.

To be acceptable, the scope of work must meet the expectations of regularly intended users for similar assignments, and it must match what the appraiser's peers would do in performing a similar assignment. If the appraiser decides to exclude any investigation, information, method, or technique that would appear relevant to the client, to another intended user, or to the appraiser's peers, the appraiser must be prepared to support that decision.

The Disclosure section of the Scope of Work Rule states that the appraisal report must contain sufficient information to allow intended users to understand the scope of work performed. This includes disclosure of research and analyses performed, and might also include disclosure of research and analyses not performed.

Jurisdictional Exception Rule

The purpose of the Jurisdictional Exception Rule is to limit the potential adverse effects of local laws on the applicability of the USPAP in the local jurisdiction. If a local law makes part of the USPAP unenforceable, the remaining parts are not affected.

> *If any part of [these standards] is contrary to the law or public policy of any jurisdiction, only that part shall be void and of no force or effect in that jurisdiction.*

Standards and Standards Rules

As we discussed earlier, there are ten Standards in the USPAP (see Figure 14.3). Standards 1 and 2 are most relevant to residential appraisal. Standard 3 is also relevant, to the extent that it focuses on the process of reviewing another appraiser's work.

Coursework specifically devoted to the Uniform Standards of Professional Appraisal Practice is generally required as part of the curriculum for appraiser licensing or certification. Although detailed knowledge of the USPAP is not necessary for a real estate agent, a person planning to become a full-time appraiser will need to study the USPAP closely and thoroughly.

Exercise 5

1. What are the four sections of the Ethics Rule of the USPAP?

   a. ______________________________

   b. ______________________________

   c. ______________________________

   d. ______________________________

2. The provision of the USPAP that requires an appraiser to evaluate his or her knowledge and experience prior to accepting an appraisal assignment is called the:

   ____

3. Indicate whether each of the following statements regarding the USPAP is true or false.

   a. A Statement on Appraisal Standards, issued by the Appraisal Standards Board, does not have the same force and effect as a Standards Rule. **T/F**

   b. If a local law makes part of the USPAP unenforceable, then the USPAP doesn't apply to the appraisal of property in that jurisdiction. **T/F**

   c. If confidential information is revealed to a peer review committee, it is no longer subject to the terms of the Ethics Rule. **T/F**

   d. It is essential that a professional appraiser communicate his or her opinions in a manner that will not be misleading in the marketplace. **T/F**

Key Terms

Abstract of title—A legal document listing the history and condition of title to a parcel of real estate.

Appraisal—The act or process of developing an opinion of value; an opinion of value (USPAP definition). A form of appraisal practice.

Appraisal consulting—The act or process of developing an analysis, recommendation or opinion to solve a problem, where an opinion of value is a component of the analysis leading to the assignment results (USPAP definition). A form of appraisal practice.

Appraisal Foundation—A nonprofit educational corporation founded by the appraisal industry to promote uniform standards of appraisal practice and appraiser qualification. It is the parent organization of the Appraisal Standards Board and the Appraiser Qualifications Board.

Appraisal practice—Valuation services performed by an individual acting as an appraiser, including but not limited to appraisal, appraisal review, or appraisal consulting (USPAP definition).

Appraisal Standards Board—A division of the Appraisal Foundation, responsible for maintaining the Uniform Standards of Professional Appraisal Practice.

Appraisal Subcommittee—A division of the Federal Financial Institutions Examinations Council (FFIEC), created by FIRREA. It is responsible for monitoring state licensing and certification programs, FFIRA appraisal regulations, and the Appraisal Foundation.

Appraiser—A person qualified by education and experience to perform appraisals.

Appraiser Qualifications Board—A division of the Appraisal Foundation, responsible for maintaining uniform standards for appraiser competence, including the Uniform State Certification Examination.

Certified appraiser—An appraiser who has satisfied the requirements of a state with respect to certification.

Client—The party or parties who engage an appraiser (by employment or contract) in a specific assignment (USPAP definition).

Closed sale—A sale in which title has been transferred from the seller to the buyer.

Comparable—A property that has been sold in the same market that currently includes the subject property, and that appeals to the same sorts of buyers. Comparables are used in many different appraisal techniques.

Effective date of appraisal—The date as of which value is estimated, distinguished from the date the appraisal report is prepared. Value estimates are always made as of a specific date, because value can change over time.

Federal Deposit Insurance Corporation—An independent government agency that manages the system of national deposit insurance for participating banks and savings institutions. It is one of the five federal financial institutions regulatory agencies.

Federal Financial Institutions Regulatory Agency—One of five federal government agencies that regulate the various types of financial institutions, including the Board of Governors of the Federal Reserve System, the Federal Deposit Insurance Corporation, the Office of the Comptroller of the Currency, the Office of Thrift Supervision, and the National Credit Union Administration. Transactions that are regulated by a FFIRA are subject to the appraisal requirements of Title XI of FIRREA.

Federal Home Loan Mortgage Corporation—One of the major intermediary organizations in the secondary market for real estate loans. Commonly known as Freddie Mac.

Federally related transaction—A real estate related financial transaction that involves a FFIRA and that requires the services of an appraiser. Federally related transactions are subject to the requirements of Title XI of FIRREA.

Federal National Mortgage Association—One of the major intermediary organizations in the secondary market for real estate loans. Commonly known as Fannie Mae.

Federal Reserve System—The central banking system of the United States. The Board of Governors of the Federal Reserve System is one of the five federal financial institutions regulatory agencies.

Fee appraiser—An appraiser who is self-employed, or who works for a company whose primary business is to provide appraisal services to others.

Financial Institutions Reform, Recovery and Enforcement Act of 1989—An act of Congress passed in response to the savings and loan crisis of the 1980s. FIRREA reorganized the system of federal regulation of financial institutions. Its Title XI (the Real Estate Appraisal Reform Amendments) established government requirements for uniform standards of appraisal practice and appraiser qualification, as well as appraiser licensing and certification.

Form report—A written appraisal report prepared on a standardized form, usually with addenda.

Licensed appraiser—An appraiser who has met the requirements for licensing established by the state where the appraiser works.

National Credit Union Administration—An independent government agency that regulates nationally chartered credit unions. It is one of the five federal financial institutions regulatory agencies.

Office of the Comptroller of the Currency—A division of the Treasury Department, responsible for regulating federally chartered commercial banks. It is one of the five federal financial institutions regulatory agencies.

Office of Thrift Supervision—A division of the Treasury Department, responsible for regulating savings institutions. It is one of the five federal financial institutions regulatory agencies.

Real estate—An identified parcel or tract of land, including improvements, if any (USPAP definition).

Real property—The interests, benefits, and rights inherent in the ownership of real estate (USPAP definition).

Refinance—A new loan or loans secured by property that is already owned by the borrower, as compared to a loan used to purchase property.

Report—Any communication, written or oral, of an appraisal, appraisal review, or appraisal consulting service that is transmitted to the client upon completion of an assignment (USPAP definition). The means by which an appraiser's value conclusions are communicated to the client.

Residential property—Property intended to be used for dwellings.

Staff appraiser—An appraiser employed by a business, government agency, or other organization, to perform appraisal services that relate to the employer's operations.

Title XI—Part of FIRREA known as the Real Estate Appraisal Reform Amendments. Title XI established federal requirements for appraiser licensing and certification, and for uniform standards of appraisal practice. These requirements apply to all appraisals performed in connection with federally related transactions.

Uniform Residential Appraisal Report—A standard form report for use in appraisals of single-family residences. The URAR is approved for use in appraisals that are governed by FNMA, FHLMC, HUD, and the VA.

Uniform Standards of Professional Appraisal Practice—Appraisal standards issued by the Appraisal Standards Board of the Appraisal Foundation, and adopted as minimum standards by Title XI of FIRREA.

Summary

I. Professional appraisal associations set standards for conduct and competence through their membership requirements.

A. Many professional associations contribute to the level of competence in the appraisal industry by sponsoring educational programs and publications.

B. Standards of conduct are enforced through a process of peer review.

C. The significance of membership in a professional association is related to the quality of the standards that the association maintains for its members.

II. The development of uniform standards of professional practice for appraisers began in the 1980s, when the crisis in the savings and loan industry occurred.

A. In 1987, major appraisal associations created the first Uniform Standards of Professional Appraisal Practice (USPAP) and established the non-profit Appraisal Foundation to oversee the standards.

1. The USPAP represented the first attempt to create industry-wide standards of practice for appraisers.

2. The Appraisal Foundation includes the Appraisal Standards Board, which is responsible for the ongoing development of uniform standards of practice, and the Appraiser Qualifications Board (AQB), which develops and promotes standards of professional training and competency.

B. The USPAP was incorporated into law by the Financial Institutions Reform, Recovery and Enforcement Act of 1989 (FIRREA), which also requires licensing and certification of appraisers.

1. Licensing or certification is required for appraisals made in connection with federally related transactions.

2. Certification requires a higher level of competence than licensing. State-licensed appraisers may only perform appraisals for transactions where a state-certified appraiser is not required by law.

3. AQB guidelines call for four appraiser classifications: certified general, certified residential, licensed, and trainee. A trainee appraiser is supervised by a licensed or certified appraiser.

III. Title XI of FIRREA (the Real Estate Appraisal Reform Amendments).

A. Title XI governs appraisals made in federally related transactions.

1. A federally related transaction is any real estate related financial transaction (sale, loan, refinance, etc.) that involves or is regulated by a federal financial institutions regulatory agency (FFIRA), and that requires the services of an appraiser.

2. A transaction with a value of less than $250,000 is not considered a federally related transaction.

B. Appraisals covered by Title XI must be performed by state-certified or state-licensed appraisers.

1. State-certified appraisers must meet the standards of the Appraiser Qualifications Board of the Appraisal Institute.

2. State-licensed appraisers must meet the standards set by the individual state in which they are licensed.

3. State-certified appraisers are required for all transactions with a value of $1 million or more, for all nonresidential transactions with a value of $250,000 or more, and for residential transactions with a value of $250,000 or more where the property to be appraised, the form of ownership, or the market conditions are not typical.

a. All other appraisals for federally related transactions may be performed by either a state-certified or a state-licensed appraiser.

C. Appraisals covered by Title XI must be performed in accordance with FFIRA-specified appraisal standards, and must be in writing.

1. The five FFIRAs are: the Board of Governors of the Federal Reserve System (the Fed); the Federal Deposit Insurance Corporation (FDIC); the Office of the Comptroller of the Currency (OCC); the Office of Thrift Supervision (OTS); and the National Credit Union Administration (NCUA).

2. The FFIRAs have issued regulations listing five standards for appraisals.

IV. In order to be able to sell their loans in the secondary market, most lenders require their appraisals to conform to secondary market (Fannie Mae/Freddie Mac) standards.

A. Fannie Mae/Freddie Mac appraisals must be performed by state-licensed or state-certified appraisers.

1. The appraiser must be selected directly by the lender.

2. Lenders must verify appraiser qualifications.

B. Certain appraisal practices are not acceptable to Fannie Mae/Freddie Mac.

1. Appraisers must use accurate data and report any negative influences on value.

2. Comparables must be personally reviewed by the appraiser. They should be as similar to the subject as possible, and comparable data must be validated by someone other than a party to the transaction.

3. Sales comparison adjustments must reflect market reactions, and conclusions must be supported by market data.

4. The appraisal may not consider discriminatory factors.

C. Fannie Mae/Freddie Mac appraisals must be reported on approved forms.

1. Appraisals must be dated within one year prior to the loan date. Appraisals dated more than four months prior to the loan date require the appraiser's certification that the property has not declined in value.

2. Completion certificates are required when an appraisal is made subject to completion of repairs or improvements.

3. Use of the sales comparison approach, based on at least three completed sales, is mandatory. Comparable sales should be no older than one year and preferably no older than six months.

V. The Uniform Standards of Professional Appraisal Practice establish the guidelines that regulate the appraisal industry.

A. The USPAP consist of several general provisions, ten Standards with associated Standards Rules, a number of Statements on Appraisal Standards, and non-binding Advisory Opinions issued by the Appraisal Standards Board.

1. The Ethics Rule of the USPAP governs conduct, management, confidentiality, and record keeping.

   a. Professional appraisal services must be performed in a manner that is not unlawful, fraudulent, or misleading.

   b. When the appraiser's role can reasonably be viewed as that of an impartial third party, the appraiser must perform in an objective and independent manner.

   c. Contingent compensation arrangements are generally unethical. An appraiser should not accept an assignment that is contingent on reporting predetermined opinions or conclusions, or any direction in value that favors the client.

   d. Undisclosed fees or payments for procuring appraisal assignments are unethical.

   e. False, misleading, or exaggerated advertising and soliciting practices are unethical.

   f. Confidential data obtained from a client, or developed for a client, may be disclosed only to the client, persons authorized by the client, persons authorized by law, and duly authorized peer review committees.

   g. Appraisal records must be kept for a minimum of five years. If the appraisal assignment involves testimony in a legal proceeding, the records must be kept at for least two years following the final conclusion of the proceeding.

2. The Competency Rule requires the appraiser to verify that he or she has the necessary knowledge or experience prior to accepting an appraisal assignment.
   a. Otherwise, the appraiser must: disclose the lack of knowledge or experience to the client before accepting the assignment; take whatever steps are necessary to perform the assignment in a competent manner; and describe the lack of knowledge or experience, and the steps taken in order to perform competently, in the appraisal report.
3. The Scope of Work Rule requires the appraiser to perform the scope of work necessary to produce credible results for the assignment. To be acceptable, the scope of work must meet the expectations of regularly intended users for similar assignments, and it must match what the appraiser's peers would do in performing a similar assignment.
4. Under the Jurisdictional Exception Rule, if a local law makes part of the USPAP unenforceable in a particular jurisdiction, the remaining parts are not affected.

Chapter Quiz

1. According to the USPAP, an appraiser may reveal confidential information to:
   a. the client
   b. an authorized peer review committee
   c. a person authorized by law
   d. Any of the above

2. In order to perform a complex appraisal in connection with a federally related transaction, an appraiser must:
   a. be state-licensed
   b. be state-certified
   c. have at least five years of experience
   d. All of the above

3. Which of the following is not a federal financial institutions regulatory agency (FFIRA) as defined in FIRREA?
   a. Office of the Comptroller of the Currency (OCC)
   b. National Credit Union Administration (NCUA)
   c. Resolution Funding Corporation (REFCORP)
   d. Federal Deposit Insurance Corporation (FDIC)

4. An appraisal is subject to the requirements of FIRREA if:
   a. the subject property is worth over $1 million
   b. the subject property is a complex residential property
   c. it is made in connection with a federally related transaction
   d. All of the above

5. If an appraisal is subject to the requirements of FIRREA, but does not require the services of a state-certified appraiser, it may be performed by:
   a. a state-licensed appraiser
   b. a state-certified appraiser
   c. any appraiser
   d. Either a) or b)

6. The purpose of Title XI (the Real Estate Appraisal Reform Amendments) of FIRREA is to:
   a. raise funds through appraiser licensing fees
   b. enhance the prestige of the Appraisal Foundation
   c. protect the public interest in real estate related transactions
   d. require all appraisers to follow the Uniform Standards of Professional Appraisal Practice (USPAP)

7. A state-certified appraiser must meet standards of competence that are defined by:
   a. the Appraisal Subcommittee
   b. the Appraisal Standards Board
   c. the Appraiser Qualifications Board
   d. the Appraisal Institute

8. The primary market for real estate loans includes all of the following, EXCEPT:
   a. Fannie Mae
   b. commercial banks
   c. savings institutions
   d. credit unions

9. When an appraisal is made subject to the completion of repairs or improvements to the subject property, Fannie Mae/Freddie Mac rules require the appraiser to:
    a. issue a certificate of completion when the construction is finished
    b. prepare a new appraisal if construction takes longer than six months
    c. review the appraisal to determine whether market conditions changed during the construction period
    d. All of the above

10. In a Fannie Mae/Freddie Mac appraisal, the appraiser may use comparable sales data provided by the real estate broker in the transaction, provided that:
    a. the appraiser independently verifies the data
    b. the broker has already received a commission
    c. the appraiser reasonably believes the data is reliable
    d. the appraiser was not selected for the assignment by the broker

11. USPAP rules governing business practices such as advertising and compensation arrangements are found in the:
    a. Ethics Rule
    b. Competency Rule
    c. Jurisdictional Exception Rule
    d. Preamble

12. According to the Record Keeping section of the Ethics Rule, appraisal records must be kept for a minimum of:
    a. 2 years
    b. 3 years
    c. 5 years
    d. 10 years

13. Which of the following practices would always be considered unethical under the terms of the USPAP?
    a. Payment of an undisclosed commission in connection with the procurement of an appraisal assignment
    b. Refusing an assignment in which the fee is contingent on reporting a direction in value that favors the cause of the client
    c. Disclosure of confidential information to a peer review committee
    d. All of the above

14. An appraiser who lacks the knowledge and experience to complete an appraisal assignment competently:
    a. must decline the assignment
    b. may accept the assignment if the appraisal will be reviewed by another appraiser who is competent
    c. must disclose the lack of knowledge and/or experience to the client before accepting the assignment
    d. may accept the assignment if the lack of knowledge and/or experience is unavoidable

15. The organization that is responsible for updating the USPAP to reflect changes in the appraisal profession is the:
    a. Appraisal Standards Board
    b. Appraiser Qualifications Board
    c. Appraisal Practices Board
    d. Uniform Standards Board

Quiz Answers

1. d) The results of an appraisal may be shared with the client, with persons authorized by the client or by law, or with a peer review committee.
2. b) A complex appraisal in a federally related transaction (for instance, one with a value of $1 million or more) must be performed by a state-certified appraiser.
3. c) The Comptroller of the Currency, the National Credit Union Administration, and the Federal Deposit Insurance Corporation are all federal financial institutions regulatory agencies (FFIRAs).
4. c) An appraisal is subject to FIRREA requirements if it is made in connection with a federally related transaction.
5. d) An appraisal that is subject to FIRREA requirements but is not required to be performed by a state-certified appraiser may be performed by either a state-licensed or a state-certified appraiser.
6. c) The intent of Title XI of FIRREA is to protect the public interest by establishing standards for conduct and competence for appraisers.
7. c) State-certified appraisers must meet qualifications established by the Appraiser Qualifications Board (AQB) of the Appraisal Foundation.
8. a) The primary market does not include Fannie Mae, which is a secondary market agency.
9. a) If an appraisal is subject to completion of repairs or improvements, the appraiser must issue a certificate of completion once the work is done, according to Fannie Mae/Freddie Mac rules.
10. a) Fannie Mae/Freddie Mac rules state that an appraiser may use data provided by a party to the transaction only if the appraiser makes an independent verification of the data.
11. a) The Ethics Rule of the USPAP regulates activities such as advertising and compensation.
12. c) According to the Ethics Rule, appraisal records must ordinarily be kept for a minimum of five years after preparation.
13. a) An appraiser must disclose a payment for procuring an appraisal assignment.
14. c) An appraiser who lacks the knowledge and experience to complete an assignment may still take the assignment if he discloses to the client that lack of knowledge and the steps that will be taken to complete the assignment correctly.
15. a) The USPAP is periodically updated by the Appraisal Standards Board (ASB) of the Appraisal Foundation.

Exercise Answers

#1
1. a. Offering seminars and courses
   b. Publishing textbooks, reports, and journals
2. a. Demonstrated competence through education, testing, and/or experience
   b. Observance of professional standards of practice, subject to peer review
3. a. Standards of competence and conduct set by association for its members
   b. Reliability of the association in enforcing its standards

#2
1. The collapse of the savings and loan industry
2. The Appraisal Foundation; Appraisal Standards Board (ASB); Appraiser Qualifications Board (AQB)
3. Financial Institutions Reform, Recovery and Enforcement Act of 1989 (FIRREA)
4. Real Estate Appraisal Reform Amendments
5. Appraisal Subcommittee of the Federal Financial Institutions Examination Council (FFIEC)
6. The Appraiser Qualifications Board (AQB) of the Appraisal Foundation
7. General certification
8. a. Must be performed by a state-certified or state-licensed appraiser
   b. Must be performed in accordance with specified standards of appraisal practice
   c. Must be written

#3
1. a. A transaction in which a federal financial institutions regulatory agency plays a role
   b. A transaction where an appraiser's services are required
2. $250,000
3. a. Transactions with a value of $1 million or more
   b. Nonresidential transactions with a value of $250,000 or more
   c. Complex residential transactions with a value of $250,000 or more

#4
1. a. Board of Governors of the Federal Reserve System
   b. Federal Deposit Insurance Corporation
   c. Office of the Comptroller of the Currency
   d. Office of Thrift Supervision
   e. National Credit Union Administration
2. All three items are unacceptable practices
3. The date of the loan by the primary lender
4. Three; one year

#5 1. a. Conduct
b. Management
c. Confidentiality
d. Record Keeping
2. Competency Rule
3. a. F
b. F
c. F
d. T

Glossary

Absorption—The purchase or lease of newly developed property from the developer. The absorption rate—the rate at which property is absorbed by the market—is an important factor influencing value.

Abstract of Title—A legal document listing the history and condition of title to a parcel of real estate.

Access—The means by which a property can be entered from a public street.

Accrued Depreciation—The amount of depreciation that has occurred between the time an improvement was built and the effective date of its appraisal.

Accrued Interest—Interest that has been paid or is due to be paid.

Acre—A unit of area equal to 43,560 square feet.

Actual Age—The amount of time that an improvement has been in existence. Also called chronological age or historical age.

Adjustments—Changes in the sales price of a comparable property to account for differences between the comparable and the subject property in the sales comparison approach to value.

Ad Valorem—A Latin phrase meaning "according to value." Used to describe general property taxes that are levied on the basis of a property's assessed value.

After Tax Cash Flow—Pre-tax cash flow, minus income taxes.

Agents of Production—Capital, land, labor, and coordination. In economic theory, these four agents work individually or in concert to create wealth.

Air Rights—Rights of ownership or use with respect to air space.

Allocation—A technique for valuing the land portion of improved property, by deriving a ratio between the value of land and improvements for similar properties, and then applying this ratio to the total value of the subject property.

Amenities—Things that make a property more desirable.

Amortization—An arrangement for the recovery of capital through a series of regular payments.

Annual Debt Service—The total of one year's payments for principal and interest on a loan.

Annuity—A series of regular periodic payments, such as regular monthly rental payments under the terms of a lease.

Anticipation—A principle of value which holds that value is affected by the expectations of buyers regarding the future benefits to be gained from property ownership, including the utility to be derived from ownership and the potential gain or loss on resale of the property.

Appraisal—The act or process of developing an opinion of value; an opinion of value (USPAP definition). A form of appraisal practice.

Appraisal Assignment—The task of appraising a particular property under specified terms and conditions.

Appraisal Foundation—A nonprofit corporation founded by the appraisal industry to promote uniform standards of appraisal practice and appraiser qualification; the parent organization to the Appraisal Standards Board and the Appraiser Qualifications Board.

Appraisal Practice—Valuation services performed by an individual acting as an appraiser, including but not limited to appraisal, appraisal review, or appraisal consulting (USPAP definition).

Appraisal Report—*See:* Report.

Appraisal Standards Board—A division of the Appraisal Foundation, responsible for maintaining the Uniform Standards of Professional Appraisal Practice.

Appraisal Subcommittee—A division of the Federal Financial Institutions Examinations Council (FFIEC), created by FIRREA. It is responsible for monitoring state licensing and certification programs, FFIRA appraisal regulations, and the Appraisal Foundation.

Appraiser—A person qualified by education and experience to perform appraisals.

Appraiser Qualifications Board—A division of the Appraisal Foundation, responsible for maintaining uniform standards for appraiser competence, including the Uniform State Certification Examination.

Appreciation—An increase in value.

Appurtenance—Something that goes along with ownership of real estate, such as mineral rights or an easement.

AQB—*See:* Appraiser Qualifications Board.

Architectural Style—A recognizable category of building design.

Area—The size of a two-dimensional object. Area is expressed in square units (square feet, square yards, etc.) or in acres.

Arm's Length Transaction—A transaction between parties who are not relatives, friends, or business associates of one another.

ASB—*See:* Appraisal Standards Board.

Assemblage—The process of combining two or more separate lots into a single ownership.

Assessed Value—The value used to calculate the amount of general property taxes. Each state has its own definition of assessed value for property tax purposes.

Assessment—1. The valuation of property for property tax purposes. 2. The amount of a property tax. 3. The process of levying a property tax.

Assessment Ratio—The numerical ratio between assessed value and market value as defined in state property tax laws. Assessed value is often calculated by multiplying market value times the assessment ratio.

Assumptions—Assertions that are assumed to be true for the purposes of an appraisal, but that the appraiser does not independently verify. *See also:* Extraordinary Assumptions.

Attached House—A house that shares one or more party walls with another house.

Attic—The area of a house between the ceiling and the rafters.

Backfill—Soil or gravel used to refill the excavation surrounding the foundation walls.

Balance—A principle of value which holds that value is maximized when the four agents of production are in balance. An overimproved or underimproved property suffers in value because of an imbalance in the agents of production.

Balloon Framing—A type of frame construction in which the floor frames are attached to the interior of continuous wall frames.

Balloon Payment—Repayment of all or a portion of loan principal at a specified time, not in the course of regular periodic loan payments.

Band of Investment Technique—A method of deriving a direct capitalization rate by combining separate capitalization rates for the equity (investor) and debt (lender) portions of a property's income.

Baseboard—A horizontal piece of interior trim attached to the base of the walls.

Base Line—The principal east-west line in a unit of the rectangular survey. Townships are numbered in consecutive tiers north and south of the baseline.

Basement—A below-ground level of a house.

Base Rent—The minimum rent due under a percentage lease.

Bathroom—A room with a sink, a toilet, and usually a bathtub and/or shower. It's a full bath if there's a bathtub; a three-quarter bath if there's a shower stall instead of a bathtub; a half bath (or powder room) if there's only a sink and a toilet.

Beam—A large horizontal framing member used to support a floor or ceiling frame.

Bearing Wall—A wall that supports the weight of some other portion of the structure, such as an upper floor or the roof.

Before Tax Cash Flow—*See:* Pre-Tax Cash Flow.

Blocking—Short boards placed between and perpendicular to studs or joists, to provide rigidity to the frame and impede the spread of fire.

Blueprint—*See:* Plans and Specifications.

Board Foot—A unit of measurement for lumber, equivalent to 144 cubic inches.

Book Depreciation—The amount of an asset's capital value that has been written off for accounting or tax purposes. Book depreciation is not relevant to an appraisal.

Book Value—The value of an asset for accounting or tax purposes.

Breakdown Method—A method of estimating depreciation that involves separately estimating the amount of each type of depreciation (curable and incurable, and physical, functional, and external). Also called the observed condition method.

British Thermal Unit (BTU)—A unit of measurement for heat. HVAC equipment is commonly rated according to the number of BTUs it can produce.

Building Capitalization Rate—A direct capitalization rate used to estimate the value of an improvement.

Building Code—A system of regulations that specifies the allowable designs, materials, and techniques for building construction.

Building Residual Technique—A technique for valuing improvements by capitalizing the portion of a property's income that is attributable to the improvements.

Built Up Roof—A type of roofing consisting of alternating layers of asphalt and roofing felt.

Bundle of Rights—A description of property ownership in terms of the various rights that ownership conveys.

Capitalization—*See:* Income Capitalization.

Capitalization Rate—The percentage rate used to convert an amount of income to value in direct capitalization.

Cash Equivalent—Financing on terms that are typical and commonly available in the market.

Cash Flow—Payments made to an investor in connection with an investment.

Cash Flow Analysis—A study of the anticipated movement of cash into or out of an investment.

Cash on Cash Rate—*See:* Equity Dividend Rate.

Casing—A type of molding used around door and window openings.

Certified Appraiser—An appraiser who has satisfied the requirements of a state with respect to certification.

Chain—A unit of distance equal to $^1/_{80}$ of a mile or 66 feet.

Change—A principle of value which holds that the forces of supply and demand are in constant flux in response to the forces that influence value. Because of this, value can only be estimated as of a specific date.

Chimney—A metal or masonry structure designed to vent smoke and fumes from a fireplace.

Chronological Age—*See:* Actual Age.

Client—The party or parties who engage an appraiser (by employment or contract) in a specific assignment (USPAP definition).

Closed Sale—A sale in which title has been transferred from the seller to the buyer.

Closing Costs—Costs other than the purchase price that are incurred in a sale of property, such as real estate commissions, sales taxes, etc.

Collateral—Property that serves as security for a debt.

Commercial Property—Property that is used for trade or business.

Community Property—A form of common ownership by a husband and wife in states that recognize this type of ownership. Each spouse holds an undivided one-half interest in all community property, and the right of survivorship applies.

Comparable—A property that has been sold in the same market that currently includes the subject property, and that appeals to the same sorts of buyers. Comparables are used in many different appraisal techniques.

Comparable Sales Method—A method of deriving a direct capitalization rate by analyzing the sales prices and incomes of comparable properties in the market. The income of a comparable property is divided by its sales price to indicate the capitalization rate.

Comparative-Unit Method—A technique for estimating the cost of improvements by multiplying the size of the improvement (in square feet or cubic feet) by a unit cost figure. Also called the square foot method.

Competition—The interactions between sellers or between buyers in a market. The principle of competition holds that competition helps to bring supply and demand into balance, either by raising prices when supply is low compared to demand, or by driving prices down when demand is relatively weak.

Compound Interest—Interest that is calculated on both principal and accrued interest.

Condemnation—The legal process by which the government exercises its power of eminent domain.

Conditions of Sale—An element of comparison that reflects the motivations of the buyer and seller in a real estate transaction. When conditions of sale are not typical of the market, the sales price is probably not a reliable indicator of market value.

Condominium—A type of ownership that combines fee simple ownership of an individual unit (and the airspace it occupies) with shared ownership of common areas.

Conformity—The harmonious blending of land uses. The principle of conformity holds that property values are enhanced when the uses of surrounding properties conform to the use of the subject property.

Consistent Use—A rule of appraisal that requires both land and improvements to be valued for the same use.

Construction Cost—The cost to build an improvement.

Consulting—The act or process of developing an analysis, recommendation, or opinion to solve a problem, where an opinion of value is a component of the analysis leading to the assignment results (USPAP definition). A form of appraisal practice.

Contract Rent—The amount of rent that is called for under an existing lease. Also called scheduled rent.

Contribution—The increase in overall property value that results from the presence of one component of the property. The principle of contribution holds that the value of a component of a property is equivalent to the amount by which it increases the value of the property as a whole.

Conventional Financing—Institutional financing that is not guaranteed or insured by the government.

Cooperative—A form of ownership in which property is owned by a corporation and individual units are leased to the shareholders.

Corner Influence—The effect on value resulting from the location of a property at an intersection.

Correction Line—East-west lines at intervals of 24 miles north and south of the base line in the rectangular survey system, where adjustments are made to account for convergence.

Cost—The actual amount of expenditure necessary to acquire or produce something.

Cost Approach—One of the three approaches to value in the appraisal process. In the cost approach, the value of the subject property is indicated by the cost to build the subject improvements, plus the value of the site, and minus any depreciation which exists in the subject improvements.

Cost Index—A statistic that tracks the relative change in construction costs over time. If the original cost of an improvement is known, its replacement cost can be estimated by dividing the current index by the index from the time of construction, and then multiplying the result by the original cost of construction.

Cost of Development Method—*See:* Subdivision Development Method.

Cost to Cure—A technique for estimating depreciation by estimating the cost to remedy the defects in the improvement.

Crawl Space—The space between the ground and the bottom floor frame of a house.

Creative Financing—Financing on terms that are not typically available in the market.

Curable Depreciation—Depreciation that can be physically and economically remedied.

Current Use—The purpose for which a property is being used at the present time.

Debt Coverage Method—A method of deriving an overall capitalization rate for a property, by dividing the debt portion of net operating income by the loan amount.

Debt Coverage Ratio—A property's annual net operating income, divided by its annual mortgage debt service.

Debt Financing—Borrowed funds that are used to finance an investment.

Debt Service—*See:* Mortgage Debt Service.

Deed—An instrument used to convey title to real estate.

Deed of Trust—A type of specific, voluntary lien. Similar in most respects to a mortgage, but with different rules of foreclosure.

Deed Restriction—*See:* Private Restriction.

Deferred Maintenance—*See:* Physical Deterioration.

Defined Value—The specific type of value that an appraiser is asked to estimate in an appraisal assignment.

Degree—An angular measurement equal to $^1/_{360}$ of a complete circle.

Demand—The amount of something that buyers in a market want to acquire at a given price.

Demography—The characteristics of a population, such as age, family size, etc.

Department of Housing and Urban Development (HUD)—A department of the federal government that manages a variety of programs relating to housing and urban issues.

Department of Veterans Affairs (VA)—A department of the federal government that, among other things, administers a mortgage loan guaranty program for military veterans.

Depreciation—The difference between cost and value, from whatever cause.

Depth—The dimension of a lot measured perpendicularly from the street on which the site address is located.

Desire—One of the four factors of value; for something to have value, it must generate the desire to own it in potential purchasers.

Detached House—A house that is not connected to any other property.

Development Cost—The cost to create a project, such as a subdivision or housing development, including the construction cost of any improvements.

Direct Capitalization—The process of estimating value on the basis of income from a single period, usually one year. The formula for direct capitalization is Value = Income ÷ Capitalization Rate, or Value = Income × Multiplier.

Direct Costs—The costs for labor and materials used to build an improvement. Also called hard costs.

Discounted Cash Flow Analysis—The process of converting the expected cash flows of an investment to present value.

Discounting—The process of calculating the present value of an expected future amount.

Discount Rate—A rate used to convert a future amount to its present value.

Dominant Tenement—A parcel of land that has the benefit of an easement.

Dormer—A structure that projects through the roof of a building to create additional usable space on the upper floor.

Downspout—A pipe or channel used to discharge water from a gutter to the ground.

Drywall—Interior wall finish material that does not require mixing with water.

Duct—A metal passageway used to circulate or vent air in a building.

Dwelling—A building designed for residential use.

Easement—A nonexclusive right to use someone else's property for a particular purpose; a type of nonfinancial encumbrance. Appurtenant easements benefit a particular piece of real estate. Easements in gross benefit individuals or organizations.

Eave—The part of a roof that overhangs the exterior walls of the building.

Economic Age-Life Method—A technique for estimating depreciation, based on the assumption that an improvement loses value at a steady rate over the course of its economic life. Also called the straight line method.

Economic Base—The economic activities that support the people living in a particular area.

Economic Forces—Factors that influence the availability and cost of capital, and the purchasing power of buyers, which affect value in the market. Economic forces are often influenced by governmental forces.

Economic Life—The length of time during which an improvement will contribute to the value of a property. Economic life ends when the improvement no longer represents the highest and best use of the property.

Economic Obsolescence—Depreciation that is caused by economic conditions or factors. *See:* External Obsolescence.

Effective Age—The apparent or functional age of an improvement, based on its current condition and current conditions in the market.

Effective Date of Appraisal—The date as of which value is estimated, distinguished from the date the appraisal report is prepared. Value estimates are always made as of a specific date, because value can change over time.

Effective Gross Income (EGI)—Potential gross income, minus an allowance for vacancies and bad debt losses.

Effective Gross Income Multiplier (EGIM)—A factor that can be used to convert effective gross income to value, or to determine a capitalization rate.

Effective Interest Rate—An interest rate expressed as a rate per compounding period.

Effective Purchasing Power—When potential purchasers have the ability to pay for a property or a product. One of the four factors of value.

Effective Tax Rate—The annual amount of general property taxes assessed against a property, divided by the property's market value.

Effective Yield Rate—*See:* Effective Interest Rate.

EGI—*See:* Effective Gross Income.

EGIM—*See:* Effective Gross Income Multiplier.

Element of Comparison—A factor that may indicate a difference in value between the subject property and a comparable. Common elements of comparison include location, size, number of rooms, etc.

Eminent Domain—The power of government to take private property for public use upon payment of just compensation. This power is exercised through the process of condemnation.

Encroachment—An improvement that is located on the property of another.

Encumbrance—A real property interest that does not include the present or future right of possession. Financial encumbrances (such as mortgages) affect title to the real estate. Nonfinancial encumbrances (such as easements) affect the use of the real estate.

Entrepreneurial Profit—The amount of profit that an owner/developer would expect to make from improving the property.

Environmental Forces—Those aspects of the physical environment, whether natural or man-made, that influence value, including the character of the land, climate, infrastructure, and location.

Equity—The value of an asset, minus the amount of any mortgage debt secured by the asset.

Equity Capitalization Rate—A direct capitalization rate used to estimate the value of the equity interest in a property in the band of investment technique.

Equity Dividend—*See:* Pre-Tax Cash Flow.

Equity Dividend Rate—A rate used to convert pre-tax cash flow to value, using direct capitalization. Also called the cash on cash rate.

Equity Residual Technique—A technique for estimating the value of the equity portion of an investment by capitalizing the income attributed to equity.

Escalator Clause—A clause in a lease that specifies periodic increases in rent.

Estate—A real property interest that includes the right of possession, i.e., the exclusive right to occupy and use the real estate. Estates may be freehold estates (ownership) or leasehold estates (tenancy).

Excavation—The removal of soil, or the resulting hole in the ground.

Excess Competition—An overcorrection of an imbalance between supply and demand, usually as a result of the availability of excessive profits.

Excess Land—Part of a parcel of land that is not necessary to support the highest and best use of the parcel, and that is adaptable for some other use.

Excess Rent—The amount by which a property's contract rent exceeds its market rent.

Externalities—Factors outside of a property that influence its value.

External Obsolescence—A form of depreciation which results from causes arising outside of the property itself.

Extraction—A technique for valuing land by deducting the depreciated value of the improvements from the total value of the property. Extraction is used most often when the value of the improvements represents a small fraction of total property value.

Extraordinary Assumptions—Assumptions directly related to a specific assignment, which could alter the appraiser's opinions or conclusions if found to be false.

Fannie Mae—*See:* Federal National Mortgage Association.

Fascia—A trim board attached to the ends of rafters.

FDIC—*See:* Federal Deposit Insurance Corporation.

Federal Deposit Insurance Corporation (FDIC)—An independent government agency that manages the system of national deposit insurance for participating banks and savings institutions. It is one of the five federal financial institutions regulatory agencies.

Federal Financial Institutions Regulatory Agency (FFIRA)—One of five federal government agencies, including the Board of Governors of the Federal Reserve System, the Federal Deposit Insurance Corporation, the Office of the Comptroller of the Currency, the Office of Thrift Supervision, and the National Credit Union Administration. Transactions that are regulated by a FFIRA are subject to the appraisal requirements of Title XI of FIRREA.

Federal Home Loan Mortgage Corporation (FHLMC)—One of the major intermediary organizations in the secondary market for real estate loans. Commonly known as Freddie Mac.

Federal Housing Administration (FHA)—A government agency that promotes homeownership through a program of mortgage insurance.

Federally Related Transaction—A real estate related financial transaction that involves a FFIRA and that requires the services of an appraiser. Federally related transactions are subject to the requirements of Title XI of FIRREA.

Federal National Mortgage Association (FNMA)—One of the major intermediary organizations in the secondary market for real estate loans. Commonly known as Fannie Mae.

Federal Reserve System—The central banking system of the United States. The Board of Governors of the Federal Reserve System is one of the five federal financial institutions regulatory agencies.

Fee Appraiser—An appraiser who is self-employed, or who works for a company whose primary business is to provide appraisal services to others.

Fee Simple—A freehold estate that is the most complete and comprehensive form of real property interest, including the entire bundle of rights.

FFIRA—*See:* Federal Financial Institutions Regulatory Agency.

FHA—*See:* Federal Housing Administration.

FHLMC—*See:* Federal Home Loan Mortgage Corporation.

Financial Institutions Reform, Recovery and Enforcement Act of 1989 (FIRREA)—An act of Congress passed in response to the savings and loan crisis of the 1980s. FIRREA reorganized the system of federal regulation of financial institutions. Its Title XI (the Real Estate Appraisal Reform Amendments) established government requirements for uniform standards of appraisal practice and appraiser qualification, as well as appraiser licensing and certification.

FIRREA—*See:* Financial Institutions Reform, Recovery and Enforcement Act of 1989.

Fixed Expense—An operating expense that does not vary depending on the occupancy of a property.

Fixture—*See:* Improvement.

Flashing—Pieces of metal used to seal joints in a building's exterior surfaces.

Flat Lease—A lease in which the amount of rent does not change during the entire lease term. Also known as a level payment lease.

Flush Door—A door consisting of a hollow or solid core sandwiched between two sheets of veneer.

FNMA—*See:* Federal National Mortgage Association.

Footing—A concrete pad or beam used to transmit the weight of a structure to the soil.

Forced Air System—A type of heating and/or cooling system that uses a fan and ducts to distribute air through the building.

Foreclosure—The forced sale of property in order to satisfy a debt that is secured by a lien against the property.

Form Report—A written appraisal report prepared on a standardized form, usually with addenda.

Foundation—*See:* Substructure.

Foundation Wall—A part of the substructure consisting of a concrete wall that is supported by a footing.

Four Factors of Value—The factors that must be present for a thing to have value; utility, scarcity, desire, and effective purchasing power.

Framing—The structural components of the superstructure, including joists, studs, headers, rafters, etc.

Freddie Mac—*See:* Federal Home Loan Mortgage Corporation.

Freehold—An estate that includes the rights of ownership or title, either presently or in the future. Freehold estates include the fee simple, the life estate, the estate in remainder, and the estate in reversion.

Frieze—An exterior trim board attached to the top of the wall below the soffit.

Frontage—The boundary of a parcel of land that abuts a street, waterway, or other desirable feature.

Front Foot—One foot of frontage. Where the amount of frontage is an important value indicator, appraisers may analyze market prices on a per-front-foot basis.

Functional Obsolescence—A form of depreciation caused by defects in design.

Functional Utility—The ability of an improvement to perform its intended use.

Furlong—A unit of distance equal to $^1/_8$ of a mile or 660 feet.

Future Value—The value of something as of some future date.

Gable—The triangular wall area formed by two opposing surfaces of a gable roof.

Gable Roof—A style of roof with two roof surfaces rising from opposite sides of the building.

General Data—Data that relate to the real estate market in which a property is located, including regional, district and neighborhood data.

General Partnership—A partnership in which each partner is fully entitled to act on behalf of the partnership.

General Property Tax—A property tax levied against all non-exempt property, usually on the basis of a property's value (ad valorem).

Gentrification—Renewal or restoration of run-down neighborhoods by an influx of more prosperous ownership.

GIM—*See:* Gross Income Multiplier.

Ginnie Mae—*See:* Government National Mortgage Association.

GNMA—*See:* Government National Mortgage Association.

Going Concern Value—The total value of a proven, ongoing business operation, which includes real property that is an integral part of the operation.

Governmental Forces—Laws, regulations, and public services that affect the value of property in the market.

Government Lot—A division of the rectangular survey system. Irregular parcels that do not constitute a full section or quarter section are identified as government lots.

Government National Mortgage Association (GNMA)—One of the major intermediary organizations in the secondary market for real estate loans. Commonly known as Ginnie Mae.

Government Survey System—*See:* Rectangular Survey System.

Grading—The process of leveling or smoothing the surface of the ground.

Graduated Lease—*See:* Step-up Lease.

GRM—*See:* Gross Rent Multiplier.

Gross Adjustment—The total of the amounts of adjustments to the sales price of a comparable, without regard to whether the adjustments are negative or positive.

Gross Building Area—The total area of a building, including above-grade and below-grade enclosed spaces, as calculated from the external dimensions of the building.

Gross Income—*See:* Effective Gross Income; Potential Gross Income.

Gross Income Multiplier (GIM)—*See:* Effective Gross Income Multiplier; Potential Gross Income Multiplier.

Gross Lease—A lease in which the lessee is responsible only for rent payments, and not for payment of any expenses.

Gross Living Area—The size of the living space in a house, calculated on the basis of the outside dimensions of the structure. Gross living area includes finished areas of the house that are at or above ground level, but does not include garages, attics, or basements.

Gross Rent—The total periodic rent for a property.

Gross Rent Multiplier (GRM)—A factor used to convert gross rent to value using direct capitalization.

Ground Lease—A long-term lease of vacant land on which the tenant constructs a building.

Ground Rent—The rent paid under the terms of a ground lease.

Ground Rent Capitalization—A technique for valuing land that is subject to a ground lease, by capitalizing the amount of the ground rent.

Guide Meridian—North-south lines at intervals of 24 miles east and west of the principal meridian in the government survey system, where adjustments are made to account for convergence.

Gutter—A horizontal channel attached to the base of the roof to carry runoff.

Hard Costs—*See:* Direct Costs.

HBU—*See:* Highest and Best Use.

Heating, Ventilating and Air Conditioning (HVAC)—The equipment used to control air quality in a building.

Highest and Best Use (HBU)—A reasonably probable use that results in the highest value for a property. It must be a use that is legally permitted, physically possible, and economically feasible.

Hip Roof—A style of roof in which a separate roof surface rises from each exterior wall of the building.

Historical Age—*See:* Actual Age.

Holding Period—The life span of an investment; the length of time from the date a property is purchased until the date the property is resold.

Homeowners Association—A nonprofit organization designed to manage the common areas of a development and to enforce the covenants of the development.

HUD—*See:* Department of Housing and Urban Development.

HVAC—*See:* Heating, Ventilating and Air Conditioning.

Improvement—An item of personal property that is added to the land by human effort, in such a way as to become part of the real estate. Also called a fixture.

Income—Money or other benefits that are received.

Income Approach—One of the three approaches to value in the appraisal process. In the income approach, the value of the subject property is indicated by the amount of net income that the property can generate. Also called the income capitalization approach.

Income Capitalization—The process of estimating value on the basis of a property's income.

Income Capitalization Approach—*See:* Income Approach.

Income Property—Property used for the production of income.

Increasing and Decreasing Returns—If one or more of the agents of production remain fixed, an increase in the other agent(s) will first result in increasing rates of return for the property, but will eventually result in decreasing rates of return once the point of diminishing returns is reached.

Incurable Depreciation—Depreciation that cannot be physically or economically remedied.

Independent Fee Appraiser—*See:* Fee Appraiser.

Index Lease—A lease that calls for periodic adjustment of the rent amount, based on changes in an economic index.

Indirect Costs—Costs other than direct costs (labor and materials) that are incurred in the process of building an improvement, such as overhead, architectural fees, construction financing interest, permit fees, etc. Also called soft costs.

Infrastructure—Public improvements that support basic needs, such as transportation and utilities.

Inside Lot—A lot that is not located on a corner.

Insulation—Material used in construction to reduce the transfer of heat.

Insurable Value—The value of property for purposes of reimbursement under the terms of an insurance policy. Insurable value is defined by the insurance policy.

Interest—1. The amount earned by an investment; return on capital. 2. The amount earned by a debt investment (loan), as compared to the amount earned by an equity investment.

Interest Rate—*See:* Rate of Return.

Interim Use—A temporary use to which a property is put when its current highest and best use is expected to change in the near future. An interim use anticipates a more productive highest and best use in the foreseeable future.

Investment Value—The value of a property to a particular investor with specific investment goals. Investment value is inherently subjective.

Jamb—The frame in which a door or window is mounted.

Joint Compound—Plaster-like material used to seal the joints in wallboard construction.

Joint Tenancy—A form of common ownership in which each owner (joint tenant) has an undivided interest in the entire property and cannot transfer his or her interest without the consent of the other joint tenant(s). Most joint tenancies include a right of survivorship, which means that if one joint tenant dies, ownership of the property automatically vests in the surviving joint tenant(s).

Joist—The primary horizontal structural element of a floor or ceiling frame.

Judgment Lien—An involuntary general lien created by a court judgment, which affects all of the debtor's property that is within the jurisdiction of the court.

Just Compensation—The payment due from the government to an owner whose property is taken under the power of eminent domain.

Land—The surface of the earth, together with all that it contains.

Land Development Method—*See:* Subdivision Development Method.

Landlord—The holder of a leased fee interest. Also called the lessor.

Land Residual Technique—A technique for valuing land by capitalizing the portion of a property's income that is attributable to the land.

Lease—A contract between a landlord and a tenant, which temporarily separates the ownership of real estate from the right of possession. The interest of the owner/landlord is called a leased fee, and the tenant's interest is called a leasehold.

Leased Fee—The real property interest of the landlord (owner) under a lease, which includes ownership but not the immediate right of possession.

Leasehold—A non-freehold estate, which includes the right of possession during the term of the lease, but not ownership or title; the real property interest held by a tenant under a lease. Also known as a tenancy. Leasehold estates include the tenancy for years (created by a term lease), the periodic tenancy (created by a period-to-period lease), and the tenancy at will (created when a tenant remains in possession with the landlord's consent after expiration of a valid lease).

Legal Description—A description of a parcel of real estate in a form that is legally approved in the state where the property is located. Common systems of legal description include the metes and bounds, government (rectangular) survey, and lot and block systems.

Legal Nonconforming Use—A use that would not be permitted under current zoning laws, but that is allowed to continue because it was permitted at the time the use was started.

Lessee—*See:* Tenant.

Lessor—*See:* Landlord.

Less-than-Freehold Estate—*See:* Leasehold.

Letter of Transmittal—A brief letter accompanying a written appraisal report and summarizing its contents.

Letter Report—A written appraisal report in the form of a letter to the client.

Level Payment Lease—*See*: Flat Lease.

Licensed Appraiser—An appraiser who has met the requirements for licensing established by the state where the appraiser works.

Lien—A financial encumbrance. The holder of a lien has the right to force the sale (foreclosure) of the liened property and use the proceeds of the sale to satisfy a debt, in the event that the debt is not paid according to its terms. Specific liens (such as mortgages) apply only to a particular piece of real estate, while general liens (such as judgment liens) apply to all real estate owned by the debtor.

Life Estate—A freehold estate that terminates automatically upon the death of the person designated as the measuring life.

Limited Partnership—A form of partnership that includes general partners who have authority to act on behalf of the partnership, and limited partners who share financial risks and rewards but do not control the partnership assets.

Limiting Conditions—A statement or explanation in an appraisal report that limits the application of the conclusions contained in the report.

Liquidation Value—A form of market value that assumes the property must be sold in a limited period of time, which probably does not constitute "reasonable" exposure to the market.

Listing Price—The price at which property is offered for sale through a real estate broker.

Loan Constant—*See:* Mortgage Constant.

Loan to Value Ratio—The amount of a loan, divided by the value of the security property; usually expressed as a percentage.

Location—An element of comparison that reflects the impact of neighborhood influences on value.

Locational Obsolescence—A form of depreciation caused by surrounding properties. *See*: External Obsolescence.

Long-Lived Item—A component of an improvement that is expected to last as long as the improvement itself.

Lot—A parcel of land.

Lot and Block System—A system of legal description of real estate, describing land by reference to an official map showing the boundaries of the parcel.

Manufactured Housing—Housing that is not constructed on the building site.

Marginal Productivity—The value of an individual component of a property, measured as the change in overall value of the property that is attributable to the presence or absence of the component.

Market—The interactions among a group of buyers and sellers who trade in a particular thing, such as real estate, within a particular area. The actions of the buyers and sellers in a market determine market value.

Marketability—The likelihood that a property will sell for its market value within a reasonable marketing period.

Market Approach—*See:* Sales Comparison Approach.

Market Comparison Approach—*See:* Sales Comparison Approach.

Market Conditions—An element of comparison that reflects the state of the market on the date a property was sold. Adjustments for market conditions take into account the changes in value over time.

Market Data Approach—*See:* Sales Comparison Approach.

Market Extraction Method—A technique for estimating depreciation, based on depreciation figures extracted from the sales prices of comparables.

Marketing Period—The length of time a property must be offered for sale on the market until a buyer can be found.

Market Price—The price for which a property is sold in an arm's length transaction.

Market Rent—The amount of rent that a property should be able to command under current market conditions.

Market Value—In general, the amount of cash (or cash equivalent) that is most likely to be paid for a property on a given date in a fair and reasonable open market transaction. Specific (but varied) definitions of market value can be found in USPAP and in many state laws. Also called exchange value or value in exchange.

Matched Pairs Analysis—*See:* Paired Data Analysis.

Metes and Bounds System—A system of legal description of real estate, describing the boundaries of a parcel using reference points, courses (directions), and distances.

Mill—One tenth of a cent. Property tax rates are often expressed in mills per dollar of assessed value.

Mineral Rights—The right to extract minerals from a property.

Minute—An angular measurement equal to $^{1}/_{60}$ of a degree.

Misplaced Improvement—*See:* Overimprovement; Underimprovement.

Molding—Finish material, relatively thin in cross section, used for decorative effect or to conceal joints.

Monolithic Slab—A type of foundation consisting of a concrete slab resting directly on the soil.

Monument—A natural or artificial object used as a reference point for land descriptions.

Mortgage—A type of specific, voluntary lien. The holder of a mortgage (the mortgagee) has the right to foreclose on the mortgaged property if the secured loan is not repaid according to its terms.

Mortgage Capitalization Rate—A direct capitalization rate used to estimate the value of the debt portion of an investment.

Mortgage Constant—The amount of annual mortgage debt service for a loan, divided by the loan amount. The mortgage constant depends on the interest rate of the loan, the loan term, and the frequency at which loan payments are due. Also called a loan constant.

Mortgage Debt Service—The periodic amount due under the terms of a mortgage loan, including payments of both principal and interest.

Mortgage Residual Technique—A technique for estimating the value of the debt portion of an investment by capitalizing the amount of income attributed to it.

Multiple Listing Service (MLS)—An organization of real estate brokers who pool listings and share commissions.

Narrative Report—A written appraisal report in narrative format; the most complete form of appraisal report, setting forth all the data relied on by the appraiser, and fully describing the appraiser's analysis and conclusions.

National Credit Union Administration (NCUA)—An independent government agency that regulates nationally chartered credit unions. It is one of the five federal financial institutions regulatory agencies.

NCUA—*See:* National Credit Union Administration.

Neighborhood—A geographical area in which land uses are complementary and in which all properties are influenced in a similar way by the forces affecting value.

Net Adjustment—The net sum of positive and negative adjustment amounts for a comparable sale.

Net Income Ratio (NIR)—The relationship between a property's net operating income and its effective gross income; the complement of the operating expense ratio.

Net Lease—A lease in which the tenant is responsible for payment of some property expenses (taxes, insurance, and/or maintenance) in addition to the rent.

Net, Net, Net Lease—A lease in which the tenant is responsible for payment of all property expenses (taxes, insurance, and maintenance) in addition to the rent. Also called a triple net lease.

Net Operating Income (NOI)—Effective gross income, minus all operating expenses.

NIR—*See:* Net Income Ratio.

NOI—*See:* Net Operating Income.

Observed Condition Method—*See:* Breakdown Method.

OCC—*See:* Office of the Comptroller of the Currency.

OER—*See:* Operating Expense Ratio.

Office of the Comptroller of the Currency (OCC)—A division of the Treasury Department, responsible for regulating federally chartered commercial banks. It is one of the five federal financial institutions regulatory agencies.

Office of Thrift Supervision (OTS)—A division of the Treasury Department that is responsible for regulating savings institutions. It is one of the five federal financial institutions regulatory agencies.

Off-site Improvement—An improvement that benefits a property but is not located on the property, such as a street or alley.

On-site Improvement—An improvement that is located on the property in question.

Operating Expense Ratio (OER)—A property's operating expenses divided by its effective gross income; the complement of the net income ratio.

Operating Expenses—The expenses associated with an income producing property, including fixed expenses, variable expenses, and reserves for replacement.

Operating Statement—A financial report that lists income and expenses for a property.

Opportunity Cost—The opportunity cost of an investment is the amount an investor could have earned by choosing a different investment. According to the principle of substitution, an investor will not make an investment that yields less profit than similar investments available in the market.

Option—The right to do something (such as purchase a property for a set price, or renew a lease on specified terms) at a future date.

Oral Report—An appraisal report that is communicated in speech, including a deposition or oral testimony.

OTS—*See*: Office of Thrift Supervision.

Overall Capitalization Rate—A capitalization rate used to convert a property's total net operating income to value using direct capitalization.

Overimprovement—A improvement that is too expensive to represent the highest and best use of the land.

Paired Data Analysis—A technique for measuring the effect on value that is caused by differences in a single element of comparison. The effect on value is estimated by comparing the prices of properties that differ in only the one element of comparison. Also called matched pairs analysis.

Paired Data Set Analysis—*See*: Paired Data Analysis.

Panel Door—A door constructed of solid wood stiles and rails that frame one or more thinner panels.

Partial Interest—Any real property interest other than the fee simple. Usually refers to a shared common ownership in real estate.

Partnership—A legal arrangement by which two or more persons or entities share rights and responsibilities with respect to property used in a business.

Party Wall—A wall that is shared by two separate properties. Houses that share party walls are referred to as attached houses.

Percentage Lease—A lease that calls for a minimum base rent plus a percentage of the tenant's income from operating a business on the leased property.

Percentage Rent—The portion of rent in a percentage lease that is based on the tenant's income.

Periodic Lease—A lease that has no fixed expiration date, but continues in effect until terminated by one of the parties.

Periodic Tenancy—The tenant's estate created by a periodic lease.

Personal Property—All property that is not classified as real estate.

PGI—*See:* Potential Gross Income.

PGIM—*See*: Potential Gross Income Multiplier.

Physical Deterioration—A form of depreciation caused by damage or wear of the physical components of the improvement. Curable physical deterioration is also called deferred maintenance.

Physical Life—The length of time an improvement would be expected to last with normal maintenance.

Pitch—The angle of elevation of a roof surface, usually expresses as the number of feet of vertical rise per 12 feet of horizontal run.

Planned Unit Development (PUD)—A subdivision in which fee simple ownership of a unit or lot is combined with common ownership of open space, recreational facilities, or other common elements.

Plans and Specifications—Construction documents that describe how a building will be constructed. Plans are drawings and specifications are text.

Plat—A map showing the boundaries of real estate.

Plate—A horizontal board at the top or bottom of a wall frame.

Platform Framing—A system of wood frame construction in which floor and wall frames are alternated.

Plottage—The increase in value that results from combining two or more lots under one ownership to allow for a more profitable highest and best use. If two lots are worth more when combined than they are separately, the added value is called the plottage value or plottage increment.

Plumbing—The system of pipes and fixtures that distribute water and drain away waste in a building.

Point—A type of charge to the borrower in connection with a loan. One point is equal to one percent of the loan amount.

Point of Beginning—The reference point from which a metes and bounds land description begins.

Point of Diminishing Returns—The point at which the four agents of production are in balance. At this point, the cost of making additional improvements to the land becomes higher than the resulting increase in value.

Police Power—The power of government to make and enforce regulations for the protection of the public health, safety and welfare. It is the basis for zoning laws, land use regulations, building codes, etc.

Post—A vertical structural member used to support a beam.

Post and Beam Framing—A system of wood frame construction using relatively large framing members, often with exposed beams and rafters.

Potential Gross Income (PGI)—The total periodic amount of revenue that a property is capable of producing at full occupancy, without any deduction for expenses; usually an annual amount. Potential gross income includes rent and any other income that the property is capable of generating.

Potential Gross Income Multiplier (PGIM)—A factor used to convert potential gross income to value using direct capitalization.

Preliminary Analysis—The first steps in the appraisal process, including defining the appraisal problem to be solved and determining the scope of work that will be needed to complete the assignment.

Present Value—The value of something as of the present time. Expected future payments or benefits may be converted to their present value by discounting.

Pre-Tax Cash Flow—Net operating income, minus mortgage debt service costs. Also called equity dividend.

Price—The actual amount paid by a particular buyer to a particular seller in an actual transaction.

Primary Data—Data that are generated by the appraiser, such as by a physical inspection of property or personal interviews.

Principal—The amount of a debt or equity investment, as compared to interest.

Principal Meridian—The principal north-south line in a unit of the rectangular survey. The name of the principal meridian identifies the unit of the survey. Ranges are numbered in consecutive columns east and west of the principal meridian.

Private Restriction—A type of non-financial encumbrance that limits the types of uses that an owner may make of real estate. They are most commonly created by developers at the time of subdivision, and are enforced by other property owners, often through a homeowners association. Also called a deed restriction.

Private Zone—The part of a residential lot that is shielded from the street.

Progression—The increase in the value of a property that is attributable to its location among more desirable properties.

Property—Anything that can be owned, including real estate and personal property.

Property Residual Technique—A method of estimating value by direct capitalization of net operating income.

Property Tax—*See:* General Property Tax; Special Assessment.

Public Restrictions—Government regulations that affect land use.

Public Zone—The part of a residential lot that can be viewed from the street frontage.

PUD—*See:* Planned Unit Development.

Purchasing Power—The financial resources to buy something. When coupled with the desire to buy, it creates effective demand, one of the four characteristics of value.

Purpose of Appraisal—The information that a client wants the appraiser to provide in an appraisal assignment. The purpose of most appraisals is to estimate a defined value for a specific real property interest in a specific parcel of real estate as of a specific date.

Quantity Survey Method—A technique for estimating the cost of an improvement by calculating the cost of labor, materials, equipment and overhead for each item in the construction.

R-Value—A measure of resistance to heat transfer. Insulation is rated according to its R-value.

Rafter—Any of the parallel structural members of a roof frame.

Range—A north-south strip of land bounded by two consecutive range lines in the rectangular survey system.

Range Line—North-south lines running parallel to the principal meridian at intervals of six miles in the rectangular survey system.

Rate of Return—The amount of income produced by an investment, divided by the amount the investor paid for the investment, usually expressed as a percentage. Also called an interest rate.

Real Estate—An identified parcel or tract of land, including improvements, if any (USPAP definition).

Real Estate Reform Amendments—See Title XI.

Real Property—The interests, benefits, and rights inherent in the ownership of real estate. (USPAP definition).

Recapture—Recovery of the amount paid for an investment; return of capital.

Reconciliation—The process by which an appraiser reduces two or more value indicators to a single indicator or estimate of value.

Reconstructed Operating Statement—A projected (future) operating statement that includes only those items that are included in the appraisal definitions of potential gross income, effective gross income, net operating income, and pre-tax cash flow.

Rectangular Survey System—A system of legal description of real estate, describing property in relation to a rectangular grid that has been established by federal government survey. The land is described by referring to the appropriate principal meridian, township, range, section, and partial section. Also called the government survey system.

Refinance—A new loan or loans secured by property that is already owned by the borrower, as compared to a loan used to purchase property.

Register—An opening at the end of a duct through which warm or cold air enters a room, often controlled by a damper.

Regression—The decline in value suffered by a property that is located in an area of less desirable properties.

Reinforced Concrete—Concrete that has been strengthened by means of embedded reinforcing steel bars (rebar) or wire mesh.

Relative Comparison Analysis—A technique for estimating whether a difference in a single element of comparison has a positive, negative, or neutral impact on value. Similar to paired data analysis.

Remaining Economic Life—The amount of time from the effective date of an appraisal until the end of the appraised improvement's economic life. Remaining economic life equals economic life minus effective age.

Rent—The amount paid by a tenant or lessee for the right to use property under the terms of a lease.

Replacement Cost—The cost to create a substitute improvement of equivalent function and utility, using current methods, materials and techniques.

Replacement Reserves—*See:* Reserves for Replacement.

Report—Any communication, written or oral, of an appraisal, appraisal review, or appraisal consulting service that is transmitted to the client upon completion of an assignment (USPAP definition).

Reproduction Cost—The cost to create an exact duplicate of an improvement, using the same design, materials, and construction methods as the original.

Reserves for Replacement—Amounts set aside to cover the cost of replacing short-lived items for an income property; a form of operating expense. The amount of reserves is usually calculated by dividing the replacement costs of the items by their remaining useful lives.

Residential Property—Property intended to be used for dwellings.

Residual—Something that is left over. Residual techniques use direct capitalization to determine the value of the left over component, when the value of the other component is known (or is estimated by some other technique).

Restricted Appraisal Report—A written appraisal report that is prepared in accordance with USPAP Standards Rule 2-2(c).

Return of Capital—*See:* Recapture.

Return on Capital—*See:* Interest.

Reversion Factor—A factor used in financial calculations to calculate the present value of a future amount.

Review—The act or process of developing and communicating an opinion about the quality of another appraiser's work that was performed as part of an appraisal, appraisal review, or appraisal consulting assignment (USPAP definition). A form of appraisal practice.

Rod—A unit of distance equal to $^1/_{320}$ of a mile or 16.5 feet.

Roof—The top portion of a building.

Sales Comparison Approach—One of the three approaches to value in the appraisal process. In the sales comparison approach, the value of the subject property is indicated by the adjusted sales prices of similar properties (comparables) in the market. Also called the market approach or market comparison approach.

Salvage Value—The value of an improvement or its components after removal from the real estate.

Scarcity—Limited availability or limited abundance. One of the four factors of value, and a key element in the principle of supply and demand.

Scheduled Rent—*See:* Contract Rent.

Scope of Work—The type and extent of research and analyses in an assignment (USPAP definition). The extent to which the appraiser collects, confirms, and reports data for an assignment. The scope of work for an appraisal depends on the complexity of the assignment and the needs of the client.

Second—An angular measurement equal to $^1/_{60}$ of a minute, or $^1/_{360}$ of a degree.

Secondary Data—Data generated by someone other than the appraiser, and obtained by the appraiser via a review of published materials.

Secondary Market—The market in which real estate loans are packaged and resold to investors. The major secondary market organizations are FNMA, FHLMC, and GNMA.

Section—A division of a township in the rectangular survey system. A section measures one mile on each side and contains 640 acres.

Self-Contained Appraisal Report—A written appraisal report that is prepared in accordance with USPAP Standards Rule 2-2(a).

Seller Financing—A loan or other financial arrangement offered by a seller to a buyer in connection with the purchase of property.

Septic System—An on-site sewage disposal system with a tank for separation of solids and a system of pipes for distribution of liquids to a porous drain field.

Service Zone—The access ways and outdoor storage areas of a residential lot.

Servient Tenement—A parcel of land that is subject to an easement.

Sewer—A underground system of pipes or channels for disposal of runoff and/or sanitary waste.

Sheathing—Structural material applied to the frame of a building to provide support for the finish materials.

Shed Roof—A type of roof with a single sloped roof surface.

Short-Lived Item—A component of an improvement that is expected to wear out and need replacement during the economic life of the improvement.

Sill—The bottom piece of a door or window frame.

Sill Plate—A board attached to the top of a foundation wall.

Simple Interest—Interest that is calculated on the principal amount only, and not on accrued interest.

Site—A parcel of land that has been prepared for use by clearing, grading, and providing access and utilities.

Site Improvement—An improvement other than a building, such as landscaping or utilities. Improvements "of" the site (such as utility access) are usually valued as part of the land. Improvements "on" the site (such as fences) are valued separately from the land.

Siting—The location and placement of a building on its lot.

Slab—A horizontal concrete surface.

Slab on Grade Foundation—*See:* Monolithic Slab.

Social Forces—The numbers, lifestyles, standards, and preferences of the people in a particular market, which affect property values in that market.

Soffit—The underside of the eaves of a roof.

Soft Costs—*See:* Indirect Costs.

Special Assessment—A form of property tax levied against properties in a special assessment district or local improvement district, in order to cover the cost of some public improvements that benefit those properties. It is a one-time tax that expires when sufficient tax revenue has been collected to pay for the improvements.

Specifications—Construction documents that specify the types of materials and techniques to be used in construction of an improvement.

Specific Data—Data that relate to a specific property, such as the subject property or a comparable.

Square Foot Method—*See:* Comparative-Unit Method.

Staff Appraiser—An appraiser employed by a business, government agency, or other organization to perform appraisal services that relate to the employer's operations.

Standard Parallel—*See:* Correction Line.

Step-Up Lease—A lease that calls for specific rent increases at specific times during the lease term. Also called a graduated lease.

Story—An above ground level of a house. If a level does not have full-height walls, it is often referred to as a half-story.

Straight-Line Method—*See:* Economic Age-Life Method.

Stud—Any of the vertical structural members of a wall frame.

Subdivision—1. The division of one parcel of real estate into two or more separate parcels. 2. A group of properties that have been developed for a particular use.

Subdivision Development Method—A technique for valuing vacant land when the highest and best use of the land is for subdivision and development. The appraiser estimates the future value of the developed lots, and then subtracts the costs of development to arrive at the current value of the land. Also called the land development method.

Subflooring—Structural sheathing attached to a floor frame as a base for the finish flooring.

Subject Property—The property being appraised.

Sublease—A lease of property from one tenant to another.

Substitution—A principle of value which holds that the value of a property cannot exceed the value of equivalent substitute properties that are available in the market.

Substructure—The part of a building that is below ground level and that supports the superstructure. Substructure includes footings, foundation walls, piers, and other elements of the foundation.

Summary Appraisal Report—A written appraisal report that is prepared in accordance with USPAP Standards Rule 2-2(b).

Superadequacy—A form of functional obsolescence, consisting of a design feature whose cost is greater than its contribution to value.

Superstructure—The part of a building that is above ground, supported by the foundation.

Supply—The amount of something that is available for sale in a market at a given price.

Supply and Demand—A principle of value which holds that the value of a property in a competitive market is determined by the relative levels of supply and demand. Property is worth more when demand is high compared to supply, and worth less when supply exceeds demand.

Surplus Productivity—The amount of a property's income that remains after deducting the income attributable to capital, labor, and coordination. The remaining income is attributable to the land, and is used to indicate the value of the land.

Tenancy—*See:* Leasehold.

Tenancy by the Entireties—A form of common ownership similar to a joint tenancy in which the co-tenants are husband and wife.

Tenancy in Common—A form of common ownership in which each owner (co-tenant) has an undivided interest in the entire property and can freely transfer his or her interest without the consent of the other co-tenant(s).

Tenant—The holder of a leasehold estate. Also called a lessee.

Tenant Improvement—An improvement of leased property made by the tenant.

Term—A length of time, such as the duration of a lease agreement (lease term), or the time for repayment of a loan (loan term).

Threshold—A door sill.

Timeshare—A shared ownership interest that includes the right to use the property only during a specified time of the year.

Title—An ownership (freehold) interest in real estate.

Title XI—Part of FIRREA known as the Real Estate Appraisal Reform Amendments. Title XI established federal requirements for appraiser licensing and certification, and for uniform standards of appraisal practice. These requirements apply to all appraisals in connection with federally related transactions.

Ton—A unit for measuring heat, equivalent to 12,000 BTUs.

Topography—The characteristics of the surface of the land.

Township—A unit of the rectangular survey system, formed by the intersection of a range and a township tier, and identified by its position relative to the principal meridian and base line. A township measures six miles on a side, and contains 36 sections.

Township Line—East-west lines running parallel to the base line at intervals of six miles in the government survey system.

Township Tier—An east-west strip of land bounded by two consecutive township lines in the government survey system.

Trade Fixture—A fixture installed by a tenant in connection with the operation of a business on leased property. Usually considered to be the personal property of the tenant, not part of the real estate.

Transferability—The quality of something whose ownership may be given or sold to another.

Triple Net Lease—*See:* Net, Net, Net Lease.

Truss—A multi-piece structural framing assembly designed to span a distance between two points.

Underimprovement—An improvement that is too inexpensive to represent the highest and best use of the land.

Undivided Interest—A shared interest in real estate that is not limited to any physical portion of the real estate.

Uniform Residential Appraisal Report (URAR)—A standard form report for use in appraisals of single-family residences. The URAR is approved for use in appraisals that are governed by Fannie Mae, Freddie Mac, HUD, and the VA.

Uniform Standards of Professional Appraisal Practice (USPAP)—Appraisal standards issued by the Appraisal Standards Board of the Appraisal Foundation and adopted as minimum standards by Title XI of FIRREA.

Unit—A portion of a multi-family dwelling designed to accommodate one household.

Unit-in-Place Method—A technique for estimating the cost of an improvement by calculating the quantities of various building components and multiplying the quantity of each component by an appropriate unit cost.

Unit of Comparison—A unit in which price is stated for comparison purposes, such as price per square foot of living area. When comparing different properties, the price of each property must be stated in the same unit of comparison.

URAR—*See:* Uniform Residential Appraisal Report.

Use of Appraisal—The reason why a client wants to know the information that an appraiser will provide in an appraisal assignment.

Use Value—The value of a property assuming it is used for a specific purpose. Also called value in use.

Useful Life—How long an improvement can be expected to perform its intended function.

USPAP—*See:* Uniform Standards of Professional Appraisal Practice.

Utility—The ability to satisfy some want or need of potential buyers. One of the four factors of value.

VA—*See:* Department of Veterans Affairs.

Vacancy Factor—An amount (usually a percentage) deducted from a property's potential gross income to account for vacancies and unpaid rents.

Valuation—*See:* Appraisal.

Valuation Date—*See:* Effective Date of Appraisal.

Value—The monetary relationship between a property and a person who buys, sells, or uses it. The theoretical worth of something, expressed in terms of something else (usually money).

Value Indicator—A piece of data or a derived conclusion (such as the adjusted sales price of a comparable) that is relevant to the value of the subject property in an appraisal.

Variable Expense—An operating expense that varies depending on the level of occupancy of a property.

Volume—The size of something in three dimensions. Volume is expressed in cubic units (cubic feet, cubic yards, etc.).

Wainscot—Separate finish material applied to the lower portion of an interior wall surface.

Width—The dimension of a lot measured parallel to the street on which the site address is located.

Yield—1. *See:* Interest. 2. The amount earned by an equity investment, as compared to the amount earned by a debt investment (loan).

Yield Capitalization—The process of estimating value on the basis of all the anticipated cash flows (the total income) over the life of an investment.

Zoning—Government regulations that specify the allowable uses for a property. Zoning laws are an exercise of the police power, and are designed to enhance property values by preventing incompatible uses.

Index

A

D

E

H

I

J

K

L

T

U

V

W

Y

Z